THE BELIEVING PRIMATE

THE BELIEVING PRIMATE

SCIENTIFIC, PHILOSOPHICAL, AND THEOLOGICAL REFLECTIONS ON THE ORIGIN OF RELIGION

Edited by

JEFFREY SCHLOSS

AND

MICHAEL J. MURRAY

OXFORD
UNIVERSITY PRESS

OXFORD
UNIVERSITY PRESS

Great Clarendon Street, Oxford OX2 6DP

Oxford University Press is a department of the University of Oxford.
It furthers the University's objective of excellence in research, scholarship,
and education by publishing worldwide in

Oxford New York

Auckland Cape Town Dar es Salaam Hong Kong Karachi
Kuala Lumpur Madrid Melbourne Mexico City Nairobi
New Delhi Shanghai Taipei Toronto

With offices in

Argentina Austria Brazil Chile Czech Republic France Greece
Guatemala Hungary Italy Japan Poland Portugal Singapore
South Korea Switzerland Thailand Turkey Ukraine Vietnam

Published in the United States
by Oxford University Press Inc., New York

British Library Cataloguing in Publication Data
Data available

Library of Congress Cataloging in Publication Data
Data available

Typeset by SPI Publisher Services, Pondicherry, India
Printed in Great Britain
on acid-free paper by
the MPG Books Group in the UK

ISBN 978-0-19-955702-8

1 3 5 7 9 10 8 6 4 2

Jeffrey and Michael dedicate this work to the following individuals, respectively:

To Stanley Ogren, John Leedy, James A. Teeri, and C. Richard Tracy—my teachers in the biosciences who inspired me with the thrill of knowing, and of not knowing yet.

To R. Preston Mason—for prodding me to follow the evidence wherever it leads, and guiding me to hear and heed the knock.

Preface

As every enquiry which regards religion is of the utmost importance, there are two questions in particular which challenge our attention, to wit, that concerning its foundation in reason, and that concerning its origin in human nature.

David Hume, *The Natural History of Religion* (1757)

This book is an attempt to foster conversation about one of the most fascinating and crucial topics in the relationship between religion and the natural sciences that, 250 years after Hume and 150 years after Darwin, is still woefully under-discussed in intellectual and civic life. The conversation we hope to stimulate, and even to enjoy, is between those interested in Hume's first question (involving the rational warrant for religion) and those applying evolutionary theory to Hume's second question (involving a causal explanation of religion). What are the religious and philosophical implications of recent evolutionary proposals to explain religion? After more than a century of debate over religious understandings of evolution, the tables have turned, and we are posed with evolutionary understandings of religion.

In order to have and to invite others into this conversation, we are seeking to overcome several obstacles. First, just discussing Hume's 'second question', and, more generally, examining the meaning–attributing dimensions of human culture by the mechanism-inferring methods of natural science, seems to make people nervous. On the one hand, we are all reticent to have our beliefs accounted for—from mathematical propositions to moral principles—in terms that make no reference to the truth but only to the cause of these beliefs. On the other hand, there has been a legacy of agenda-driven explanations of religion—from Feuerbach to Marx to Freud—that have somewhat devalued the currency of such totalizing modes of explanation. However, in the last several decades, and even in the last few years, significant breakthroughs in both cognitive science and evolutionary theory have opened up this conversation with empirically grounded and immensely fruitful new approaches. We are fortunate to have a number of leading contributors to these areas participating in this volume.

Second, there seems to be lingering ambivalence over how evolutionary explanations, in particular, should participate in this conversation. In part, this may reflect the fact that evolutionary theory has only recently honed its tools to engage these questions, and a new discussant threatens existing guilds. But also, within evolutionary biology itself there has been prominent and virulent controversy both about whether the central tendencies of human cognition and culture are tractable to Darwinian explanation and, if so, which tools apply. The emerging field of evolutionary religious studies offers promise of more cautious and ecumenical approaches to these questions. And, again, we are fortunate to have contributors representing a range of perspectives from the evolutionary and behavioral sciences.

Third, and most important, the streams of commerce between evolutionary and religious thinking are notoriously turbid with incivility and mistrust. Notwithstanding the regrettable politicization of the evolution–religion conflict in some regions of the world, there are clearly two more general reasons for this mistrust, both involving Hume's first question. The primary source of effluent is the fact that many religious thinkers have tied the attempt to buttress reasons for religious belief—primarily via arguments from design—to a wholesale rejection of evolution. This is not an option we entertain in this volume. On the other hand, and more recently, several prominent exegetes of evolutionary theory have wedded it to the assertion that there are no reasons for religious belief.[1] This is an issue we do discuss, both as an assumption and as a conclusion linked to evolutionary accounts of religion. We are particularly fortunate to have contributions from scholars representing naturalistic and varied theistic perspectives, and who have, within both traditions, differing understandings of the implications for religion of evolutionary proposals to explain religion.

The book therefore seeks to raise, though by no means resolve, three questions for an interdisciplinary readership. One, contributors describe several of the major questions in the evolution of religion, and sample, if not

---

1. For example, Richard Dawkins, *The God Delusion* (New York: Houghton Mifflin, 2007), or Daniel Dennett, *Darwin's Dangerous Idea* (New York: Simon and Shuster, 1995). Contrary to many criticisms, Dennett does not wed his evolutionary examination of religion in *Breaking the Spell: Religion as a Natural Phenomenon* (New York: Viking Penguin, 2006) with the assertion that religion must be false. In fact, he explicitly says that an evolutionary account of religion could be adequate, and religion still be true.

survey, a range of current proposals. Two, we ask what religiously significant philosophical assumptions—if any—underlie or arguably ought to underlie evolutionary accounts of religion. Three, we assess the consequences for religious belief of different theories currently being proposed to explain religious belief.

The book begins with an introduction that surveys the landscape and comments on the major issues to be engaged in each of the above three areas. This is followed by a series of chapters that describe and advocate various approaches to explaining religion evolutionarily. Finally, several sections, which include contributions by philosophers, theologians, and behavioral scientists, engage the implications of current theories. As will be evident, most of the chapters—regardless of the section or the author's background—pick up the gauntlet of interdisciplinary conversation and address several of the questions above. As will also be evident, many of the contributors—including several who engage each other directly—distinctly disagree. Indeed, the editors themselves disagree with several of the arguments, on both sides of the theism–naturalism divide. Pieces were solicited from recognized scholars in an attempt to provoke conversation, with the expectation that each contribution—on its own—will stand or wither under the heat of criticism.

Finally, we should describe how the conversation this book represents has come about, and acknowledge the support that has enabled it. Many of the contributions reflect literal conversations that have been occurring over several years, in a variety of venues. Calvin College hosted a couple of month-long, interdisciplinary faculty workshops on the evolution of morality and the evolution of religion, and follow-up international conferences on each of those themes.[2] Most of the contributors have participated in one or more of these collaborative gatherings.[3] Although not contributing to this volume, we wish to acknowledge the helpful participation of Richard Alexander, Larry Arnhart, Marc Bekoff, Chris Boehm, Donald Cronkite, Laura Ekstrom, Bruce Gordon, Niels Gregersen, James Hurd, Joseph Laporte, John Mullen, Tim Morris, Holmes Rolston III, Michael Ruse, William Struthers, Ralph Stearley, Ray van Arragon,

2. 2002–5. The Calvin project on the evolution of morality resulted in a book: Philip Clayton and Jeffrey Schloss (eds.), *Evolution and Ethics: Human Morality in Biological and Religious Perspective* (Grand Rapids, Mich.: Eerdmans, 2004).

3. Justin Barrett, John Haught, Dominic Johnson, Michael Murray, Alvin Plantinga, Del Ratzsch, Peter Richerson, Jeffrey Schloss, Charles Taliaferro, David Sloan Wilson.

David vander Laan, Jitse vander Meer, Kevin Vanhoozer, Keith Ward, and Rob Waltzer. Additional exchange between contributors occurred at the Templeton Research Lectures on 'the Cognitive Science of Religion' hosted by the Evolution, Cognition, and Culture Project at Johns Hopkins University (Spring 2008); the Pursuit of Happiness Project hosted by the Center for the Study of Law and Religion at Emory University (Oct. 2007); the workshop on 'the Social, Political, and Religious Transformations of Biology', hosted by the Faraday Institute, St Edmund's College, Cambridge (Sept. 2007); the interdisciplinary panel on the evolution of religion, hosted by the Metanexus Institute (June 2007); the Workshop on the Evolution and Theology of Cooperation, hosted by the Program in Evolutionary Dynamics at Harvard University and the Harvard Divinity School; and the International Conference on the Evolution of Religion (Makaha, Hawaii, Jan. 2007). Several of the chapters in this volume have benefited from and/or represent in modified and expanded form, ideas presented in these venues.[4] We want to thank the John Templeton Foundation and Calvin College for their generous funding of this project and also Emory University, Harvard University, Johns Hopkins University, St Edmunds College, Cambridge, the Metanexus Institute, and the Collins Foundation for supporting exchange that has contributed to the present volume. Last, we want to express appreciation to Philip Clayton, Robert Hinde, Michael Rea, and Dean Zimmerman for their helpful comments on parts of the manuscript.

We express our thanks to Metanexus.net for permission to reprint the essay by David Sloan Wilson. This essay was originally published by the Metanexus Institute in the *Global Spiral*, (www.globalspiral.com). Our thanks also to Edge.org for permission to reprint a much expanded version of the essay by Jonathan Haidt, first published on *Edge* (www.edge.org).

JPS

Westmont College, Santa Barbara, California

MJM

Franklin and Marshall College, Lancaster, Pennsylvania

May 2008

---

4. Justin Barrett, Paul Bloom, Joseph Bulbulia, Dominic Johnson, Michael Murray, Peter Richerson, Jeffrey Schloss, David Sloan Wilson, Peter van Inwagen.

Contents

List of Contributors   xiii

Introduction   I

1. Hand of God, Mind of Man: Punishment and Cognition in
   the Evolution of Cooperation   26
   Dominic Johnson and Jesse Bering

2. Religiosity as Mental Time-travel: Cognitive Adaptations for
   Religious Behavior   44
   Joseph Bulbulia

3. Cognitive Science, Religion, and Theology   76
   Justin Barrett

4. Is Religion Adaptive? Yes, No, Neutral. But Mostly
   We Don't Know   100
   Peter J. Richerson and Lesley Newson

5. Religious Belief as an Evolutionary Accident   118
   Paul Bloom

6. Explaining Belief in the Supernatural: Some Thoughts on
   Paul Bloom's 'Religious Belief as an Evolutionary Accident'   128
   Peter van Inwagen

7. Games Scientists Play   139
   Alvin Plantinga

8. Scientific Explanations of Religion and the Justification of
   Religious Belief   168
   Michael J. Murray

9. Evolutionary Accounts of Religion: Explaining and
   Explaining Away   179
   Michael J. Murray and Andrew Goldberg

10. Explaining Religious Experience   200
    Charles Taliaferro

11. Humanness in their Hearts: Where Science and Religion Fuse   215
    Del Ratzsch

12. Theology and Evolution: How Much Can Biology Explain?   246
    John Haught

13. Cognitive Science and the Evolution of Religion: A
    Philosophical and Theological Appraisal   265
    Nancey Murphy

14. Moral Psychology and the Misunderstanding of Religion   278
    Jonathan Haidt

15. Does Naturalism Warrant a Moral Belief in Universal
    Benevolence and Human Rights?   292
    Christian Smith

16. Evolutionary Social Constructivism: Narrowing
    (but Not Yet Bridging) the Gap   318
    David Sloan Wilson

Bibliography   339
Index   363

List of Contributors

Justin Barrett, Institute of Cognitive and Evolutionary Anthropology, Oxford University

Jesse Bering, Institute of Cognition and Culture, Queen's University, Belfast

Paul Bloom, Department of Psychology, Yale University

Joseph Bulbulia, Department of Religious Studies, Victoria University of Wellington

Andrew Goldberg, Mt. Sinai School of Medicine, New York

Jonathan Haidt, Department of Psychology, University of Virginia

John Haught, Department of Theology, Georgetown University

Dominic Johnson, Department of Government, Harvard University

Nancey Murphy, Fuller Theological Seminary

Michael J. Murray, Department of Philosophy, Franklin and Marshall College

Lesley Newson, School of Psychology, University of Exeter

Alvin Plantinga, Department of Philosophy, University of Notre Dame

Del Ratzsch, Department of Philosophy, Calvin College

Peter J. Richerson, Department of Environmental Science and Policy, University of California, Davis

Jeffrey Schloss, Department of Biology, Westmont College

Christian Smith, Department of Sociology, University of Notre Dame

Charles Taliaferro, Department of Philosophy, St. Olaf College

Peter van Inwagen, Department of Philosophy, University of Notre Dame

David Sloan Wilson, Department of Biological Studies, Binghamton University

Introduction: Evolutionary Theories of Religion

Science Unfettered or Naturalism Run Wild?

Jeffrey Schloss

> The sciences long remained like a lion-cub whose gambols delighted its master in private; it had not yet tasted man's blood... Science was not the business of Man because Man had not yet become the business of science... when Darwin starts monkeying with the ancestry of Man, and Freud with his soul, and the economists with all that is his, then indeed the lion will have got out of its cage.
>
> C. S. Lewis, 'Inaugural Lecture', Cambridge University (1954)[1]

Explanation on the Prowl

In a sense this is a book about the uncaged lion. While the oft-cited explosion of scientific knowledge is striking (Rescher 1978; Gilbert 1978), it also understates the character and cultural significance of recent developments. What has happened beyond a mere increase in amount of information is, of course, that entire regions of human experience previously considered off-limits or at least seemingly recalcitrant to scientific elucidation have become fair game for its explanatory prowess. Moreover, and perhaps more significantly, the life and behavioral sciences have become progressively unified under the single explanatory rubric of evolutionary theory. Darwinism is not just about 'ancestry' anymore (as if it ever were—Dewey 1910). Nor, contra the above quote, do theories

---

1. Lewis 1969: 7.

of the human psyche or economics involve separate disciplines. Over the last several decades, and even over just the last few years, there has been a proliferation of evolutionary proposals for consolidating previously disparate explanatory approaches to human cognition and behavior, including the crucial phenomenon of religion.

These developments have been enabled—the cage has been 'unlocked' as it were—by important theoretical keys, particularly in population genetics, cognitive science, and game theory. But there is more at work than this. A second lock comprised of social reticence to developing biological accounts of human behavior, due, in part, to a reaction against overly zealous attempts in the first half of the twentieth century, has been pried open in a couple of stages (Sahlins 1977; Segerstrale 2001). First, the emergence of sociobiology and evolutionary psychology in recent decades has involved, as Mary Midgley somewhat facetiously but accurately observes, the break-down of a 'precarious truce' between evolutionary theorists and human behavioral scientists, in which it was 'agreed not to deny the reality of human evolution, so long as nobody attempted to make any intellectual use of it' (Midgley 1982: p. xi). Second, and the subject of this volume, evolutionary analysis has very recently focused specifically on religion: 'Up to now, there has been a largely unexamined mutual agreement that scientists and other researchers will leave religion alone . . . pioneers are now beginning, for the first time really, to study the natural phenomena of religion through the eyes of contemporary science' (Dennett 2006: 19, 31).

What precisely is going on for the 'first time'? Of course, the attempt to understand the rational and natural foundations of religious belief is not in itself new. Two hundred years before Lewis's observation and a century before Darwin, Hume opened his *Natural History of Religion* with, 'As every enquiry which regards religion is of the utmost importance, there are two questions in particular which challenge our attention, to wit, that concerning its foundation in reason, and that concerning its origin in human nature' (1956: 21). Moreover, contemporary evolutionary accounts are not completing a job that only began with Hume. Prior to Hume's vig-ilant skepticism, there was a longstanding tradition within the community of faith—from Pascal to Aquinas to Anselm and Augustine—of debating the adequacy of rational arguments for belief, the root of faith in native dispositions, and the relationship between reason and nature (Porter 2005).

Nevertheless, current research on religion is indeed quite new in at least two ways. First off, the traditional critical emphasis on Hume's 'two questions'—religion's foundation in reason and its origin in human nature—has largely been pared down to just one. This understandably ensues from the fact that current discussions are primarily scientific, and looking for natural causes, not assessing metaphysical arguments, is simply what science does. But more is at work than the metaphysical neutrality of science. There is also a widespread confidence that science is able to provide an explanation that is not just necessary but sufficient for understanding religious belief: when rational justifications for religion are widely understood to constitute a null set, all that is left to investigate are its causes. In *Naturalism and Religion*, Kai Nielsen makes the claim that

> by now it has been well established that there are no sound reasons for religious belief: there is no reasonable possibility of establishing religious beliefs to be true; there is no such thing as religious knowledge or sound religious belief. But, when there are no good reasons for religious belief... and yet religious belief, belief that is both widespread and tenacious, persists in our cultural life, then it is time to look for the *causes* of religious beliefs...
>
> (2001: 35)

Now even this is not a wholly new enterprise. Spinoza viewed the assurance that God directs things toward His purposes as illusory, and set out to explain 'why so many fall into this error, and why all are by nature so prone to embrace it...' (1910 [1677]: 30). What seems to be unprecedented, in the public domain, is leveraging this position with the modern cultural authority of science, and, in the scientific domain, the relinquishment of neutrality on issues that, by both the logic of its method and tradition of its employment, science has not heretofore adjudicated. Daniel Dennett, the most philosophically sophisticated public exegete of evolutionary theories of religion, rightly laments the 'unfortunate pattern in the work that has been done. People... either want to defend their favorite religion from its critics or want to demonstrate the irrationality and futility of religion...' (2006: 32). Actually, in evolutionary studies of religion there are prominent examples of the latter and virtually none of the former. But my point concerns not so much the ends to which the science is put, but the assumptions with which it begins. While there are plenty of overt and acerbic attempts to use science to discredit religion (Dawkins 2007; Stenger 2007), this by no means characterizes the field. What does characterize it is the a priori emphasis on the adequacy of natural causal explanations.

I am not speaking here merely of the methodological commitment to eschew employment of supernatural causes in scientific explanation, but of the prevailing assumption that *reasons* for belief in supernatural entities can safely be uncoupled from an explanatory account of why people hold such beliefs. In the spirit of emphasis on Hume's second question, Dennett himself dissociates causal explanations of religious beliefs from consideration of their truth or falsity. Not arguing one way or another, he indicates 'I decided some time ago that diminishing returns had set in on the arguments about God's existence, and I doubt that any breakthroughs are in the offing, from either side' (2006: 27). While this would seem to embody the very methodological neutrality he endorses, matters are more complicated. For one thing, proffering an explanation for why someone holds a belief independent of its rationale—positing causes and dismissing reasons—is not itself a neutral posture toward the belief. Moreover, it turns out that 'diminishing returns' does not refer to an argument that has mired in stalemate, could go either way, and is best not to get ensnared in, but rather to one that has been decisively settled and does not warrant further investment: 'flattening all the serious arguments for the existence of God' is a feat that has been adequately accomplished (Dennett 2007).

None of these comments are meant to be remonstrative. Indeed, if religious (or other) beliefs are either false or groundless, and are nevertheless widely held—as many beliefs about the paranormal and supernatural demonstrably are—this surely warrants both recognition and explanation. My point is simply that such recognition represents a salient, recent, and prominent (though by no means invariant) feature of evolutionary approaches to religion. And it is an issue on which contributors to this volume disagree.

The second significant aspect of current theories is that not only do they emphasize natural causes over reasons for religious belief, but also they understand the latter *in terms of* the former. And, unlike earlier Freudian and Marxist naturalistic explanations of religion, evolutionary accounts involve causal processes that have empirical ramifications and are posited to be universally influential—across all aspects of human behavior and in all biological phenomena. 'Everything we value—from sugar and sex and money to music and love and religion—we value for reasons. Lying behind, and distinct from, our reasons are evolutionary reasons, free-floating rationales that have been endorsed by natural selection' (Dennett 2006: 93).[2]

2. This was anticipated in Dewey's claim nearly a century ago that 'the influence of Darwin upon philosophy resides in his having conquered the phenomena of life for the principle of transition, and thereby freed the new logic for application to mind and morals and life'

This second distinctive is by no means entirely worked out or uncontroversial. Even within evolutionary biology, there is considerable debate over the extent to which and in what sense human reasons can be adequately understood in terms of selection's 'rationales' (Buller 2006; Dennett 2003; Gould 1997a; Gould 1997b; Maynard Smith 1995; Orr 1997; Rose and Rose 2000). Or, to use the language of game theory, how well psychological utilities map the utility of fitness. Moreover, the relationship between evolutionary reasons and the endorsement of selection is not always clear. This involves prominent debates over the adaptationist paradigm. But also, even when the adaptive rationale for a trait is unquestionable—as in sexual reproduction or the genetic code—we still may have no explanation for how the characteristic evolved to begin with: function does not provide an account of a trait's origin. Stephen Gould's admonition on this point is especially relevant when it comes to evolutionary accounts of religion: 'a crucial, but often disregarded, distinction [exists] between "reasons for historical origin" and "basis of current utility". The common conflation of these entirely separate notions has engendered enormous confusion in evolutionary theory' (2002: 671).

The above issues are much larger than, but set the general context for, evolutionary theories of religion. In what follows, I will describe more specifically the landscape of current discussion on which contributions to this volume are situated.

Scientific Accounts

Although the philosophical literature on scientific demarcation is vast and unsettled, most scientists are not philosophers and most of their work does not involve the need to identify, much less publicly justify, what about it is properly 'scientific'. This has not been the case when it comes to evolutionary theory in general and scientific explanations of religion

(1910: 15). E. O. Wilson asserted this with more bravado if less nuance at the beginning of his seminal *Sociobiology*, which formally launched the field: 'self-knowledge is constrained and shaped by the emotional control centers in the hypothalamus and limbic systems of the brain...What, we are then compelled to ask, made the hypothalamus and limbic system? They evolved by natural selection. That simple biological statement must be pursued to explain ethics and ethical philosophers, if not epistemology and epistemologists, at all depths' (1975: 3). Dennett's notion of a 'free-floating rationale' that is both 'behind and distinct from human reasons' is a considerably more elegant framing (Dennett 2003; 2006).

in particular. 'Creationist' attempts to refashion the meaning of science, widespread ambivalence (if not resistance) to applying its methods to the study of religion, and the history of distorting science for the sake of discrediting or advancing religion by those with a metaphysical 'ax to grind' (Dennett 2006: 32; Stark and Finke 2000) have caused working scientists to be quite explicit though not always nuanced in delimiting what makes an explanation scientific. Over and against these challenges, science is characterized as providing explanations in terms of natural rather than supernatural causes. In a widely cited and representative recent critique of 'Creationism', evolutionary biologist Jerry Coyne opines: 'science simply doesn't deal with hypotheses about a guiding intelligence, or supernatural phenomena like miracles, because science is the search for rational explanations of natural phenomena' (2007).

This sounds fair enough; virtually no scientist would disagree. To offer a scientific account of religion, then, would seemingly be to assess it, like any other object of inquiry, with the view that 'religion is natural as opposed to supernatural, that it is a human phenomenon composed of events, organisms, objects, structures, patterns, and the like that all obey the laws of physics or biology, and hence do not involve miracles' (Dennett 2006: 25). At the very least, a scientific approach to religion would involve the commitment—as with all scientific research—to get as far as possible with naturalistic explanation (and to provide another kind of account would be to do something other than science). While this may generate challenges to, it does not have to be inimical to religious belief. In their social scientific account of religion, Stark and Finke advocate navigating between, on the one hand, 'the old atheistic approach to religion' that assumes it is irrational and, on the other hand, the 'fallacy that to be true, religions must be immune to social scientific analysis, being inexplicable enigmas' (2000: 20).

While the commitment to natural versus supernatural explanation is the undisputed if unadorned starting-point of the present research program, it involves several questions that are not much discussed in this literature but have import for both the study of religion and the implications of such study for religious belief itself.

First, the distinction between 'natural' and 'supernatural' has been made in profoundly contrasting ways in different historical periods and intellectual contexts,[3] and even in the specific context of modern scientific inquiry

---

3. Porter (2005) provides an extensive historical survey of the manifold meanings of 'natural'. Nielson (2001), Rea (2004), and Brooke and Cantor (1998) give contrasting accounts of the

it is both permeable and ambiguous. Coyne (2007) cites 'alchemy, faith healing, astrology, creationism', as quintessential examples of the supernatural, which have not 'advanced our understanding of nature by one iota'. Their ultimate lack of empirical confirmation and explanatory fruitfulness is indisputable. But it is a jingoistic view of scientific history to suggest that—from phlogiston to Lamarkianism to phrenology—only the ideas that survive contribute to advance: it is the *winnowing process* and not just the *winning proposals* that facilitate advance. Now we might want to employ differential diagnoses for failure, and say that history has taught us that some kinds of proposals—notably those that involve the supernatural—have been so consistently unproductive that they do not deserve to enter the process of scientific winnowing.[4] Yet that still leaves us with the problem of demarcating the 'supernatural'. Alchemy and particularly astrology, for example, have complex social histories of mystical and occult, or naturalistic formulations, and in any case have, until recently, always been deeply intertwined with empirical science of the day. 'In the hands of Ptolemy', historian of astronomy Owen Gingrich observes, 'astrology became a scientific topic' (2003: 347). Moreover, to say that astrology—from Ptolemy's *Almagest* and *Tetrabiblios* on—has not contributed one iota to 'our understanding of nature' is to be as insensitive to the history of celestial science as current advocates of astrology are indifferent to contemporary science (Whitfield 2001; Gingrich 2003).

role of the natural and of natural causes in scientific explanation. Over and against this, Shea (1984) offers an especially thoughtful discussion of the historical and contemporary meanings of 'supernatural', distinguishing between epistemological, ontological, and theological conceptions: 'We have seen two senses of supernatural. In the first, the term means the unnatural or an occurrence beyond the laws of nature in contrast with the expected, the ordinary, or the event in accord with the laws of nature. The second sense intends a distinction between orders of beings, supernatural and natural. The first sense is basically Greek. The second usage of the term entered the Christian tradition in the fifth century . . . These two are the inherited and popular meanings. The third was developed in the medieval debate during the eleventh to thirteenth centuries on the relation between grace and free will' (204). Given the debated 'nature of the natural' and the role of background beliefs in distinguishing it, McGrath concludes—no doubt also debatably—' "Nature" is thus not a neutral entity, having the status of an observation statement: it involves seeing the world in a particular way—and the way in which it is seen shapes the resulting concept of "nature". Far from being a "given", the idea of "nature" is shaped by the prior assumptions of the observer. One does not "observe" nature; one constructs it . . . the concept of nature is, at least in part, a social construction. If the concept of nature is socially mediated—to whatever extent—it cannot serve as an allegedly neutral, objective, or uninterpreted foundation of a theory or theology. Nature is already an interpreted category' (2001: 113).

4. In fact, I would want to say that. But for a more nuanced assessment, see Hull 1978.

Reflecting on a more defensible list than Coyne's, philosopher Michael Rea nevertheless observes that we

> disagree about what it is for something to count as natural or supernatural. There are common paradigms: men, beasts, plants, atoms, and electrons are natural; God, angels, ghosts, and immaterial souls are supernatural. But even these paradigms are controversial; and in any case, it is not clear what items on each list have in common with their other list-mates that makes them examples of natural or supernatural entities.

> (2004: 54)

There are, of course, a variety of process, panentheistic, and other proposals for souls (though not immaterial souls), for miracles, and even for God that are fully committed to a uniform system of materially instantiated causes not open to interruption from outside—in fact committed to there being no such thing as 'outside'. Such understandings emphatically reject supernaturalism. Although I have no interest here in assessing, much less defending, their conceptions of the above entities or of the natural, the point is that understandings of the natural do vary, and, even accepting a fairly stringent definition, it is not always clear what qualifies for the list. No less a naturalist than Quine comments that, 'Descartes' dualism between mind and body is called metaphysics, but it could as well be reckoned as science, however false' (1995: 252). These arcane issues don't matter much at all, in fact they are arcane by very virtue of not mattering, when it comes to conducting most science. But they may matter a great deal when it comes to the study of religion 'as a natural phenomenon'.

Second, let's assume for argument that the absence of conversation about this issue in the science of religion literature reflects not just neglect, nor even mere compliance, but actual clarity about what does and does not qualify as natural. We still have the question of warrant for the methodological canon of not employing the supernatural, and under what circumstances, if ever, it could be relaxed.[5] Prominent evolutionary biologists operate with and publicly express very different understandings of this issue. Jerry Coyne (2007) takes an instrumentalist approach, claiming: 'We don't reject the supernatural merely because we have an overweening philosophical commitment to materialism; we reject it because entertaining the supernatural has never helped us understand the natural world.' But,

---

5. I am not questioning the warrant for methodological naturalism in science (although some contributors to this volume do). But I am suggesting that how this warrant is articulated influences how the method is applied to phenomena that are taken to represent the supernatural.

if this is the case, could we accept a supernatural cause if it produced fruitful explanation? Quine thinks so: 'If I saw indirect explanatory benefit in positing sensibilia, possibilia, spirits, a Creator, I would joyfully accord them scientific status too, on a par with such avowedly scientific posits as quarks and black holes' (1995: 252). In this volume, David Sloan Wilson and Christian Smith take very different approaches to this matter.

On the other hand, Richard Lewontin argues for a position diametrically opposite Coyne's, identifying it as the very

> key to an understanding of the real struggle between science and the supernatural. We take the side of science ... because we have a prior commitment, a commitment to materialism. It is not that the methods and institutions of science somehow compel us to accept a material explanation of the phenomenal world, but, on the contrary, that we are forced by our *a priori* adherence to material causes to create an apparatus of investigation and a set of concepts that produce material explanations ...
>
> (1997: 31)

But if *that* is the case, and one excludes supernatural explanations based on prior metaphysical commitments, is it justifiable to allow the supernatural, or at least its possibility, if starting with different background assumptions? This is a question Alvin Plantinga and Del Ratzsch explore in this volume.

Third, let's set aside the above issues for a moment and acknowledge the fact that, although current scientific research on religion involves workers from a wide spectrum of religious, non-religious, and anti-religious commitments in conversation with one another, such research is empirically rooted and theoretically fruitful, and—even though (perhaps because) these issues have not been deeply addressed—there is nevertheless a broadly shared methodological approach. That approach simply involves not invoking the supernatural; it can be characterized as not using the existence of the objects of religious beliefs in explanations of those beliefs. Pascal commented on the 'God-shaped vacuum' in each human heart.[6] In one sense, scientific theories of religion can be understood as describing the contours of 'Pascal's vacuum', assessing the individual and social consequences of various prescriptions for filling it, and analyzing the conditions that generate various kinds of assurance that it has been filled. It does

6. Actually, this phrase is absent from his writings, though it may be consonant with his considerably more elegant description of 'seeking from things absent the help he does not obtain in things present. But these are all inadequate, because the infinite abyss can only be filled by an infinite and immutable object, that is to say, only by God Himself' (Pascal 2004: 98).

(or ought) not, however, assess the metaphysical reality of what is believed to fill it. Stark and Finke, themselves religious believers, claim 'our fundamental quest is to apply social scientific tools to the relationship between human beings and what they experience as divine. Science may examine any aspect of that relationship except its authenticity' (2000: 21). Daniel Dennett, who frankly acknowledges his atheistic commitments in his book on religion, nevertheless maintains that a scientific study of religion need not deny the truth of religious belief, claiming 'that it could be true that God exists, that God is indeed the intelligent, conscious, loving creator of us all, and yet still religion itself, as a complex set of phenomena, is a perfectly natural phenomenon' (2006: 25).

This is a good starting-point, but there are two different problems with these representations of neutrality, having to do with an unstated incongruity between Stark and Dennett. Some will say that Dennett goes too far; indeed, in this volume Haught and Taliaferro say just that. Yes, if religion is '*perfectly* natural' it could be that God exists, but not the God that most theists in most times have believed in, and not the God of the religious traditions that Dennett and other researchers most wish to explain. Dennett is not just proposing that we subject religion to unflinching scientific analysis, but that we start already having reached the conclusion that there is nothing at all to religion or the objects of its beliefs that is not fully amenable to such analysis: it *is* 'natural as opposed to supernatural' and does 'not involve miracles'. This clearly entails a metaphysical rather than a methodological commitment, and up front, judges as false the beliefs of anyone who thinks that there are or have been miracles (at least, if miracles are 'supernatural'), or, especially, anyone who believes *because* of a purported miracle. A famous example of the latter is Pascal's renewal of faith at witnessing the healing of his niece in Port Royal: 'scio cui credidi—I know whom I have believed'. But, of course, the Christian tradition in general believes not only that there is a 'loving creator of us all' but that this Creator has acted in history, and definitively in the resurrection. A thoroughgoing scientific explanation of religion along the lines outlined on this account would set itself the task of explaining the existence of a tradition founded on belief in an event that is presumed never to have happened.

On the other hand, there is a case to be made for doing just this. It could well be that 'neutrality' does not go nearly far enough. The qualities of an explanandum should not be ignored but accounted for by the explanans: if a proposition is demonstrably false, and yet believed, it is not just the fact of believing a certain kind of proposition, but also the fact of believing a falsehood that warrants explanation. When the patent falsity of a belief is 'tolerably plain to informed and impartial persons not crippled by ideology and neurosis . . . it is of crucial importance to look for [its] causes and indeed to find them, if we can' (Nielsen 2001: 35).

Moreover, the very falsity (or the indemonstrability) of some beliefs is not only something to be explained but also serves as part of the explanation in some accounts of religious beliefs. For example, in some 'costly signaling' proposals, massively fictional or socially marginal beliefs are posited to be adaptive in virtue of these very qualities' ability to convey shared commitment. Stark and Finke's comment that science cannot investigate the 'authenticity' of the relationship between humans and their experience of the divine would seem to entail a woefully constrained notion of authenticity, if it ignores the question of whether experience itself is delusional.

Richard Dawkins is sure that belief in the virgin birth is a delusion. He comments that if he had a time machine he would go back, get some Jesus DNA, and use the Y-chromosome to demonstrate who the real father was. The same thing could be said about the empty tomb, a centerpiece of religious belief for Christians. Of course, we don't have a time machine. But, unlike notions of the Trinity or an afterlife or the salvific value of faith vs works, these are phenomenal claims about the material world, amenable in principle to empirical assessment and, in the absence of direct access to the events in question, appropriate subjects for some kinds of evidential argument. Should assessment, on the basis of textual analysis, historical records, sociological and psychological principles, and scientific understanding, etc.—not for the existence of deity, but for whether or not an *event* occurred—figure in to an explanation of religious belief in the event? But now we are back to questions of (a) the relationship between reasons for belief and causal explanations for belief, (b) distinguishing the natural and supernatural (including the possibility of natural causes for 'miracles'), and (c) the a priori exclusion of the supernatural in causal accounts of religion.

Just raising these issues risks subverting the very conversation we wish to convene. There are those who understandably view the questions as non-questions—being both simple and settled, there is no need for discussion. Others will understand them to be much more complicated than can be done justice by a non-philosopher in a brief introduction. And, perhaps most difficult, the well of conversation has been poisoned by tripartite 'Creationist' abuses: ignorance and misrepresentation of empirical data, the explicit goal not of explaining but of proselytizing, and seeking to obscure rather than clarify the very distinction between natural and supernatural. This is the first book on evolutionary theories of religion that attempts both to give proper weight to a wide range of fully naturalistic scientific accounts and also to foster comment from a comparably wide range of philosophical and theological perspectives.

Religion

The Yale ecologist G. Evelyn Hutchinson is reputed to have remarked: 'the most important decision an ecologist ever makes is where to get out of the car'. This is surely true of scientific studies of religion as well. How one defines religion, and under what conditions it is studied, will influence the explanations proffered. (And of course the reverse is also the case.) Although I will not undertake an assessment of different ways of construing religion here, I do want to make two comments on how this construal influences current theorizing.

First, different explanatory approaches tend to emphasize different definitions of religion. Many cognitive science approaches understandably focus on religious concepts, particularly concepts of supernatural agents. For example, Paul Bloom (2005) cites Tyler's famous 1876 'minimum definition of religion: the belief in spiritual beings'. Other cognitive science accounts similarly emphasize supernatural or counter-intuitive agents (Atran 2002a; Boyer 2001; Barrett 2004), or belief in magnified agent qualities such as an afterlife.

On the other hand, many evolutionary adaptationist approaches to religion employ definitions that emphasize its contribution to human flourishing, from the social functionalism proposed by theorists like Durkheim to the meaning-making value posited by contemporary accounts like Peter Berger's (1990) notion of a socially constructed 'sacred canopy'. Clifford

Geertz's (1973) influential definition is widely cited: 'A religion is a system of symbols which acts to establish powerful, pervasive, and long-lasting moods and motivations in men by formulating conceptions of a general order of existence and clothing these conceptions with such an aura of factuality that the moods and motivations seem uniquely realistic.' Geertz himself clearly acknowledges that while definitions do not answer questions they do control the direction of inquiry. In fact, his approach has been both praised and criticized as an attempt to 'rescue religion from the ravages of positivism' (Frankenberry and Penner 1999: 618; McCutcheon 2004).

Each of these formulations has therefore tended to yield the explanations proposed by those invoking the definition. In his more inclusive treatment that considers both cognitive and adaptationist proposals, as well as memetic virus accounts, Dennett combines the above two by proposing to 'define religions as social systems whose participants avow belief in a supernatural agent or agents whose approval is to be sought' (2006: 9). Even this definition leaves out those belief systems that do not posit supernatural beings, and leaves out of religion the notion of divine reality or the sacred. It turns out that the approach few evolutionary inquiries seem to take is that taken by William James in defining religion as 'the feelings, acts, and experiences of individual men in their solitude, so far as they apprehend themselves to stand in relation to whatever they may consider the divine' (1902: 31). Nevertheless, one must begin somewhere: if one augments Dennett's definition—which is both ecumenical and parsimonious—to include living in accord with not just supernatural agents but also transcendent reality, it would encompass the range of approaches taken by contributors to this volume.

Second, of course there are many aspects of religion that warrant an explanation, and the above differences, in part, reflect this. There are cognitive propositions about beings, or transcendent moral realms, or an afterlife, or the origins of the world. There are religious or numinal experiences, and (not the same) emotional affect that attends experience. There are individual spiritual disciplines, corporate rituals, and sanctioned social behaviors. There are religious institutions and knowledge workers. And for all of the preceding phenomena there exists both the human *capacity* to produce them and the specific *content* of beliefs, emotions, behaviors, etc.—all of which are potentially amenable to evolutionary explanation in the same way there are evolutionary proposals for the capacity for and the content of moral beliefs, behaviors, and social systems. Finally, there are personal ontogenies of religious faith, ecological life histories to the development of particular religious traditions, and evolutionary trajectories of religious change across cultural epochs. If religion is pathological, it is not a disease, but a syndrome with a decidedly mixed etiology!

Evolutionary Explanations

As with any new area of study, evolutionary accounts of religion involve a wide range of varying and vigorously debated approaches. I want to characterize briefly the major positions and their attendant controversies, each of which will be individually assessed by other contributors to this volume.

A number of taxonomies have recently been proposed for evolutionary accounts of religion (Atran and Norenzayan 2004; Dennett 2006; David Sloan Wilson 2005). Like all schemes of classification, they both reflect and direct judgments about what constitute key differences. Much of the contemporary discussion tends to emphasize the distinction between adaptationist and non-adaptationist accounts (David Sloan Wilson 2005; Atran 2002a). On the one hand, this makes good sense because the question of whether or not religion has biologically relevant function is crucial for the development of an evolutionary explanation of its origin (though bear in mind Gould's admonition: while the former is relevant to the latter, it does not provide the latter). This distinction also makes sense because it highlights a significant and largely unanticipated break between current adaptationist theories and the dominant naturalistic approaches to religion for much of the last century (e.g., Marx and Freud) that have characterized religion as pathological.

On the other hand, dichotomizing current theories by locating them at two poles along an adaptationist axis is problematic for several reasons. For one thing, what it means to be adaptive is still a matter of some ambiguity in both the philosophy of biology and evolutionary theory (Brandon 1995; Plotkin 1994b; George Williams 1966; Richerson and Newson, this volume). It can be understood to involve traits evident at different, and debated, scales of function (e.g., organism, group, species). And the meaning, even viability, of functional language in naturalistic explanation is itself debated (Allen, Bekoff, and Lauder 1998; Ariew, Cummins, and Perlman 2002; Buller 1999; Fodor 2000). 'Adaptive' can be understood without referent to traits and solely in terms of the successful transmission of replicators. Moreover, with humans, there are debated proposals for non-genetic replicators, or 'memes'. All this means that distinguishing an adaptationist from non-adaptationist proposal is not a black and white issue, and emphasizing this distinction may even end up obscuring the implications of different accounts. For example, explaining religion as a memetic virus that infects human minds, to the detriment of both the individual human and the society, may be considered either an adaptationist account from the perspective of the meme, or a non-adaptationist account in terms of human flourishing. Religion could be 'adapted to' but not 'adaptive for' human life.

Even if we assume a workable understanding of adaptation, the question of whether a widespread trait that varies highly in both environmental context and phenotypic expression *is or is not* adaptive is just too wooden in its formulation. Even a single-locus polymorphism like sickle-cell anemia has some phenotypes that are adaptive in some environments and not in others. A complex phenomenon like religion, which exists in varied social and ecological contexts, with many different attributes (see above), each of which has many different manifestations, would almost certainly be expected to vary in adaptive character. And, notwithstanding polemics on both sides, this is exactly what seems to be the case.

But perhaps we can at least ask whether or not religion is *primarily* or *typically* adaptive or favorable to human flourishing? David Sloan Wilson has sought to address this question empirically through a random sample of world religions (2005), and argued provisionally for an adaptive role of religion. Richard Dawkins argues strongly for the reverse, from a somewhat less randomly chosen sample. And Daniel Dennett just wants to make sure the question is emphatically posed and no longer dodged:

> Yes, I want to put religion on the examination table. If it is fundamentally benign, as many of its devotees insist, it should emerge just fine; suspicions will be put to rest and we can then concentrate on the few peripheral pathologies that religion, like every other natural phenomenon, falls prey to. If it is not, the sooner we identify the problems clearly the better.
>
> (2006: 39)

While the question of whether religion generates behaviors that promote fitness (or human flourishing broadly conceived) is both scientifically and religiously important, asking whether it *is or is not fundamentally so* is probably naive. How would we reckon? Is it the number of adaptive versus maladaptive religions: majority wins? Or the total number of adherents? Or its net influence (by some hedonic or eudemonic index) on total number of lives? Or its integrated influence on the trajectory of history? Or perhaps we are to identify a fundamental essence, and distinguish this from 'peripheral' impacts—benign or pathological—that represent the corruption of religion by other, non-religious factors. And all of this construes 'religion' as one thing, the fundamental character of which can be identified and assessed. Posed dichotomously, the question of virulence is methodologically impenetrable and inescapably vulnerable to what definition and aspect of religion one focuses on, and what understanding of human *telos* is utilized to make the judgment of benign versus pathological. Moreover, it is bound to conscript science in the very attempts to discredit or advance religion, which the insistence on unflinching assessment seeks to avert.

For all of the above reasons, plus the actual content of the major scientific proposals under consideration, I would suggest that the legitimately important question of religion-as-adaptation needs neither to be dichotomized nor to dominate discussion of evolutionary explanations. Rather than being strict alternatives, current approaches can be understood as representing explanation at different causal scales: proximal cognitive mediation, Darwinian selection, and cultural innovation (see Table 0). It turns out that adaptationist versus non-adaptationist interpretations exist

Table 0. Evolutionary accounts of religion

Cognitive accounts	Darwinian accounts	Co-evolutionary accounts
Extended attachment	'Spandrels'	Memetic pathogen
Emotional compensation	Vestigial traits	Memetic symbiont
Obsessive-compulsive disorder/harm avoidance	Sexually selected displays	Cultural group selection
Anthropomorphic projection	Internalized sanctions	
Hypersensitive agency detection device (HADD)	Costly cooperative signals	

within each tier, and interactions between tiers are expected. What we would like, of course, is an integrated account of the selective regime that gave rise to and maintains religiously salient cognitive dispositions, cultural innovations, and interactions between the two. Notwithstanding, these three theoretical domains are presently characterized by proposals that view religion, respectively, as a non-adaptive 'spandrel', a cooperative adaptation, and a memetic pathogen. I will briefly comment on each, leaving subsequent chapters to provide more detailed assessment.

Cognitive Science

Current approaches in the cognitive science of religion view religion as involving innate cognitive dispositions that have evolved along with all of our cognitive capacities, but religion itself is not understood as an evolutionary adaptation. Rather, it is a 'spandrel' or by-product of other cognitive capacities that do have selective value. There are a number of proposals to explain different aspects of religion as cognitive incidentals. Religious ritual is suggested to ensue from the reification of obsessive contagion or harm avoidance behaviors (McCauley and Lawson 2002); religious emotions and imagery from unconstrained extrapolation of capacities and longings for attachment (Kirkpatrick 2004); the nearly universal belief in supernatural agents, from anthropomorphic projection (Guthrie 1993) or from a bias toward false attribution by innate mechanisms for agency detection (Atran 2002a; Barrett 2004; Bloom 2005; Boyer 2001b). While these proposals are by no means mutually exclusive, the last proposal—involving a 'hypersensitive agency detection device' (HADD)—has arguably received the most attention within and outside the field.

Several issues merit pointing out, which will be further explored from different perspectives by later chapters. First, the empirical observations underwriting these approaches are extensive and impressive. There can be little question that the detection of agency, the magnification of certain aspects of agency (e.g., immortality, omniscience), and a bias toward false positives entail innate cognitive dispositions. On the other hand, there is little empirical work demonstrating that these cognitive mechanisms and the religious mentation they contribute to 'are not adaptations and they have no evolutionary functions...' (Atran 2002a: 4). The Darwinian question of what selective regime accounts for these dispositions is largely separate from and considerably less addressed than the empirical demonstrations of their existence and operation.

Second, and whether or not HADD and related phenomena are 'spandrels', these empirically supported proposals for cognitive innateness of religiously salient concepts are surely necessary to the scientific understanding of religion. But they are by no means sufficient. Notwithstanding the ambitious title of a prominent exposition of 'spandrel' theory—*Religion Explained* (Boyer 2001)—there are numerous questions about religion that HADD does not explain. Why do religious entities have numinal or deeply sacred qualities that go far beyond those ascribed to other magical or super-agents that many people really believe exist, like leprechauns? What about religious beliefs is able to exact such demanding investment—arguably one of the most expensive investments human beings make—especially if it is a 'spandrel'? And while the promiscuity of innate cognitive dispositions may make unseen agents conceivable, and their minimally counter-intuitive nature may make them memorable, what makes them continue to be credible (a question pressed by Murray in this volume)? Having worked hard to develop a scientific account, it will not do to lapse into ad hominem assertions of religion's supposed immunity to self-analysis (Dennett 2006). Empirical work indicates that religiously relevant agency concepts are assessed and winnowed over the course of both individual cognitive development (Barrett 2004) and historical cultural development (Whitehouse 2004a; Whitehouse 2004b). A comprehensive explanation of religious belief must include an account of how it is confirmed, relinquished, and, yes, sometimes stubbornly or indifferently clung to in the face of reason and experience.

Last, theories of cognitive innateness have been employed—I would suggest unconvincingly—for both natural theology and atheology. James Ashbrook's evocative phrase (1994)—'the cry for the other'—refers to innate cognitive and neurological desires for deep connection, and is even reminiscent of Pascal's vacuum. It has been invoked to suggest that this cry is a cry for something that is real, since fundamental features of perception and cognition typically refer to things that are so. Ed Oates (2007) argues that just as wings and lungs evolved 'into' or in virtue of atmospheric air, so mind—including its moral and religious concepts—evolved into 'mental air'. The problem is 'air' is not just a feature of the environment that lungs evolved into: the fact that air has enough free oxygen to make possible lungs and the lifestyle they support is due to photosynthesis and therefore is itself a product of evolution. *Air evolved*. Moreover, although in the last analysis lungs would not evolve if there were no such thing as air, cognitive dispositions can evolve as long as the behaviors they motivate serve (or are pleiotropically associated with serving) reproduction, regardless of whether or not their referent is 'there'. The existence of innate proclivities to believe in God is certainly concordant with His existence. But it doesn't demonstrate it.

In fact, the same observations of innateness have been used to argue for the reverse. For one thing, if religion is due to a cognitive mechanism that is vulnerable to false positives (HADD), then perhaps religious belief itself is innately unreliable. Michael Murray considers this problem at length in this volume. For another thing, even if religious belief-forming mechanisms are not unreliable, we may have no warrant for confidence in their accuracy. This would seem to be a consequence of any naturalistic explanation of belief that uncoupled cause from rationale: 'to turn the Darwinian explanation into an "explaining away" the Nihilist need only add the uncontroversial scientific principle that if our best theory of why people believe P does not require that P is true, then there are no grounds to believe P is true' (Sommers and Rosenberg 2003: 67). This point deserves to be taken seriously, though it should be taken seriously in the context of three qualifications. First, there is an interesting rhetorical game going on here. We begin the scientific study of religion by uncoupling the assessment of religious truth claims from a search for biological causes of religious belief, seeing how far we can get with this religiously neutral method. We end by concluding that only a different kind of explanation, ruled out from the start—one that entails the truth (or falsity) of beliefs in an account of their acceptance—is congenial to warrant for religious belief. Second, clearly this is a game that could be played with any beliefs, including those about scientific or mathematical propositions, and even evolutionary theories of religion (see Murray and Plantinga in this volume for more on this theme). Third, when it comes to religious belief, it is not yet clear whether we can explain it 'all the way down' in a way that is indifferent to whether or not it is true. Some kinds of beliefs may require that the belief be true as a precondition for having the belief: e.g., any explanation of my belief, P, that I was born, requires as part of the explanation that P be true. To explain belief in a God who made all things, including people who believe in Him, in a way that does not require the truth of that belief, would involve having an adequate explanation for minds' inclination to hold the belief, and the origin of minds that hold it, and a universe with characteristics that gave rise to minds, and something rather than nothing at all which does not require there be a God. Whether or not we have such an account and, if so, whether it constitutes 'our best theory' is an issue that many view as settled. Unfortunately, those who are most sure of this don't seem to agree on the outcome.

Darwinian Accounts

Darwinian accounts of religion explain it as a biological characteristic that has resulted from natural selection. This does not mean that religion is adaptive. Religion could be a behavioral fossil, a vestigial trait that is the same as it was in an ancestral environment in which it was originally adaptive, but no longer is in the current environment. Or its phenotypic plasticity could have allowed originally adaptive characteristics to be distorted, having been a very different phenomenon in primordial environments with different population densities, social structures, or resource availability. Or, famously, it could be an evolutionary 'spandrel', an incidental or pleiotropic by-product that has no adaptive value but is associated with other traits or underlying genes which do. Before 'spandrel' accounts for religion became prominent, similar accounts for morality had already been proposed (Ayala 1987; Ayala 1995). These non-adaptive proposals are all fully Darwinian and are all postulated in the context of the aegis of natural selection.

Like the above, biologically adaptationist accounts view religion as a genetically endowed characteristic (or suite of characteristics) but posit it to have evolved because it confers reproductive benefit. There are manifold proposals for how religion serves this role, including sexual selection, or enhanced ability to attract mates (Slone 2007), self-enhancing displays of status or manipulative employment of signals (Cronk 1994), reduction of stress related to fear of death or the unknown (an adaptationist construal of some cognitive theories that are often linked with 'spandrel' interpretations), and an adaptation for cooperation in much larger groups with more at stake than other mammals (Alexander 1987; Roes and Raymond 2003; Schloss 2004; Schloss 2007; David Sloan Wilson 2002).

The cooperative adaptation hypothesis has generated the greatest number and variety of both theoretical and empirical studies, which emphasize variations on two themes. One possibility is that religion may serve as an adaptation for detecting and controlling cooperative defection (Bulbulia 2004a; Irons 2001; Johnson and Bering 2006; Johnson and Kruger 2004). Cooperative systems are vulnerable to destabilization by defectors. Cooperators may accrue fitness advantages in situations where defectors are penalized through mechanisms of social control, including coercion and punishment, or in situations where cooperators are reliably able to recognize and interact with one another. Religion may facilitate the former both by institutional sanctions and by internalized beliefs in supernatural punishment (Bering and Johnson 2005; Johnson and Bering 2006). It may achieve the latter by a variety of costly signals of commitment (Irons 2001; Gintis, Smith, and Bowles 2001; Sosis 2000; Sosis 2003; Sosis and Alcorta 2003) or hard-to-fake displays of interior disposition (Bulbulia 2004a; Frank 2001; Schloss 2007). The second possibility is that religion may function to coordinate cooperative strategies and goals (Atran and Norenzayan 2004; Roes and Raymond 2003; David Sloan Wilson 2002). Cheater control and interactive coordination are the two challenges that must be met for any cooperative system, from genomes to multicellular organisms, to social groups and formal economic systems.

In principle, any or all of the above solutions to the challenges of cooperation may be implemented as individual or group-level adaptations. They are established, respectively, by selective regimes that confer reproductive advantage to individuals having a trait relative to those lacking it within a group (you are the top scorer and hence the most highly paid player on your team), or by situations in which there may be a within-group decrement in fitness to a cooperating individual that is offset by inter-group benefit (you feed the ball to others and make less, but get a bonus for being on the championship team). Religious adaptations have been proposed to accrue from both individual (Johnson and Bering 2006) and group (David Sloan Wilson 2002) selection. For example, costly signaling could work as either an individual or group level adaptation (or it could do both, having an ambiguous history of selection at each level). If it were an individually selected trait, a religious adherent would not be predicted to invest more deeply or believe more consistently in religious exhortations to cooperate than would be likely to accrue reproductive benefit to the individual believer (Alexander 1987). If group selected, religious belief could be anticipated to underwrite genuine sacrifice on behalf of the group (but not for those outside the group), in conditions where the sacrifice was compensated for, by the benefits of prevailing in inter-group competition. Though still vigorously debated, these processes, operating at different scales, are not incommensurable with one another. However, they do have differing implications for both the degree of cooperative investment and the mode by which it is maintained in religious groups. Johnson, Bulbulia, and Richerson explore differing aspects of adaptationist explanations in this volume.

Finally, I should mention that a good deal of both the scientific literature and interdisciplinary reflections on the religious implications of evolutionary accounts of religion view adaptationist approaches as somehow more friendly or less hostile to religion. Interestingly, this seems to be true in terms of the tone taken by prominent proponents of 'spandrel', vestige, and adaptationist approaches. But it is surely not true in terms of the proposals' implications. With respect to the truth or falsity of religious claims, neither explanation has anything to say. With respect to warrant for religious belief, as I have discussed, both approaches (and any account that uncouples reasons from causes) entails challenges. And, with respect to whether religion is a 'good' or valuable enterprise, while the adaptationist perspective might seem more amenable to this conclusion, it is not. All sorts of things are capable of enhancing fitness at the cost of individual health, personal happiness, or widely shared moral judgment. On the other hand, a non-adaptive trait may enhance all three while still being fitness neutral. Ayala (1995) argues that by-product accounts are actually more honoring of morality than adaptationist theories that reduce it to reproductive pay-off; one might make the same observation of religion. In any case, there is little reason here to be tempted to choose or resist a theory for its consequences.

Coevolutionary Accounts

Coevolutionary approaches to religion (and other aspects of culture) take the previous two approaches—proximal explanations in terms of cognitive mechanisms and ultimate Darwinian explanations in terms of selection—as necessary but insufficient for a natural account of religion. For humans it is not just innate cognitive proclivities or genetically selected central tendencies that account for behavior but also culturally transmitted and archived information that is not reducible to, or even wholly constrained by, the former two processes.

There is a wide range of proposals for understanding the relationship between genetic and cultural evolution (Boyd and Richerson 1985; Boyd and Richerson 2005; Cavalli-Sforza and Feldman 1981; Dugatkin 2001; Durham 1992; Maynard Smith and Warren 1982; Plotkin 2003). There are debates over whether cultural information may best be construed as particulate replicators, or 'memes' (Blackmore 1999; Coyne 1999; Sperber 2000). Transmission may be understood to involve primarily imitation, or cognitive insight, and may or may not be amenable to the logic of differential replication or selection without being 'completely tautological, unable to explain why a meme spreads except by asserting, post facto, that it had qualities enabling it to spread' (Coyne 1999: 768; Coyne 2003). Moreover, there are varied ways cultural information or memes may be 'adaptive'. Several ways among many: it may enhance biological reproduction and be propagated through familial descent; it may enhance social integration and be transmitted laterally through the growth of human populations or through the dissemination of successful cultural innovations; or it may contribute in neither of these ways but may 'parasitize' human cognitive and cultural systems, causing individual and social pathology, while (like drug addiction or a literal virus) being highly successful at getting itself transmitted.

By far the most prominent approach posits religion to be a pathogenic but highly infectious memetic virus that is transmitted to human hosts at the expense of biological and cultural flourishing: 'religious ideas are virus-like memes that multiply by infecting the gullible brains of children' (Dawkins 2007: 205; Dennett 2006). Famously, '*faith* is one of the world's great evils, comparable to the smallpox virus but harder to eradicate' (Dawkins 1997: 26). Regrettably, this is one approach for which we do not have an advocate contributing to this volume. In part, this reflects the fact that although the memetic pathogen thesis has received wide public attention it has not generated a substantial amount of theoretical or empirical work. Nevertheless, it is an important option and warrants several brief comments.

First, memetic theory in general represents a significant acknowledgement if not a dramatic concession by evolutionary reductionism: for the first time in a century, humans are in some sense viewed as both unique and biologically transcendent. Daniel Dennett (2006: 4) comments that 'Like other animals, we have built-in desires to reproduce and to do pretty much whatever it takes to achieve this goal...But we also have creeds, and the ability to transcend our genetic imperatives. This fact makes us different.' Even more strikingly Richard Dawkins closes his introducing the idea of memes in *The Selfish Gene* with the exuberant exhortation: 'We have the power to defy the selfish genes of our birth . . . something that has no place in nature, something that has never existed before in the whole history of the world' (2006 [1976]: 200).

Second, while the above claims constitute a significant acknowledgement of the limits of genetic explanation, they do not actually constitute an explanation in their own right. We do not yet have an operational or empirically assessable definition of a meme; agreement on whether cultural information is particulate and replicatable; an account of how to quantify transmission and whether or not successful transmission of memes is analogous to fitness of genes, or whether it is 'completely tautological, unable to explain why a meme spreads except by asserting, post facto, that it had qualities enabling it to spread' (Coyne 1999: 768; Coyne 2003); an agreement on whether memetic transmissibility requires epidemiological as opposed to rational models of dissemination (Dawkins 1993; Dawkins 1997) or merely involves successful spread, in which case science and meme theory itself would be memes (Dennett 2006). And, most importantly, there is no proposal for how it is that memes exert their impressive causal leverage on behavior. In fact, it is not entirely clear how it is that positing unseen and undefined entities that infect human minds by unassessed processes involving the entities' own quest for transmission and that cause people to do things that transcend their genetic imperatives is fundamentally different from medieval demonology or, in any case, qualifies as an empirically grounded explanation in terms of natural causes. 'The existence of a God meme is no better established than the existence of God' (Orr 2006).

Finally, I should point out that just as the question of 'spandrels' is distinct from cognitive explanations of religious belief, so the question of pathogenicity is separate from memetic proposals for their transmission. If memetic accounts of religion prove fruitful there are at least five theoretically plausible and empirically observed options for the relationship between memetic and genetic information (Durham 1992). Religious memes could be beneficial symbionts rather than parasites, enhancing biological fitness or cultural function, or both. In fact, the relationship could be an obligate mutualism—humans being unable to live 'by bread alone'. Or memes could be commensalists, sustained by human biology but conferring no net benefit or detriment to their hosts. Yet another option, implicit in the notion of memetic irreducibility to genetic imperatives (Dawkins 2006

[1976]; Dennet 2007), is that religious memes may be 'pathological' relative to the biological *telos* of fitness, but beneficent in their contribution to other construals of human flourishing, including the moral *telos* of love. Whatever one makes of the as yet unsettled concept of memes, the relationship between the cultural dissemination of religious ideas and the flourishing of an evolved humanity is a larger question to be settled.

Although the three major approaches described above are often represented as competing alternatives, they need not be. They often employ different definitions of religion and/or focus on different aspects of religion (Alcorta and Sosis 2005). And the approaches emphasize different and non-exclusive levels of causation—cognitive function, Darwinian selection, and cultural transmission. In fact, there are numerous ways these processes may interact. An innate cognitive disposition could arise as a 'spandrel', but be 'exapted' by voraciously entrepreneurial natural selection. It could also be readily infected by memes, which by the process of 'memetic drive' (Blackmore 2000) subject the original cognitive inclination to directional selection, even hypertrophy. Proposals for the adaptive internalization of supernatural sanctions and other aspects of religious commitment (Bulbulia; Johnson and Bering, this volume) are amenable to just this analysis. At this point, theory choice is happily under-determined by data. There is lots of room for exploring which scientific account is, or which combinations are, most promising (Orr 2006; Dennet 2006) and for discussing the entailments for religion, should promise be fulfilled.

I

Hand of God, Mind of Man

Punishment and Cognition in the Evolution of Cooperation

Dominic Johnson and Jesse Bering[1]

Introduction

> We're in hell...they never make mistakes and people are not damned for nothing.
>
> Inez: Jean-Paul Sartre, *Huis Clos* (1967)

The Puzzle of Human Cooperation

To put it bluntly, all life on Earth is based on selfishness. Genes that replicate fastest spread at the expense of others. Any that incur costs by sacrificing self-interest disappear from the gene pool, gobbled up by the inexorable mill of natural selection. This is how life has been for 3.5 billion years. Whether an amoebic blodge or a zebra, the struggle for existence has always been a bloodbath of death and displacement, without sentiment, without compassion. If this sounds extreme, pay a visit to the Serengeti and watch a pride of lions tear the life from a frail or newborn wildebeest, its fellow herd members fleeing without a second thought. Watch as each lion scrambles to steal the prize cut, snarling and slashing at their conspecifics

1. We thank Justin Barrett, Terry Burnham, Gordon Gallup, Stewart Guthrie, Brian Hare, Roger Johnson, Alvin Plantinga, Gabriella de la Rosa, Todd Shackelford, Jeffrey Schloss, David Sloan Wilson, Richard Sosis, Dan Sperber, David Voas, and Richard Wrangham for comments and criticisms on the ideas in this chapter. We also sincerely thank Jeffrey Schloss and Michael Murray for the invitation to contribute.

as though they would never eat again. This is the reality of nature. At some point in the dark days of our ancestral past, we were exactly the same. Selfishness would have been our genetic guiding lantern: look out for yourself, or die.

But this image of nature is shocking precisely because we, modern humans, do not seem to be bound by this inevitable logic. We are not wholly selfish. Indeed, we are a species characterized—defined, perhaps—by altruism, self-sacrifice, and charity (Schloss 2004). How, therefore, can such behavior be squared with selfish genes? The point of this chapter is to argue that this apparent paradox can, in fact, be reconciled with evolutionary biology. The central proposition is that something happened since the dark days of our selfish evolutionary origins to purge us of sheer selfishness, and instill instead a keen sense of caring, cooperativeness, and compassion.

Cooperation is, of course, widespread among mammals, birds, insects, cells, microscopic organisms, even different organs of the body (David Sloan Wilson 2000). Sometimes cooperation results from mutual pay-offs to all individuals or genes involved, and can therefore be easily understood as each pursuing their own selfish interest (Dawkins 1986). However, other instances of cooperation are more surprising, because individuals help others despite incurring a cost in doing so. In the last half century, a number of theories have come to understand such behavior as the result of motives that, while they may be apparently altruistic at first glance, ultimately serve selfish genetic interests (they incur an immediate cost, but result in a net gain to inclusive fitness overall). The four dominant theories are: 'kin-selection', in which cooperation is genetically rewarded by favoring kin (Hamilton 1964); 'reciprocal altruism', in which altruistic acts are returned later on (Trivers 1971); 'indirect reciprocity', in which one's reputation for cooperation is rewarded indirectly through the favor of third-party observers (Alexander 1987; Nowak and Sigmund 1998); and costly signaling, in which generosity serves as an advertisement of high fitness to would-be mates or allies (Gintis, Smith, and Bowles 2001; Zahavi 1995). Formerly puzzling examples of animal cooperation have now been routinely explained in terms of these theories (see, for e.g. Dugatkin 1997).

By contrast, cooperation *among humans* is still not understood. Although people do increase cooperation when kin-selection, reciprocal altruism, indirect reciprocity, and costly signaling are at stake, we also continue to cooperate when they are not (Fehr and Fischbacher 2003; Gintis 2003).

In the words of two leading scholars, 'people frequently cooperate with genetically unrelated strangers, often in large groups, with people they will never meet again, and when reputation gains are small or absent', leaving human cooperation as an 'evolutionary puzzle' (Fehr and Gächter 2002: 137). The key evidence for such puzzling behavior comes from controlled laboratory studies demonstrating that people cooperate even when any possible self-interested pay-offs via existing theories are carefully eliminated one by one. The result is that, when asked to play simple games that represent everyday social dilemmas, people from both modern and pre-industrial societies around the globe cooperate to a greater extent than can be accounted for by traditional theory—a phenomenon dubbed 'strong reciprocity' (Fehr and Fischbacher 2003; Henrich, et al. 2004). So far, no one has come up with a consensus explanation for this phenomenon. A number of scholars have invoked group selection as a possible explanation (Boyd, et al. 2003; Gintis 2000). Another explanation may be that our psychology simply fails to optimize behavior in evolutionarily novel circumstances (such as laboratory experiments or big cities) and better reflects the constraints of our former 'environment of evolutionary adaptedness' (EEA) where we lived in small groups of extended kin, few strangers, strong hierarchies, and lasting reputations (Burnham and Johnson 2005; Johnson, Stopka, and Knights 2003). In this chapter, we take an entirely new approach. We suggest that religious beliefs, specifically the moralizing and sanctioning behavior they generate, may serve as a common origin for human cooperation.

Religion as a solution to the puzzle

It would be incredible to suggest that religion has nothing to do with cooperation—either in ancient or modern societies. Anthropologists have long noted such links, and over the years have both championed and criticized functionalist accounts of religion's apparently numerous socially beneficial functions (Morris 1987; Weber 1978). However, scientific progress on the topic reached a 'theoretical impasse' until the advent of approaches that explicitly couched the benefits of religion in terms of natural selection (simply observing possible benefits ignored the problem of how the prerequisite costly beliefs were initiated, and why cheats did not thrive: Sosis and Alcorta 2003). The new evolutionary approach has given rise to a number of theories arguing that religion was a key promoter of within-group cooperation during human evolution (e.g. Cronk 1994; Irons 2001; Roes and Raymond 2003), but this work remains totally absent from the literature on 'strong reciprocity' and the puzzle of cooperation (Johnson, Stopka, and Knights 2003).

In fact, economists have specifically denied any link between cooperation and religion (e.g. Fehr and Gächter 2003), despite mounting empirical evidence supporting such an intuitive link. Sosis has shown that, among a large sample of nineteenth-century communes, religious groups with more costly rituals out-survived secular groups and religious groups with fewer rituals (Sosis and Bressler 2003). Among Israeli kibbutzim, groups with more religious rituals also demonstrated higher levels of cooperation than secular groups and religious groups with fewer rituals (Sosis and Ruffle 2003), which may explain why religious kibbutzim are economically successful while secular ones have faced bankruptcy (Fishman and Goldschmidt 1990). That religious beliefs are associated with higher levels of cooperation is not in doubt. What remains intriguing is why.

A New Theory

We outline a precise, proximate cognitive mechanism that suggests it is the expectation and fear of supernatural punishment that serves to promote cooperation. We also argue that this mechanism evolved via individual selection (any group selection effects, though they are not necessary, would help drive the system). The theory builds on two recent and complementary ideas: (1) supernatural punishment as a positive impact on cooperation (Johnson and Kruger 2004); and (2) human cognition as an evolutionarily novel canvas for the workings of natural selection (Bering and Shackelford 2004).

Supernatural punishment and cooperation

It is increasingly accepted that punishment is key to ensuring cooperation (Andreoni, Harbaugh, and Vesterlund 2003; Clutton-Brock and Parker 1995; Fehr and Gächter 2002; Sigmund, Hauert, and Nowak 2001; Trivers 1971). However, the act of punishing cheats entails costs, so punishment itself represents a 'second-order' public good (Hackathorn 1989; Yamagishi 1986). The original puzzle of cooperation therefore just reappears at a new level: 'second-order' cheats may cooperate towards the public good, but then defect from contributing to punishment. So how is cooperation enforced? Four solutions to this conundrum have emerged in the literature. Three are deemed unsatisfactory (Henrich and Boyd 2001: 80), and the fourth is contested: (1) punishment is administered by an external institution (however, while this may be true in Western societies today, cooperation evolved long before modern institutions existed, and is evident even in remote societies that are not subject to state regulations); (2) punishment is not costly after all (however, administering punishment must incur some cost, however small, of time and/or effort which combined with the risk of reprisals from punished individuals or their allies simply returns us to the original dilemma); (3) both regular defectors and those who refuse to punish are punished (however, as Boyd and Richerson put it (2005: 190): 'Do people really punish people who fail to punish other nonpunishers, and do people punish people who fail to punish people, who fail to punish nonpunishers of defectors and so on, ad infinitum?'); (4) Some fraction of people altruistically punish defectors for the good of the group (Fehr and Fischbacher 2003; Fehr and Gächter 2002), and this trait is propagated by group selection (however, this requires that humans are genuinely altruistic, a claim that is problematic for a number of reasons; see Burnham and Johnson 2005; Johnson, Stopka, and Knights 2003). The puzzle therefore remains: without institutions of law and order, and without a good incentive for people to punish each other, how could early human societies establish cooperation with a credible deterrent threat against cheats?

We believe solution (1) is discounted too readily. Although most legal and law enforcement institutions are indeed modern inventions, Henrich and Boyd (2001) neglect another 'external' category of norm setting and enforcement that reaches as far back as we can see into human history: religion.

Johnson and Kruger (2004) argued that over our evolutionary history individuals would be dissuaded from free-riding if they feared supernatural retribution as a consequence of their actions. Religious codes, taboos, and mythology provided the 'laws'—the rights and wrongs which defined the norms of conduct promoting, among other things, cooperation. These norms were enforced by the threat of supernatural punishment, either in the present and/or in the afterlife (commonly endorsed by folklore, explanations for other people's misfortune, and supernaturally sanctioned worldly punishment by real group members). If supernatural punishment is held as *a belief*, then this threat becomes a deterrent *in reality*, so the mechanism can work regardless of whether the threat is genuine or not (following the Thomases dictum: 'If men define situations as real, they are real in their consequences' (Thomas and Thomas 1928: 572)).

Cooperation enforced by the threat of supernatural punishment has four major selective advantages that evade the classic public goods problems troubling current theoretical work: First, there is no second-order freerider problem (supernatural agents are envisioned as administering the punishing). Second, since other group members do not have to be vigilantes they do not risk reprisals that could undermine future cooperation. Third, (believing) defectors can expect to be automatically caught (the idea is encapsulated in Matt. 5: 28: 'whosoever looketh on a woman to lust after her hath committed adultery with her already in his heart', see Bering and Johnson 2005). Fourth, (believing) defectors can expect to be automatically punished (the act itself triggers the punishment).

Considerable ethnographic evidence suggests that the threat of supernatural punishment for norm transgressions exerts a powerful effect on people's behavior—believers literally alter their everyday decisions in order to avoid supernatural retribution (see examples in Boyer 2001). Not only is supernatural punishment commonly feared in diverse cultures around the world, both ancient and modern, it is also commonly linked to taboos concerning life or death collective action problems, such as scarce resources, food sharing, hunting, who can have sex with whom, divisions of labor, defense, or warfare (see Boyer 2001; see Earhart 1993; Weber 1978).

Supernatural punishment may come from any mix of gods, dead ancestors, witches, or sorcerers. One or more feature prominently in hunter-gatherer societies, and all are commonly attributed to the cause of ill fortune (Boyer 2001: 160; Murdock 1980). Dead ancestors are commonly offered gifts and attention specifically to avoid their retribution (Bonsu and Belk 2003). In medieval Europe thoughts of the dead were prevalent in the conduct of daily life to such an extent that one historian treated them as a separate age group (Bering 2006). In ancient Hawaii, the 'souls' of the dead (akua), once unconstrained from bodily limitations and senses, could be in several places at one time, know the thoughts of others, and were in constant interaction with the living (Dudley 2003). There are some cultures that are apparently not particularly concerned about supernatural punishment, such as the Amazonian Yanomamo whose spirit of judgment after death can be lied to about one's worldly conduct because he is stupid (Chagnon 1997). Nevertheless, such cases appear to be exceptions to an otherwise widespread significance of supernatural punishment in the world's pre-industrial cultures.

The idea of supernatural punishment is common in modern religions as well. Christians who act contrary to God's will expect divine retribution either immediately, by sanctions (e.g. struck down with an affliction or some other misfortune), or later, in hell. Even if they don't believe that, they commonly attribute positive and negative life events to their conduct before God. Either way, 'it is plain from the Bible that sin will be punished' (Harrison, Bromiley, and Henry 1960: 196). Supernatural punishment is also a central theme in Islam, where salvation depends on 'human effort as well as God's mercy in following the Qur'an's teachings' (Coward 2003: 164–5). Similar concerns for the afterlife are prominent in East Asian and Indian religious traditions, and as well in ethnographic evidence on the far more numerous and diverse pre-industrial cultures (for some preliminary examples and evidence, see Bering 2006; Bering and Johnson 2005; Dominic Johnson 2005; Johnson and Kruger 2004).

Why punishment is more important than reward

It may seem odd to focus on punishment, because most religions also offer the prospect of rewards for good behavior (in fact, many people, religious or not, see positive events as well as negative ones as felicitous signs of supernatural forces—e.g., 'it was *meant* to be' (Bering 2002a; Gilbert, et al. 2000)). Such beliefs would, like punishment, serve to induce cooperative behavior if one was rewarded for pro-social actions.

However, the effects of carrots and sticks on the level of cooperation are not symmetrical, even when of equivalent magnitude: punishment is inherently *more* effective at promoting cooperation than rewards. Carrots are not enough because, although they may encourage *some* people to cooperate, they do not prevent *all of them* from cheating. Even if the rewards of cooperation are large and obvious to everyone involved, they provide no credible deterrent against defectors—cheats will not be deterred if they can gain even more by shirking the costs of cooperation (Schelling 1960; Sigmund, Hauert, and Nowak 2001). This reflects the fundamental paradox behind the famous 'Prisoner's Dilemma' game. Even though the two players know that they could be better off if they both cooperate, rational actors defect because this is the only way to avoid exploitation—and there is no credible deterrent against doing so (Axelrod 1984; Poundstone 1992). In other contexts, too, rewards turn out to be less effective than equivalent levels of punishment in promoting cooperation. Empirical experiments bear out this claim: within real-life groups, cooperation collapses without additional binding agreements to prosecute or punish dissenters (a single cheat can cause otherwise cooperative agents to withdraw their own contributions (Fehr and Gächter 2002; Ostrom, Walker, and Gardner 1992; Yamagishi 1986)). Such results have led to a convergence of opinion among economists, game theorists, and evolutionary biologists that—wherever self-interest conflicts with group outcomes—cooperation will emerge only if defectors are punished.

Rewards may contribute to promoting cooperation, but it is the weaker of the two complementary forces: punishment has an intrinsic leverage. While rewards clearly play an important part in religious behavior (a Christian, for example, may be motivated by eternity in heaven as much as by the fear of hell), the punishment aspect is likely to have the more potent influence on the dynamics of cooperation. As one theologian pointed out: 'the very proclamation of hell indicates that the defenders of religion found it necessary to balance the attraction of its promise with a threat for the "others", who rejected it or failed to meet its tests' (Bernstein 1993: p. x). This resonates with the observation that while there are many hunter–gatherer societies in which the only supernatural agents are antagonistic, there are few, if any, whose only supernatural agents are beneficent. The effectiveness of sticks over carrots also concords with accumulating evidence that negative psychological events and phenomena are much more potent in their effects than positive ones (Baumeister, et al. 2001).

Human cognition and supernatural agency

The supernatural punishment theory, outlined above, offers the plausible hypothesis that a fear of supernatural punishment is the proximate mechanism that maintains cooperation, but it begs the all-important question of how the system initiates in the first place. Johnson and Kruger (2004) pointed out that the mechanism could originate via the 'green beard effect' (Dawkins 1986), via a purely cultural innovation, or via group selection processes (Sober and Wilson 1998; Wilson and Sober 1994). None of these mechanisms may be necessary, or sufficient, however. As has been recently pointed out, 'supernatural punishment can only be an effective deterrent insofar as individuals are capable of reasoning that negative life events are caused by supernatural agents who have explicit reasons for bringing about such events' (Bering 2004: 434).

Recent work by Bering (2002; 2006) offers precise reasons and evidence suggesting that humans do indeed reason in this way about negative events. We appear to have an inherent cognitive tendency to search for reason and intentionality in life events, and to attribute positive and negative outcomes to supernatural agency. Keleman suggests that children are 'intuitive theists' because of their commonplace teleological reasoning that things usually exist 'for' something (e.g. clouds are for raining; see Keleman 2004). Bering and Bjorklund's (2004) study on children's reasoning about the psychological states of dead agents also hints at a default 'afterlife' stance that may only be usurped by explicit scientific understanding about biology and death—knowledge that was of course limited in our pre-scientific environment of evolutionary adaptedness. Such tendencies, we argue, may have specific selective advantages at the individual level. The logic is set out below and illustrated in Figure 1.1.

Novel selective pressures on human sociality

Unlike most other primate species, humans possess an 'intentionality system', which is the capacity to represent mental states as the unseen causes of behavior (Bering 2002a; Povinelli and Bering 2002). This system is foundational for a true human cognitive specialization: 'second- and third-order representation'—the ability to know what others know, and to know that they know what we know, or did (i.e. A knows that B knows what A knows, or did). Humans also differ from other species in having language (allowing information about specific social behaviors to spread among the group). Consequently, B can inform C by word of mouth about A's actions, information that can profoundly influence the nature of subsequent interactions between A and C, with significant fitness consequences (e.g., if A stole from B in the absence of any social others, then retaliation against A might come from C, D, or E and so on, perhaps days, weeks, or months later). Through the lens of this evolutionary novelty, many higher-function and premeditated human behaviors take on great adaptive significance, including murder of witnesses, revenge, suicide, and generosity (Bering and Shackelford 2004). With humans, therefore, natural selection has a new

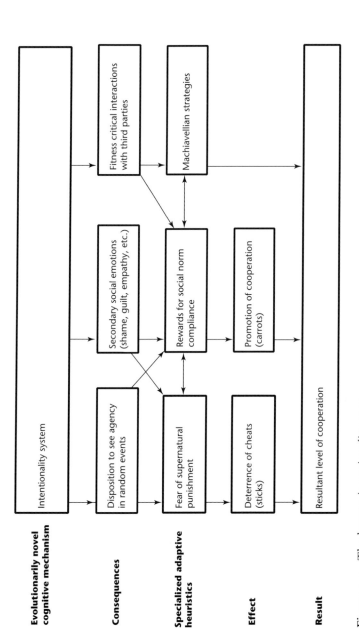

Figure 1.1. The human intentionality system

The human intentionality system has three key consequences: disposition to assign agency to events; secondary social emotions (shame, guilt, empathy, etc.); and fitness–critical interactions with third parties. These lead to a fear of supernatural punishment (which deters potential defectors), rewards for social norm compliance (which promotes cooperative tendencies), and Machiavellian strategies (which exploit the intentionality system). In combination, these effects determine the resultant level of cooperation.

workbench to shape human behavior that Darwin did not consider. No other species is subject to its effects.

Before these social cognitive processes evolved, selfish behavior would be consistently selected for as long as it conferred a net pay-off (even when this occurred in full view of others). As an analogy, chimpanzees can be selfish in front of other chimpanzees without their behavior being reported to absent others. There can therefore be no negative repercussions from absent third parties because such individuals could not entertain others' knowledge states (nor could they learn such complex information by communication).

After the co-evolution of language and higher-order social cognition, by contrast, it was in the genes' interests to avoid selfish behavior in contexts that could bring negative repercussions (now one had to worry about the consequences of other actors, wholly removed from the scene of the crime, learning of the act and responding later). People could hear, discover, infer, remember, report, gossip, hypothesize, and act on others' behavior—even long after the event. What are the consequences?

God-fearing strategies

Selfish behavior is evolutionarily ancient, whereas higher-order social cognition and language are evolutionarily novel. So, while selfish behaviors might have paid off in the simpler social life of our prehistoric ancestors, many of them (or too many of them) would bring a net fitness loss in a cognitively sophisticated, whispering society. The advent of these novel cognitive abilities increased the likelihood of public exposure for selfish behavior which, in our EEA, could bring high costs of retaliation by other group members (involving death, physical harm, imprisonment, seizure of property or kin, social sanctions, or ostracism from the group).

Specific mechanisms might have evolved to rescue inclusive fitness *after* the individual committed a social offence in this new Big Brother society (e.g. cognitive processes underlying confession, blackmail, killing witnesses, suicide, and so forth (Bering and Shackelford 2004)). However, these de facto strategies tax reproductive success, so there would be novel selective pressures for more efficient traits that constrain selfishness to some extent in the first place (indeed we see such traits in human interaction every day—restraint, self-control, sacrifice, sharing, patience, etc.). Those that carried on being indiscriminately selfish would be outcompeted by prudent others who were able successfully to inhibit their more ancient selfish motives and refrain from breaching social rules to begin with.

According to Bering and Shackelford (2004), the human intentionality system allowed the selection of traits that militated against public exposure. Because the temptation to cheat remained, however, we add that something extra—a belief in supernatural punishment—which was an effective way to caution oneself against transgressions and thereby avoid 'real' worldly retribution by other group members. God-fearing people may, therefore, have had a selective advantage over non-believers because the latter's more indiscriminately selfish behavior carried a higher risk of real-world vengeance by the community.

Machiavellian strategies

So far we have focused on the disadvantages of the novel aspects of human social cognition—selfish actions now bring an increased risk of detection and retaliation. However, these new traits also brought opportunities: selective pressures for traits that exploit these novel aspects, since one can manipulate others' knowledge as well as suffer from it (as a result of these two mechanisms, the overall selective effect might be expected to be quite strong, effectively 'pushed' and 'pulled' simultaneously in the same direction by evolution—exposed transgressors are selected out, prudent exploiters of the social cognitive system are selected in). As an example of manipulation, one can conceal the transgressions of kin, or preferentially cooperate with those who have established a good reputation with others— examples which hint at significant implications for the evolution of kin-selection and direct or indirect reciprocal altruism among humans. In short, these new psychological forces gave humans, for better or worse, a new capital stock to trade in—social information. Our ancestors became highly invested in this stock because it exerted a significant influence on reproductive gain. Profits came from effectively gathering, retaining, and regulating (through whatever means possible, including deception, threats, and violence) the flow of social information that had the potential to impact inclusive fitness. One may therefore postulate Machiavellian strategies that did exploit the human intentionality system for personal gain, but which were not God-fearing.

Which strategy wins?

Table 1.1 compares the performance of the above two strategies (God-fearing and Machiavellian) and the ancestral state, following the advent

Table 1.1. The human intentionality system

Strategy	Intentionality system?	Result in post-intentionality system social setting	Can exploit intentionality system for personal gain?	Probability of detection (p)	Cost of punishment (c)	Cost of missed opportunities (m)	Pay-off
ancestral	no	pure selfishness	no	high	same	none	lowest
Machiavellian	yes	devious selfishness	yes	high	same	none	highest (if $pc < m$)
god-fearing	yes	reduced selfishness	yes	low	same	some	highest (if $pc > m$)

Three strategies come into competition with the advent of the human intentionality system. Grey shading indicates features that act against genetic fitness. Machiavellians would clearly outcompete ancestral individuals because, while everything else is identical between them, ancestrals cannot reap the spoils of exploiting the intentionality system for personal gain. More importantly however, the table indicates that God-fearing strategists can outcompete Machiavells. They differ in just two respects: God-fearing strategists have a lower probability of detection, but miss out on some opportunities for selfish rewards. Therefore, God-fearing strategists will outcompete Machiavells as long as the probability of detection (p) multiplied by the cost of punishment (c) is greater than the cost of missed opportunities for selfish rewards (m). In other words, when the inequality $pc > m$ is true. Moreover, where $pc > m$, we should expect exaggerated estimates of p (such as a belief that supernatural agents are watching) to outperform accurate estimates of p, given that the latter will engender more mistakes (see logic in Nettle 2004).

of the mental representational features of human social cognition. Machiavellians would clearly outcompete ancestral individuals because, while everything else is identical between them, ancestrals cannot exploit these new representational features for personal gain. More importantly, however, Table 1.1 indicates that God-fearing strategists can outcompete Machiavellians. They differ in just two respects: God-fearing strategists have a lower probability of detection but miss out on some opportunities for selfish rewards. Therefore, God-fearing strategists will outcompete Machiavellians *as long as* the total expected costs of punishment (i.e. the probability of detection (p) multiplied by the cost of punishment (c)) is greater than the cost of missed opportunities for selfish rewards (m): in other words, when the inequality $pc > m$ is true. This would occur wherever the rewards of selfishness were relatively small compared with the costs of public exposure (which include injury, ostracism, death, or worse: punishment of one's kin as well). Even a small p can mean selfishness does not pay on the average. Moreover, where $pc > m$, we should expect *exaggerated* estimates of p (such as a belief that supernatural agents are watching) to outperform *accurate* estimates of p, given that the latter will engender more mistakes (see logic in Haselton and Nettle 2006; see logic in Nettle 2004).

Summary of the model

To summarize, humans often act on selfish motives (and sometimes inadvertently due to emotionally charged situations)—acts which, thanks to the human intentionality system, carry a far greater chance of social exposure than in previous stages of evolution. If the chance and costs of exposure are high enough, individuals who were more likely to refrain from cheating for fear of supernatural agents concerned with group norms (indeed, such agents are often the proposed authors of these norms) and who punish defectors by inflicting misfortune (on both the self and innocent others) could have out-reproduced otherwise equal—and more indiscriminately selfish—individuals. Of course, Machiavellian, non-believing cheats who do not get caught would do best of all, but we suggest that the heightened chance and costs of exposure by virtue of the intentionality system favored the evolution of traits that suppress selfish behavior, and favored instead the kind of moralistic behavior that is, after all, empirically common among human societies (Alexander 1987; Trivers 1971). Interestingly, recent criminal evidence indicates that convicts tended to underestimate the probability of being caught and punished (Robinson and Darley 2004).

Conclusions

The supernatural punishment theory of Johnson and Kruger (2004), combined with the powerful implications of the human intentionality system (Bering and Shackelford 2004), offer a novel theory for the origins of human cooperation—a solution that has a specific proximate mechanism and that precisely defines the cognitive processes involved. Our proposition is not mutually exclusive of other theories of religion, nor of other theories of cooperation. The mechanism we describe would complement many of them. However, our proposal offers a more complete and plausible mechanism than many, and an intuitive and circumstantially supported one. Although we have highlighted a central role for individual selection in our theory, any inter-group advantages leading to the group selection of such morally bound cooperative behavior would augment the process. Indeed, group selection could lead to the dominance of god-fearing strategies in one fell swoop, since groups with Machiavells will suffer by comparison.

An additional lever in our proposed mechanism comes from a consideration of third parties. Over and above any personal experience, third parties will draw lessons from supernatural agency apparently befalling others (again, a faculty made possible by higher-order social cognition). Someone else's misfortune or fortune (e.g. illness, gifted children) may tend to be seen as evidence of wrongdoing or virtue (e.g. selfishness, generosity). Whether the victim really *is* bad or virtuous is of little consequence for selective pressures to operate, if the events are perceived as the 'evidence' (especially where other group members corroborate that interpretation; cultural learning is clearly important here). Such perceived connections will steer onlookers away from behavior that would bring the same fate—not just because of the fear of supernatural punishment (as we proposed in our general argument above), but also because of how one learned that such negative life events would be viewed by other group members. Thus, supernatural agents are seen not only as communicating to the self through life events, but in so doing they are also seen as communicating to other group members about the moral (in)aptitude of the self. The gods effectively call out the wicked, exposing them to the group to impose its own social punishments.

How does our theory fit with existing literature? Sosis and Bressler (2003: 227) found that on the basis of their comparisons of secular and religious communes the costly signaling theory of religion fails to 'capture some critical elements of religious belief that distinguish it from belief in a secular ideology'. In their study, variation in costly signaling explained variation in *religious* commune survival. However, variation in costly signaling did *not* explain variation in *secular* commune survival. The underlying reason for this, they suggest, is the special 'sanctity' of religious rituals, which simply cannot be matched by secular rituals (see also Whitehouse 2000). Religious rituals are superior to secular ones in their ability to build solidarity among group members, it appears, *because* they are directed towards a supernatural being, which authenticates them beyond logical analysis—a critical component of their success (Rappaport 1999). Sosis and Bressler predict as a consequence that, among different religious doctrines, those that are more reliant on the supernatural should exhibit higher levels of cooperation (a prediction partially supported by a recent empirical test of a large sample of pre-industrial cultures; Johnson 2005). Other evolutionary studies arrive at similar appeals to some as-yet-unexplained, special feature of religion: Dogon women in Mali, for example, are obliged to visit 'menstrual huts' to advertise their fertility cycle and thereby reduce cuckoldry. Although this conforms to theories based on ritual, the study's author noted that 'the threat of supernatural sanctions is crucial for enforcement' (Strassmann 1992). We offer an explanation for *why* such a supernatural component may be so fundamental to understanding the power of religion in achieving cooperation.

Clearly, cooperation in the modern world cannot be explained solely by any religious theory because cooperation is prevalent among atheists as well as believers (although we must remember that 79 per cent of Americans expect a day of judgment when God decides whether they will go to heaven or hell and, depending on religious affiliation, 74 per cent or more believe in an afterlife, as do 58 per cent of adults *who have no religious affiliation* (Pinker 2002; religioustolerance.org)). Many instances of social cooperation today are no puzzle at all because modern institutions impose strong social contracts to cooperate (and punishment if one does not). However, many of these modern institutions, and their founding morals, ethics, and norms, are in fact deeply rooted in local traditions that are essentially religious. Indeed, religious traditions continue to underlie fundamental aspects of law, political discourse, appeals to public action problems, and social life, even if the modern proponents are no longer themselves believers (consider marriage, swearing on the Bible in court, charity, many national constitutions, and calls for US unity against an 'evil empire' or 'axis of evil'—it is not inconceivable that these norms originated and persevered because of their historical selective success and cognitive salience). Certainly, most people today—even atheists—continue to behave in accordance with a set of values which, although they may appear as self-evident, are directly analogous to many religious codes (and evoke the same secondary emotions of shame, empathy, guilt, etc., that supervise one's own actions). Our mechanism can be generalized to suggest similar adaptive advantages in superstition, folklore, or just world beliefs.

Speculations about modern society aside, the real puzzle is still the *evolutionary origins* of cooperation behavior—independent of the forces governing cooperation today. How did early human societies achieve cooperation? Future studies of the evolutionary origins of cooperation must focus on analogs of that point in our history, the best window onto which comes from evidence on contemporary hunter-gatherer societies. At the same time, recent studies of twins indicate that aspects of religiosity are heritable, and that this influences adult behavior over and above influences in environmental conditions while growing up (Koenig, et al. 2005). Certainly, there is something deep in biology and human nature that predisposes us to religious beliefs (Atran and Norenzayan 2004; Barrett 2004; Boyer 2001).

Imagine every single Bible in the world vanished, along with all memories of what it said, in all people. Imagine the next generation growing up without any religious reading or teaching at all. What would their belief system be like? We predict: that they would believe in supernatural agents; that natural events would seem to have meaning and purpose; that others' fortune and ill-fortune would seem to betray moral conduct or misconduct; and, lastly, that they would successfully curb their ancient primeval selfishness for fear of greater forces observing and judging their actions. If this is what human nature is, then it bodes well for eliciting these natural sentiments and channeling them to good use. Evolution by natural selection does not appear to be the bugbear of altruism, self-sacrifice, charity, after all. God is no accident, and no mere by-product of large brains. On the contrary, religious beliefs are highly adaptive for the cooperation that is essential to and that defines human social life.

Much of the literature on religious beliefs and evolutionary biology focuses on squaring religious behavior with economic 'rational-actor' assumptions or, at the other extreme, the physiological responses of the brain. What has been lacking, however, is a careful consideration of the 'black box' in between—our *minds*—and how the cognitive processes involved interact with the natural selection of behavior. We suggest that, by virtue of our unique social cognitive abilities, the evolution of cooperation may have been influenced more than currently appreciated by the hand of God at work in the mind of man.

2

Religiosity as Mental Time-travel

Cognitive Adaptations for Religious Behavior

Joseph Bulbulia[1]

Introduction

In this chapter, 'religiosity' describes belief in superhuman reality, as well as motivations, emotions, and practices closely related to these beliefs. I assume supernatural beings play no causal role in the explanation for why religious agents commit and react to them. This assumption follows from methodological naturalism. While I will not defend this stance here, I observe that methodological naturalism is consistent with non-scientific forms of discussing and understanding religion. It is probably consistent with being religious—though I leave this discussion for theologians.

By 'supernatural' I mean non-natural beings, places, and forces— Jehovah, Krishna, The Pure Land, Hades, Num, Zeus, Mana, Jizo, Buddha, and innumerable others of these kind. There are problems both in viewing religion as concerned with the 'supernatural' and also with the term itself. For it is unclear whether 'supernatural' cuts the concepts of our understanding at any joint. Boyer and Ramble have data suggesting that it does—that regardless of our affiliations and traditions we reliably recognize supernatural concepts in roughly the same way (Boyer and Ramble 2001).

1. I would like to thank Aarhus University's Laboratories on Religion and Cognition for their support. I'd also like to thank Laura Feldt and Rich Sosis for commenting on an earlier draft.

Let's accept the view, then, that 'supernatural' is a natural kind, though surely more evidence is needed.

A significant problem in human evolutionary biology is explaining how evolutionary processes—both cultural and genetic—could have tolerated religious commitments. For naturalists, religious beliefs are at least partially unfounded. Agents attribute beliefs to gods; we have assumed the gods play no causal role in activating these beliefs. How could religious persons go so badly wrong? More puzzling: how can they go so badly wrong without injuring themselves, in the way schizophrenics do? For there is no evidence that adult religious agents are cognitively impaired, globally irrational, or immature. Unlike schizophrenics, religious agents flourish. Whatever one thinks about the sanity of religious belief, religious persons are sane.

Moreover, we must explain why religious commitments are typically linked to powerful norms and emotions. Why did selection tolerate the behavioral costs that flow from religious commitments and behaviors (Atran 2002a; Sosis 2003; Bulbulia 2004a; Dennett 2006)?[2]

In section I, I explore a plausible model in which evolutionary processes favor religious architecture susceptible to local religious ideas and norms, and which link these to powerful emotional and motivational states. The model is sometimes called the 'costly signaling' model for religion, but I shall call it the 'commitment-signaling' model. The model makes sense of the costs of religion as adaptations. In section II, I use evolutionary task analysis to predict that motivational states must be *disconnected* from most practical action domains (causing little harm). Here I specify a plausible design for accomplishing these tasks, and review data supporting its presence. In section III, I use the model to explain how religious persons are able to experience superhuman agents while remaining otherwise functionally engaged with distal realities—ecological and social.[3] I shall conclude that religion is a variety of mental time-travel, one that relies on very specially contrived fictions and encapsulated self-deception over their reality.

---

2. 'Cost' here and throughout will mean reproductive cost. The literature on commitment signaling sometimes describes hard-to-fake signals as 'costly'. But such signals do not always bring reproductive costs. Faking a genuine smile is difficult for most people, yet not reproductively costly. To denote signaling costs I use the slogan 'hard-to-fake'. What others (including Bulbulia 2004a) have called the 'costly-signaling theory' I call 'commitment-signaling theory'.

3. Finding an ancestor spirit in a lake, or a sprit in the sky, or a deity in a configuration of paint and clay requires extremely loose inferential standards. We would not mistake a photo of a sexual partner for the real target, and present accordingly.

I. The Commitment-signaling Hypothesis for Religiosity

I begin by reviewing the reasons to think selection tolerated, enhanced, and elaborated religious dispositions—tendencies to form emotionally powerful religious commitments—or their adaptive benefits.

The commitment-signaling theory holds that being religious in religious society helped our ancestors to manage the cognitive burdens of social living. It is uncontroversial that cooperative groups bring significant advantages to the individuals who compose them. It is also uncontroversial that humans have lived in cooperative groups for at least a million years, well before the arrival of modern humans between 150–250 thousand years ago (Boehm 1999). Human social organizations function to increase resource extraction capacity and efficiency. Cooperating and coordinated groups provide vigilance against predation threats. They allow agents to organize divisions of labor and expertise, create economies of scale, and establish networks for the distribution and defense of resources. Group living also brings tremendous epistemic advantages. Human societies may be arranged to store, perfect, and transmit locally useful knowledge by divisions of intellectual labor; our capacity for social learning facilitates this transmission with a relatively high degree of fidelity (Tomasello 1999). No single individual need learn the collective wisdom of a tribe. Children receive adaptive information from their parents—through an inheritance of ideas, not merely genes—and they also receive wisdom from parental cohort and peers. Oblique and horizontal transmission enables us to learn about the labile local environments that situate us. Such transmission selects for behavioral and developmental plasticity (Sterelny 2003). Much locally adaptive knowledge is traded freely, without deception, and this too is a kind of cooperation. Parents do not generally sabotage the beliefs of their neighbor's children (Sterelny 2004; Sterelny 2006). Our spectacular capacity to transmit and improve practical knowledge has enabled humans to support life in nearly every terrestrial circumstance. Our ability to manage cooperative life has enabled us to survive together in scorching deserts and on frozen seas and it has left a trail of mass extinctions in our wake (Richerson and Boyd 2005).

The benefits accessible to individuals living in cooperative groups are significant. But such benefits are notoriously difficult to obtain; for the benefits of social life are typically accessible only when all or most pay a price. Frequently, defectors can benefit from the toil of others without themselves toiling, thereby undermining cooperation. Together we can bring down the Mammoth. If one or two defect, the beast will fall. Where many defect, the cooperative pay the price of assaulting a large target alone. Rational incentives often favor defection, but where many defect group benefits vanish. So, cooperation is often available only to the degree that it is policed. However, policing often comes at a cost, and these too bring fresh cooperation dilemmas (Bulbulia 2004a; Dominic Johnson 2005).

In our lineage, policing is helped through a variety of psychological mechanisms. We track past behavior and punish defection by withdrawing cooperation, thus incentivizing exchange (Boyd and Richerson 2001). We jealously guard our resources, even when doing so brings costs in excess of their loss, and so deter aggression. We are emotional hagglers who refuse to accept unfair offers, even when refusal is costly. We form strong affective bonds. Our capacity for language enables us to establish very powerful and precise information gradients. This capacity when combined with tendencies to gossip enables us to spread socially relevant news (Dunbar 1998). Within a short time, the indiscretion known to one is known to all. The perturbation of social information reduces defection by ramping up its risks (Jolly 1966). Moreover, an inclination to accord prestige to socially benefiting acts loads further incentive to cooperation. When an altruistic reputation brings rewards, an agent has an incentive to acquire one.

According to the 'social complexity hypothesis' a key driver of human intelligence was the emergence of large, functionally integrated social units. As a society grows, so too do the demands imposed by social cognition. Dunbar observes that an increase in the number of agents with whom a focal agent interacts sharply increases the amount of socially relevant information she must store and track for effective policing, prediction, and effective social maintenance (Humphrey 1976; Byrne and Whiten 1988; Humphrey 1992; Dunbar 1998; Dunbar 2005). A focal agent needs to monitor information about each new agent introduced to a group—that agent's resources, behavioral tendencies, physical capacities, reliability, mate choices preferences, expertise, social status, and other information. And, critically, a focal agent must monitor, store, and update information about how each new agent interacts with potentially every other agent. 'Horizontal' complexity of social groups rises much faster than group number. Moreover, because the social agents also align themselves with various subgroup structures—kin groups, totems, hunting groups, political and economic hierarchies, religious units, and a number of informal alliances and friendships—a focal agent must understand and potentially remember how each new agent relates to each of these subgroups, and how these subgroups relate to each other, and to the largest group unit taken as a whole. This 'vertical' complexity increases as groups become more socially differentiated. (For extended discussion see Sterelny 2007.)

The complexity of social life drives the evolution of enhanced storage and tracking skills, and predictive abilities. To accommodate a Machiavellian mind, our chimp-like ancestors required a massive memory upgrade. And they became increasingly skilled theorists of mind, understanding how the motivational and epistemic states of their cohort were linked, and how these vary with circumstance for specific agents. Social complexity further selected for enhanced linguistic competence—perhaps also facilitated by enhanced memory and agent-tracking skills—as agents needed to convey and interpret increasingly precise and substantial social and ecological information. And, with these upgrades, a still further elaboration of social complexity was made possible, thus creating new and more intricate cognitive demands on increasingly social agents. Over time, cognitive and social complexities were mutually elaborated (Boyd and Richerson 1985).

Religiosity as an adaptation that reduces the cognitive load of cooperative social life

As the informational demands on agents rise, so too do the advantages of technologies equipping agents to *reduce* the computational complexity of social living. Cooperation is policed by Machiavellian minds, but it is also policed by a variety of cognitive mechanisms and cultural innovations that diminish the cognitive load of strategic socializing. As Chris Boehm has emphasized, a significant factor in the explanation for the success of forager groups lies in their power to specify and propagate egalitarian norms (Boehm 1999). Norms regulate exchange by standardizing expectations, thereby reducing Machiavellian complexity. We know the pig's hindquarter goes to the killing hunter's family, the back and chest is divided among the hunting party, the entrails go to the spear maker, and so forth. And as Richerson and Boyd have emphasized, violations of norms are often immediately and cheaply punishable, and so norms appear to be self-policing (Boyd and Richerson 2001; see also Fehr and Fischbacher 2004).

Sterleny uses the rather vivid example of drunkenly groping a superior's mate at a Christmas party, a norm whose violation brings immediate disutility (Sterelny 2007).

We are also a symbolic species who mark social worlds in a variety of ways relevant to action and exchange, and this marking also reduces a weighty cognitive load. For, given a marking convention, we are better able to understand social affiliations, and so better able to predict future behaviors. That skinhead with the swastika tattoo on his forehead has pre-committed himself to the fate of his neo-Nazi cohort. His prospects are truly dim if they fail. His fate and those of his group converge, substantially diminishing his cooperation dilemma. With symbolic labeling, intricate computational problems are reduced to perceptual and emotional problems we are well equipped to solve. With norms and symbolic conventions, it appears we do not need to evolve minds capable of running massively intricate social chess programs. Thus, through the convergence of norms and symbolic marking, computationally intractable problems are tamed. Boehm and others find it no accident that the first evidence of symbolic marking coincides with the rapid expansion of the hominid lineage into formally inhospitable domains (Boehm 1999; Mithen 1999). Through a tremendous reduction in cognitive demands afforded by normative and symbolic life, it appears human society grew its feet, and ran.

But commitment-signaling theorists believe normative and symbolic marking give only part of the story for the human transition to the ultrasocial niche. Let us consider why.

The commitment-signaling theory of religion

Norms and symbolic marking foster reliable exchange by cheaply punishing defection. But, in a Machiavellian world this effect can only be temporary. *For extrinsically motivating social conventions select for more effective Machiavellian agents.* Instead of drunkenly groping a superior's spouse at the party we take the adultery underground. Defectors may use the cover of night and other screens and props effectively to deceive. The gossip gradient may be polluted with mistaken or exaggerated information (Geertz 2009; Geertz 2007). Defectors may contrive various schemes and technologies to assist in swindling their norm-following cohort: shell games, card hustles, snake oils are common in every culture. Thieves often strike and honor private deals at the expense of group welfare. Cabals and juntas form. Not every action can be policed by a norm. And to the degree that defection remains difficult to detect, there will be incentive to dodge and exploit the rules.

Furthermore, we are prone to 'matching law' fallacies. Our preference for immediate reward over future reward is (approximately) inversely proportional to the timing of the reward (Frank 1988). We often select immediate pleasure at the expense of future pain. Were we to experience a hangover *before* imbibing, few would drink to excess. We do not always act as we know we should. So, at the time, even risky norm-violating behavior may seem worth it. Moreover, where defection stakes are high, and the threat of discovery is low, defection in even well policed societies may pay.

Norms commit agents to cooperation through extrinsic benefits and costs. But they do not *pre-commit* agents. And for this reason they do not secure commitment where an agent perceives an interest to defect. Norms do not reliably reduce Machiavellian complexity unless they are *intrinsically motivating*. The standard solution to social evolution does not solve its problem.

It seems religion may rescue norms. For religion appears to afford cheap policing. Even if an actual return favors defection, a perceived supernatural return (now or soon) or a strong emotional desire to please a norm-supporting supernatural agent will be capable of inducing cooperation. When individuals face cooperation dilemmas, it is not the actual pay-off schedule that predicts cooperation. What matters is their preference schedule. If the distortion brings more advantage than accuracy then selection will favor distortion in our understanding and feelings relative to a reward matrix. And if a god or ancestor or karmic power *is believed* to reward cooperation or punish defection then defection may be rationally disfavored (Bering 2004; Dominic Johnson 2005). Where a religious agent acts out of self-interest, or a sense of duty, or love for a god, social transgressions become less desirable. It may be very easy to access the boss's spouse, but if you have reason to believe that a castrating god or your dead mother is watching the tactic may seem ill advised (for a 'spandrelist' account of 'full access strategic agents' see Boyer 2001). Moreover, the idea that gods and other supernatural powers are agents to whom we owe duties and obligations can motivate exchange when the idea becomes genuinely and commonly believed. For, given the rest of human psychology, we feel those obligations without calculating conditional strategies and natural outcomes. For religionists, honoring social commitments will seem desirable. Or so it may seem.

Unfortunately religious policing is unevolvable. Supernatural illusions cannot police exchange. For such a tendency to supernatural policing cannot become common when the illusion-trait is rare. Against defectors, religionists will only get cheated. And even where religion is common religious persons remain exploitable by defectors impersonating religionists: in time, defecting wolves dressed as cooperative sheep keep company only with other wolves in theological drag (see, e.g., Irons 1996). Religious cooperators face a *recognition constraint* (Bulbulia 2005; Bulbulia 2006). Critically, religiously motivated cooperation is evolvable only if co-religionists can find each other, while at the same time spotting religious impostors.

Religious emotions as pre-commitment signals

The commitment-signaling theory of religion suggests we can solve this problem. At the core of the theory is the idea that solving the recognition constraint relies on the deployment and interpretation of signals that reliably and perceptibly distinguish genuinely religious agents from defecting frauds. If religious cooperators are able to produce a characteristic signature that identifies them as different from religious impostors, religiously motivated moralities become possible. Yet, what could function as such a signal? What can religious agents do that would-be defecting agents impersonating religious agents cannot?

Commitment theory suggests many candidate signals. Participation in religious practices frequently brings costs that only the religiously committed will accept (Irons 1996; Irons 2001; Sosis 2003; Sosis and Alcorta 2003; Sosis 2004; Bulbulia 2004a). Some of these costs are very striking indeed, for ritual agents immolate themselves in dramatic and dangerous ways (Atran 2002a; Bulbulia 2004b). Many costs are less vivid, and come through resource expenditure and forsaken opportunities. For cost outlays themselves give information about the nature and degree of commitment. If Hajji is willing to swing on a flesh hook for his god, there can be little doubt he is committed. The core prediction of ritual-signaling theory is that if an agent produces evidence of commitment to a god, that agent is committed to a group (for empirical evidence supporting ritual-signaling theory see Sosis 2000; Sosis and Bressler 2003; Bulbulia 2007).[4]

4. Sosis and his colleagues have built an impressive empirical case for looking at rituals as amplifiers of cooperation signals. But I (and they) want to emphasize that commitment signaling may not be the primary function of ritual action. To the extent that rituals permanently mark us, they

There are other signals religious agents may send that defectors will not easily match. Theological knowledge is a hard-to-fake signal of group affiliation; it identifies past resource investments and developmental histories. For theological knowledge is hard to learn. Indeed, theology may serve few utilities apart from its signaling capacity, for religious agents do not appear to employ it to reflect about their gods (Barrett 1996; Barrett 1998; Barrett 2004). Moreover, permanent symbolic markers—those that come both through 'assent' and 'dissent' communities—may pre-commit individuals through permanent marking, as the swastika example illustrates. Where individuals lack permanent signals they will often import various contrivances to signal their affiliation—headpieces, unusual clothing, scarves, masks, and headdresses, various charms and emblems, specific and unconventional configurations of body hair. They may adopt a special gait or stride. These paraphernalia and habits signal commitment through conventional meanings that many defectors would be reluctant to accept; especially where such affiliations are public and exclusive (extensive display disrupts the join–defect–leave strategy). True believers may shed much information as a by-product of their normal activity, for religious commitments impinge on life outside of symbolic contexts. Paying attention to what religionists do when they are distressed may give clues about their convictions. An athlete who thanks and praises a god on national television gives a somewhat difficult-to-fake signal of commitment, and this kind of example, so familiar in public life, may reflect a deeper disposition to shed hard-to-fake evidence of group identity and commitment in non-religious contexts.

So there are many signals potentially relevant to solving the recognition constraint. Here, I wish to focus on emotional signaling, for emotions illustrate the most basic and ancient reliable signaling technology, one that has long been a legacy of primate flesh.[5] Moreover, our ancestral signaling system helps to explain the cognitive binding of religious beliefs and powerful motivation states. Let us consider emotional signaling generally, before considering how religious emotions give evidence of commitments to

powerfully pre-commit us to acting in pro-social ways. For, if group competition is fierce, our prospects for survival may well coincide with the success of our tribe, as the parable of the tattooed Nazi suggests. And there may be other crucial non-signaling functions (see discussion below).

5. Primates signal emotion through cries and facial expressions, and through postures and ritual gestures (Griffiths 1997b). See also Zahavi and Zahavi 1997.

norm-supporting superhuman agents. There are three significant properties of emotions that collectively work to make emotions reliable as signals of cooperative (or defective) intent (Frank 1988; Zahavi and Zahavi 1997; Frank 2001).

First, emotions are linked to motivations. To feel lonely suggests a motivation to seek company. To feel fear suggests a motivation to escape. Of course, we do not always act on our emotions. But, where an emotion is present, there is at least a prima facie motivation to act or respond (or to inhibit response) in a certain way. Notice that evidence of motivation gives clues about future behavior. This connection between display, motivation, and signal enables emotions to function prophetically. A strong emotion— say, fear at being dragged to the fire—will accurately predict activation of a characteristic response pattern. Facial expressions of basic emotions—fear, joy, anger, sadness, shock, disgust, and others—are human universals. They are unlearned and universally understood (Darwin [1872] (1965); Ekman 1994). No one needs to explain the haunted expression of terror in the torture victim's eyes.

Second, emotions manifest themselves in ways that are hard to fake. Emotionally salient fear is not difficult to detect. And, though other emotions may be masked, for most of us they are difficult to obscure for long, and some cannot be manipulated. A blush expresses self-consciousness, and the response may be very difficult to control. The muscular orchestration of a smile is both complex and produced outside of the neo-cortex, in regions of the brain dedicated to emotional processing (Ramachandran and Blakeslee 1998). Most of us have a hard time producing a genuine smile for the camera. The face is not the only emotional projector. Our voice too gives evidence. Speakers find fear and anger difficult to suppress. Profuse sweating suggests high autonomic arousal. Posture and gait also give emotional clues. Someone advancing rapidly with his chin forward probably means business. In short, though our emotions may be damped down, emotional states are very often credibly paired with motivations that are signaled through clear perceptual cues. Audiences are able to use these clear cues to discern emotional signatures, and so are better outfitted to predict behavior.

Third, audiences scrutinize emotional displays. The data here are less decisive for we are not perfect at detecting liars (see, e.g., Ekman 1975). Nevertheless, Frank's studies indicate that experimental subjects in even artificial, data-impoverished settings do far better than random prediction

(1988). Considering emotions in the wild, Frank argues that our inter-pretive and discriminatory capacities will give even better results, as the information presented to them is more substantial, differentiated, and informed by other channels of information (the gossip gradient, accolades, emblems of success, reputations, and others). Moreover, most of us find it difficult to suppress and control emotion for long. In the evolutionary arms race between signaling and detection systems, our capacities to dis-cern emotional signals as reliable indicators of motivational states endow emotions with a fragile prophetic power. In scanning an emotional display we are better able to anticipate how an agent will behave, and so to adjust our plans. But deceptive agents will always have incentive to mimic these signals and, for this reason, biologically wired signaling technologies must be configured to remove them as much as possible from deceptive control (including self-deceptive control). For discussion of how ritual helps to combat evolutionary arms races in signaling technology, see Sosis 2003; Bulbulia 2004a. If Frank is right, our emotional responses are relatively reliable and transparent because they evolved to pre-commit agents to cooperation. To a rough approximation, emotional displays function as signals potentially relevant to social interaction.

The literature on emotional signaling bears on an important feature of religious commitment. It helps us to understand how intrinsically moti-vating norms would have been supported over hominid evolution through emotional displays relative to supernatural beings. We begin to understand how religion supports norms by looking to the evolutionary problems our immediate ancestors had to solve before acquiring rich normative morality. Without a doubt, our emotional signaling system evolved much earlier than did our capacities for normative and symbolic living. While our nearest primate relatives have nothing remotely approaching normative and symbolic society, they nevertheless register emotional displays in response to other primates (and natural agents) as Darwin long ago observed ([1872] (1965); see also Griffiths 1997b; Sterelny and Griffiths 1999).[6] Our capacity for managing intricate social worlds emerged in a lineage already equipped with the cognitive wares to express pre-commitments through hard-to-fake emotional display.

Notice that this commitment-signaling system provides a powerful pre-adaptation for norm-supported society. *Agent–emotion signaling bridges*

---

6. Not always other primates. A chimpanzee will recoil violently from a snake, etc.

an evolutionary trench that primates must cross before beginning the ascent of norm-building fitness peaks. For, once norms were associated with norm-supporting agents, normative commitments could have been marked by an agent–emotion display system whose complex and coordinated efficiency already had been honed by millions of years of evolutionary organization. That link would have been forged not because supernatural agents are intrinsically norm supporting (we shall see in section III how the gods behave appallingly). Roughly, the opposite was true. The link was forged because emotions evolved in our primate ancestors as a mechanism of response to agents. Thus, for an intrinsic signaling system to evolve from its primate predecessors, the representational inputs feeding that system would have benefited greatly by describing agent-like beings. And those agents are optimally effective only if they are all knowing, emotionally and morally compelling, potentially everywhere, and eternal. They are optimized, that is, when they are imagined as *supernatural* parents, ancestors, and masters. For the system to be stable, belief in those agents would have benefited through regular emotionally charged encounters, that is, through religious experience. (In section III we shall see how cognition manages this trick.)

Conviction → Norm-supporting Agents → Emotional Signal →
Predicts Cooperative Intent

The connection of emotions to beliefs in norm-supporting gods would have unleashed tremendous advantages to individuals facing significant cooperation dilemmas. For, again, norms remain imperfectly reliable when they are not supported through intrinsic commitment. In an increasingly Machiavellian social world the recognition constraint threatens extensive, reliable exchange. By registering emotions relative to norm-supporting gods we were able to express pre-commitments to a god-supporting social group.[7] Moreover, where such agents form the targets of emotional concern—when we love or respect the gods—then violating their laws will not only seem unwise but also shameful.[8] And these pre-commitments will

---

7. Emotions may be centered on various natural objects—the props and prompts of religious culture, priests and priestesses, striking natural objects like mountains, or the sun and moon, and others. While my interest here is on explaining supernatural commitments relative to supernatural agents, a full treatment requires understanding the enchantment of nature. A full treatment would link supernatural agents to the larger class of 'sacred agents'.
8. Given the matching law, supernatural rewards must be paid in either the immediate or near future, or be enormously substantial to work. But intrinsically felt emotions alter preference schedules without a need for extra reward.

then be decoded by perceptional systems already evolved for the task of defector detection, thereby bypassing the computational intractability of a Machiavellian world. A substantial barrier to social living was crossed.

Is there any evidence for this evolutionary conjecture? The theory predicts that emotional responses to norm-supporting gods will be difficult to fake absent actual belief in such gods. And it predicts that morally motivating gods will never be merely represented: they will also be feared, adored, ingratiated, respected, loved, and honored. Perhaps unsurprisingly there is little experimental data on the role of emotional signaling in the literature on religion. Indeed, without the commitment-signaling hypothesis, it is unclear why anyone would look for it. More data are needed here. Intuitively it would seem difficult for most of us to manage emotions of religious piety towards superhuman agents that strike one as preposterous, under the hard scrutiny of religious observers. The relevant emotions are difficult to prompt and even harder to sustain. Moreover, the emotional dimension of religiosity is commonplace to anthropologists and historians of religion. And it is a repeated theme in religious theologies from Augustine through Edwards, Schleiermacher, Otto, and their contemporary followers. Finally, the commitment-signaling model of the emotions is well supported in the ordinary exchange contexts (Frank 2001). So, it appears safe to back the emotional-signaling horse in religious contexts.

At present, the commitment-signaling theory of religious emotions, then, takes the form of an inference to the best explanation. It explains the otherwise puzzling fact that religious agents inhabit emotion-drenched supernatural worlds. It explains the link between belief in false reality and strong motivational social commitment, and so explains the integration of religious belief with emotion to produce powerfully motivating conviction. I want to stress again, however, that the emotional dimension of religious signaling gives only part of the story. Emotions do more than signal commitment. Emotions motivate the search for specific kinds of information relevant to development and success. For example, aesthetic emotions may direct the search strategies of religious agents, indicating what sort of super-human information to seek out. An intense interest in gossip, for example, better enables us to understand our social context (see Tooby and Cosmides 2001 for an account of 'aesthetic' emotions and their importance to developmental contexts).

Moreover, a more detailed explanation of religious emotion would require submersion in the details of the highly structured religious contexts that prompt, cultivate, revise, edit, assess, and amplify religious emotions. Cultural variation will organize different emotion-regulation systems in different contexts. The spasmodic ejaculations that are expected in an evangelical church will appear out of place in a dour Presbyterian service. Moreover, religious emotions are not stable absent *any* religious context, and without continued exposure to religious practice, religiosity as a whole degrades (Francis and Kay 1995). So, religious commitment substantially relies on locally configured religious practice for enduring epistemic support. Finally, without platforms for broadcasting commitment signals we would have no means for detecting them in the social collectives; for we cannot scan the religiosity of our peers without public, collective expressions of religious commitment.[9] In short, there is far more to the explanatory story than has been suggested here. Nevertheless, I hope to have made a credible case for investigating religious emotions as strategic adaptations for social exchange.

II. Religious Decoupling

Having sketched an evolutionary account for the integration of supernatural commitment to powerful emotional and motivational states I now consider how the systems that mediate that connection disengage religiosity from non-social practical domains. For, when religious conviction seeps into practical domains, an otherwise adaptive trait becomes damaging. Religious agents face an *encapsulation constraint* (see Bulbulia 2006 for discussion)

Consider our capacity for decoupled representation (or 'metarepresentation'). Organisms do not merely respond to their immediate circumstances with stereotyped behaviors. Instead, their perceptual representations of distal reality are 'decoupled' from automated response strategies. Perceptual

---

9. For religious signaling to function it clearly needs to be projected through cultural technology. In a tribe of 150 cooperators laced with defectors, a focal agent cannot move from shelter to shelter inducing and then evaluating the religiosity of each of her cohort. An organism whose life dissolves into an everlasting series of produced and observed religious seizures is not viable. Moreover, the computational demands imposed by constant emotional signaling remain too high. Each individually observed religious signal would need to be filed, retained, and updated as social dramas unfold. There is no substantial reduction of a cognitive load here. In place of everlasting emotional scrutiny, however, we have social practices that at one time routinely display the religiosity of a collective. Moreover, such amplification technologies allow for other credible signals of religious motivation apart from emotional display, and these too provide a means for securing reliable exchange.

information may be stored and accessed for future purposes, perhaps presently unknown. Perceptual information may also prompt a range of behaviors. And, for any single behavior, a range of signals may activate initiation (Sterelny 2003). Other organisms decouple thought from behavior. A cat monitoring prey may attempt reconnaissance before pouncing. But, in the hominid lineage, this capacity operates with truly astounding richness and intricacy. We do not merely register distal affairs, we reflectively consider the extent to which our representations are true. We form moral and epistemic attitudes to our thoughts. We remember the source of certain information—as self or other (and who)—and modify our commitments in light of new information. We mark representations with time tags as well— locating events within the space–time matrix of personal autobiography. We recall and re-experience these representations with vivid emotional detail. And we update autobiographical knowledge with the receipt of new and relevant information. 'Jane wanted John the moment she discovered his unseemly defect.' Robust decoupling capacity enables us to manipulate and mark our thoughts for a range of purposes, many of which we cannot determine in advance. Such capacity brings massive, portable behavioral flexibility (see especially Cosmides and Tooby 2000).

In developing my story about religious decoupling I wish to consider the special advantages we obtain through counterfactual metarepresentation (and the simulation systems that inform it.) Through counterfactuals we are able to manipulate specific representations for special consideration offline.

(1) 'What would happen if the door to the aircraft cabin just now opened at 12,000 meters?'

(1) can receive a reliable though non-actual answer. In contemplating this scenario, an agent may access epistemic databases and utilize simulation-based inference machinery to bear on the task. She may produce and compare various scenarios, according a degree of probability to each. The relevant information processing may be very complicated indeed. For example, an agent's knowledge may change in light of how she imagines the counterfactual cases, and this change, in turn, may inform further deliberation. Stable panhuman resources such as folk physics may be invoked—in the present case, the law of gravity acting on the trajectories of falling bodies. Novel knowledge may give advice: Second World War bombardiers improved their accuracy by retraining their folk intuitions (McCloskey 1983). A 'phonological loop' and 'visual sketch pad' may be

deployed (Cosmides and Tooby 2000). We rehearse ideas and hatch plans in quasi-perceptual formats.

It is significant that through counterfactual inference, agents are frequently able to produce reliable answers to non-actual but possible scenarios. They do so without incurring the substantial risks and costs of live experimentation. In understanding and predicting their world, counterfactual-enabled agents are liberated from the deliverances of actual fortune. And they may devise plans appropriate to their novel, local circumstances. How may this happen?

In the first instance, counterfactual reasoning involves separating and marking a set of propositions for consideration as 'imagined but not actual'. To dignify ignorance with a name, let us call the scope operator that binds this set the IMAGINE WHAT IF operator. (I will suppose conditional counterfactuals give a THEN WOULD scope operator in inferences acting on arguments bound by the WHAT IF operator):

(1*) IMAGINE WHAT IF [(The door to the aircraft cabin just now opened) THEN WOULD (I fall to my death, bringing others with me)]

Though understood as not literally true, the contents bound by the counterfactual operator are allowed to migrate freely, as if they were true. We can produce a range of potential outcomes and assess their conditional probability through this invented knowledge (a form of individual learning). Propositions within the scope of the operator are treated differently than they would be were they admitted without the operator. Critically this isolation of information within a domain prevents false information from damaging our inferential capacity in unrelated domains. The information encoded in the hypothetical (1*) would produce schizophrenic terror were it represented or read in the unmarked form as:

(1**) The door to the aircraft cabin just now opened at 12,000 meters.

Moreover, counterfactual decoupling combines with other metarepresentational capacities, for we are able to do more than mark propositions for special consideration as 'not literally true'. We are able to form emotional attitudes to hypothetical propositions and accord them a degree of certainty. The source of a representation—say, as 'self' rather than as 'other'—can be identified and pinned to its representational contents. Robust combinatorial inflection enables us to generate richly structured representational outputs:

(1***) SELF // NOW // IMAGINE WHAT IF [(the door to the cabin just now open...) VERY LIKELY // THEN WOULD (I fall to my death, bringing others with me)
→ inference: WOULD BE // UNDESIRABLE (I fall to my death...)
→ inference: mark antecedent of the conditional UNDESIRABLE

The rich inflectional character of thought also helps us to produce strikingly precise strategies. With it, we travel through time to fictional futures, running experiments to improve our own.

2. PLAN (Do not open the door)

Massive decoupling enables us to plan in ways unavailable to the literal-minded. We consider alternatives and limn future possibilities. We scheme, trading immediate discomfort for future return: 'If I endure the tooth drilling, the chronic pain will dissipate.' As with any creature, the shadow of the future falls on us. Yet, through 'remembering a future'—in Cosmides and Tooby's apt phrase—we can alter which shadows fall. We anticipate destiny and so are not enslaved by it.

The power of non-literal thinking also emerges in the analysis of fiction. For the present purposes, consider fiction as extended counterfactual cognition deploying a matrix of representations explicitly understood to be not literally true. It is interesting, and puzzling, that we should desire to contemplate such representations (Tooby and Cosmides 2001), for the extensive contemplation of fiction imposes opportunity and other resource costs, and it dwells in falsehoods. There is no possible future in which we will face the Minotaur, the Little Mermaid, or Vader's Death Star. Moreover, in fiction, non-literal thinking is none the less represented in quasi-literal format (Brock 2002). We know the *Shining* is only fictional, but nevertheless we fear for the boy as he flees to the snowy maze. We know Godzilla has never afflicted Japan—indeed we know the 100-meter dragon cannot be physically realized—yet hope the Japanese army will deter it. Moreover, though we fear the fictional Godzilla, we do not run from the theater as we would from a real 100-meter dragon. And, even as we hope for its success, we may not even know if Japan has an army.

There has been lively debate over the utility and evolutionary history of fictional capacities (Crews, Gottschall, et al. 2005). Some see purposes, e.g. Carroll 2004. Others see fiction as 'mental cheesecake', attractive but not functionally so (Pinker 1997: 525). But it cannot be doubted that a substantial information management system needs to be in place to prevent the cognition of fiction from becoming maladaptive. For fiction to work we require something roughly approximating the following meta-representational design:

IMAGINE + [Fiction]

We define 'IMAGINE' as the ordinary counterfactual decoupler that marks a collection of non-actual representations for hypothetical and conditional consideration. We identify the argument of this operator (the bounded non-actual collection) with the notation [Fiction]. To prevent fiction from harming us, the IMAGINE operator must keep fictional information from spilling into practical inferential domains. It erects cognitive firebreaks between the representations it binds and practically relevant ontological commitments. It marks the contents within its scope as 'not literally true'. We judge that

(3) Scarlet O'Hara is beautiful

but also that

(3*) Scarlet O'Hara does not exist.

Paradox is resolved when we note that (3) falls within the scope of a fiction. (3) should be read as

(3**) IMAGINE [(*Gone with the Wind*) → LICENSE fictional inference: (Scarlet O'Hara is beautiful)]
  → practical inference: NOT TRUE (Scarlet O'Hara exists)

The IMAGINE scope operator guides the interpretation and motivational integration of fiction cognition.[10] It enables us to understand both that fictions are invented and that genuine inferential relations hold for their contents. If fiction is adaptive the systems that export fictional information to practical problem solving domains do so without the contents of fiction ever being believed.[11]

---

10. Advocates of the 'fiction as adaptation' idea observe that the knowledge and emotion released through fictional contemplation allow for a more rapid accumulation of locally adaptive knowledge than is possible were we restricted to learning from the vagaries of actual experience. See esp. Tooby and Cosmides 2001.

11. The marking of fiction as only quasi-true allows for inferences within the boundaries of a fictional marking to flow freely. This leads to some peculiar effects. We can ask whether

I have avoided the 'fiction as adaptation' debate. But, in section I, I urged that religiosity manifests the complex and coordinated structure of an adaptation for cooperative exchange. Its function is not to help us learn about social complexity but rather to reduce it. It does so by making social relations more reliably predictable. Thus, the task requirements further constrain the cognitive organization of religious commitment, and structure the metarepresentational systems that manage them.

I have discussed the distinctive functions of highly motivating religious commitment. The most parsimonious supposition—in evolutionary and cognitive terms—is to suppose that the capacities that enable us to produce decoupled religious representation resemble the capacities that underwrite counterfactual and fictional thinking (see Atran 2002a and Pyysiäinen 2003a for similar but non-adaptationist analyses). For, the functional tasks in many respects resemble each other. Religious cognition contemplates fictional realities in ways that drive domain-specific motivations and responses. Information held within the scope of the religiosity operator must not migrate into many practical domains of interaction. Religiosity, like counterfactual and fictional reasoning, faces a significant encapsulation constraint. Functional religious decoupling, however, differs from fiction counterfactual decoupling.[12] These differences stem from the functions of religiosity as a pre-commitment and signaling device.

The most important and obvious difference is that religious conviction is not self-consciously represented as fiction. It is self-consciously represented as true. We begin with the simplest conjecture:

$$^{®}\text{IMAGINE} + [\text{Fiction}]$$

where $^{®}$IMAGINE is a special counterfactual scope operator. Like the naked IMAGINE operator we assume that the religious decoupler binds a fiction so that it is read by the motivation and behavior systems as not actual. This prediction follows from the encapsulation constraint. An

Holmes is brighter than Watson and form an opinion, though this fact is never directly stated within Conan Doyle's work. But we cannot sensibly ask the color of Watson's eyes or the number of wives he has had. For nothing in the propositions given in Doyle's books allows inferences to these conclusions. We tolerate inferences (and perhaps debates) over the first case, whereas the second meets a blank stare of incredulity. There is a fact of the matter about how many wives Jeppe Jensen (an actual person) has had. But there is no such fact for Watson. Fictional characters are in this respect ontologically gappy.

12. I am not committing to an 'out of fiction' conjecture for the origins of religiosity. Rather, I merely note that both capacities share very similar structural features, for both are powerfully constrained by the demands of encapsulation.

evolutionary task analysis predicts that ®IMAGINE is read by most psychological systems in ways similar to the IMAGINE scope operator. The simplest hypothesis is that religious representations are read by the systems that regulate practical involvement with the world similarly to the way they read fictional marked representations. Metarepresentational binding allows religious information to be fenced off from harming a religious agent.

(4) ®IMAGINE [Zugroo is Lord Creator]
   → practical inference: NOT TRUE [Zugroo is Lord Creator]

Yet, given the functional constraints on adaptive religiosity, we assume that in the workspace where representational contents are *consciously accessed* and manipulated religion is represented as 'true', or even as 'certainly true'. *For the strength of a pre-commitment signal hinges on the emotionally detectible certainty of a religious belief.* Hence, self-consciousness is constrained to read ®IMAGINE counterfactuals as it would read factual representations. We can say that religiosity operates under a *self-deception constraint*. Here I use 'self deception' in Trivers' sense of a biasing and distorting of information flow to produce adaptive outcomes (Trivers 1991). We must *consciously believe* and we must also *unconsciously not believe* that religious representations are true. Needless to say, this division of a religious mind imposes strict demands on the metarepresentational system that controls and isolates religious fictions.

To a religious agent the scope operator will give something like the following permission to autobiographical consciousness:

(4*) ®IMAGINE [Zugroo is Lord Creator]
   → practical inference: NOT TRUE [Zugroo is Lord Creator]
   → workspace inference: CERTAINLY TRUE [Zugroo is Lord Creator]

Whether we are able to claim that agents believe in gods rather than 'believe in believing' has recently been subject to lively dispute (Palmer and Steadman 2004; Dennett 2006), for there is no obvious referent to that to which religious agents express commitment. But if the commitment signaling theory is in the right ballpark, there can be little doubt that religious agents consciously believe that what they are representing is true. For, such a conviction is required to produce the hard-to-fake emotional commitment to a norm-supporting god. Indeed, for the system to remain functional, we must believe with emotional zeal (Dennett is correct to note that religious agents 'believe in believing' but wrong in thinking that the 'religious memes' explanation sufficiently explains why (2006)). A non-trivial prediction of commitment signaling theory, then, is that persons will genuinely believe that they believe, even if this belief is inferentially unbounded. They will, for example, pass polygraph tests and galvanic skin response measures for lying.

Let us examine the interplay between self-conscious belief and encapsulation more fully. In a karma-bound world an agent expresses intrinsic pre-commitment by expressing moralistic emotional beliefs in karmic powers. Yet, consider an agent who truly believes in karma (that what goes around comes around). In a karmic world there is no point in punishing our enemies, for they shall get theirs anyway (as the karmic wheel turns). But karma doesn't exist. An organism that fails to punish its enemies will have lots of delighted enemies, and it will also be short for this world. Consider the thought that there is a perfect life of bliss after this one where all the faithful will go. A natural inference from this thought is: 'Give up caring very deeply about what happens in this life.' Yet, not caring about the hard labor of living is a bad idea for survival. Like a contradiction, almost anything follows from unconstrained supernatural commitment. And that makes any dispositions to it very dangerous indeed. So, religious commitments must be surrounded by cognitive firewalls similar to those that prevent our counterfactual and fictional musings from collapsing into a split-minded failure to distinguish actual from non-actual representations. The theory predicts that while religious persons express religious beliefs such persons will act in many ways as if they do not believe—for example, they will punish their enemies and fear death.

Furthermore, commitment-signaling theory predicts that religious fictions will be expressed with a moral valence. This further constrains its outputs. [®]IMAGINE fictions must be visible both to consciousness and to the systems that control moral normative emotions, motivations, and responses. While the outputs of religious belief must be fenced off from practical domains, they must be highly salient in cooperation domains. For religiosity to function adaptively those outputs must be integrated to normative exchange domains. Thus, religiosity not only faces an *encapsulation constraint* it also faces an *integration constraint* (Bulbulia 2006; Bulbulia 2007).

(4**) ®IMAGINE [Zugroo is Lord Creator]

    → practical inference: NOT TRUE [Zugroo is Lord Creator]

    → workspace inference: CERTAINLY TRUE [Zugroo is Lord Creator]

    → emotional response: Zugroo is real display

    → morally normative inference: Follow Zugroo's norms (including norms of sacrifice).

The integration constraint predicts that agents will come to believe that the rules and social orientations that religious fictions describe and motivate are intrinsically good and right. Hence religious fictions will be cast to prevent or minimize challenges to the moral authority of religious fictions. It is worth observing that in all religious cultures, to challenge norm-supporting inferences from religious fictions typically results in harsh and immediate social punishment. Religious narratives are norm supporting, but they are also norm supported. Religious morality thus scours the fictions that support it. This moral casting can produce very strange interpretive strategies. Very often religious characters will be seen through a moralizing lens that we do not apply to fictional characters. Consider this story.

> There is a very rich man named Mr Z who wants you to worship him. He lives in a nearby town though no one has seen him. Those who worship Mr Z are given a million dollars. No one has ever seen this, but trust me it is true. Mr Z repeatedly breaks the legs and burns those who do not worship him. If you love Mr Z, he will give you a million dollars. If you do not love him, Mr Z will savage you. [13]
>
> Some Ignorant Shepherd

It makes sense to ask whether this story licenses the inference 'Mr Z is a good man' or the inference 'Mr Z is deserving of praise and worship he demands.' More basically, it makes sense to ask why Mr Z would make such outrageous demands, and why he would care to be worshiped. But often it does not make sense for believers to ask these questions of deities who behave in similar ways. (Indeed far more horrendous ways, as in the Book of Job.) For the religious story is interpreted in such a way that God's command must be good. Moreover, for most believers it does not make sense to question a deity's practical judgment. It would be strange to ask of the Judeo-Christian fiction why God sent his all-important messages of

---

13. This story is adapted from <http://www.jhuger.com/kisshank>.

salvation to uneducated shepherds, at a time when there were no printing presses or mass media. The question is obvious, but does not come up. Similarly, it makes no sense to ask why, if God is invisible but omnipotent, God did not write his name on the moon or in the stars.[14] Moreover, religiously inflected accounts of religious history are not typically revised in light of new knowledge, and resist placement into a wider context. We may doubt the veracity of 'the Legend of Mr Z' transcribed by Some Ignorant Shepherd. But, to refer to Christianity as invented by scientifically ignorant pastoral peoples in the ancient Near East may well offend solemn Christian believers.

Notice I do not claim that the gods of religious fictions will always be interpreted as good and righteous.

(5) → Moral normative inference: Follow Zugroo's norms
    is compatible with but not equivalent to

(5*) → Morally normative inference: Follow Zugroo's norms because Zugroo is morally perfect.

The inference (5*) is not the only one capable of supporting a norm. There may be a variety of reasons agents supply for why they follow Zugroo's demands—for example, terror of crossing a cosmic tyrant. Moreover, the morally normative inference may well be basic, given the integration constraint religious norms likely deliver for every believing agent, absent the need for supplementary reasons.

The data suggest that few religious fictions support norms through reliance on representations of perfectly moral gods. Indeed, in vastly many traditions, the gods are explicitly represented in morally questionable ways. Human morality and the gods' morality are sharply distinguished. To repeat, this property of religious fictions is striking when compared with ordinary fictions. Even very powerful fictional characters (Mr Z) are held morally accountable by our standards. Ordinarily we apply to fictional characters standards we would apply to ourselves.

The religious fictions of ancient Greece ably illustrate this pattern: Greek gods are explicitly represented as ruthless, capricious, and cruel. Similarly,

---

14. Children do sometimes ask this question, for which they are generally dissuaded if not harshly punished. It appears they do not know whether to group a narrative bundle with an IMAGING THAT scope operator or an IMAGINE THAT® scope operator, perhaps because their religiosity system remains immature. This is very interesting and deserves close consideration in the developmental psychology of religion.

the Hindu god Kali is represented as arbitrary and vicious, yet nevertheless remains the object of mass veneration. Nevertheless, in both ancient Greek and Hindu societies very strong morally normative inferences run from religious mythologies to pro-social (and sacrificial) behavior. These facts comport well with commitment-signaling theory, which predicts an active integration of religious commitment to cooperative domains. For religion to enhance solidarity, religious commitments must promote distinctive motivational and behavioral states. While religiosity is insulated from (non-social) practical behavior, it must be reliably integrated to social behavior. Otherwise, religiosity will be rejected, not targeted and amplified by evolutionary selection pressures (see Bulbulia 2004a). [15]

To draw the threads of this section together, the commitment-signaling model predicts that religious persons will emotionally believe in gods, and moralistically believe in believing, for believing in a norm-supporting god signals a commitment to each other. The ®IMAGINE operator therefore defines a moral expectation about the fiction it bundles, in intricate and often bizarre ways. The convention of interpreting stories to have norm-supporting consequences frequently distorts and biases the interpretation of religious fictions. Explicit 'why do we celebrate nailing day?' questions will be discouraged or punished.

III. Religious Experience and Confabulation

I finally consider an application of the religious scope operator hypothesis to the domain of religious experience. Religiosity involves the active interpretation of reality as god-infested. While the gods are passively represented through shared religious stories and through public testimony, many religious agents report that the gods are personally encountered (James 1902).

I suggest that religious conviction is best explained as a kind of confabulation. We know that individuals have poor access to the true causes of their judgments, emotions, and behaviors. In a classic experiment Nisbett and Wilson (1977) showed that when faced with an arbitrary decision

---

15. While religious fictions support norms by allowing for emotional pre-commitment signaling, I do not think that religious fictions are necessary for supporting such norms. The fact that Asperger's patients can learn and strongly commit to religious norms without understanding other minds suggests that the relevant domains are to some degree dissociated. See Atran 2002a: 193. In Asperger's we find normative bracing without psychological content.

between identical objects (nylon stockings), agents nevertheless invented reasons for their choice, defending these reasons even after being informed the objects were identical.[16] Dennett suggests that confabulatory practices are extremely common, for concocting ad hoc stories is a fundamental part of interpreting who we are. In expressing our personal pasts we invent reasons and fill missing gaps, supplying a coherence and control to our autobiographical selves that we do not actually possess. Hirstein observes that the response 'I don't know?' is a complicated cognitive feat, one that involves the active suppression of conjectural thoughts that flood knowledge and response systems. The breakdown of these systems in a range of cognitive disorders suggests that critical cognitive stopgaps mediate the relationship between how we imagine ourselves to be and how we finally acknowledge ourselves to be. Hirstein notes that the effect of confabulatory response is particularly strong when agents are asked to respond to questions for which they *ought* to have answers. When asked by a romantic partner, 'why do you love me?', agents will typically supply *some* explanation— 'your eyes', 'your kindness', 'your sympathy'—when in fact they may not understand or have access to their reasons. It would be inappropriate in such instances to reply 'Honestly, I don't know why I love you' (Hirstein 2005: chap. 1). Thus, given well-documented confabulatory response effects, it would be astonishing if believers were unable to supply reasons for their strong religious conviction; it would be astonishing if they were to reply 'I don't know why I have strong religious conviction', all the more so where there are strong social expectations that they ought to know. Such expectations pervade many religious contexts.

While the reasons religious agents give for their belief may be sheer confabulation, it is nevertheless interesting that religious agents often describe some of their experiences as of supernatural beings. That is, the experience of some religious agents seems to be confabulatory in the present tense. Religious persons describe how they encounter religious beings in the course of their lives—typically, though not always, in the course of private and public religious practices (James 1902). Here I want to understand whether the minimalist-scope syntactic architecture I sketched in section II sheds any light on how such characterizations are organized. 'Spandrel' theories suggest that religiosity endures through the transmission of arresting

---

16. When given a set of choices, most people tend to pick the rightmost object. While only those with psychological training have access to this reason, nearly everyone will supply a reason.

or otherwise compelling concepts (e.g., Boyer 2001; Atran 2002a). Here, the claim is that religious information comes second hand, by a kind of conceptual transfer. But I have urged that the minimum unit of transfer is not the concept, but a scope-restricted fiction that embeds religious concepts (see also Feldt 2009). Agents acquire the religious fictions of their cohort in the context of social learning. But it seems they also acquire religious information through powerful emotional experience, in groups, but also alone by a kind of individual learning.[17] We have assumed that the gods play no explanatory role in agents' experiences. Thus, it is perplexing how religious agents are able to describe some of their experiences as caused by supernatural beings.

Given the scope-syntactic model presented above, the simplest explanation is that religious experience is ordinary counterfactual simulation in which the relevant simulations are marked and bounded by the ®IMAGINE scope operator. That is, religious simulations are *internally generated* religious fictions. Such representation can undoubtedly produce powerful affect. For a capacity to imagine religious agents as CERTAINLY TRUE makes it possible to engage with supernatural agents as more than abstract concepts. Through religious experience, agents are able to *commune* with supernatural beings. The simplest explanation for this experience is that religious agents produce counterfactual representations of sacred realities, which they consciously interpreted and store 'as true' (*the self-deception constraint*). These representations are formatted so that they do not split-mindedly influence practical action (*the encapsulation constraint*) outside of normative social exchange (*the integration constraint*).

The model sketched above also gives an initial answer for why religious agents produce religious experience. Given an absolute poverty of experience, it is difficult to understand how religious commitments to superhuman agents could be long sustained. Yet, religious experience gives emotionally powerful episodic support to religious commitment. For in most instances the best reason for believing in something is having directly experienced it. Thus, on the scope-syntactic model advanced here, we can view religious experience as a kind of *adaptive confabulation*. It is adaptive because it produces emotionally powerful evidence for religious pre-commitment and signaling. It is confabulation because religious evidence flows from a heavily structured biasing and distorting of information.

---

17. Individual learning, of course, may be developmentally scaffolded by social learning.

Let us explore this hypothesis. Moving from an imagined possibility to an unlicensed belief is extremely common. Such occurs every time one slips from a belief that x might be the case ('the tyrant might be holding weapons of mass destruction'; 'the chairman might be trying to thwart my progress'; 'she might love me') to an affirmation that x is true [thus, → infer: CERTAINLY (Invade!); thus, → PLAN (Hit the chairman with a chair); thus, → MEMORY (She struck me from love)]. Such confusion manifests itself in peculiar clinical situations. Patients significantly and obviously impaired by stroke sometimes truthfully deny their condition (anosognosia) or concoct and believe with rigid certainty wildly implausible stories for why they cannot do what is asked of them (as in Korsakoff's syndrome). Capgras disorders also lead afflicted agents to express convictions in vastly unwarranted claims. Such agents regularly invent fabulous stories in which loved ones are claimed to be impostors who have killed and are now impersonating their loved ones, or are alien clones. Here again the stories are so remote as to seem expressed in jest or as lies. But the afflicted agents are dead serious, sometimes to the point of attacking those they take to be doppelgangers (for discussion see Hirstein 2005: 124–34).

Exploring this model further, observe that in practical domains the systems that internally generate counterfactual representations will mark and bind counterfactual ruminations with 'the self' as their source. (The contents are marked and bounded as 'only imaginary' and 'invented by me'.) When I imagine Judgment Day, I register and record the simulation as mine. But ®IMAGINE marking of internally generated counterfactual simulation allows for the authority of religious counterfactuals to lie *outside* the religious agent. Here 'Judgment Day' is experienced as uniquely real, and endowed with moral importance. Given this authority, it would be unsurprising if religious imagination were frequently registered with the source tag 'supernatural other' and mistaken for an objective, external encounter.

There is much evidence suggesting that religious experience is registered as supernatural-other generated (James 1902; Taves 1999). The ethnographic and historical literature is also animated with examples of powerful and vividly represented supernatural experiences (e.g., Richard Katz 1984). On the model proposed here, we find that religious experience stems from an adaptive marking error. It is a kind of powerfully motivating, moralistic confabulation.

Notice that the religious decoupling of imagination makes it possible to have religious experience without visual or auditory hallucinations. The model predicts that when a believer generates a simulation of Judgment Day the argument (bundled representation set) produced is approximately similar to that of a disbeliever. But, different scope operators bind the believer's argument by very different rules, according them very different permissions than do the scope operators inflecting a non-believer's argument. For the believer, these representations are read as 'CERTAINLY TRUE'. And this gives imagination an experiential quality without a requirement for ordinary sensory experience.

Moreover, the model predicts that internally generated religious fictions will be marked and accessed by episodic memory as *morally relevant* experience. For the capacity for experiential storage enables religious simulation to generate norm-supporting motivational power. Religious experience not only obeys the integration constraint; it also *supports* integration by *generating* supernatural evidence. But, because religious scope operators restrict 'as true' interpretations of religious experience to the confines of moral emotion and motivation (cooperative pre-commitments) religious experiences, though false, will not typically harm religious agents. Indeed, if the model proposed here is correct, these experiences benefit religious agents over the long haul. They do not, for example, produce behavior characteristic of schizophrenia, because religious scope operations encapsulate their content.

The literature on sensory deprivation and religious experience provides a fertile ground on which to explore this model. From the late 1950s to the 1970s researchers conducted experiments on participants whose sensory inputs were significantly reduced, often through immersion in warm dark saline baths placed in soundproof rooms. Participants in such conditions frequently described altered states of consciousness and imagery, which they almost universally interpreted positively (Lilly 1977; Lilly 1956; Suedfeld 1975). But they did not interpret such experiences as 'hallucinations' (Suedfeld and Vernon 1964). They did not literally see and hear as they would in ordinary experience.

In an experiment examining reports of religious imagery in sensory deprivation tanks, Hood and Morris compared the responses of intrinsic and extrinsic religious participants in a double-blind procedure. Intrinsic participants value religion for its own sake (they are cooperators, in my terminology). Extrinsic persons value religion for their worldly/practical benefits such as access to mates or as a means to impress high-status community members (defectors). (As Maynard Smith 1982 noticed long ago, most cooperating populations are stably composed of a mixed group of cooperators and defectors!) Half the participants were instructed to imagine religious figures, situations, and settings, whereas the other half were asked to imagine cartoon figures, situations, and settings. The researchers theorized that the intrinsic religious persons would produce more religious images because for them such images are more 'relevant'. Analysis revealed that indeed intrinsically religious persons reported more cued religious imagery than did their extrinsic counterparts. But, strikingly, the intrinsic religious persons produced more spontaneously religious images in the cartoon control setting than extrinsic persons produced in the religious setting! Intrinsic agents were finding religion even where they were primed to find only cartoons (Hood and Morris 1981). Interestingly, Hood and Morris did not observe this effect in response to ambiguous drawings, suggesting that the effect was limited to *experiential* simulations.

The finding suggests that the systems that control simulation in intrinsically religious persons may be strongly primed to read ambiguous experience with something like the ®IMAGINE scope operator. Critically, there is an important developmental story relevant to this marking disposition, for mere exposure to religious fictions is insufficient to produce the relevant effect. Nevertheless, once acquired, intrinsic religiosity initiates an experiential search protocol for religion.[18]

I do not suggest that these data fully vindicate the experience-as-religiously-inflected-imagination hypothesis. But they produce intriguing evidence for it. And a negative result (religious experience as hallucination) would undermine the hypothesis. Moreover, sensory deprivation experiments illustrate how a well-motivated theory of religious experience enables us to place already known facts into a wider explanatory frame. This is important because we are not only interested in fragments of a puzzle about religiosity but also in whether those fragments form part of a larger complex and functionally integrated composition.

We can hazard several more predictions. If religious experience is ordinary counterfactual simulation bound by a religious scope operator, then

---

18. I think this research program also casts some doubt on the proposition that repetitive and sensory impoverished rituals lack sensory pageantry—a key dogma of contemporary cognitive ritual theory. But I will leave this point unexamined for now.

religious persons will represent the characters of religious experience as they do fictional characters. That is, they will describe and remember religious experiences as something akin to 'true fiction'. In the simplest case, those who have religious experiences will be unable to tell you whether God has thick eyebrows or walks with a limp. They will not be able to say whether the God they converse with in prayer speaks with a heavy foreign accent. Gods here are ontologically gappy, like ordinary fictional characters. Such questions, of course, can be asked after encounters with ordinary agents. Having met him, I can tell you whether Sosis walks with a limp. This, of course, does not rule out that more robust confabulatory simulation may occur. A schizophrenic religionist can really tell you whether God's eyes are blue because she has seen them. But, even in very robust experiential simulation—for example, that cultivated by meditation, trances, psychedelic drugs, or simply very specifically manipulated sensory contexts—the model predicts that for non-clinical common-or-garden religionists, such extreme experiences, nevertheless, will be restricted by religious scope operators to prevent inferential damage. Religious persons will say and believe mad things, but they will generally not act as if they are mentally impaired.

Conclusion

I began with a review of the commitment-signaling hypothesis for religiosity. I suggested that this hypothesis is important because it postulates psychological and cultural mechanisms for supernatural cognition that differ somewhat from many popular cognitive approaches. In particular, it postulates emotionally salient commitments to superhuman agents capable of motivating moral exchange. The signaling hypothesis explains the otherwise puzzling link between religious cognition, moral cognition, and emotional display. Supernatural commitments help to predict cooperative exchange by endowing norms with strongly enhanced motivational support. They enable the conversion of extrinsically motivated normative commitment to intrinsically motivated pre-commitment. Yet, I have urged that religious pre-commitment is only evolvable if religious agents are able to solve the *recognition constraint*. To find each other, such agents must be capable of producing and decoding signals whose production is easy for religious persons but difficult for religious impostors. I urged that the barriers to religious cooperation are surmountable. The affective dimension of religious cognition—visible signs of love, devotion, piety, or fear for the gods—provides signals of cooperative commitment that help to resolve the demands of recognition. Religious emotions, on this view, are not noise created by otherwise functional mental architecture, they are adaptations for rewarding trade. I suggested that many of the costs surrounding religious practice, then, may be fruitfully explored as scaffolding for cooperative exchange.

In the second section, I used the commitment-signaling theory sketched in section I to sketch a metarepresentational design for processing religious information. I observed that our capacities to commit to a moralizing supernatural reality appear to be minimal modifications of our capacities to represent counterfactuals and fictions. A strong *encapsulation constraint* on the functionality of religion suggests that—like counterfactual and fictional thought—cognitive firewalls stand between religious information and most practical motivation/action domains. Religiosity, I suggested, exhibits something approximating the functional elaboration of fictional decoupling, for, in religion, emotionally salient false beliefs are nevertheless massively insulated from most practical action domains. But the similarity stops there. A *self-deception constraint* suggests that, unlike ordinary fictions, religious fictions will nevertheless be represented as true. For if religious agents are to manage emotional and other signals of belief in non-actual moralizing agents they must *really* believe in them. An *integration constraint* suggests that religious scope-operators will support normative inferences linking religious commitment with moral pre-commitment. For if religious beliefs are to support normative pre-commitments, that informational channel must be opened and maintained. I noted that the integration constraint leads to moralistic inferences from religious fictions that are strikingly different from those we would ordinarily derive from stories explicitly represented as fictional. For example, morally appalling gods appear praiseworthy.

In the final section, I applied the structured scope operator developed in section II to the domain of religious experience, urging that religious experience is best explained as the religious confabulation of ordinary imagination—mental time-travel mistaken (though restrictedly) as true. I urged that anomalies in the data on sensory deprivation and religious imagery are best explained by the confabulatory model of religious experience.

Much of the preceding argument has been offered as an inference-to-the-best-explanation. I have sketched a model that explains why religiosity is common, emotionally powerful, believed as true, and connected to cooperative exchange. The model also explains why non-actual superhuman agents are experienced, and how this experience is prevented from damaging those who produce it. And, finally, the model showed how these three explanations are linked by commitment-signaling theory.

This chapter presents a guardedly optimistic view about the ability of biological theory to shed light on some very basic and pervasive structural features of religious cognition. This adaptationist picture of religion presented here does not gaze at religion through straws. It is a broad picture, and some may reject it as imprecise. But such rejection would be too hasty. For, in my view, we desperately need plausible alternatives to the 'spandrelist' conceptions of religion that have dominated the cognitive study of religion over the past fifteen years. For a similar criticism see Bering 2004. I have sought to develop a model that makes it apparent why emotional religiosity is no accident, and why otherwise rational and functional persons experience supernatural realities and stake their lives on these experiences. Only after it becomes credible to view religiosity as richly adapted for human flourishing can we begin to assemble the sundry, disparate fragments of empirical data on religion into a more coherent picture. I have advertised a way to begin putting the puzzle together, one that strikes me as fruitful.

3

Cognitive Science, Religion, and Theology

Justin Barrett

The antagonism between Christianity and evolution continues. For over 100 years numerous anti-theists have bludgeoned Christianity using evolution by natural selection as a bat. Christians have assailed evolutionary theory as bad science advanced only for ulterior motives. Inspired by observations from molecular biology, the battle has crested again in terms of 'Intelligent Design' versus unguided materialist evolution (e.g., Behe 1996). The end of this struggle remains nowhere in sight. And then there's the 'science of religion . . .'.

With the new millennium a new scientific study of religion has emerged that some opponents of religion might regard as the surest way for evolution finally to defeat Christianity and other theistic faiths. Rather than try to show that evolution is true and then assert that Christianity must therefore be false, this new scientific study of religion attempts to use evolution to show that religions generally (and hence, Christianity, too) are by-products of natural selection or 'accidents' (Bloom 2005). Evolution has endowed humans with particular mental facilities and social arrangements that prop up religious illusions. If evolution can explain religious belief, then we have no need to appeal to the reality of gods to account for these beliefs. Game over.

Not so fast. Rather than seeing cognitive and evolutionary explanations of religion as hostile to Christianity, I see much promise in the cognitive sciences to enrich our understanding of how humans might be 'fearfully and wonderfully made' (Ps. 139: 14) to readily (though not inevitably) understand God sufficiently to enjoy a relationship with Him. Though the particular explanations of Scott Atran (2002a), Pascal Boyer (2001b),

D. Jason Slone (2004), Ilkka Pyysiäinen (2002; 2004), and David Sloan Wilson (2000) contain elements that rub believers the wrong way, a treatment of religion using the cognitive science of religion need not be viewed with defensiveness or hostility.

Below I sketch an account of why belief in superhuman agents (gods) is historically and cross-culturally common by appealing to the naturally occurring properties of human minds as they function in historically and cross-culturally ordinary natural and social environments. First, I discuss the nature of belief generally; then I propose some particular features of human minds that make belief in superhuman agents natural. I share some observations about the development of human minds in childhood that make several divine attributes championed by Christian theology even more likely to be understood, believed, and spread.

After this introduction to the cognitive science of religion I share some of my reasons for optimism that this new science for exploring religion need not be an enemy of Christianity. Rather, the cognitive science of religion might prove compatible with orthodox Christian theology.

How People Come to Believe

According to cognitive scientists, the mind is no brute all-purpose processing device. Instead, its normal function compares to a workshop. The workshop features numerous specialized tools for processing particular classes of information. These mental tools arise with built-in biases that influence to which bits of information will be attended and how that information will be distorted systematically. These mental tools and their characteristic biases provide insights on how many beliefs arise including beliefs in gods.

Two Types of Belief

Reflective beliefs

I find it helpful to distinguish between two classes of belief: reflective and non-reflective beliefs.[1] Reflective beliefs approximate what we colloquially

1. Dan Sperber (1997) makes a similar distinction: he labels reflective and intuitive beliefs.

call *beliefs*. We hold consciously reflective beliefs and may arrive at them through deliberate reflection. When asked if we believe something in particular, a reflective belief is what we reply. That is, statements of belief typically provide fair representations of reflective beliefs.

To illustrate, when people say they believe that insects are more plentiful than mammals; $E = mc^2$; bananas are yellow; Lance Armstrong is the reigning Tour de France champion; or Tom Cruise is six feet five inches tall; they are expressing reflective beliefs. Whether a belief is reflective does not bear on its truth-value or whether it is justified.

Non-reflective beliefs

Non-reflective beliefs, in contrast, operate without our conscious awareness in the background. Not consciously accessible or arising through deliberation, our minds produce non-reflective beliefs automatically all the time. Though speech acts may suggest the nature of non-reflective beliefs, other behaviors may prove more informative. Intuitions map closely onto non-reflective beliefs.

Non-reflective beliefs include:

- People act in ways to satisfy desires.
- Rainbows exhibit six bands of color.
- Raccoons and Opossums are very similar animals.
- People from outside my group are more similar to each other than people inside my group.
- Animals have parents of the same species as themselves.
- Unsupported objects fall.

Like reflective beliefs, non-reflective beliefs may or may not be true, empirically verifiable, or rationally justifiable.

Often, non-reflective beliefs match reflective beliefs, but need not. For instance, research suggests it is quite natural to form stereotypes non-reflectively (Hirschfeld 1996). This tendency may include a belief that others' groups are more uniform than our own. Reflectively we may become convinced that this non-reflective belief is flawed, but the non-reflective belief often remains (non-consciously). This observation gives us a hint as to the relationship between reflective and non-reflective beliefs.

Because non-reflective beliefs may be gauged non-verbally, we know a considerable amount about an infant's non-reflective beliefs. Based on observing their eye gaze, for instance, we know that babies non-reflectively believe that solid objects cannot pass directly through other solid objects (Spelke and Van de Walle 1993). They likewise believe that unsupported objects fall (Needham and Baillargeon 1993), that inanimate objects must be contacted to be launched whereas people need not be, and so forth (Spelke, Phillips, and Woodward 1995). Note that these non-reflective beliefs from infancy tend to match adult reflective beliefs. This conclusion provides yet another clue regarding the relationship between these two types of beliefs.

Whence Non-reflective Beliefs Come

Beliefs about the existence and properties of mundane, ordinary things come from numerous mental tools. Sometimes called *intuitive inference systems*, these mental tools operate automatically on specialized domains of information.

The existence of these mental tools has been supported by research in the brain and behavioral sciences as well as evolutionary and developmental cognition (e.g., Gazzaniga 1995; Pinker 1997). Mind-brains are highly structured with various subsystems designed to carry out particular tasks that are important for our species' survival.

These mental tools automatically and non-reflectively construct most of our beliefs about the natural and social world. Non-reflective beliefs arise directly from the operation of these mental tools on inputs from environment. The majority of these beliefs are never consciously evaluated or verified. They just seem intuitive.

To illustrate, consider four mental tools: Naive Physics, Naive Biology, Agency Detection Device, and Theory of Mind. Naive Physics generates the non-reflective beliefs that objects tend to move on inertial paths, cannot pass through other solid objects, must move through the intermediate space to get from one point to another, and must be supported or they will fall downward (Spelke, Phillips, and Woodward 1995). Among others, Naive Biology generates the non-reflective beliefs that animals bear young similar to themselves, and living things act to acquire nourishment (Keil 1995). The Agency Detection Device automatically tells us that self-propelled, goal-directed objects are intentional agents (Baron-Cohen 1995). Theory of Mind gives us non-reflective beliefs concerning the internal states of these intentional agents and their behaviors: agents act to satisfy desires, actions are guided by beliefs, beliefs are influenced by percepts, and satisfied desires prompt positive emotions (Wellman, Cross, and Watson 2001).

None of these non-reflective beliefs is the sort of things that children are taught through explicit verbal instruction. If asked about these beliefs most children and most adults would think the questions peculiar. Children rapidly and uniformly acquire these non-reflective beliefs by virtue of being the sort of animal that they are living in the sorts of environments they live in. They do not require special environments, training, or instruction.

Whence Reflective Beliefs Come

As the examples already given demonstrate, non-reflective and reflective beliefs do not arise in isolation. Rather, non-reflective beliefs are the primary stuff from which our minds construct reflective beliefs. Specific mental tools generate non-reflective beliefs relevant to a given domain but then more general mental processes draw upon available non-reflective beliefs to form reflective beliefs. To illustrate, if I were asked if a raccoon is more similar to an opossum or to a cow, I would be forced to form a reflective belief. If I had never considered these taxonomic relations, without conscious awareness of what I was doing, I would *read off* my non-reflective belief (that opossums are more similar to raccoons than cows) (Atran 1995). In absence of salient, consciously accessible reasons to the contrary, I would simply adopt the non-reflective belief as my reflective belief. This process of *reading off* mental tool outputs is the primary mode of reflective belief formation.

Some reflective beliefs arise from the converging outputs of several mental tools or multiple outputs of a single mental tool. For instance, if I observe a man with a bulge under his shirt trot out of a store, not pausing for a store worker standing in his path but running right over her, what am I to believe? My well-rehearsed human form detector tells me the bulge is not part of human anatomy (I don't even consider the man has a tumor). My Theory of Mind tells me automatically that a bulge under a shirt is not visibly accessible to others and because intentional agents behave purposefully, the man desired to obscure the object. As my Agency Detection Device knows that intentional agents need not continue on inertial paths, I non-reflectively assume the man did not intend to stop for the store worker. Theory of Mind tells me the man must have desired to run over the store worker and sends me searching for an explanation of this behavior (since, unlike inanimate objects, we don't typically attempt to move others through contact). The explicit suggestion that the man was stealing from the store makes sense intuitively given the outputs of all these mental tools working in concert. Hence, I am likely firmly to adopt this reflective belief even though I have no conclusive evidence. It just seems to make sense. In general, the more different non-reflective beliefs that converge on a particular reflective candidate belief the more likely the reflective belief becomes held.

Sometimes strategies for overriding non-reflective beliefs become available. Most simply, we may 'consider the evidence' for a given belief candidate. But the evidence (if available) is always filtered and distorted by the operation of mental tools. We never have direct access to evidence but only processed evidence—memories.[2] When asked 'how many colors are in a rainbow?' I might recall the last time I saw a rainbow and what it looked like. But this 'evidence' has already been tainted by non-reflective beliefs. Memory for a rainbow's appearance is actually a memory for how our perceptual and conceptual systems interpreted the visual stimulation. The biased processing of mental tools has already molded all memories for events, objects, and ideas (including memories just formed). No reflective data remains uninfluenced by intuitive mental tools.

To summarize, mental tools automatically generate non-reflective beliefs continually. Reflective beliefs typically come from the cumulative weight of non-reflective beliefs converging on the same candidate belief. The more non-reflective beliefs that converge the more likely a belief becomes reflectively held. Memories, already shaped by non-reflective beliefs, may contribute to the credibility of the belief as well. Without salient reasons for disregarding or overriding the non-reflective beliefs, they become reflectively held. Consequently, the bulk of explicitly believing most of what we do comes from the non-conscious, automatic functions of mental tools in our minds.

Given the critical role of non-reflective beliefs in informing reflective beliefs, any account of why people believe in gods must start with how

2. Even the claim of a science teacher at the moment of our attempt to form a reflective belief is only accessible as the interpreted memory of what was just said. What was said has already been processed by our auditory perceptual systems, our language-processing systems, and any higher-order semantic processing relevant to the topic of the utterance. There is no such thing as pure experience from which to draw.

well such beliefs are grounded by the non-reflective beliefs generated by naturally occurring mental tools. Not every religious belief is anchored to non-reflective beliefs and arises because of them. For instance, that the Christian God is believed to be a Trinity and non-temporal has little or no non-reflective foundation. Nevertheless, fundamental religious beliefs such as the existence of gods that are intentional beings with beliefs, desires, and perceptual systems that guide their activities have firm non-reflective support as I sketch below. This non-reflective support accounts not only for their prevalence but also their general uniformity.

Why People Believe in Gods

In brief, people believe in gods because gods gain tremendous support from the natural and ordinary operation of mental tools. Note that as mental tools and their processing biases arise primarily as a consequence of biological endowment plus essentially universal features of human environments the same factors that prompt belief in gods in Canada are similar to those that prompt belief in Cameroon. Below I sketch several ways in which god concepts receive this support.

Minimally counter-intuitive (MCI) concepts

Recall the principle that the more non-reflective beliefs with which an idea agrees the more likely it is to be embraced reflectively. Another way of expressing this is that concepts that are largely *intuitive* are generally more plausible. Conversely, concepts that are highly *counter-intuitive*—in the technical sense of violating mental tools' automatic expectations—tend to be less plausible.

God concepts that are commonly held are not as highly counter-intuitive as might be assumed. As anthropologist Pascal Boyer observed, most religious beliefs held by ordinary folk in real-time thinking and problem-solving are largely intuitive (Boyer 1994; Boyer 2001b). A statue that listens to prayers involves a simple transfer of mental properties to an artifact. Otherwise, the artifact meets ordinary intuitive expectations for artifacts (that is, non-reflective beliefs), and the mind of the statue meets ordinary non-reflective beliefs about minds. Anthropologists often come across artifacts that hear prayers but not artifacts that hear prayers not yet uttered or hear prayers no matter where the person praying is located or hear prayers but wholly misunderstand them, and so on. Such concepts would be highly counter-intuitive. Similarly, the concept of ancestor-spirits seems to meet intuitive assumptions for people, with the exception of not having a material body. Compared to how massively counter-intuitive concepts could be, successful religious concepts tend to be rather intuitive. They conform to non-reflective beliefs governing their intuitive ontology, hence maintaining general plausibility. Being only partly or *minimally counter-intuitive* also provides god concepts with facilitated transmission.

For an idea to be more than an idiosyncratic belief it must be shared. Only recurrent beliefs reach the status of 'religious' or 'cultural'. Consequently, a crucial consideration pertaining to belief in gods is why some ideas or beliefs spread better than others do from person to person. If people remember and communicate ideas about a given god, that god will more likely be believed than gods and concepts are that are not remembered or communicated.

A critical factor for whether concepts become remembered and transmitted is their complexity. More precisely, concepts that satisfy most mental tools' expectations or biases are most easily remembered and transmitted. That is, concepts that are largely intuitive spread well. Because the concept *horse* fits Naive Biology's expectations on living things, *horse* is readily remembered. Likewise, if someone told you about a horse that is like other horses but is also the size of a rabbit, you would probably find the concept easy to grasp, remember, and tell to someone else. An unusually small horse still fits Naive Biology's expectations relevant to animals.

Concepts that too greatly violate intuitive expectations generated by mental tools would be difficult to understand, remember, and communicate at a later time. For instance, a horse that experiences time backwards, is born of a goldfish mated with a bullfrog, sustains itself on crude oil, speaks through singing Italian opera, and changes into spaghetti on Thursdays would be a difficult concept faithfully to transmit. Such a concept's primary limitation is that it so greatly violates mental tools' expectations (non-reflective beliefs) regarding horses that the conceptual structure is undermined. This massively counter-intuitive concept is no longer a portable concept but a laundry list of features that do not hang together coherently.

This horse is counter-intuitive in the technical sense that it violates intuitive assumptions or non-reflective beliefs.[3]

But, as experiments have shown, some counter-intuitive concepts make strong candidates for successful transmission (Boyer and Ramble 2001). Those that violate a small number of intuitive assumptions may actually transmit better than completely intuitive concepts (in certain conditions). Concepts that balance meeting most non-reflective beliefs, while violating just a small number (e.g., one or two at a time) have been called minimally counter-intuitive (MCI) concepts (Barrett 2004; Barrett and Nyhof 2001). A cow that speaks Spanish would be a minimally counter-intuitive concept. A cow that gives birth to kittens or a cow that can never die would also be MCI. MCI concepts enjoy good conceptual integrity. As such, MCI concepts are easily remembered, recalled, and shared. Additionally, the counter-intuitive feature often helps the concepts to stand out against more mundane concepts, hence improving their salience and the attention devoted to remembering them. Experimental results support these claims (Barrett and Nyhof 2001; Boyer and Ramble 2001).

Note that whether a concept is *counter-intuitive* in this technical sense is largely or entirely independent of cultural context. As the features of our relevant mental tools are largely independent of cultural context the non-reflective beliefs they generate remain essentially uniform across cultural context, as does whether a concept is counter-intuitive.

But not all minimally counter-intuitive concepts make strong candidates for religious concepts (or any other cultural concepts, for that matter). Take, for example, a cucumber that vanishes whenever observed versus a cucumber that speaks. Both cucumbers are counter-intuitive but the vanishing cucumber possesses weak *inferential potential*. Some concepts more readily generate predictions, inferences, and explanations than others, exciting more mental tools. Consequently, they carry more reflective credibility and may arise as relevant in more contexts, providing more opportunity for transmission.

Items such as vanishing cucumbers and horses sustained on oil do not populate religious belief systems. Rather, religious belief systems center on counter-intuitive *intentional agents* with special features. Unlike many other counter-intuitive properties, adding agency or modifying it in a counter-intuitive fashion often generates rich inferential potential.

3. Science and theology both generate numerous massively counter-intuitive concepts. Being counter-intuitive in this technical sense does not imply false, fictitious, or even unusual.

Advantages for Agent Concepts

Compared with other concepts, intentional agents (such as gods) have more *inferential potential*—ability to inject explanation or meaning into a broad array of human concerns—and connect a large number of mental tools and salient outputs. Recall that the more mental tools that converge on a belief, the more likely it is to become reflectively held. The broad-reaching character of these concepts gives them a selective transmission advantage over other classes of concepts (such as physical objects, substances, abstracts, etc.). I amplify this claim in three areas: the detection of agency; the role of agents in reasoning about fortune, misfortune, and morality; and the fate of agents after death.

Agency detection

The mental tool responsible for agency detection is the agency detection device (ADD). Research involving shapes on computer screens and other artificial and more natural displays (e.g., Barrett and Johnson 2003; Rochat, Morgan, and Carpenter 1997; Scholl and Tremoulet 2000) supports the notion that the ADD is touchy or hypersensitive. That is, even given ambiguous or incomplete information, ADD often finds agency. To emphasize this hypersensitive character of ADD I sometimes refer to it as the 'hypersensitive agency detection device' (HADD).

HADD and objects

Anthropologist Stewart Guthrie argues that our tendency to find agency (especially human) around us has arisen for survival reasons (1993). In our evolutionary past our best opportunities for survival and reproduction and our biggest threats were other agents, so we had to be able to detect them. Better to guess that the sound in the bushes is an agent (such as a person or tiger) than assume it isn't and become lunch. If you reacted unnecessarily (e.g., because of the wind blowing in the brush), little is lost. This 'hypersensitive agency detection device' produces (non-reflective) beliefs that agency is present. The Theory of Mind tool then generates non-reflective beliefs about beliefs, desires, and perceptions of the alleged agent.

It is HADD that makes us non-reflectively believe that our computers deliberately try to frustrate us, that strange sounds in a house mean an intruder, and that light patterns on a television screen are people or animals with beliefs and desires. But more relevant to religious belief are situations in which a wisp of mist or smoke gets recognized as a ghost or spirit. This function of HADD, identifying objects as agents, has begun to receive a fair amount of attention from cognitive scientists. Receiving less attention, but probably more relevant to religion, are two other functions of HADD: registering an event as being caused by agency and recognizing an object or pattern as being caused by intentional agency.

HADD and events

Many events lead to agency detection without a known agent as a possible candidate. Suppose a woman walking alone through a deep gorge rounds a bend in the trail and rocks tumble down the steep wall and nearly hit her. HADD might reflexively search for the responsible agent. A man hiking through an unfamiliar forest hears something behind a nearby shrub. HADD screams, 'Agent!'

If, after detecting agency in these sorts of cases, a candidate superhuman agent concept is offered and seems consistent with the event, belief could be encouraged. Similarly, when a god concept is already available as a good candidate, events that HADD might have overlooked become significant. For instance, a child in California prays for snow in May and a blizzard drops two feet of snow the next day. The context suggests agency. Or a man in New York is told by doctors that he is dying but he feels a tingling all over his body and a sense of peace that all will be well. The man recovers and attributes the miraculous healing to God.

Because the agency detection device is so eager to find agency when other intuitive explanatory systems (such as Naive Physics or Naive Biology) fail, many different events may be attached to superhuman agency. These events then support belief.

HADD and traces

In addition to objects (such as wisps of fog or computers) and events (such as falling rocks), HADD may find agency in *traces*—those physical changes that an agent may have left behind. Mysterious markings, tracks, or configurations of objects could count as traces of agency. Crop circles, the intricate geometric patterns mysteriously left in crop fields around the world, present a striking example of a trace that HADD typically identifies as caused by intentional agency. Indeed, the apparent agency behind crop circles are so compelling that the debate surrounding them typically focuses only on what kind of agent left the trace. Was it aliens or mischievous farm boys?

Contextual factors

Context matters for HADD. Thresholds for HADD to register a non-reflective belief in agency vary as a function of the environment and personal relevance. In brief, contexts which possess more urgency cause HADD to be more sensitive. By *urgency* I mean the salience of survival demands. A soldier on the battlefield will have a more sensitive HADD than a person strolling through a park. A hungry subsistence hunter will find HADD registering more positives than a well-sated recreational hunter.[4]

HADD's ability to reinforce belief

HADD might play only a very minor role in reinforcing beliefs in super-human agents if HADD's false positives easily get overridden and ignored. Exactly how much of a role HADD plays is an empirical matter demanding further research. But, even if HADD experiences alone rarely propel belief in superhuman agents they likely encourage beliefs in superhuman agency even when HADD's initial agent detection is reflectively rejected.

Consider the woman and the falling rocks. Someone with such a HADD-experience might initially think someone had thrown rocks at her and search for the responsible agent. Not finding a culprit, she might aban-don HADD's agent detection. Perhaps a return to the scene demonstrates that walking on that stretch of path causes vibrations that radiate up the gorge wall and could have shaken the rocks loose.

But, then again, perhaps someone explains to the woman at a later time that the gorge is haunted by territorial spirits known to throw rocks. The memory for the HADD experience may be revived as evidence for a reflective belief in the spirits. Similarly, if the woman were to return to the gorge and a different HADD experience occurred, the first experience

4. HADD's sensitivity could vary across individuals and perhaps across lifespan and sex, in part accounting for differences in religiosity as a function of age and sex (Barrett 2004). These claims, however, demand considerably more empirical support.

might be recalled. The two experiences together could fortify belief in an unseen agent whereas each one independently might have been ignored.

It might be that HADD rarely generates specific beliefs in ghosts, spirits, and gods by itself, and hence does not serve as the origin of these concepts. Nevertheless, HADD likely plays a critical role in spreading such beliefs and rejuvenating them. Christians devoted to their faith often refer to answered prayer, special communications, and other events they attribute to God's activity thanks to HADD at work. Without HADD, these experiences that support belief would never register on the reflective ledger. They would remain peculiar, inexplicable happenings instead of being remembered as possible actions of an intentional being.

Connecting agency with fortune, misfortune, and morality

One recurrent mark of religions is that gods (broadly construed) frequently become connected with moral concerns. Why this connection?

First, humans are chronic meaning makers. Humans search the environment for causal explanation and meaning. Mental tools such as Naive Physics and Naive Biology initially attempt to explain events, but when these explanatory systems fail to account for the evidence at hand our minds attempt to apply social or intentional causation. HADD, Theory of Mind, and other mental tools engage.

Second, fortunate and unfortunate events inevitably happen. People experience inexplicably good crop yields or famine, great wealth or sudden sickness and death. Intuitively, such unusual events demand an explanation. Reasoning that the event has arisen merely by chance rings hollow to our intuitive desire for explanation.

Gods enter the picture due to their particular minimally counter-intuitive properties. Many have unusual powers or invisibility that would allow them to bring about the fortune or misfortune without being directly detected. Likewise, their invisibility or super-knowledge gives them *strategic information* about what people do secretly (Boyer 2001b). Hence, gods may act to punish or reward moral failings that no human could know about. In this way, salient fortune or misfortune can be seen as the action of an agent that is motivated by moral concerns. These moral concerns, too, are cross-culturally recurrent because of *Intuitive Morality*, another mental tool.

Intuitive Morality generates non-reflective beliefs about what constitutes moral behavior. From an early age, children appear intuitively to differentiate between moral codes and social conventions (Turiel 1998). It appears as though people converge upon general rules of behavior that typically frown on murder, adultery, theft, deception, treachery, and cowardice, especially as directed toward one's own group, though the precise catalog of moral intuitions is a matter of continued empirical research. People regard these moral intuitions as immutable and not merely arbitrary and changeable conventions (Leonard D. Katz 2000).

Marry Intuitive Morality with otherwise inexplicable dramatic events, and an explanatory niche arises that gods naturally fill. God concepts gain reflective plausibility by working in concert with these non-reflective beliefs. Recall that the more non-reflective beliefs that converge upon a candidate reflective belief the more likely it is to become reflectively believed.

Agency after death

Briefly, research on children's and adult's intuitions concerning death suggests that while humans readily understand biological cessation our Theory of Mind readily continues supposing minds continue functioning after death (Bering 2002b; Bering, Hernández-Blasi, and Bjorklund 2005). The available data from children and adults in different cultural settings suggest that two of our mental tools, Naive Biology and Theory of Mind, offer conflicting non-reflective beliefs concerning death—perhaps especially the death of a loved one (Bering 2002b; Boyer 2001b). When someone dies, Naive Biology registers that the person will no longer move, no longer require nourishment, and so forth. Accustomed to reasoning without a body present, Theory of Mind finds the physical absence of a person of little consequence and wonders what the deceased wishes, thinks, feels, perceives, and so forth. This intuitive dualism non-reflectively makes people sympathetic to agency after death. Couple 'hypersensitive agency detection' with a Theory of Mind tool that does not fully register someone has passed on, and you have a recipe for detecting agency after death.

Why People Believe in Particular Divine Attributes

Belief in gods is natural. Belief in religious entities is encouraged by the dynamics of a number of intuitive inference systems I call *mental tools*. Minimally counter-intuitive concepts enjoy a transmission advantage over other comparable concepts. Further, agent concepts possess great inferential potential and activate a number of receptive reasoning systems concerning morality, fortune, misfortune, and death. In the next section I will expand this 'naturalness of religious belief' thesis to consider how belief in the divine attributes of a supergod such as those in Abrahamic traditions receives special support from cognitive structures. Specifically, super-knowledge, super-perception, superpower (especially to create natural things), and immortality all benefit from the operation of mental tools in childhood development. In all four of these cases, the relevant mental tools assume super-abilities for all agents, human or otherwise. Subsequently, through the course of development, relevant mental tools restrict these abilities for people and other natural agents. Because children seem to assume super-properties on these four dimensions of agents (knowledge, perception, power, and mortality), children need not learn these divine attributes as much as have them simply affirmed or left unchallenged (Barrett and Richert 2003).

Super-knowledge

In the enormous area of research concerning children's developing Theory of Mind, data strongly support the position that before around five years of age (and sometimes later) children assume that everyone's beliefs about the world are infallible (e.g., Wellman, Cross, and Watson 2001). That is, if a three-year-old child knows that he has a coin in his pocket, he assumes that his mother, too, will know that he has a coin in his pocket. He will fail to consider that his mother might not have had the prerequisite perceptual information to form such a belief. Colleagues and I replicated this finding using versions of a paradigm that has come to be called a *false-belief task* (Barrett, Richert, and Driesenga 2001; Knight, et al. 2004).

In one such study experimenters showed three- to six-year-old American Protestant children a closed cracker box (Barrett, Richert, and Driesenga 2001). Experimenters then asked children what they thought was inside the box. Familiar with that sort of container, children all answered 'crackers'. After being shown the box actually contained rocks, the box was closed and the experimenter asked the children what their absent mothers would think was inside the box if they saw it for the first time. Consistent with previous research, the vast majority of three- and four-year-olds reported that their mother would think that the box contained rocks. But more than 80 percent of five- and six-year-olds reported that their mothers would think the box contained crackers. That is, not until age five did children tend to understand that their mothers would have a false belief. Asked about other potential observers (e.g., bear, elephant, tree), children answered essentially identically as for their mother. Four-year-olds assumed infallible beliefs but five-year-olds understood false beliefs. God proved an exception. When asked what God would think was inside the closed cracker box, children at all ages examined showed the same strong tendency to say that God would know the box contained rocks. That is, three- or six-year-olds 'accurately' (theologically speaking) predicted God's infallible knowledge.

Experimenters replicated these sorts of results using different Theory of Mind tasks and different populations (Barrett, Newman, and Richert 2003; Knight, et al. 2004). Importantly, Knight, et al. showed that Mayan children living on the Yucatan Peninsula differentiated among the probable knowledge of different deities in a way that closely mapped on to adult theological conceptions. Cumulatively, these studies suggest that children find a super-knowing god readily comprehended and used to generate predictions while they still struggle with understanding the boundaries on human (or animal) knowledge and beliefs. Children may find super-knowing gods relatively easy to understand because of Theory of Mind's default assumption that agents are super-knowing. Children must learn when this default does not apply with humans, but no such boundaries require construction for understanding God.

Super-perception

A similar account has emerged from research concerning children's under-standing of others' perception. Three- and four-year-olds tend to assume others perceive objects how they perceive them, whereas five- and six-year-olds tend to understand that this is not always the case. But children of all these ages tend to represent God as having perceptual access to everything (including smells, sounds, and sights) (Richert and Barrett 2005). As with knowledge, children's default is to assume full perceptual access for other agents and through development they pare back these generous allowances. They need not pare back for super-perceiving gods.

Super-power

Since Jean Piaget, developmental psychologists have noted children's tendency to treat adults as god-like by overestimating their strength and power
(Piaget 1929). Further, a formidable amount of research supports that
children intuitively embrace gods as the designers and creators of the natural
world. As with mental attributes, children begin with lofty expectations on
intentional agents' power and must then learn the boundaries for humans.
These developmental biases make super-powerful god concepts readily
adopted by children. The concept of an omnipotent Creator-God requires
no boundary learning comparable to understanding humans.

From childhood, humans remain keenly sensitive to evidence of pur-
posefulness in objects and the environment. Deborah Kelemen has found
that children tend to attribute design and purpose not only to biological
kinds but also other natural kinds such as rocks. Rocks are pointy, for
instance, to keep from being sat upon rather than because of some series of
natural or random factors (Kelemen 1999a; Kelemen 1999b). Kelemen has
suggested that people possess a *promiscuous teleology*—a tendency to over-
attribute design even given scant evidence—akin to 'hypersensitive agency
detection' (Kelemen 2004).

Given this promiscuous teleology, 'Creationist' and 'Intelligent Design'
explanations for natural origins should prove readily adopted and transmitted. Margaret Evans' research on children's relative preferences for different
origins accounts of animals has shown that children eagerly embrace 'Creationist' accounts and are very resistant to evolutionary accounts, even if
their parents and schools advance evolutionary origins (Evans 2001). It is
no wonder that Creator-God concepts are so widespread. These cognitive
factors are so powerful as to lead some to suggest that children are 'intuitive
theists' (e.g., Kelemen 2004).

Immortality

Naive Biology and Theory of Mind generate conflicting non-reflective
beliefs regarding human death which complicate children's understanding
of mortality. Hence, children begin appreciating God's immortality before
they have a robust understanding of human mortality. As mortality appears

more firmly tied to biological reasoning than reasoning about minds, children easily grasp that God, who is not a biological being, may be immortal.

The developmental privileges of some god concepts

These biases in mental tools regarding knowledge, perception, creative power, and mortality provide additional transmission advantages to god concepts that have the divine attributes of being super-human along these dimensions. Once supergod concepts are introduced into a population they are likely to spread ably within generations and to future ones. Perhaps this, in part, explains the success of Abrahamic god concepts.

Do not, however, misunderstand me as arguing that all attributes attributed to the Christian God have more 'fitness' than those attributes of other god concepts. Being non-temporal or a Trinity, for instance, are likely liabilities rather than assets in terms of brute transmission. Further, strict monotheism is not favored. As parsimony does not appear to be a value of intuitive reasoning systems, few strict monotheists exist. Even in the so-called 'Great Monotheisms' adherents believe in God plus devils, angels, ghosts, and other counter-intuitive superhuman agents.

The Naturalness of Religious Beliefs and Theological Implications

Cumulatively, the way human minds work in historically prevalent natural and social environments prompts belief in gods.

Mental tools and belief

General beliefs typically arise through the activity of implicit mental tools feeding their outputs to reflective systems. Beliefs consistent with the biases of mental tools seem intuitive on a reflective level and become believed.

Minimally counter-intuitive concept

God concepts transmit easily and retain plausibility by virtue of being minimally counter-intuitive. They count among a subset of counter-intuitive concepts that exchange complete intuitiveness for counter-intuitive features that enhance the concepts' inferential potential (ability to predict and explain). These minimally counter-intuitive concepts demand more attention and more readily factor into reasoning about a wide range of human concerns. Minimally counter-intuitive agent concepts are particularly rich in inferential potential.

One upshot of minimally counter-intuitive concepts having transmission advantages is that overly complex theological concepts stand a weak chance of survival among ordinary believers. A tension will always exist between what theological specialists advance and what concepts ordinary people use to make decisions and produce explanations (Slone 2004). Even though children might easily acquire ideas about super-knowing and super-perceiving gods, adults find it difficult to maintain too many counter-intuitive properties in mind when drawing real-time inferences (Barrett 1998; Barrett and Keil 1996; Barrett and VanOrman 1996). Consequently, simpler, more anthropomorphic properties of gods get used in parallel with the 'theologically correct' versions (Barrett 1999).

Agents and inferential potential

By virtue of being agents, gods share strong inferential potential. People may use them to explain a broad range of phenomena. This ability of gods non-reflectively to make sense of events encourages belief in them. It follows that changing intellectual and environmental conditions may differentially impact belief in specific gods. For instance, forest spirits that are helpful for understanding hunting and other forest activities may prove irrelevant in the face of urbanization. Further, fertility gods may prove dispensable in the face of fertility technologies whereas gods that maintain natural laws and processes may be more immune from technological advances. That is, while individuals do not necessarily affirm the truth of a god's existence for utilitarian or intellectualist reasons, the more a god connects with real-life concerns the more belief is reinforced. Hence, opponents of religion should strive to partition religious beliefs from day-to-day activities, whereas proponents of religious commitment should encourage full integration of religious beliefs and daily activity.

Given observations from the cognitive science of religion, it comes as no surprise that atheism has most successfully taken root in urbanized, post-industrial communities with relative stability and affluence. Communities such as these, particularly in North America and Europe, provide a relatively broad separation between human cognitive activities and natural survival concerns. Further, these artificial environments offer non-religious candidates for HADD experiences. In urban settings with powerful technologies and government entities, strange experiences, fortune, and catastrophe may all be attributed to human agency. People in these places rely on humans to solve problems and blame humans for creating problems from poverty to hurricanes. The affluence of these communities allows for detached reflection and institutions that make a point of undermining intuitive belief-making: formal education.

Strategic information, morality, fortune, and misfortune

Most gods that occupy central positions in religious systems have *strategic information* important to human survival and reproduction. They gain this information by virtue of special properties such as mind reading, omniscience, or invisibility. Strategic information allows them knowledge of the moral triumphs and failings of humans. Consequently, they may be invoked as plausible causes for otherwise inexplicable events such as cases of extreme fortune or misfortune. Death is no exception. Being theoretically active in so many important issues, gods become supported by yet more mental tools that may produce god-consistent non-reflective beliefs.

Suppose someone proposed a god that had no concern for human moral failings or triumphs. Such a god would not compete well against other gods to capture the minds of humans. Similarly, a god that supported a moral code violating Intuitive Morality would find itself fighting a losing battle. Religions may sharpen and reinforce moral systems but cannot wholly create them.

Super-attributes and development

Super-properties of gods receive further encouragement from early-emerging biases in mental tools to favor the attribution of super-knowledge, super-perception, creative power, and immortality to agents. Children's minds nudge them toward understanding these divine properties but they must labor to learn human limitations along these same dimensions. Similarly, mental tools encourage children (and adults) to find design in the natural world. So, the suggestion of a creator-god or -gods that accounts for the cosmos carries great intuitive plausibility.

Once, psychologists of religion advanced the idea that children could not be expected to learn about divine attributes until around age nine. God is too abstract for the younger mind, it was thought. Now, sufficient evidence exists to suggest that theological education may fruitfully start much earlier (Barrett and Richert 2003). Children need opportunities to exercise their intuitive default assumptions about God's super-properties so that they do not so easily fall prey to the anthropomorphism that plagues adult folk theology. Further, children (and often adults) do not need to be given reasons to believe as much as reasons to love God and submit to Him.

Further Implications and Speculations

Though the cognitive science of religion has evidential and theoretical thin spots, its naturalness of religious belief thesis is complete enough to begin exploring its implications for religious belief and relationship with theological commitments. Indeed, some of the excitement generated by this field of scholarship concerns whether it successfully defeats theistic belief, or at least weakens it.

The thinking of anti-theists seems to be that if a scientific (naturalistic, materialistic) explanation shows why religious beliefs are so prevalent, then that so many people hold religious beliefs no longer counts as evidence for these beliefs. This reasoning carries a number of flaws. First, explaining how beliefs come about—no matter how complete the explanation—says nothing about whether a belief is *true* or justified. If cognitive neuroscientists manage some day fully to explain the brain activity and evolutionary history of those brain functions responsible for people believing that seventeen times eleven equals 187, seventeen times eleven would still equal 187. Similarly, a complete scientific explanation for why humans nearly universally believe that other people have minds would not suddenly count against whether humans *should* believe that others have minds. Belief in other minds and belief in gods are both highly intuitive consequences of cognitive architecture operating on ordinary inputs. Both are non-empirical, widespread beliefs. Neither is directly weakened by increasing scientific knowledge about how these beliefs come about any more than knowledge of the visual system makes us suspicious that the visual world is not really out there.

In general terms, then, the cognitive science of religion does not give aid and comfort to opponents of religion. Nevertheless, thinkers that wish to embrace these scientific accounts of religion *and* particular theological commitments have some work to do. Placing aside whether evolution of human minds is consistent with biblical Christianity, can one consistently hold such an account of belief (presented above) along with a Christian theology?

The atheist may suggest that the evolved human mind happens to encourage belief. If Christian theology teaches that God created humans so that they might enjoy a relationship with Him, why would God leave such important cognitive capacities to chance plus natural selection? A couple of responses exist for the Christian. First, God could have instantiated this world out of all the possible worlds because in this world natural selection brought about the kind of creatures capable of a loving relationship with Him. Second, God could have guided natural selection to develop the sorts of minds humans have. Perhaps the 'random mutations' from which natural selection selected were not random after all. The environmental contingencies that favored one organism over another could have been designed or directed to bring about humans with their particular minds.[5]

But, if God chose this sort of mind for us—either through instantiating this world or through supernatural or guided selection—why do the documented conceptual biases only encourage belief in superhuman agents generally and not one true, accurate god concept? Further, if God created humanity to enjoy a loving relationship with Him, why not hard-wire into our brains a fully formed belief in God?

One possible answer is that a perfectly adequate concept of God does come as part of our biological heritage but that living in a sinful, fallen world this concept grows corrupt as we grow. If not for broken relationships, corrupt social structures, flawed religious communities, and the suffering that people inflict upon each other, perhaps children would inevitably form a perfectly acceptable concept of God.[6] The diversity in god concepts we see is a consequence of human error and not divine design.

---

5. I have heard it asked, if God directed the formation of our minds, why not make them infallible instead of clumsy and limited? Such a question assumes that cognitive capabilities beyond simply living and loving are a good. One could argue that more powerful minds open the potential for more horrendous moral failings.

6. I once had a similar explanation offered to me by a Brahman on a train in India. Children have been with the divine more recently than adults and this world corrupts their purer knowledge.

The biblical story of Adam and Eve suggests a similar account. When Adam and Eve rebelled from God's reign, one consequence was banishment from His direct presence. Never again could they know Him directly. Adam and Eve might have known all that was needed about God to love Him obediently and be loved by Him, but their decision to make their own decisions—to be like gods—created not just relational separation from God but cognitive separation as well. Hence, cognitive architecture is only receptive to God's revelation but does not entail it.

Another biblical hint regarding the adequacy of human cognitive architecture appears in Romans. Paul writes:

> because that which is known about God is evident within them; for God made it evident to them. For since the creation of the world His invisible attributes, His eternal power and divine nature, have been clearly seen, being understood through what has been made, so that they are without excuse. For even though they knew God, they did not honor Him as God, or give thanks; but they became futile in their speculations, and their foolish heart was darkened.

> (Rom. 1: 19–21 New American Standard Version)

To paraphrase and amplify, cognitive capacities plus environmental data are sufficient for knowing God enough appropriately to respond to Him. Continued rebellion further undermines accurate belief.

Whatever the reasons for these cognitive biases to serve as imperfect guides to God, a Christian version of the cognitive science of religion remains possible. The Christian may argue that through some means (perhaps including evolution) God has equipped people with the prerequisite cognitive equipment to have an appropriate relationship with God. Clearly, this relationship has been disrupted and perhaps one of the consequences of this falling out is distorted thinking about God and problematic cognitive architecture. But God has not given up on the relationship. Rather, God has revealed Himself in a variety of ways that trigger these cognitive capacities to suspect superhuman agency. Belief in Him does not require lots of effortful deliberation but rather an intuitive response to the natural world. Further, He has used scriptural and other forms of revelation to clarify confusion—not primarily to share *that* He is but *who* He is. Then, ultimately, He became human in the person of Jesus of Nazareth. Recall that one of the conceptual difficulties people have is representing and using a concept of God that too greatly deviates from intuitive biases—one that is not mostly anthropomorphic. Perhaps one of the motivations for God to reveal Himself in the form of a human is that an anthropomorphic form is one that our fallen cognition could conceive. And maybe it is in the state of fallen cognition that God must meet us for us to have hope of reunion with Him. Part of our salvation and eventual transformation is to get beyond these cognitive limitations.

Ultimately, the cognitive science of religion and other scientific treatments of religion that draw from the psychological and biological sciences do not necessarily support or challenge any particular world view. Believers and non-believers alike must marshal reasons beyond the science of religion for or against belief. Nevertheless, the tough mind will insist that, whatever world view one embraces, it takes seriously the findings and explanations offered by this exciting new field.

4

Is Religion Adaptive?

Yes, No, Neutral. But Mostly We Don't Know

Peter J. Richerson and Lesley Newson

Introduction

We view human culture to be an evolving part of human biology and this gives us a new approach to understanding aspects of culture like religion. But gene-culture evolutionary analysis doesn't simplify the matter of explaining them. Biological phenomena generally are complex and diverse (Richerson and Boyd 1987). For example, each species is typically a complex meta-population of complex organisms with a complex evolutionary history. In addition, biologists have to worry about millions of species in total and dozens to hundreds of interacting species even in small biological communities. In the case of humans, culture complicates the evolutionary process, and humans are diversified into thousands of cultures and subcultures. In the complex societies of the past few millennia, internal differentiation has become quite extreme. Human communities are typically as complex as natural ones. Odd as it may seem, the complexity of biology very often restricts us to understanding particular cases in terms of quite simple models (Burnham and Anderson 2002). In truth, we can often understand biological phenomena when Nature is kind and the phenomenon of interest is dominated by relatively few processes.

Using evolutionary theory as a way to gain an understanding of religion gives us access to concepts and theoretical and empirical tools that have been very successful in explaining biological diversity. Of course, the tools of evolutionary biology have been mostly developed through the study of non-human living organisms with the assumption that it is *genes* that are evolving. The evolutionary study of human behavior adds an important wrinkle. In all living things, information is transmitted down the generations coded in genes. Humans also pass on a vast amount of information culturally, by teaching and imitating one another. To get an idea of the scale, consider that the human genome has perhaps 20,000 structural genes while the vocabulary of high school graduates numbers about 60,000 words. Kids do not invent those words, at least not most of them; they pick them up or inherit them from the people they associate with. And of course vocabulary is only a modest part of their cultural inheritance.

The cultural and genetic inheritance systems in humans both carry a large amount of information but one important difference is that human genes vary only slightly across our species. Our cultural characteristics, on the other hand, are highly variable. Our understanding of how cultural characteristics evolve to create this huge diversity is quite modest in some respects. Historians, paleoanthropologists, archaeologists, and other scholars have provided us with a good descriptive picture of how various cultural characteristics have changed over time. Anthropologists and other scholars have given us a good qualitative picture of cultural diversity. But this is very different from the quantitative and mechanistic understanding of evolution that has been pursued by biologists looking at how genes change.

When Darwin began to develop his theories, naturalists and fossil-hunters had built up reasonable descriptive accounts of the diversity and change in living organisms. Darwin saw that this hotchpotch of data made sense if the diversification of living things had occurred through *descent with modification*. Darwin saw several ways that modification could occur. There were three types of selection (natural, sexual, artificial), random variation, and the inheritance of acquired changes. Darwin saw humans as a special case and developed his ideas on human evolution at some length in the *Descent of Man* (1874). Biologists energetically pursued the Darwinian approach to the evolution of genes but social sciences developed in a quite un-Darwinian direction as they emerged in the early twentieth century. Only in the last quarter of the twentieth century did scholars begin to turn their minds to developing a quantitative, mechanistic theory of cultural evolution and most of the pioneers were biologists, not mainstream social scientists (Cavalli-Sforza and Feldman 1981; Lumsden and Wilson 1981). Most twentieth-century social scientists saw little use in trying to derive a basic theory of human behavior from biology or evolution. An important exception was the psychologist Donald Campbell (1965; 1975). Today Darwinian social science is perhaps as mainstream as any other variety in this unfortunately fragmented field of inquiry (Gintis 2004; Laland and Brown 2002).

That religions are part of culture can be seen by the way they are inherited. If a baby, whose parents were Buddhist, is adopted by a Christian family in the United States, he or she will grow up to know about Christianity and will maybe consider him or herself to be a Christian. Just as a child of Chinese-speaking parents adopted by English speakers in an English-speaking community receives no knowledge of Chinese words from its genes, neither will it have Buddhist teaching coded in its genes. But, on the other hand, the *capacity* to learn a language *is* inherited genetically, even if the vocabulary and rules of grammar are not. Being able to learn to communicate through language is adaptive. People lacking in this ability were less fit than those who were good at it. The genes of adept language learners were more likely to be passed on than were those of people who could not use this mode of communication. If possessing religious beliefs also made people more fit, the *capacity* to acquire such beliefs is likely to be genetically coded.

So we can use an evolutionary approach to look at whether being religious enhances fitness or detracts from it. If it enhances fitness, it is likely the inclination to be religious is adaptive and therefore somehow coded in the genes. We can also use an evolutionary approach to look at specific kinds of religion or components of religion to see how they change: which were passed on generation after generation in their culture, and which rapidly become extinct? Clearly, the two ideas are linked. The kinds of religion or components of religion which brought net benefits to its members and allowed them to 'go forth and multiply' more effectively were the ones most likely to survive in the culture.

As with most biological phenomena, religion immediately bombards us with complexity. Any given religion is an amalgam of beliefs, practices, institutions, and organizations. To complicate matters even further, religions are webbed up with other domains of culture—art, social and political organization, family life, practical knowledge, and so on. Religions are diverse. We have polytheisms, monotheisms, and atheistic spiritual, ethical, and mystical systems. Religions also differ in what they consider to be important. Some insist that adherents maintain a proper set of beliefs, some consider carrying out proper ritual to be all important, and some emphasize common commitment to ethical ideals. Some restrict entry to a select few. Others are evangelical and open to all who want to join. Some religions are bureaucratic and authoritarian and some are entirely the product of egalitarian local groups. It is likely that almost any human behavior we can imagine has turned up as a component of religion, sometime, somewhere.

The Basics of Evolution I: Adaptation

The idea that natural selection favors genetic variations that cause their bearers to survive better or reproduce more is familiar to everyone who has had a good high school biology course. But Richard Dawkins (2006 [1976]) pointed out that genes are not the only entities that can respond to selection. Cultural elements, ideas, or bits of information—Dawkins coined the term 'memes'—can be selected just as genes can. Historical examples such as those given by Rodney Stark (1997) suggest that religion could be a cultural variant that persists because it brings advantages. Stark argues that early Christianity grew rapidly in the late Roman period in part because it generated congregations that engaged in mutual helping in a very uncertain world. This helping caused Christians to be more likely to survive and reproduce than pagans. In time, therefore, Christians began to outnumber pagans. QED: religion is adaptive?

The question, however, is less straightforward. The notion of adaptation becomes quite complex once we venture very far onto the seas of biological complexity and diversity. Culture adds newer and greater depths to explore. Consider sexual selection. Darwin paired his discussion of humans with his discussion of sexual selection because he wanted to argue that the conspicuous differences between the races like skin color and nose form were due to sexual rather than natural selection. Mate choice sexual selection was a lot like fad and fashion. Arbitrary aesthetic displays like peacock tails evolve to attract the opposite sex, but are otherwise useless or even costly. So, can a peacock's tail be considered an adaptation? Biologists differ in their answers to questions like this. Some see an adaptation as something which increases survival while others define an adaptation as being whatever selection has favored, in which case a peacock's spectacular tail is an adaptation on the part of males for mating success.

We will use a basic definition of adaptation that derives from what the great twentieth-century evolutionary biologist Ronald Fisher called the 'fundamental theorem of natural selection' (Grafen 2003). According to this theorem, natural selection builds adaptations by favoring genetic variants that increase the mean fitness of individuals or of communities of cooperative individuals. By the way, this is *not* all that selection does and certainly not all that evolution does. For example, sexual selection may decrease the fitness of male peacocks because of the fitness costs of carrying a ridiculously large and cumbersome tail. It may decrease the fitness of peahens as well. Quite conceivably, hens often fail to mate because the local male population has been depleted by predation on encumbered males. Thus, sexual selection can favor variants that decrease rather than increase mean fitness. But whenever we refer to 'adaptation' we will exclude such things and refer to *any genetic or cultural variant that increases the mean genetic fitness of a population*. Normally, complex adaptations are built up incrementally by selection or other processes but the 'atom' of adaptation is some heritable variant that increases mean fitness compared to alternate variants. This definition will serve as a sort of lighthouse, a point of reference for an adventure on the dark and stormy seas of evolutionary complexity that follow. So note it well!

The Basics of Evolution II: Selection at Multiple Levels

Competition is the engine of natural selection and this has lead many people to suggest that taking an evolutionary approach demands that we see individuals as fundamentally competitive. This is not necessarily the case because selection can work at different levels of organization. Classically, biologists talk about survival of the fittest organism; in other words, selection at the level of the individual organism. Selection is seen to favor traits that increase the mean fitness of individuals, to favor variants that increase the survival and reproduction of individuals. But this introduces a problem because many organisms, amoeba for example, consist of a single cell, while others, humans for example, consist of billions of cells organized in a way that allows them to cooperate to produce a single thriving organism. Because of this, Richard Dawkins (2006 [1976]) proposed that it is more helpful to think of selection taking place at the level of genes. It is the genes that are selfish not the organisms that contain them. By this reckoning, selection at the level of the individual organism is really group selection, the selection of an organization of cooperating genes.

Eors Szathmary and John Maynard Smith (1995) argued that the history of life over that last three billion years could be read as a series of major transitions, which allowed the assembly of larger and larger groups—individual genes grouped to form cells made up of many cooperating genes, individual cells grouped to form larger organisms made up of many cooperating cells, and so on. Why is the assembly of groups so rare as to be considered a major life transition? And why does it take millions of years to achieve? It is because such an assembly can only be stable once mechanisms emerge that ensures that the individuals within cooperative groups continue to work together to achieve a common goal.

We take it for granted that the genes that make up our genome are each contributing to the work of our cells. But as molecular biologists gained a more detailed understanding of life at the sub-cellular level they discovered the kinds of nefarious behaviors genes are capable of. Some have been identified that act like selfish parasites at the expense of the cell as a whole, doing things like disrupting cell division by inserting multiple copies of themselves at the expense of other genes. You have a full complement of necessary genes because the well-behaved genes of your four grandparents were divided up reasonably fairly to produce the egg and sperm that united to created your genome. This is because the cells of sexually reproducing organisms have mechanisms for making cell division an orderly process that usually doesn't allow rogue genes to get away with anything. There is also a problem of roguish behavior on the part of cells within the body of a multicellular organism. Mutations in certain genes can make our body cells cease to play their role. Again, we have mechanisms to deal with this. Much of the work of our immune system is dedicated to detecting and destroying body cells that fail to cooperate and begin to live like parasites. It is only when these mechanisms fail that we get cancer.

Transitions to a higher level of organization are unusual events because the probability is low that a combination of random changes will occur that produces mechanisms that succeed in preventing non-cooperating individuals getting the upper hand. But once such a mechanism exists a cooperative group of genes or cells can usually exploit the environment better than the many individual components competing on their own. After that, selection between groups will drive the evolution of organization and control systems that are increasingly effective. Members of better-organized groups will cooperate more fully so the likelihood of their survival and reproduction will be higher.

In theory, cooperation can also occur at the next level up, within communities of individual multicellular organisms. Group selection can operate to encourage cooperation whenever a reliable statistical association exists between being a cooperator and being in a group composed of other cooperators (Henrich 2004). In other words, groups can only work together if a high enough proportion of its members are working hard enough for the group as a whole. Making sure that happens is not easy when the group members are free to move around. Up to now in the evolution of life on Earth only limited degrees of cooperation are seen at the level of the organism. A mechanism for maintaining cooperation within a community of organisms would need to ensure that a sufficiently high proportion of the members are behaving cooperatively rather than competing. This means well-behaved members must be retained, encouraged to reproduce, and, if possible, new cooperators must be recruited from outside the community. Members who fail to cooperate must be recognized and either rehabilitated or expelled from the community. Uncooperative outsiders must be recognized and barred from entry.

Game theoretical simulations have shown that if cooperative behavior is genetically inherited (i.e. genes induce the cooperative behavior) then cooperative communities are only likely to emerge in two circumstances: (1) If the individuals in the community have the same or very similar genes; (2) in small groups between individuals who have established long-term reciprocal relationships. In the latter cases, the genes encourage reciprocal behavior rather than cooperation.

Humans are rare if not unique in having cooperation within large communities of unrelated individuals. Our unusual form of cooperation is part of our genetic inheritance. We are endowed with the mental tools for operating a cultural inheritance system. We may not have genes that force us to cooperate but we can learn to cooperate. This does not mean learning to cooperate with anyone anyhow; we learn in what situations being cooperative would be appropriate. We also become very adept at recognizing the kinds of behavior our culture would consider inappropriate or unacceptable. Cultural institutions can emerge within human communities that reward high levels of cooperation and punish or expel non-cooperators. So, just as organisms have genetically evolved mechanisms that work to maintain communities of cooperating cells, groups of humans have culturally evolved behaviors and institutions that provide mechanisms that do the same thing.

Robert Boyd and Peter Richerson have developed what they call the 'tribal social instincts hypothesis' to explain human cooperation (Boyd and Richerson 1985; Richerson and Boyd 2005). It argues that cooperation evolved hand in hand with the human capacity for culture. At the core of the hypothesis is the idea that group selection is a more potent force on cultural variation than on genetic variation (Henrich 2004). Populations in semi-isolation rapidly evolved cultural differences. Symbolic boundaries limited the flow of ideas between groups. Individual members were inclined to copy the behavior most common within their group and this decreased the differences within the groups and increased differences between the groups. Individuals who failed to conform were punished and fared badly within the group.

As these processes continued for generation after generation in the remote past, primitive cooperative institutions arose. These institutions formed an environment in which genes were selected that conveyed the capacity to thrive and to make the most of culture. This eventually led to an innate social psychology. The successfully social human was relatively docile, prepared to conform to social institutions and prepared to cooperate, especially with members of a symbolically marked in-group. The phrase 'tribal social instincts' was coined because the kinds of groups in which they evolved are commonly called tribes, although anthropologists often use other terms for them.

Modern complex societies betray the nature of the tribal instincts. Religion is often employed as a way of making the in-group. Even very large systems like nations are usually united by a common language, and nations in the modern sense only became possible after mass literacy and mass communication made it possible for the mass of people to sense a cultural kinship with each other (Anderson 1991). Tribal scale social institutions are still the building blocks of complex societies. Armies, civilian bureaucracies, companies, voluntary organizations almost always have units much like the residential bands of hunter-gatherers (academics, think 'department') and like the tribe (academics, think 'universities'). Or disciplines and sub-disciplines. The religious will think congregation and sect. We shall use what we think of as the least value-laden term: 'cooperative community'.

Group selection between communities gradually improves the communities' cultural mechanisms that promote cooperation. Those with the more effective mechanisms will be more successful and this means that their institutions (as well as their members) will have a higher rate of reproduction. This can happen through a number of means. The more successful communities may conquer less successful ones and impose their institutions. The more successful communities may have greater growth of membership through reproduction and immigration. Overcrowding might then cause members to migrate and set up new communities with similar institutions. Other communities with less-effective institutions may well abandon them and adopt the more successful cultural mechanisms. The different cooperative groups will continue to compete and their cooperative institutions will change. In time, these processes should cause the evolution of increasingly effective institutions.

The honing of these mechanisms will not necessarily lead to the increased fitness of individual members of the cooperative community. On top of the cost invested in the cooperative effort there are the costs of running the mechanisms, and the more effective the mechanisms the more costly they are likely to be. Cooperators within groups must signal that they are members in good standing to avoid being expelled from the community as uncooperative outsiders trying to freeload. Such signals must be difficult to give or imposters would find it easy to cheat the detection system. By the way, a system of signaling belonging is also needed for the body cells within an organism. Your cells manufacture and display a combination of complex protein markers that is characteristic of your genome and denotes your 'tissue type'. These proteins are difficult for infectious agents to make. And should tissue be implanted in your body made up of cells with the wrong combination of markers on their surface, it could be attacked and 'rejected' by your immune system. Hence the need for immunosuppressant drugs for transplant patients. The patient's body is just trying to make sure that no non-self DNA is invading to take advantage of the products of the cooperation between its cells.

Religion as a Promoter of Cooperation

Human communities have evolved a number of ways of keeping the proportion of cooperators to non-cooperators as high as possible. Religions are clearly among these; but what elements of religion operate to maintain cooperation and how effective are they? And do the institutions enhance the members' welfare and fitness? Many religions teach a moral code and prescribe cooperation. But the members of some faith groups display a diversity of behavior which can range from great heights of altruism to cavernous depths of selfishness. If this goes unnoticed by the members of the religious community, or they tolerate it, the institutions of this religion are not effective promoters of cooperation. Members are not likely to experience tangible welfare benefits from belonging to such an organization.

Iannacone (1994) argues that strict faiths can generate higher levels of cooperation and mutual help than lax ones because the practices of strict churches are too costly for cheaters to fake. The beliefs of strict churches are complex and difficult to learn. The ongoing expenditures of time and resources to conform to the practices of strict faiths are high. Subscribing to outlandish beliefs handicaps members from reasonably considering the evidence and judging what might really be in their best interest. Belonging to a strict faith is a conspicuous commitment that makes it difficult for members to maintain strong ties with members of other belief systems. Few are willing to pay such high costs unless their commitment to the religious community is genuine. The group is therefore protected from impostors.

But, on the other hand, the higher the costs that members of a community must pay, the less cooperative product the strict church provides. So, belonging to a strict church may also provide no tangible benefits or even have net costs. The membership might be so engaged in maintaining rituals and ritual objects that they can devote no effort to helping one another. Furthermore, the levels of practical commitment that might sometimes be required of devout faith group members may be detrimental to their welfare. As we know very well from the Middle East today, the Balkans a few years ago, and from Western Europe in the sixteenth and seventeenth centuries, unless overarching institutions exist that promote tolerance between religious groups, members of groups might be expected to engage in violence to protect or avenge fellow group members.

Religions can therefore both enhance and detract from the welfare of their members. Examples of this are provided by Sonya Salamon (1992). She reports that German-ancestry farming communities in the American state of Illinois have a single church in each community, either Catholic or Lutheran, but never both in any one community. The churches here are institutions that foster local solidarity. However, British ancestry communities in the state have a number of small Protestant churches in each community. Congregations here typically compete for members, so religion is a divisive rather than a unifying influence on the community.

Arguments made by historians and social scientists about the positive or negative influences of religion can be confusing. For example, Edward Gibbon (2006) argued that the Christian Church persuaded its members to transfer resources to the humble and unproductive members of society. This, he said, contributed to the decline and fall of the Roman Empire—a negative outcome. Rodney Stark (1997) argues that early Christian congregations grew rapidly because of the welfare services that were provided for members and hence Christianity gained acceptance in Roman society—a positive outcome. These may, in fact, amount to the same argument: What was good for the Christian Church was not necessarily good for the Roman Empire. An evolutionist's approach avoids such confusion by agreeing that the outcome being monitored is fitness—the size and welfare of subsequent generations. The Christian Church contributed to the health of subsequent generations by transferring resources to humble families. On the other hand, so did the Roman Empire, by providing the infrastructure for trade and a larger economy. Since the fall of the Roman Empire resulted in widespread depopulation in the West, the net fitness effect of Christianity was arguably negative. (Arguable, because the rise of Christianity is only one of a number of plausible hypotheses about the causes of Roman collapse (Diamond 2005).)

Frequency-dependent Selection and the Established Church

When religion promotes welfare because it unifies a community under a common set of customs, institutions, and organizations, such as Sonya Salamon observed in the German communities of Illinois, it is only effective when the majority of people in the population are members of the religious community. And, the larger the majority, the more effective it is. Throughout the history of civilization, many conquerors and leaders have attempted to unify a population by declaring one form of religion to be official, often with them as the official leader. The teachings in the Qur'an unified Arab clans and eventually many different national groups despite the schisms that soon developed. Many societies, be they historically Buddhist, Christian, Jewish, or Islamic were and still are hostile to unofficial ideologies. And in the case of Hinduism the system of assigning families to castes has a religious basis, and to some extent it still constitutes the fundamental organizing institutions of Indian society (Gadgil and Malhotra 1983; Srinivas 1962).

The fact that so many populations throughout history have had official religions suggests that it is often effective as a means of bringing net advantage to a population. Once a faith has exclusive access to a population, it can promote cooperation on a wider scale and coordinate larger groups. This can bring important benefits to the members of a wide religious community. To the extent of its ability to do this, we can say that religion might also be most adaptive when it is more common in the population. On the other hand, established churches often become hidebound, bureaucratic, and corrupt. Sometimes they are the handmaidens of predatory elites. Sociologists of religion Roger Finke and Rodney Stark contrast America's vibrant religious economy based upon a plethora of entrepreneurial churches and sects with the feeble established churches of Western Europe (1992).

Evolutionary analysis can reveal some counter-intuitive effects. If possessing a characteristic is very beneficial to an individual's welfare, one might expect this characteristic to be very common in a population. If belonging to a religion brings great benefits, it seems as if everyone will eventually become a member. This is not always the case, however. The outcome of selection can sometimes be very far from the outcome that would maximize fitness. In biology, this can be seen by considering the sex ratio of babies born in a species like cattle. A bull is able to produce far more offspring than a cow. A cow can only become pregnant about once a year while a bull can impregnate many cows during that time. In theory, then, having the 'male' characteristic brings far more fitness than having the 'female' characteristic and this advantage to males should mean that more males should be born than females. But, of course, males can only enjoy this kind of advantage when there are far more females than males. As the proportion of males

increases, their average fitness decreases. A 50 : 50 sex ratio turns out to
be roughly where selection comes to rest in most species. Ranchers, who
want to maximize the offtake of animals from their pastures, maintain only
enough bulls to do their proper work, about one to twenty cows. Female
fig wasps do roughly the same thing when laying eggs in a fig, but only
when no males from competing females are likely to introduce competing
males into the fig.

That 50 : 50 distribution of sexual characteristics is a special case of what
evolutionists call frequency-dependent selection. Commonly, a characteristic is most beneficial to its bearers when its frequency in a population
is low. Possessing the cultural characteristic of being 'a doctor' means a
person can command a high income, but only because their numbers
are few. Doctors know this and take various measures to ensure that the
characteristic remains rare.

This is also the case for religions. Amish communities are currently
growing rapidly in the United States and Canada, mostly because of their
very high birth rates. In the case of this religion the biological-fitness
benefits to being a member are really substantial. The fitness of the Amish
and other religious sects in first-world countries that are resisting the demographic transition is probably the highest in the world. Families of nine or
more are not uncommon. However, most Amish, do not pursue education
past the age of 13 and this sharply limits the number of occupations that
Amish can pursue. The proportion of Amish in the population is increasing
and as they become more common three things might happen: and all
three will lead to a decline in the mean fitness of the Amish. First, Amish
economic success might drop as they need to compete more fiercely for
the limited number of occupations that can be performed by people with
little education. The Amish have moved into various craft and factory
occupations in recent years as land has become too expensive for all of them
to remain in farming. Eventually Amish family sizes might be limited by
falling wages in the occupations they are able to serve. Second, the Amish
population might continue to rise, eventually reducing the skilled labor
force enough to handicap the economies of the United States and Canada.
Third, the Amish might decide to become less strict and allow members to
pursue higher education. This might introduce influences in the members'
lives that are likely to compete with producing large families. The Amish
remain distinctive and resist modernization in part by eschewing educated
professionals who are the epitome of modernity. Whatever the outcome,

the adaptedness of the Amish and other high-fertility religious groups is certain to change as they rise from an insignificant part of the population to a major component.

Another advantage of belonging to a rare religion is that small sects may be less at risk from penetration by selfish impostors. When a sect is small, few non-cooperators will know enough about it to fake membership. Quite cheap occult signals may be sufficient to differentiate members from non-members. The doctrines and practices of large churches tend to be common knowledge. Hence they are easy to penetrate. Also, large churches are inevitably bureaucratic and may tend to become excessively top-down organizations. Small sects may much more effectively tap the local enthusiasm and esprit.

Cultural Evolution

We have discussed a number of ways in which it is useful to think of the culture of a population as being similar to the gene pool of the population. By this analogy the various cultural elements (ideas, skills, languages, social institutions, and so on) that are available to the population can be seen as genes. We inherit these cultural elements by learning them, through imitating others, and by being taught by others, just as we inherit genes from our parents. Thus, all the complexities of adaptation discussed above apply to genes as well as culture, albeit with many differences of detail.

The analogy becomes more useful if we also keep in mind the many ways that the inheritance of cultural elements differs from the inheritance of genes. For our purposes here, it is sufficient to concentrate on just a few of these—the ones that give rise to the most interesting differences regarding adaptation.

The most fundamental difference perhaps is that cultural evolution is 'Lamarckian'. It includes the inheritance of acquired variation. Humans are not necessarily passive participants in transmission of culture. From the many cultural elements available to our population we can to some extent make decisions about which to adopt and which to ignore or forget. We can also decide which to keep to ourselves and which to teach (or how actively to teach) and to whom they should be taught. We may decide to reject all the cultural variants on offer and make up our own. These sorts of behaviors enable individual members of a culture to make the most of being a member. The behaviors create what we see as 'forces'—'decision-making forces'—that operate to push culture to evolve in a direction. Donald Campbell (1965) argued that the decision-making forces constituted 'vicarious selectors'. Presumably, human psychology was under selection in the past to have rules for acquiring culture that enhanced genetic fitness, at least under conditions that approximate to those that we evolved under. Much of the work on the evolution of human behavior takes it for granted that human decisions of all sorts will be fitness optimizing (Laland and Brown 2002). In accord with this argument, humans are a spectacularly successful species based on our culturally transmitted technology and social institutions (Richerson and Boyd 2005).

In religion as in any other realm of culture, individuals use their decision-making abilities to try to invent and adopt variants that are favorable to themselves. Thus, if individuals have any choice at all of church, pastor, or doctrines they are liable to adopt those that benefit them. It is not difficult to see why natural selection favored those who were better at choosing between the cultural variants available to them.

Cultural evolution, however, also allows plenty of scope for the emergence of variants that are 'maladaptive', that are detrimental to the welfare and fitness of the members of the culture (Richerson and Boyd 2005). As with adaptations, all of the potential maladaptive processes that exist for genes also have cultural analogs. Some of these probably have greater force in the case of culture, most notably the potential for virus-like selfish memes to arise and spread among the members of a population. One example that occurred recently was the idea that the new 'MMR' triple vaccine for mumps, measles, and rubella causes autism. Adopting this piece of scientifically unfounded piece of information caused many parents not to have their children vaccinated. As a result, many of them succumbed to the biological viruses, with a few suffering permanent damage.

The evolution of cultural maladaptations is a particular risk because of another important difference between cultural evolution and the evolution of genes: the pattern of the transmission of information. Genetic transmission is constrained to be vertical—from parents to offspring. This, thanks to the cellular mechanisms that keep rogue genes at bay, makes biological evolution relatively orderly. Cultural variants can be transmitted vertically (from parent to offspring), but oblique transmission (unrelated adults to children) and horizontal transmission (among peers) are also important.

Individuals equipped with some reasonable decision-making rules can hope to harvest some good ideas by imitating people other than their parents. But there is always a risk. The scope for the evolution of attractive-seeming but ultimately harmful information in obliquely transmitted cultural elements is great, and it is even greater when the information is horizontally transmitted, that is from individuals who are as inexperienced and untested as oneself.

Some students of cultural evolution imagine that culture is largely made up of what they consider to be 'parasitic memes' (Blackmore 1999). Richard Dawkins (2006 [1976]) argues that religion is such a maladaptive cultural element—typically transmitted to children at young ages when their minds are impressionable and their decision-making powers not yet fully functional. He subscribes to a by-product hypothesis to explain most if not all of religion. Young minds have to be impressionable so as rapidly and accurately to acquire essential information from parents. Parasitic religious memes take advantage of this impressionability. Evolutionary psychologists have advanced similar ideas (Atran and Norenzayan 2004).

One doesn't have to follow these authors in suggesting that *all* religious ideas, institutions, and organizations are maladaptive to realize that some may be. Extreme examples of religious sects espousing maladaptive ideas do certainly exist—for example, the cult led by Jim Jones that committed mass suicide in 1978. Modern societies have much greater rates of horizontal and oblique cultural transmission compared to traditional ones. The scope for the evolution of pathological memes is consequently greater than in the past. The rapid decline in fertility in modern and modernizing societies is explicable on this basis (Newson, et al. 2005). Religious groups like the Anabaptists that still have high fertility comprehensively reduce their exposure to modern memes and maintain tight kin networks. Even quite pronatalist denominations like Catholicism have not been very effective in the face of the demographic transition.

Other cultural-evolutionary mechanisms may generate specific sorts of maladaptations. For example, symbolic culture can evolve exaggerated traits by a mechanism much like sexual selection (Richerson and Boyd 1989). Exaggerated, costly, religious rituals could be examples. The Protestant Reformation's charge that the Roman Catholic Church's lavish expenditure on buildings and ornaments was dysfunctional is a potential example. Perhaps costly religious behavior often has little or nothing to do with guaranteeing honest signals and is mostly or entirely costly competitive exaggeration. On the other hand, such initially symbolic variation perhaps generates the raw material for cultural group selection. Roy Rappaport advanced an interesting hypothesis along these lines (1979). He thought that 'supernatural veils' were necessary to protect group-functional adaptations from the corrosive attack of individually selfish rationality. Random exaggeration may be the group-level analog of mutation, ultimately a raw material for adaptation. For every Jacob Amman or Joseph Smith there must be hundreds of religious innovators like Ann Lee, the founder of the celibate Shakers, whose sects at best prosper briefly and then disappear.

Having culture brings net benefits or humans would not have it and nor would we be such a successful species. Unalloyed maladaptive cultural variants are the exception rather than the rule. We attribute this to the ability of humans to decide between cultural elements and to create new ones. Religious conversion and religious innovation are important examples. An innovator like Mormon founder Joseph Smith was able to invent a quite novel new religion, though in truth he mainly selected a novel combination of ideas that were current in his community in the early nineteenth century (Brooke 1994). Clearly, many people decided that adopting those ideas would benefit them and clearly many feel they have benefited. Currently, the Latter Day Saints are one of the most actively proselytizing religions in the world and enjoy rapid growth as a result (Iannaccone, Olson, and Stark 1995).

David Sloan Wilson (2002) provides a number of examples of religious ideas being adopted because they provided fitness benefits. The formation and spread of Calvinism is his central example. He describes in some detail how the problem of corruption in the Catholic Church led Calvin to propose, and the people of Geneva eventually to adopt, a religiously inspired code of conduct that effectively ended the disruptive factionalism in the city. Calvin's model inspired much imitation based on its success in Geneva. Karen Armstrong (1991) gives a similar account of Muhammad's religiously inspired code aimed at regulating the intertribal anarchy of the Arabs. Stephen Lansing (1993) shows how Balinese Water Temples function to organize scarce water and coordinate rice planting on Bali so as to optimize rice yields. Religions also seem to have many individually adaptive benefits. For example, Hill and Pargament (2003) review the literature on the connection between religion and spirituality and physical and mental health.

Conclusion

In the face of biological and cultural complexity and diversity, phenomena like religion are unlikely to support sweeping generalizations about adaptation versus maladaptation. Theory tells us that many things are possible. Any generalizations will have to be based upon careful empirical work. The basic task is to tot up the various kinds of costs and benefits that accrue to religious variants. This project has barely begun in any domain of culture. Students of religion have done some exemplary studies in this regard. Roof and McKinney (1987) showed how demographic data could be mobilized to show the relative importance of differential birth rates and differential conversion and apostasy in the growth and decline of religions. Differential birth rate (natural selection) tends to be more important than differential conversion and apostasy. Hout, Greeley, and Wilde's careful work (2001) along these lines shows how progress can be made despite the problems of complexity and diversity. Our own unpublished work with Brian Paciotti using experimental games suggests that different forms of religiosity make small positive and negative contributions to pro-social behavior.

5

Religious Belief as an Evolutionary Accident

Paul Bloom[1]

Religious belief and religious practice are human universals. There are no atheist communities and, as far as we know, there never have been. Even within the most secular societies on Earth, the countries of Western Europe, many people are religious to at least some extent, holding certain supernatural beliefs (such as life after death) or engaging in certain religious practices (such as prayer). And in the rest of the world—in Asia, Africa, and the Americas, for instance—religious rituals and ideas are at the core of people's day-to-day lives. It is impossible to make sense of most of human existence—including law, morality, war, and culture—without some appreciation of religion and how it works.

Religious belief is puzzling in certain regards. Consider other beliefs that people universally possess: objects are solid; unsupported things fall to the ground; people have minds; two plus two equals four. These are all true of the world in which we live. This makes it plausible that they could arise through natural selection, because it is adaptive for animals to know true and useful things, or that they could arise from observation, because we have evolved fairly accurate mechanisms of perception and learning.

It is considerably harder to explain the origin of beliefs such as: God created the universe; God listens to prayer; when people die, they go to heaven or to hell. As H. L. Mencken put it, the existence of religion illustrates humanity's 'stupendous capacity for believing the incredible' (<http://www.positiveatheism.org/hist/quotes/mencken.htm>). Mencken was an

1. This chapter is a substantially modified version of Bloom 2007. I thank Steven Gross for his very helpful comments on an earlier version of this chapter.

atheist, but even a theist must agree that these beliefs really *are* incredible, in the sense that they do not arise in any clear sense from systems for perceiving and observing the physical world. We can see dogs and trees; we cannot (in any literal sense) see God. And, from the standpoint of evolution, it is hard to see how having such beliefs could lead to increased reproductive success, and so—unlike intuitions about gravity, say—religious belief is an unlikely candidate for a biological adaptation.

Some scholars disagree with the last part, arguing that there really is some adaptive value to holding religious beliefs. Perhaps belief in a supernatural entity makes people more moral and hence more desirable as mates and social partners (e.g., Bering 2006; Johnson and Bering 2006). Perhaps societies whose members hold religious beliefs outlast and outgrow those who don't, and hence these beliefs might evolve through group selection (e.g., David Sloan Wilson 2002).

A different alternative is that religion is the product of culture. Religious belief is acquired by individuals through social learning, and is not reducible (in any non-trivial sense) to facts about biology or evolution. Belief in God is not akin to the perception of dogs and trees; rather we learn about religion as we might learn about Roman history or the rules of baseball. The universality of certain religious beliefs occurs, under this view, because they are especially learnable and memorable. The Christian notion of God, for instance, is a perfect mix of the expected and the remarkable, and hence sticks in people's minds (e.g., Boyer and Ramble 2001). Under one variant of this view, religion might be a cluster of memes, a cultural parasite that has evolved to infect and manipulate the human brain (e.g., Blackmore 1999).

This chapter will explore a third view. I will suggest that humans possess certain highly structured systems that have evolved for understanding the social world. Religion emerges as a by-product of these systems (for different versions of this proposal, see, e.g., Atran 2002a; Barrett 2004; Bloom 2004; Bloom 2007; Boyer 2001b; Guthrie 1993; Kelemen 2004; Pinker 1997; Pyysiäinen 2001b).

Religion is not an adaptation, then; it is not like color vision or the love we feel toward our children. Rather, it should be seen as similar to the ability to understand calculus or the pleasure we get in playing video games—something that did not emerge due to its adaptive value, but rather is a by-product (or 'spandrel', see Gould and Lewontin 1979) of pre-existing adaptations.

I should stress that this is not a complete theory of religion. For one thing, it focuses only on belief (for discussion of ritual, see Alcorta and Sosis 2005; Boyer and Lienard 2006). For another, it focuses only on universal beliefs, leaving unexplained those that vary from culture to culture. Nobody is born with the idea that the birthplace of humanity was the Garden of Eden, or that the soul enters the body at the moment of conception, or that martyrs will be rewarded with sexual access to scores of virgins. This has to be learned—though such learning might have interesting and non-intuitive properties that distinguishes it from other types of social information gathering (see Bloom and Weisberg 2007 for discussion).

Universals of Religion

Human psychological universals might emerge because of deep facts about the human mind, but they don't have to. All languages have a word for 'hand', for instance, but this is probably because it is important for people everywhere to talk about hands, not because of a specific innate capacity. Similarly, belief in gods, the afterlife, and so on, may be universal, because such beliefs emerge naturally in all societies, perhaps in response to certain universal needs or desires. From this perspective, these universals are cultural inventions, created by adults and learned by children.

This is perhaps the dominant view in the social sciences, but over the last couple of decades there has been a growing body of work suggesting that it is mistaken. While culture plainly plays some role, some universals of religion have innate roots. I will present some evidence for this below, arguing that the universals exist because of two more general habits of the human mind.

Habit 1: Agents and designers everywhere

Humans have what the anthropologist Pascal Boyer has called a 'hypertrophy of social cognition': a willingness to attribute psychological states, including agency, even when it is inappropriate to do so. This is a perfectly rational strategy (see Barrett 2004). It pays to be trigger-happy with regard to animacy-detection, because the cost of over-attributing animacy is low (if you turn your head when you hear the rustling of the bushes, and it is just the wind, you've lost nothing) while the cost of under-attributing animacy can be high (if you fail to turn your head, and there is a lion there, you might get eaten).

The classic demonstration of our propensity for intentional attribution is that of Heider and Simmel (1944), who made a simple movie in which geometrical figures—circles, squares, triangles—moved in certain systematic ways, designed, based on the psychologists' intuitions, to tell a tale. When shown this movie, people instinctively describe the figures as if they were specific people (bullies, victims, heroes) who have goals and desires, and they repeat back much the same story that the psychologists had intended to tell. Further research finds that you do not even need bounded figures—you can get much the same effect with moving dots, as well as in movies where the 'characters' are not single objects at all, but moving groups, such as swarms of tiny squares (Bloom and Veres 1999). This capacity to attribute agency based on minimal cues is not a late-emerging developing accomplishment. It exists even in babies (e.g., Csibra, et al. 2003; Hamlin and Bloom 2007).

The anthropologist Stewart Guthrie was the first modern scholar to notice the importance of this tendency as an explanation for religious thought (Guthrie 1993). In his book *Faces in the Clouds* Guthrie presents anecdotes and experiments showing that people attribute human characteristics to a striking range of real-world entities; his list includes: airplanes, automobiles, bags, bells, bicycles, boats, bottles, buildings, cities, clouds, clothing, earthquakes, fire, fog, food, garbage, hats, hurricanes, insects, locks, leaves, the moon, mountains, paper, pens, plants, pottery, rain, the sun, rivers, rocks, sirens, swords, tools, toys, trains, trees, volcanoes, water, and wind. We are hypersensitive to signs of human agency, so much so that we see intention where all that really exists is artifice or accident. As Guthrie puts it: 'the clothes have no emperor' (Guthrie 1993: 5).

Guthrie's proposal is that this bias is at the root of animistic religious beliefs. It might also contribute to the more general tendency to be swayed by the argument from design—the claim that the design that is apparent in the natural and biological world is evidence for a designer. We are natural-born 'Creationists'.

'Creationism' is particularly popular in the United States. A 2007 poll conducted for *Newsweek* presents us with the standard findings: about half of Americans claim that evolution did not occur at all—God created humans in their present form—and most of the rest concede that evolution might occur, but think it is guided by God. Only a minority believes that evolution occurred without divine assistance; more Americans believe in the virgin birth of Jesus Christ than in natural selection.

Even among the minority of those who claim to endorse Darwinian evolution, many distort it in one way or another, often seeing it as a mysterious internal force driving species towards perfection. As the biologist Richard Dawkins bemoans, it almost appears that 'the human brain is specifically designed to misunderstand Darwinism and find it hard to believe' (Dawkins 1986).

Natural selection is like quantum physics: we might intellectually grasp it, with considerable effort, but it will never feel right to us. When we see complex structure, we see it as the product of beliefs and goals and desires. We chew over the natural world with our social mode of understanding, and it is difficult to make sense of it any other way.

Our gut feeling that design requires a designer is no secret, and is understandably exploited by those who argue against Darwin, such as Michael Behe, who, in a (2005) *New York Times* Op-Ed piece, wrote: 'the strong appearance of design allows a disarmingly simple argument: if it looks, walks and quacks like a duck, then, absent compelling evidence to the contrary, we have warrant to conclude it's a duck'.

What reason is there to believe that this bias toward 'Creationism' is a natural one, as opposed to being taught? There are three sources of evidence.

First, the psychologist Deborah Kelemen has found considerable evidence for 'promiscuous teleology', a bias to see the world in terms of design and purpose (see Kelemen 2004, for review). Four-year-olds insist that everything has a purpose, including things like lions ('to go in the zoo') and clouds ('for raining'). When asked to explain why a group of rocks are pointy, adults prefer a physical explanation, while children choose functional answers, such as 'so that animals could scratch on them when they get itchy'.

Second, the psychologist George Newman and his colleagues have found that young children and even babies expect that agents, and not inanimate processes, create order. In one study they showed 3-year-olds a messy pile of blocks and asked who could have caused this—a gust of wind or a little sister? The young children said either one could do it. But when shown blocks in a neat pile, the children, like adults, say that this has to be the sister. Only an intelligent being could create order. In another study, Newman and his colleagues found that even babies look longer, indicating surprise, when a neat pile is shown to be caused by a rolling ball (Newman, et al. manuscript).

Finally, the psychologist Margaret Evans did a series of studies in which she simply asked children and adults about the origins of animals, offering them different options, including evolutionary accounts and 'Creationist' accounts. Adults differed along predictable lines—those from fundamentalist communities favored 'Creationism'; the secularists favored evolution. But Evans found that children raised by both sorts of communities tended to favor explanations that involve an intentional creator (Evans 2000; Evans 2001). If there is a natural default, then, it is 'Creationism', not evolution.

Habit 2: Common-sense dualism

Young children naturally think about inanimate physical entities in a different way from psychological entities: naive physics is different from naive psychology. But some investigators, including myself, have made the stronger proposal that we think of bodies and souls as *distinct*: we implicitly endorse a strong substance dualism of the sort defended by philosophers like Plato and Descartes (see Bloom 2004).

Under one variant of this account, our dualism is a natural by-product of our possession of two distinct cognitive systems—one for dealing with material objects, the other for social entities. These systems have incommensurable outputs, and dualism emerges as an evolutionary accident.

Dualism comes naturally to children. When asked, in implicit and explicit ways, preschool children will say that they believe the brain is only responsible for some aspects of mental life, typically those involving deliberative mental work, such as solving math problems. But the brain is not essential for activities such as pretending to be a kangaroo, loving one's brother, or brushing your teeth (e.g., Gottfried, et al. 1999; Johnson 1990; Lillard 1996). This is done by people, not their brains.

If bodies and souls are thought to be separate, you can have one without the other. Most things, such as chairs, cups, and trees, are thought of as bodies without souls, not possessing goals, beliefs, will, or consciousness. More significant for religion, dualism makes it possible to imagine souls without bodies. Christianity and Judaism, for instance, involve a God who created the universe, performs miracles, and listens to prayers. He is omnipotent and omniscient, possessing infinite kindness, justice, and mercy. But he does not, in any literal sense, have a body.

Our dualism also opens the possibility that people can survive the death of their bodies. Religions provide different accounts as to the fate of the soul: it might ascend to heaven, descend to hell, go off into some sort of parallel world, or occupy some other body, human or animal. Indeed, a belief that the world teems with ancestor spirits, the souls of people who have been liberated from their bodies through death, is common cross-culturally. And there is some evidence that, like 'Creationism', it is the natural default of children. Bering and Bjorklund (2004) told children of different ages stories about a mouse that died, and asked about the persistence of certain properties. When asked about biological properties of the mouse, the children appreciated the effects of death, including that the brain no longer worked. But when asked about the psychological properties, most of the children said that these would continue— the dead mouse can feel hunger, think thoughts, and hold desires. The body was gone, but the soul survives. And children believe this more than adults.

Implications

The proposal explored here is that humans possess early emerging and universal cognitive biases, including hypersensitivity to agency, a natural propensity to see non-random design as caused by an intelligent designer, and body–soul dualism. These make it natural to believe in gods and spirits, in the divine creation of the universe, and in an afterlife. These are the seeds from which religion grows.

This proposal is controversial. Some would argue that it attributes too much to young children and that I am underestimating the role of culture and learning. Others would argue that it attributes too little: that there are specific adaptations that are unique to religion. Distinguishing between such candidate theories is perhaps the main research program of the cognitive science of religion.

There is a more general objection that can be raised about this research. Many see this sort of psychological inquiry as fundamentally anti-religious. To put the argument in its crudest form, one might worry that the project of explaining why people believe in God is necessarily an atheistic one, because such an explanation would entail that God does not actually exist.

In this crude form, the argument is untenable. There are psychologists who explore how people come to know that five plus five equals ten, and none of them doubts the truth of five plus five equals ten. Psychologists are just as interested in the origin of true beliefs as false ones. More generally, the question 'Why do people believe X?' is different from 'Is X true?' This is obvious when you consider other domains. Psychologists who study why people believe there is intelligent life on Mars would be very confused if they thought that their findings would bear on the debate over the actual existence of extraterrestrial life.

A weaker form of this argument is more reasonable, however. While it is true that nothing from the empirical study of human psychology can *refute* religious belief, certain theories can challenge the rationality of those who hold such beliefs (see Mackie 1983).

Suppose you meet someone who believes in intelligent life on Mars, and you discovered that she holds this belief based on wishful thinking—she believes in life on Mars because she wants this to be true. It would be pretty cool if there were Martians, she explains. There is no consensus among epistemologists as to the precise conditions that have to hold for a belief to be justified, but whatever these are, surely wishful thinking does not satisfy them. Wanting X to be true is a terrible reason to believe X to be true. While it is possible that there is intelligent life on Mars (that is, she could be right by accident), still, she is unreasonable in holding this belief, and you would be unreasonable if you found yourself persuaded by her.

There are many potential routes to theistic belief. Some routes involve reasons, such as the argument from design. Indeed, when Frank Sulloway and Michael Shermer asked people about the source of their belief, the most common answer fell into the category: 'good design / natural beauty / perfection / complexity of the world or universe' (Shermer 2003). Other theists don't have reasons at all—they simply know that God exists. This is expressed in the second most common answer that people give: 'experience of God in everyday life / God is in us'.

As one would imagine, there is a lot of debate over what to make of such answers (e.g., Mackie 1983; Plantinga 2000). But, again, there are some routes to belief that are unreliable and irrational under any account. If a psychologist were to tell theists that, in fact, their belief in God is actually due to a wishful desire for a father figure, they would be offended, and rightfully so. Wishful thinking is a silly reason for believing anything, and nobody wants to be silly.

Admittedly, theological explanations are often unfalsifiable, and this is particularly true of theological proposals about the origin of religious belief. If there is an omnipotent God, then he could have orchestrated the universe so that belief in him could have emerged in any fashion whatsoever. In particular, the proposal developed in this chapter could be correct and religious belief might be an accident in an evolutionary sense (it would be a by-product of an adaptation; not itself the target of selection), but it might not be an accident in the grander sense—rather, it would reflect a divine plan. Plainly, no finding from the cognitive science of religion can refute either the existence of God or a theistic account of the origins of religious belief. But, even so, psychological inquiry can still tell us something about the rationality, or lack thereof, of religious believers, in the same sense that it can tell us about the mental status of those who believe in life on other planets.

Plantinga (1991) provides a characteristically perceptive discussion of this issue. He concedes that certain views about the origin of religious belief do portray the believer as cognitively defective, an 'intellectual gimp', but goes on to argue that under a different psychological account the same accusation—or worse—can be made about the *atheist*. He endorses a Calvinist theory in which belief in God is innate:

> [the conviction] that there is some God, is naturally inborn in all, and is fixed deep within, as it were in the very marrow . . . From this we conclude that it is not a doctrine that must first be learned in school, but one of which each of us is master from his mother's womb and which nature itself permits no man to forget.
>
> (Calvin 1960: 43–4, cited in Plantinga 1991)

For Calvin, atheism is born out of sin; lack of righteousness motivates some people to deny the clear truth of God. If so, then it is the atheist whose rationality (and morality) are challenged by the facts about human nature.

This Calvinist theory is a substantial and interesting—and testable—nativist claim about human nature. Plantinga (2000) expands on it, arguing that this belief in God requires some maturation (it is not present at birth), and might manifest itself only when triggered by exposure to certain experiences, such as glories of the natural world. In these regards, this theory of belief in God looks a lot like Chomsky's theory of language. It is a theory that some contemporary researchers might endorse (e.g., Johnson and Bering 2006)—though without accepting Calvin's theistic account of the origin of this innate belief.

I am more skeptical. I have reviewed above evidence for innate biases that might motivate certain religious ideas, and argued that such ideas are universal, natural defaults in all cultures. But there is no evidence that a belief in a single God—a God in the sense that Calvin is discussing—is unlearned. As best we know, such a belief is not universal, and it does not emerge without social contact. Plantinga (2000: 197) asserts that 'awareness of God is natural, widespread, and not easy to forget, ignore, or destroy', but these properties apply better to supernatural belief more generally, not to belief in God.

These are, in any case, empirical issues. And they are important ones, given what they might tell us about the rationality of both theists and atheists. Such research is of interest, then, to anyone who cares about whether it is reasonable to believe in God.

6

Explaining Belief in the Supernatural

Some Thoughts on Paul Bloom's 'Religious Belief as an Evolutionary Accident'

Peter van Inwagen

Naturalistic explanations of religion are as old as Xenophanes (570–480 BC). The most famous are probably those of Feuerbach, Marx, and Freud. I must confess that I don't find these three famous explanations of religion very interesting.[1] Large parts of them are unintelligible (this is particularly true of Feuerbach's writings on religion) and the parts that are intelligible are vague and untestable (Feuerbach and Freud), or else they demand allegiance to some very comprehensive theory that has been tried and found wanting on grounds unrelated to religion (Marx's theory of the dialectics of history and Freud's psychology).

Paul Bloom's theory, however, is very interesting indeed, and it certainly has none of the defects I have ascribed to the theories of Feuerbach, Marx, and Freud. Bloom's theory, or the part of it that is set out in 'Religious Belief as an Evolutionary Accident', is an explanation of a certain fact, the fact that supernaturalistic belief—belief in the reality of the supernatural— is so widespread among human beings that it may properly be called a universal.[2] (I will take it for granted that Bloom's contention that this is a

---

1. Not as explanations of religion, that is. I concede that they represent interesting episodes in the history of thought.

2. I say supernaturalistic belief; Bloom's term is religious belief. I prefer my term. For one thing, a supernaturalistic belief is not necessarily a religious belief. (I would say that someone's belief is a religious belief only if it is in some straightforward way connected with that person's religion.) People who frequent mediums presumably believe that those mediums are able to establish

fact is correct.) The fact that most human beings have some sort of belief in the supernatural is, to my mind, a fact that is much more likely to have a simple, unified explanation than the much more complicated fact that there is such a thing as religion.

And why does this fact need an explanation? Might not the universality of a belief in the supernatural be due simply to chance? Might the answer to the question, 'Why is supernaturalistic belief a human universal?' be simply 'Well, why not?'? The answer to this question is that the universality of supernaturalistic belief is an evolutionary puzzle. Most universal human beliefs (the belief in 'other minds', the belief that unsupported bodies fall…) have some simple, immediately evident connection with evolutionary fitness, but a human being's being without supernaturalistic beliefs does not decrease his or her evolutionary fitness in any obvious way. And supernaturalistic beliefs are not without their cost: they have an obvious tendency to lead to actions (rituals, prayer) that involve an expenditure of resources that might have been devoted to survival and reproduction. And it is a commonplace of evolutionary biology that any feature of a species that is costly in terms of energy and resources requires some sort of explanation. (The colorful plumage of the males of many species of birds is an example.)

The fact that supernaturalistic belief is a human universal, a feature of our *species*, therefore requires an explanation. But what fact, exactly, is this fact? The concept of the supernatural is a difficult one,[3] but nothing I say in these comments will require a sophisticated understanding of this concept. It will suffice for present purposes to understand a supernaturalistic belief as follows: 'A belief is a supernaturalistic belief if it implies the existence of invisible and intangible agents[4] whose actions sometimes have significant

---

contact with beings that most people (if not sophisticated philosophers and theologians) would classify as 'supernatural', but I should not want to call their belief a religious one. Bloom has pointed out (in the discussion following an oral presentation of some of the material in his chapter) that although Iceland is generally conceded to be the least religious of all nations 80 per cent of Icelanders believe in reincarnation. A religious belief, moreover, is not necessarily a supernaturalistic belief. My belief that Anglican orders are valid is a religious belief, but its truth or falsity depends only on whether certain human beings have performed certain actions with certain intentions.

3. As is the concept of the natural, and therefore of a naturalistic explanation.

4. These agents are to be thought of as non-human intelligences possessed of more-than-human power. By calling them invisible and intangible, I mean that they normally have these features; it is consistent with what I mean by 'invisible and intangible agents' that invisible and intangible agents have the power to make themselves visible to human beings—and even (a favorite

effects on human life,[5] or implies that human beings have a post-mortem existence.'

I will not recapitulate Bloom's naturalistic explanation of the universality of belief in the supernatural among human beings. His own exposition of this explanation is very clear, and anyone who is reading these comments can be presumed to be familiar with it—and can in any case find it by turning back a few pages. I will, however, remind you that the thesis that supernaturalistic belief is a 'universal' does not imply that everyone has supernaturalistic beliefs—a fact that does not need to be pointed out to Professor Bloom, since he himself has none, and he daily moves in social and professional circles in which the belief that there are invisible and intangible agents is not much more common than the belief that absolute monarchy is the ideal form of government.

It is also worth pointing out that Bloom's explanation of the universality of supernaturalistic belief is not intended to imply that the causal factors that it appeals to are operative in the case of every particular person who has supernaturalistic beliefs. If the explanation did imply that, it would be wrong. I am a case in point. My own supernaturalistic beliefs are extensive and elaborate (they differ from those of the Pope only in respects that would interest theologians). And yet I have no tendency to see purpose or teleology everywhere. Indeed, I have no tendency to see teleology *anywhere* other than in human actions and their consequences. If I witnessed a notoriously wicked landlord being struck dead by lightning at the moment he was giving the order to evict a weeping single mother, my natural inclination would be to believe that his death was accidental and meaningless in every sense of those words. (I suppose I do believe that many things that happen have a meaning or purpose that is not grounded in the desires and intentions of human beings, but that belief is for me a sort of theological theorem—a logical consequence of certain very general theological propositions I affirm; and I certainly do not claim to be able to identify even one thing that serves some non-human purpose.) Nor do I claim to see any design in the world other than the design that is obviously due to human beings. At any rate—I must be careful about how I put this— I do not see any design that is independent of or prior to my belief that

activity of Zeus), to present themselves to human beings in so 'tangible' a form as to be able to engage in sexual intercourse with them.

5. These effects might be anything from guiding a shepherd to a lost sheep to being responsible for the existence of the heavens and the earth and all that they contain.

there is a Designer.[6] I frequently quote Cardinal Newman on this point: 'I believe in design because I believe in God, not in a God because I see design.' I think I am right to look at the world and see design, but I do not think that the cognitive apparatus of atheists and agnostics is somehow defective because they look at the world and see no design (or 'see' it in a way, but regard the experience as illusory, like the experience of seeing one line in the Müller-Lyer figure as longer than the other). Finally, I have no tendency to mind–body dualism at all. I believe that I am a physical thing; a living animal shaped like a statue of a human being and made entirely of up-quarks, down-quarks, and electrons. And not only do I believe that I am a physical thing I *feel* it: I can find within myself no tendency to regard myself as something non-physical, and it seems to me to be entirely natural to suppose that when something has touched my head or my hand or my foot it has touched *me*.

If Bloom's explanation of the universality of supernaturalistic belief is right, therefore, he is an atypical specimen of humanity in that he has no supernaturalistic beliefs. And I am an atypical specimen of someone who has supernaturalistic beliefs in that my supernaturalistic beliefs have atypical causes.

What I want to discuss in these comments is not whether Bloom's explanation of the universality of supernaturalistic belief is correct but, rather, what the implications of its being correct would be for the epistemological status of supernaturalistic belief. This is a question that Bloom has considered and which he takes very seriously. He correctly points out that no naturalistic explanation of the universality of supernaturalistic belief can *demonstrate* that there are no invisible, intangible agents or that human beings cease to exist when they die. Having said this, he goes on to say:

> While it is true that nothing from the empirical study of human psychology can *refute* [supernaturalistic] belief, certain theories can challenge the rationality of those who hold such beliefs...

> Suppose you meet someone who believes in intelligent life on Mars, and you discovered that she holds this belief based on wishful thinking—she believes in

6. I will admit that I find the argument from design to be a very interesting argument—particularly in the form that appeals to the apparent 'fine-tuning for life' of the parameters of the laws of physics. Interesting, but far from conclusive (like all philosophical arguments for substantive conclusions). And I would say that it has no more to do with my belief in the existence of God than the analogical argument for other minds (also a very interesting argument) has to do with my belief in the existence of my wife's inner mental states.

life on Mars because she wants this to be true. It would be pretty cool if there were Martians, she explains. There is no consensus among epistemologists as to the precise conditions that have to hold for a belief to be justified, but whatever these are, surely wishful thinking does not satisfy them. Wanting X to be true is a terrible reason to believe X to be true. While it is possible that there is intelligent life on Mars (that is, she could be right by accident), still, she is unreasonable in holding this belief, and you would be unreasonable if you found yourself persuaded by her.

As I read Bloom, he does not mean what he says in this passage to imply that if his own explanation of the universality of supernaturalistic belief is correct then such beliefs are based on wishful thinking. His thesis is rather that certain theses about the causes of someone's holding a belief can imply that that person is irrational in holding that belief—and 'because she wants this to be true' is put forward only as an indisputable example of such a thesis.

I assent to the spirit of this passage, but I have some pedantic quibbles about the letter. The target of my quibbles is the sentence 'Wanting X to be true is a terrible reason to believe X to be true.' It is not that I suppose that wanting X to be true *is* a good reason for believing X to be true; it is rather that it does not seem to me to be a reason at all. I shall try to explain. Let us call the irrational believer Alice. As the example is set up, wanting there to be Martians is the *cause of Alice's belief* that there are Martians, and not *Alice's reason for believing* that there are Martians. Alice's reason for believing that there are Martians is the reason she would give if you asked her 'Why do you think that there are Martians?' That question *could* be a request for the cause of her belief, but would naturally be taken as a request for a reason. And she did her best to provide a sincere and reflective answer to this question. As Bloom has set the example up, Alice's answer would not be 'Because I want there to be Martians' but, rather, 'Oh, it would be pretty cool if there were Martians.' That *is* a reason for believing that there are Martians—and a terrible one (so Bloom would say and so I would say and so anyone likely to be reading these words would say; Alice, of course, sees matters differently). Here is perhaps a more realistic example of someone who believes that there are Martians, whose belief is caused by his wanting there to be Martians, and who states his reason for that belief.[7] Alice's friend

---

7. More realistic, but 'it would be pretty cool if there were Martians' is a *possible* reason for believing in Martians. Consider the following exchange (from Evelyn Waugh's *Brideshead Revisited*):
'But my dear Sebastian, you can't seriously *believe* it all.'

Fred responds to the question 'Why do you think that there are Martians?' in these words: 'Oh, their existence is a scientific fact. I read about the Martians and their canals in a book by a famous astronomer.' (But the book was by Percival Lowell and was published in 1906. Because Fred wants to believe in Martians he simply ignores all other relevant evidence—and his reason for believing that there are Martians is thus a very bad one.)

In my view, Bloom should not have mentioned reasons at all. The point that he should have made, the point that is really relevant to the question of the relevance of his explanation of supernaturalistic belief to its rationality, has to do with causes, not reasons. And the point is this. It is at least very plausible to suppose that its having causes of certain kinds can render a belief irrational: if a person's belief is caused in certain ways, that fact about the causes of the belief *entails*—quite independently of the content of the belief—that that belief is irrational. If, for example, Alice believes that there are Martians because—*simply* because—she wants there to be Martians, it follows that her belief in Martians is irrational. This conditional statement may not be true (scrupulous epistemologists may want to qualify it in some way) but it will serve as an example of what I mean: it may be that among the causes that a belief may have, *some* are such that any belief that has those causes is perforce irrational—and wishful thinking is at the very least a strong candidate for a cause that has that undesirable property.[8]

Bloom has postulated certain causes for the fact that supernaturalistic belief is a human universal. Are *those* causes of the sort that render beliefs with those causes irrational? Put the question this way: Jane believes that there are invisible and intangible agents—non-human intelligences of great power—who sometimes interact with human beings. If she becomes convinced that Bloom has correctly explained the fact that belief in such agents is a human universal should she conclude that her belief in them is irrational—or that it is in any other way epistemologically dubious?

'Can't I?'
'I mean about Christmas and the star and the three kings and the ox and the ass.'
'Oh yes, I believe that. It's a lovely idea.'
'But you can't *believe* things because they're a lovely idea.'
'But I *do*. That's how I believe.'

8. But only some. All rational beliefs must have causes of some sort—for a belief that had *no* causes, a belief that popped into one's head 'out of the blue', would certainly be irrational even if it happened to be true. A rational belief must be one that has *causes of the right sort*. One of the central problems of epistemology is that of supplying some non-circular account of 'causes of the right sort'.

Let me make a couple of obvious but important points. If there are no supernatural (invisible, intangible) agents, then, to a near certainty, the fact that almost all human beings believe that such agents exist will have some naturalistic explanation or other (presumably an evolutionary one). If, on the other hand, there *are* supernatural agents, and if, at most times and in most places, they have interacted causally with human beings, that fact might well have a lot to do with the fact that belief in such agents was a human universal. If that were the case, this belief might be a human universal even if it had no evolutionary explanation—just as the fact that almost all human beings believe that there are birds has no evolutionary explanation.[9] But if there are supernatural agents it does not *follow* that the explanation of the fact that human beings believe in them has no evolutionary component. It might be, for example, that the local presence of one of these supernatural agents was a very hard thing for human beings to detect (they are, after all, invisible and intangible), and it might be that if human beings did not have some innate disposition to believe that there were supernatural agents they would never have interpreted anything they perceived as signaling the presence of such an agent.

Naturalistic explanations of supernaturalistic belief offered by naturalists like Professor Bloom (and they are not very often offered by anyone who is not a naturalist; see, e.g., Barrett 2004) tend to covey the implication that they are 'all the explanation there is'. But this implication is not logical. Any naturalistic explanation of any phenomenon[10] can be incorporated without logical contradiction into a 'larger', more comprehensive supernaturalistic explanation of that phenomenon.[11] A theist (or other 'supernaturalist')

9. Which is not to say that the human sensory apparatus, and the fact that human beings attend to things *like* birds have no evolutionary explanations. Put the point this way: if birds had somehow suddenly appeared all over the world *after* human beings had evolved into their present form all normal human beings would thereafter have believed that there were birds.

10. Unless it explicitly contains some such clause as 'and this is all the explanation there is; in particular, this phenomenon has no supernatural causes'. One might raise the question whether it is the business of a naturalistic explanation to go beyond nature in this way: whether it is allowable for a naturalistic explanation to do more than appeal only to natural causes; whether a naturalistic explanation can properly *deny* that the phenomenon it purports to explain has any supernaturalistic causes. This is no doubt a verbal question. But it does seem—and this is *not* a verbal point—that an explanation that contained such a clause would not be a (purely) *scientific* explanation, for it would have a metaphysical component. This is an elementary point, but, elementary though it is, it is consistently ignored by those who contend that the Darwinian account of evolution is logically incompatible with the thesis that a supernatural being is responsible for the apparent teleology exhibited by living organisms.

11. In this way if no other. Let N be any naturalistic explanation of some phenomenon P. Consider a timeless God contemplating (timelessly) the creation of a cosmos. Since he is omniscient, all

may therefore accept any naturalistic explanation of supernaturalistic belief (or of any other phenomenon) without logical contradiction.[12] But this point verges on the trivial, for avoiding logical contradiction is not all that impressive an epistemological achievement. Some naturalistic explanations of a fact or phenomenon *resist* being incorporated into a larger, more comprehensive supernaturalistic explanation. And this resistance is no less real for not being a matter of logic.

An example may be helpful. Suppose that a statue of the Virgin in an Italian church is observed to weep; or, at any rate, that is how it looks. It is eventually discovered, however, that the apparent tears are bat urine (it seems that some bats have made their home in the dim recesses of the church ceiling). This account of the tears is of course logically consistent with their having a partly supernaturalistic explanation (maybe God wanted the statue to appear to be weeping and He so guided the bats that they took up residence in just the right spot). Still, it *resists* being incorporated into a larger supernaturalistic explanation—it strongly suggests that there's 'nothing more to it' than ordinary causes and chance. (If Father Guido, the beloved rector of that church, is being considered for canonization, the Roman Catholic Church will certainly not let the 'tears' pass as a miracle that could be ascribed to God's special favor to Father Guido.) I cannot think of any very informative way to give a general account or definition of the concept this example is supposed to illustrate. I cannot provide a useful definition of 'resists being incorporated into a larger, more comprehensive supernaturalistic account'. The idea is simply that a naturalistic explanation of a phenomenon would have this feature if any possible attempt to incorporate it into a supernaturalistic account of that phenomenon would be regarded by any unbiased person (including those unbiased persons

possible distributions of matter and radiation in space–time are present to his mind. Consider the one among them that is displayed by the actual cosmos. God chooses that one and says, 'Let it be!' or 'Let there be a cosmos that consists of matter and radiation distributed in space time in *that* way!' And, by that act, a complete four-dimensional whole—from the Big Bang to, well, whatever—timelessly *is*. If the thesis 'N explains P' is true, and if N is a naturalistic explanation, the truth of 'N explains P' must have been established by this timeless act of creation: its truth must 'supervene' (as philosophers like to say) on the distribution of matter and radiation in space–time. If the truth or falsity of 'N explains P' does not supervene on—is not 'settled by'—the distribution of matter and radiation in space–time N is not an explanation that can properly be called 'naturalistic'. The right description of N in that case would be 'metaphysical explanation'.

12. As Bloom says, 'If there is an omnipotent God, then he could have orchestrated the universe so that belief in him could have emerged in any fashion whatsoever.'

who believe in the supernatural)[13] as unreasonable, contrived, artificial, or desperate. Although I cannot give any very informative explanation of this idea it seems to me to be a real and useful idea, and it seems to me that I have given a clear example of one case in which it applies. As Justice Potter Stewart said in another connection, 'I know it when I see it.'

The famous naturalistic accounts of religious belief that I have alluded to (those of Feuerbach, Marx, and Freud) are certainly over on that side: any of them would resist being incorporated into a larger, partly supernaturalistic account of religious belief. (In their entirety; in my view, significant parts of the Marxian and Freudian accounts of religious belief could be incorporated into larger, supernaturalistic accounts.)

Is Bloom's naturalistic explanation of the universality of supernaturalistic belief like that? Does it resist being incorporated into a larger, supernaturalistic account of the universality of supernaturalistic belief? It certainly doesn't seem to me to have that feature. (As Justice Stewart went on to say, 'And this isn't a case of it.') Suppose that God exists and wants supernaturalistic belief to be a human universal, and sees (he would see this, if it were true) that certain features that it would be useful for human beings to have—useful from an evolutionary point of view: conducive to survival and reproduction—would naturally have the consequence that supernaturalistic belief would in due course become a human universal. Why shouldn't he allow those features to be the cause of the thing he wants?—rather as the human designer of a vehicle might use the waste heat from its engine to keep its passengers warm.

There are two aspects of Bloom's chapter that might seem to suggest that it does 'resist incorporation'. One of them is certain of his incidental remarks and turns of phrase, remarks that reflect his belief that supernatural belief in fact does have a (purely) natural explanation. (For example, 'these are the seeds from which religion grows'.) But this aspect of the chapter does not represent any of the working content of his explanation of supernatural belief. A psychologist who was a religious believer (and hence not a metaphysical naturalist) might have presented the same theory without using language that suggested that all correct explanations of any phenomenon are purely naturalistic explanations.

13. That is, those believers in the supernatural who have no special reason to want the phenomenon in question to have a supernatural explanation. In the 'Father Guido' example, a staunch advocate of Father Guido's canonization would be 'biased', but a devout Roman Catholic who didn't care one way or the other whether Father Guido was ever declared a saint might well be 'unbiased'.

The other aspect of the chapter is this: its appeal to the concept of an evolutionary accident. If a theory represents a phenomenon as an 'evolutionary accident', does that not strongly suggest—if it does not logically imply—that, according to the theory, the phenomenon has only natural causes? I think the answer to this question is simply, No. For what does it mean to say that some universal or widespread feature of a species is an evolutionary accident? It means only that possession of that feature by members of the species does not increase the fitness of the organisms that have it, and that, therefore, its presence in the members of the species does not have a straightforward explanation in terms of natural selection. (But it may well have a non-straightforward explanation in terms of natural selection: it may be—metaphorically speaking—an unintended consequence of a complex of more-or-less unrelated features—'fitness friendly' features—exhibited by the species, features that do, individually, have straightforward explanations in terms of natural selection.) A feature of a species that is an 'evolutionary accident' in this sense could certainly be part of the Creator's plan for that species. I offer a simple proof-in-principle of this thesis, without meaning to imply that I endorse the particular theology of creation that it incorporates. Consider an omniscient Creator of the sort that figured as an example in note 12. This Creator decrees 'complete' distributions of matter and radiation in space–time. Many of the features of the four-dimensional cosmos such a Creator produces will be intended features of that cosmos (others, no doubt, will be 'don't cares'). If we knew that our world had such a Creator, and if we were convinced, on scientific grounds, of the correctness of the Darwinian theory of evolution, there would be no barrier, no barrier at all, to our supposing that many features of living organisms were both intended by the Creator and evolutionary accidents. (Any distribution of matter and radiation in space–time that is remotely similar to ours must contain organisms with features that are evolutionary accidents. In choosing one particular distribution our omniscient Creator chooses the evolutionary accidents 'along with everything else'. Many of the accidents he chooses are don't-cares, but many others are—we suppose—intended.)

It is important to realize that nothing I have said implies that (nothing I have said is addressed to the question whether) supernaturalistic belief *is* rational. There are all sorts of well-known and powerful arguments for the conclusion that belief in the supernatural is irrational. The best of these arguments are versions of or elaborations on this simple argument:

there is no evidence for the existence of any supernatural beings, and it is irrational to believe in the existence of things for which there is no evidence.[14] I have been addressing, rather, this question: is there anything about Professor Bloom's naturalistic explanation of supernaturalistic belief that would—if this explanation were correct and known to be correct—imply or strongly suggest that supernaturalistic belief is irrational or in any other way epistemologically defective? I have identified this question with the following question: is Bloom's explanation of the sort—and there are naturalistic explanations of this sort—that resist incorporation into some larger, more comprehensive supernaturalistic account of the universality of human belief in the supernatural? And I have suggested that Bloom's explanation is not of that sort, or at any rate that there is no evident reason to suppose that it is. Perhaps there are causes a belief can have that have the following property: a belief that had causes of those sorts would necessarily be irrational—irrational no matter what else was true of the believer's history and circumstances. Wishful thinking is certainly a plausible candidate for a cause with that property. I do not see that evolutionary causes of the kind Bloom has proposed are like that. If they indeed have that property they do not wear the fact that they have it on their sleeve: some non-trivial argument would be required to show that they had it.

14. For my thoughts on arguments of this sort, see my 'Is God an Unnecessary Hypothesis?' (Dole and Chignell 2005: 131–49).

7

Games Scientists Play

Alvin Plantinga

K arl Popper and Imre Lakatos speak of 'the game of science'; one of my fundamental questions in this chapter is whether scientists play one game or many different games. But this question is in the service of a larger question: what should Christians think of (how should Christians think about) sociobiology or evolutionary psychology? This is a problem because (a) Christians, I think, are committed to a high view of science, committed to taking it seriously and being utterly enthusiastic about it, (b) sociobiology and evolutionary psychology (EP) are or at least appear to be examples of science, and (c) there are apparent conflicts between many theories proposed in EP and Christian belief. In the larger piece of work of which this is a part I will try to answer that question.

I will argue first that there are apparent and, upon analysis, real conflicts between some of the theories proposed in evolutionary psychology and Christian belief. Then I will ask why these scientists propose theories that are incompatible with Christian belief. The answer, I think, has to do with 'methodological naturalism'. Philosophical naturalism *tout court* is the idea that there is no such person as God or anything or anyone at all like God. Methodological naturalism (MN), however, is a horse of a different color. MN is proposed as a constraint upon science: it is the claim that proper science, real science, as opposed to ersatz science—such as, for example, 'Creationism' or 'Intelligent Design'—must proceed *as if* philosophical naturalism were true. After distinguishing several forms of MN I will ask whether it is really true that MN is a constraint on science: is it really true that an alleged scientific project is *real* science, *genuine* science, only if it conforms to MN? I will argue that in fact there are many different scientific activities, many different games scientists play or could play; MN constrains some of these but not others. Now, suppose some of these games are such that when they are properly played the results are theories or claims in conflict with Christian belief—suppose, that is, that some genuine and legitimate scientific projects issue in theories incompatible with Christian belief: what attitude should Christians take to such projects and theories? Should they see here a defeater for the Christian beliefs incompatible with those theories or, more moderately, an intellectual problem, a source of cognitive dissonance? And, secondly, should they see here a faith–reason conflict? My answer to both questions is, No; and the reason has crucially to do with the fact that these scientific projects are indeed constrained by MN.

Evolutionary Psychology and Christian Belief

Even a cursory glance at the literature shows that many theories from this area of science seem, at least on first inspection, to be deeply problematic from a Christian perspective. For example, Rodney Stark (Stark and Finke 2000) has proposed a theory according to which religion is a kind of 'spandrel' of rational thought, an attempt to acquire non-existent goods—eternal life, a right relationship with God, salvation, remission of sins—by negotiating with non-existent supernatural beings.[1] The idea is that rational thought, that is, means–ends or cost–benefit thinking, comes to be in the usual evolutionary way. But having the capacity for such thought inevitably carries with it the capacity to pursue non-existent goals, like the pot of gold at the end of the rainbow, or the ones connected with religion. Taken neat, this theory is clearly incompatible with Christian belief, according to which at least some of the supernatural beings and some of the goods mentioned do indeed exist. David Sloan Wilson suggests that religion is essentially a means of social control employing or involving fictitious belief. Again, taken neat, this is incompatible with Christian belief. Michael Ruse and E. O. Wilson suggest that morality is, or rather our moral intuitions are, in Ruse's words, a trick played on us by our genes. A group with our moral intuitions will clearly do better, from the point of view of

---

1. As David Sloan Wilson (Wilson 2002: 52) puts it, '[For Stark] Religion is envisioned as an economic exchange between people and imagined supernatural agents for goods that are scarce (e.g., rain during a drought) or impossible (e.g., immortal life) to obtain in the real world.'

survival and reproduction, than groups that lack those intuitions.[2] What has been selected for, then, are people with a twofold belief on this head. First, they have the sense that there really is this objective obligation, this objective and categorical *ought* that holds, whatever you and others think or desire, whatever your goals or aims; and, second, they think that it involves, for example, something like the Golden Rule: treat others (or at least others in your group) as you yourself would like to be treated. Thus, we are inclined to think this is an objective and categorical requirement of morality. According to Ruse and Wilson, our thinking this is a trick played on us by our genes to get us to cooperate; in fact, there aren't any such objective requirements.

Still another example: Herbert Simon proposes that altruistic behavior— i.e., behavior that promotes the fitness of someone else at the expense of the altruist's own fitness—is to be explained at the individual level in terms of two mechanisms. First, there is unusual docility, so that the altruist—Mother Teresa, for example—is unusually disposed to believe what her society or group tells her. The second mechanism is limited rationality; because of this limited rationality she is unable to see that this sort of behavior is in conflict with her inclusive fitness or reproductive interests. ('Limited' certainly seems to be the right word.) From a Christian perspective, of course, this explanation is wildly off the mark.

Now, there are fascinating questions to ask here, and fascinating lines of thought to pursue. For example, consider the Stark proposal—the proposal that religion is a 'spandrel' of rational thought and is devoted to the pursuit of non-existent goods by way of negotiation with non-existent supernatural agents. This proposal is inconsistent with Christian thought or commitment just because it declares these goods and agents non-existent. But wouldn't there be another theory, perhaps just as good and even empirically equivalent to Stark's, that was non-committal on the existence or non-existence of these goods? And would one really want to say that it was part of *science* to declare these goods non-existent? So, delete the offending bit from Stark's theory and call it Stark minus: would Stark minus be inconsistent with Christian belief? Stark minus would be something like the claim that (a) religious belief is the pursuit of certain kinds of ends or goods—salvation, eternal life, and the like—by way of negotiating with alleged supernatural

---

2. There has been controversy about whether the notion of group selection is viable; for a spirited and convincing argument that it is, see Sober and Wilson 1998.

beings, and (b) that it arises as a kind of by-product or 'spandrel' of the evolution of the capacity for rational thought. Is *that* theory incompatible with Christian thought? Not obviously.[3]

Or, consider Wilson and Ruse minus, which is the theory that results from theirs when we delete the bit according to which there really is no such thing as objective moral obligation. The resulting theory says only that morality, belief in an objective obligation to treat others the way we would like to be treated, together with the resulting tendency to behave in accordance with this belief to at least some extent has become ubiquitous among human beings by way of group selection. Is that incompatible with Christian belief? Not obviously. Similarly, for Wilson minus, the theory that results from deleting the idea that the beliefs involved in religion are fictitious: it is the theory that religion arises, or at least becomes ubiquitous among human beings by way of group selection, because it is a useful form of social control that involves beliefs of a certain kind. Is this theory incompatible with Christian belief? Again, not obviously.

I want to look a bit further into this question of the compatibility of these theories from EP with Christian thought and belief. This question is not entirely straightforward: there are several ways in which EP theories could conflict with Christian belief. Some of these theories might not be explicitly inconsistent with Christian belief but inconsistent with Christian belief together with propositions that can't sensibly be rejected. Others might be formally consistent with Christian belief, but might still be massively improbable with respect to a set of beliefs or noetic structure more or less like that of most contemporary Christians, or most contemporary Christians in the Western world (and for that matter, most Christians in the non-Western world). Such Christians will typically believe some propositions F by way of faith, and other propositions R because they are (or are thought to be) deliverances of reason (including memory, perception, rational intuition, and so on). A given theory might not be improbable with respect to F and also not improbable with respect to R, but massively improbable with respect to F and R, and hence with respect to a noetic structure that contains both F and R. Such a theory might be so unlikely with respect to such a noetic structure that it wouldn't be a real candidate for belief. An example would be the theory that if human beings have come to be by way of natural selection winnowing

---

3. Indeed, in more recent work Stark seems to have moved to Stark minus, no longer insisting that the beliefs involved must be false.

genetic variability, then no rational human being knowingly sacrifices her reproductive prospects in favor of advancing someone else's welfare. This isn't incompatible with F, and also not incompatible with R. However, a Christian will think the consequent massively improbable, and might also be inclined to accept the antecedent. This theory, then, would be incompatible with the noetic structures of such Christians, even if not logically inconsistent with Christian belief as such. There are still other forms of conflict, as I will argue below.

In order to look into this question of conflict or compatibility, I want to examine one particular EP theory more carefully: David Sloan Wilson's theory of religion.[4] This theory is a so-called 'functional interpretation' of religion. Both terms deserve comment. First, Wilson explicitly says many times that his theory is an *interpretation* of religion. This is a bit surprising: one wouldn't think of Newton's Laws, for example, or Special Relativity as an interpretation of something or other. What is involved in the theory's being an interpretation? *Understanding* of one sort or another, presumably; the thought is that once you see religion as having the function ascribed to it in the theory, then you understand it, or understand it more deeply. You understand why there is such a thing as religion, why religions arise and persist, and what they are *for*—what their function or purpose is. In the particular case of Wilson's theory, the idea is that religions play an important role in group selection. 'Many features of religion, such as the nature of supernatural agents and their relationships with humans, can be explained as adaptations designed to enable human groups to function as adaptive units' (David Sloan Wilson 2002: 51). (So a crucial difference between his theory and that of Rodney Stark is that according to the latter religious belief isn't in fact an adaptation.) He aims to 'see if the detailed properties of Calvin's Church can be interpreted as adaptation to its environment' (David Sloan Wilson 2002: 91); and he summarizes his theory as follows:

> I claim that a knowledge of the details (of Calvin's Geneva) clearly supports a group-level functional interpretation of Calvinism. Calvinism is an interlocking system with a purpose: to unify and coordinate a population of people to achieve a common set of goals by collective action. The goals may be difficult to define precisely, but they certainly included what Durkheim referred to as secular utility—the basic goods and services that all people need and want, inside and outside of religion.
>
> (David Sloan Wilson 2002: 118)

4. To be found in Wilson 2002: 48. See also Hinde 1999: 553 ff.

So Calvinism is an interlocking system with a purpose: 'to unify and coordinate a population of people to achieve a common set of goals by collective action'. This sounds a bit as if he thinks of Calvinism as an intentional project or activity undertaken by people, all or some of whom undertake it in order to achieve a common set of goals, these goals at least including that secular utility. If this were what he means, he would be wrong: Calvin and the other Calvinists weren't (and aren't) embracing Calvinism in order to achieve some kind of secular utility. In fact it is doubtful that Calvinism, or Roman Catholicism, or Christianity, or for that matter Judaism or Islam are (wholly) intentional activities in that way at all. Are they human activities undertaken in order to achieve a goal? What is the purpose or aim of being a Calvinist? What is the purpose or aim of believing in God? Well, what is the purpose or aim of believing in other people, or believing that there has been a past? The right answer, one thinks, is that believing in God, like believing in the past or in other people, typically doesn't have any purpose or aim at all. It isn't that you believe in God or other people in order to achieve some end or other. You might as well ask me what my purpose or aim is in believing that I live in Indiana or that seven plus five equals twelve. These are intentional activities, of course, but they are not undertaken in order to achieve some end or other.

You might reply that there is more to Christianity in general and Calvinism in particular than holding beliefs. This is certainly true: there is also love of God and prayer and worship, for example. These are activities one intentionally undertakes. But, again, it is not clear that there is some *purpose* for the sake of which one undertakes to love God: you love God because he is attractive, such as to compel love. You pray because it seems the right thing to do, or because we are instructed to pray, and how to pray, by our Lord Jesus Christ. The same holds for worship. When worship is going properly it isn't something done in order to achieve some end outside itself: it is more spontaneous and immediate than that. (Of course, you *might* engage in worship to please your parents or spouse or children: but then in a case like that it *isn't* going properly.) This is a complex subject, and this is not the place to go into it. What is clear, however, is that there isn't any goal or purpose or end involved, typically, in accepting the central tenets of Calvinism or Christianity, and even if there is a purpose or goal or end involved in worship and prayer it most certainly is not the achievement of the secular goods Wilson mentions.

But, perhaps Wilson isn't really proposing that Calvinists engage in the practice of Calvinism in order to achieve certain goals. This practice has goals, all right, but they aren't the goals or purposes of the people engaged in the practice. It is rather that the aims or goals are provided, somehow, by evolution. And, of course, it isn't that these aims or goals are those of evolution, or natural selection; as Wilson is thinking of it, those processes don't really have any aims or goals and aren't really aiming at the actualization of some state of affairs. Still, the idea is that some of the structures and processes that result from natural selection do have purposes, purposes they acquire from their roles in maximizing fitness. The ultimate purpose of the heart, he presumably thinks, is to enhance or maximize fitness; its proximate purpose is to pump blood (and pump it in a certain way), and the idea is that it fulfills the former purpose by fulfilling that latter. The proximate purpose of the immune system is to overcome disease; this purpose is in the service of its ultimate purpose of maximizing fitness. Whether one can really speak of purpose and proper function for organs such as the heart or liver or brain absent a designer and outside the context of theism is of course a matter of dispute; I say you can't.[5] But this isn't the place to enter that discussion.

So, let's suppose that a heart or a liver, and also an activity like a religion, can have a purpose conferred upon it by natural selection, even if God is not orchestrating and guiding that process. The purpose of a religion says Wilson is, at least in the case of Calvinism, 'to unify and coordinate a population of people'. That isn't a purpose endorsed by those who practice the religion; still, he thinks, that is its purpose. Here it is instructive to compare Wilson's views on religion with those of that great master of suspicion, Sigmund Freud. On Freud's view, religion (and here we are thinking especially of theistic religions) is an illusion, in his technical sense. This sense is not such as to entail the falsehood of religious belief, although in fact Freud thinks there is no such person as God. Still, illusions have their uses and indeed their functions. The function or purpose of religious belief is really to enable believers to carry on in this cold and hostile or at any rate indifferent world in which we find ourselves. The idea is that theistic belief arises from a psychological mechanism Freud calls 'wish-fulfillment';[6] the wish in this case is father, not to the deed, but to the belief. Nature rises

---

5. See Plantinga 1993a: chap. 11.
6. And in such a way that it (or its deliverances) rather resembles Calvin's *sensus divinitatis* (see Freud 1955: 167 ff.).

up against us, cold, pitiless, implacable, blind to our needs and desires. She delivers hurt, fear, pain; and in the end she demands our death. Paralyzed and appalled, we invent (unconsciously, of course) a Father in heaven who exceeds our earthly fathers as much in power and knowledge as in goodness and benevolence. The alternative would be to sink into depression, stupor, paralysis; and finally death.

This illusion enables us to carry on and survive: perhaps we could put it by saying that it contributes to our fitness. Is this Freudian claim incompatible with Christian belief? Could I accept Christian belief and also accept Freud's explanation or account of it? Well, maybe. For it is at least possible that God gets us to be aware of him by way of a mechanism like wish-fulfillment. According to Augustine, 'Our hearts are restless till they rest in you, O God.' But then it might be that the way God induces awareness of himself in us is through a process of wish-fulfillment: we want so much to be in God's presence, we want so very much to feel his love, to know that we are loved by the first being of the universe, that we simply come to believe this. I don't say that is in fact the way things go; I say only that it is possible and not incompatible with Christian belief.

But there is more to Freud's account than just that we come to believe in God by way of wish-fulfillment. If that were all he thinks there would be no reason to call theistic belief an *illusion*. What more does Freud say here? The more he says, and that which makes Christian belief an illusion, is that wish-fulfillment isn't *reality oriented*, as we might say. We human beings display a large number of belief-producing processes or faculties or mechanisms. There is perception, memory, a priori intuition, credulity, induction, and much else. We ordinarily think these faculties or processes are aimed at the production of true belief: that is what they are for, and that is their purpose or function. There are some cognitive processes, however, that are not aimed at the production of true belief, but at some other desideratum. Someone may remember a painful experience as less painful than it actually was. According to John 16: 21, 'A woman giving birth to a child has pain because her time has come; but when her baby is born she forgets the anguish because of her joy that a child is born into the world.' You may continue to believe in your friend's honesty long after evidence and cool, objective judgment would have dictated a reluctant change of mind. I may believe that I will recover from a dread disease much more strongly than is warranted by the statistics of which I am aware. William James' climber in the Alps, faced with a life or death situation, believed more strongly than his evidence warranted that he could leap the crevasse.

In all of these cases, there is no cognitive dysfunction or failure to function properly; but the processes in question don't seem to have as their functions the production of true beliefs. Rather, they produce beliefs that are useful in the context in one way or another. And exactly this is the way things stand with Freud's explanation: an essential part of his account of theistic belief is that it is not produced by truth-aimed cognitive processes, but by a process with a different sort of function. At this point the Christian or any serious theist will disagree with him: the serious theist will think that God has created us in such a way that we come to know him; and the function of the cognitive processes, whatever they are, that produce belief in God in us is to provide us with true belief. So, even if she agrees with Freud that theistic belief arises from wish-fulfillment, she will think that this particular instance of wish-fulfillment is truth-aimed; it is God's way of getting us to see that he is in fact present and in fact cares for us. At this point she will have to disagree with Freud.

Something similar goes for Wilson. He holds that the purpose or function of Calvinism and Christianity generally is to enhance fitness; a group with a religion of that sort will do well in competition with groups without any such religion (or anything similar). And, specifically religious *belief* plays a particular role here. The role of such belief is not to reflect reality, he says, but to play a part in the production of what religion produces. As he says: 'our challenge is to interpret the concept of God and his relationship with people as an elaborate belief system designed to motivate the behaviors listed . . . ' In a very interesting passage he proposes that religious belief isn't reality oriented but, unlike Freud, goes on to defend it. The passage is worth quoting in full:

> In the first place, much religious belief is not detached from reality . . . Rather, it is intimately connected to reality by motivating behaviors that are adaptive in the real world—an awesome achievement when we appreciate the complexity that is required to become connected in this practical sense. It is true that many religious beliefs are false as literal description of the real world, but this merely forces us to recognize two forms of realism: a factual realism based on literal correspondence and a practical realism based on behavioral adaptiveness.
>
> In the second place, much religious belief does not represent a form of mental weakness but rather the healthy functioning of the biologically

and culturally well-adapted mind ... Adaptation is the gold standard against which rationality must be judged, along with all other forms of thought. Evolutionary biologists should be especially quick to grasp this point because they appreciate that the well-adapted mind is ultimately an organ of survival and reproduction ... factual realists detached from practical reality were not among our ancestors.

(David Sloan Wilson 2002: 228)

This account of religion, then, is like Freud's in that, like Freud, Wilson sees the cognitive processes that produce religious belief as not aimed at the production of true belief, but at belief that is adaptive by way of motivating those behaviors. Religious belief in general and Christian and Calvinistic belief in particular is produced by belief-producing processes that are aimed, not at the production of true belief, but at the production of belief that will motivate those adaptive behaviors. And here someone who accepts Christian belief will be forced to demur, just as with Freud. For, if Christian belief is in fact true as, naturally enough, the Christian will think, it will be produced in us by cognitive processes that God has designed with the end in view of enabling us to see the truth of 'the great things of the Gospel' (as Jonathan Edwards calls them). She will no doubt think that these processes essentially involve what Calvin calls 'the internal witness (or testimony) of the Holy Spirit' and what Aquinas calls 'the internal instigation of the Holy Spirit'. And, of course, these processes will then be truth-aimed: they are aimed at enabling us to form these true beliefs about what God has done and about the way of salvation. So there is indeed a conflict between Wilson's theory of religion and Christian belief.

Why Do Scientists Come Up with Theories that Conflict with Christian Belief?

Wilson's theory of religion, as I have argued, is incompatible with Christian belief. But of course that is nothing special or exceptional about Wilson's theory: the same can be said for a wide variety of theories in evolutionary psychology: theories of religion, but also theories of morality and altruism. Why is it that scientists come up with such theories? Why do they come up with theories that are incompatible with Christian belief? Why do they come up with theories according to which the goods Christians seek are non-existent, or the beliefs they hold are fictitious or are deceptions foisted upon us by our genes? Why do they come up with theories according to which religious belief is not produced by truth-aimed cognitive processes? Have they discovered, somehow, that Christian belief is in fact false? Well, no; but then why? The short answer, I think, is that this feature of their scientific activity is connected, in one way or another, with the *methodological naturalism* (MN) that characterizes science and, indeed, according to many, *necessarily* characterizes science.

I don't have the space here to outline the various varieties of methodological naturalism. But, first, MN is not to be confused with philosophical or ontological naturalism, according to which there is no such person as God or anything at all like God; there is no supernatural realm at all. The methodological naturalist does not necessarily subscribe to ontological naturalism. MN is a proposed condition or constraint on proper science, not a statement about the nature of the universe. (Of course, if philosophical naturalism were true, then MN would presumably be the sensible way to proceed in science.) The rough and basic idea of MN, I think, is that science should be done *as if*, in some sense, ontological naturalism were true. Of course, this rough and basic idea can be developed in various ways; and those who endorse MN do not typically go into much detail. For our purposes, I will characterize MN as follows. First, following van Fraassen, we note that for any scientific theory there is its data set, or data model; roughly speaking we can think of this as the data that are to be explained by the theory in question. The data must be presented or stated in terms of certain parameters or categories. And, according to MN, the data model of a proper scientific theory will not refer to God or other supernatural agents, or employ what one knows or thinks one knows by way of revelation. Thus, the data model of a proper theory would not include, for example, propositions entailing that someone was suffering from demon possession. Secondly, there will also be constraints on the theory itself, although the theory can properly employ categories or parameters not permitted the data model. But, according to MN, the parameters are not to include reference to God or any other supernatural agents; and the theory, like the data set, also cannot employ what one knows or thinks one knows by way of revelation. Still further, there will presumably be a constraint on the body of background knowledge or belief with respect to which the initial plausibility or probability of a proposed scientific theory is to be estimated. That background information, presumably, will not contain propositions obviously entailing[7] the existence of God (or other supernatural beings); nor will it include propositions one knows or thinks one knows by way of revelation. Hence, rejecting a theory like Herbert Simon's theory of altruism because it is massively improbable with respect to a body of background information, including the existence of God, or Christian belief more generally, would presumably not be proper science—not, at least, if proper science involves methodological naturalism.

Interesting further questions arise here—does the relevant body of background information not only lack propositions obviously entailing the existence of God and other supernatural beings, but also include propositions entailing the non-existence of God? This would fit in well with such theories as Stark's and Ruse's, mentioned earlier, where the theory includes a part entailing the falsehood of Christian belief. If the relevant background information includes the non-existence of supernatural beings, then, relative to that background information, a theory like Stark minus or Ruse minus will be just equivalent to Stark or Ruse *simpliciter*.[8] On the other hand, while it is clear that, according to MN, no proper scientific theory can obviously entail the existence of God, can a proper scientific theory, according to MN, obviously entail the denial of the existence of God or other supernatural beings? Or is the idea that science just isn't to say anything one way or the other about God and other supernatural beings?

Games Scientists Play

These questions cry out for investigation; for now, they shall have to cry unheeded. I want to turn instead to investigating this question: what really is the relationship between MN and science? Many people claim that MN is essential to science, part of the very nature of the scientific enterprise. The idea is that science necessarily involves MN, whether weak or strong;

---

7. 'Obviously': if, as many theists have thought, God is a necessary being, the proposition that there is such a person as God is necessarily true and thus entailed by every proposition.

8. These two versions of the constraint laid on background information are reflected in historical biblical criticism in scripture scholarship by the distinction between Troeltschian scripture scholarship, where one assumes that no miracles occur and God never acts in history, and Duhemian scripture scholarship, where one simply brackets both beliefs to the effect that God acts in the world and miracles do occur and the denials of these beliefs. See my Plantinga 2000: 390 ff.

MN is a constraint on science, and a theory that doesn't conform to it isn't science, whatever its virtues. Is this correct? If so, how does it work? EP, being scientific at least by aspiration, proposes naturalistic theories and accounts of human behavior and enterprises. That is what in some way accounts for its proposing theories incompatible with Christian belief. But is it really true that MN is essential to science? How would one tell? Ask the president of the American Association for the Advancement of Science? Take a poll among scientists? That seems wrong, but then what would be the right way to tell?

Now, MN is not, of course, the only constraint that has been suggested as essential to science. In an early and important statement Francis Bacon declares that explanation by way of teleology or final causes plays no role in proper science:

> Although the most general principles in nature ought to be held merely positive, as they are discovered, and cannot with truth be referred to a cause, nevertheless the human understanding being unable to rest still seeks something prior in the order of nature. And then it is that in struggling toward that which is further off it falls back upon that which is nearer at hand, namely, on final causes, which have a relation clearly to the nature of man rather than to the nature of the universe; and from this source have strangely defiled philosophy.[9]

Much more recently, Jacques Monod concurs: 'the cornerstone of the scientific method is the postulate that nature is objective . . . In other words, the *systematic* denial that 'true' knowledge can be got by interpreting nature in terms of final causes . . . ' (Monod 1971: 21).

Many other constraints on the nature of science, or its proper practice, have been proposed: science cannot involve moral judgments, or value judgments more generally; the aim of science is explanation (whether or not this is put in the service of truth); science does not merely describe, but asks questions of nature; science asks *precise* questions of nature (of those officially on the rolls, what proportion responded to the questionnaire with 'yes'?); scientific theories must in some sense be empirically verifiable and/or falsifiable (although it is difficult *in excelsis* to say what either consists in); scientific experiments must be replicable; science cannot deal with the subjective, but only with what is public and shareable (and thus reports of consciousness are a better subject for scientific study than consciousness

9. Quoted Kass 1985: 250.

itself, which may tempt people like Daniel Dennett to claim that there really isn't any such thing as consciousness, but only reports). Richard Dawkins and Daniel Dennett say that the aim of biology is the explanation of the complex (i.e., living things) in terms of the simple (i.e., the sorts of things dealt with in contemporary physics.) Some say that good scientific theories don't propose singularities. Some say the aim of science is the attempt to discover and describe natural laws; others, equally enthusiastic about science, think there aren't any natural laws to describe. According to Richard Otte and John Mackie, the aim of science is either to propose accounts of how the world *ordinarily* goes, or to give theories that are empirically adequate *for the most part*, apart from miracles, etc.; others reject that 'for the most part'. How does one tell which, if any, of these proposed constraints actually do hold for science? And why should we think that MN really does constrain proper science?

Michael Ruse and Nancey Murphy answer this question by declaring that it is simply *true by definition* that science involves methodological naturalism. According to Murphy, 'there is what we might call *methodological atheism*, which is by definition common to all natural science' (Murphy 2001: 464). She continues: 'this is simply the principle that scientific explanations are to be in terms of natural (not supernatural) entities and processes' (her term 'methodological atheism', therefore, is close to my term 'methodological naturalism'). Similarly, for Michael Ruse:

> Furthermore, even if Scientific Creationism were totally successful in making its case as science, it would not yield a *scientific* explanation of origins. Rather, at most, it could prove that science shows that there can be *no* scientific explanation of origins. The Creationists believe that the world started miraculously. But miracles lie outside of science, which by definition deals only with the natural, the repeatable, that which is governed by law.
>
> (Ruse 1982: 322, emphasis added)

So Murphy and Ruse think MN is true by definition—by definition of the term 'science', one supposes. Thus, Ruse apparently holds there is a correct definition of 'science' such that from the definition it follows that science deals only with what is natural, repeatable, and governed by law. I have argued elsewhere (Plantinga 1995) that this cannot possibly be right. According to Ruse, science by definition deals only with the repeatable: if it turns out that the Big Bang isn't repeatable, does it follow that it cannot be studied scientifically? And, consider his claim that science, by definition, deals only with that which is governed by law—natural law, one supposes. Bas van Fraassen has offered an extended and powerful argument for the conclusion that there *aren't* any natural laws: if he is right, would it follow that there is nothing at all for science to study?

What is most puzzling about this claim, however, is that it is hard *in excelsis* to see how one could hope to settle a disputed claim by declaring that one of the disputants is wrong just by definition. The realist claims that the aim of science is the discovery of the truth about the world and the provision of true theories; the constructive empiricist instead holds that its aim is the proposal of empirically adequate theories. Suppose the former declares that his position is just true by definition. Does he really mean to suggest that the dispute can be settled just by looking up the term 'science' in the dictionary, even a very large dictionary? On the other hand, if the realist is just proposing his *own* definition—the definition of 'science' as it occurs in *his* idiolect—there is no reason for him or others to think this will be of more than autobiographical interest. Why should the anti-realist—or anyone else, for that matter—care how the realist uses that term? If I use the term 'Democrat' to mean 'creature of darkness', should Democrats everywhere hang their heads in shame? And of course the same goes for MN. Here too we cannot just look up the answer in the dictionary. While no doubt there are uses of the term 'science' with respect to which MN is indeed true, there are plenty of other uses of the term with respect to which it is not. Set aside the broader sense (if there is one) of the English word 'science' that corresponds to the German 'Wissenschaft' and the Dutch 'Wetenshap', the sense in which Aquinas argues that theology is a science (even if not the queen). In the narrower English sense, Newton, for example, no doubt used the term 'science' in such a way that his hypotheses involving divine adjustment of the planetary orbits counted as scientific. Something similar, presumably, went for the authors of the Bridgewater Treatises. The same goes for those contemporaries who, like Michael Behe (1996), propose scientific inference from 'irreducible complexity' to 'Intelligent Design'. So this argument by definition doesn't seem a promising way to discover whether MN really is or is not a constraint on science. How then do we tell whether a proposed constraint on science really is a constraint on science?

Here it may be useful to investigate more closely a long-standing and currently lively dispute between scientific realists: those who see the aim of science as the pursuit and production of *true* theories, and scientific anti-realists. Anti-realists with respect to universals believe that universals do not exist; anti-realists with respect to science believe not that science does not exist but that its aim is not the production of true theories. Instrumentalists, for example, think a good scientific theory is *useful* in one way or another, and need not be true or even true-or-false to be useful. A particularly sophisticated and well-developed anti-realism is Bas van Fraassen's *constructive empiricism* (van Fraassen 1980; van Fraassen 1989) according to which science aims at the production of *empirically adequate* theories. Such theories are adequate to all of experience: past, present, and future; whether they are also *true* is not (from the perspective of science itself) important; a theory need not be true to be good. To accept a scientific hypothesis, furthermore, is not to believe it is true, but to claim instead that it is empirically adequate; it is also to 'live in the world' of the theory. But what exactly *is* it to say that the aim of science is thus and so? Van Fraassen compares this question to the question 'what is the aim of chess?' The answer, he says, is that the aim of chess is to checkmate one's opponent. This is to be distinguished from one's motive or reasons for engaging in the activity—you might play the game because you want fame or fortune, or to demonstrate your remarkable intellectual powers, or to please your grandson; still, the aim of the game, even as you play it, is not fame or fortune or pleasing your grandson, but to checkmate your opponent. Of course, things don't stand, here, quite the same for chess and science: there are plenty of books containing a statement of the official rules for chess, but where will you find the official rules for playing the game of science?

Van Fraassen notes that *criteria of success* are at the least intimately related to the aim of science. An intentional human activity of this sort is at least partly defined in terms of its criterion of success. The same would go, presumably, for religion(?), art, politics, war, education, philosophy, architecture, cookery, and other intentional human activities. And perhaps this helps a little. But, again, how do we determine when we have a *successful* piece of science? More exactly, what is it that makes a given bit of science successful, what is it that distinguishes a successful piece of *science* from some other, perhaps closely related activity? A scientist *d'un certain age* is likely to write a book that is really philosophy, often in that book denouncing philosophy (see, e.g., Weinberg 1992; Fodor 1998: 167). Writing such books is presumably not science and not part of what scientists do as scientists; but, again, what makes the difference? Many scientists (e.g., Dawkins, Simpson, Gould, etc.) declare that modern evolutionary theory shows that human beings are not designed; are these declarations part of science? Do they make them in their capacity as scientists? The suggestion about the criterion of success doesn't really help as much as one would like: someone who thought these declarations were part of science would of course think of them as conforming to the criterion of success.

But think a bit further about the criterion of success. I once complained to the then director of the Stanford Linear Accelerator that I wasn't able to make sense of quantum mechanics. He told me that he couldn't make sense of it either, that in fact no one could really make sense of it (that there wasn't a sensible interpretation of its formalism). That didn't matter, he said; what mattered was that it was useful and extremely well confirmed. This strongly suggests that, as he saw the matter, the criterion of success for science isn't truth or even intelligibility (of some so far unspecified kind); instead it is something much more like empirical adequacy or at any rate usefulness. Consider, on the other hand, theories in biology, perhaps theories that explain the large bones found in various parts of the earth as the bones of dinosaurs. Here, one guesses, empirical adequacy would not be considered sufficient; here the aim would be to propose *true* theories as to how it is that there are these bones.

Van Fraassen argues that we cannot determine whether the aim of science is the construction of true theories (as opposed to theories that are empirically adequate and may be true or false) just by asking scientists whether *they* aim at true theories or only at empirically adequate theories. What the aim of science is, he says, depends in *some* way on what scientists and others aim at and believe, but not in any simple way. This seems right; but what about asking them, not what *their own* aims are, but what they think the aim of *science* is, in an effort to discover what the 'conscious understanding' of scientists (all or most) is with respect to this question of the aim of science? This too won't work, he says. First of all it is a little unimaginative:

> Let me suggest at least some more delicate probing as a little sociological experiment. Approach some scientists you know and mention some of their most valued scientific colleagues. Then tell them (taking the liberties of such empirical psychology) that as a matter of fact those colleagues are not pursuing the aim of finding true theories, but are privately concerned only to construct empirically adequate ones. Now ask them whether, with this new information in hand, they still regard those men and women as real scientists?

> (van Fraassen 1994: 187)

Here, I suspect, we would encounter different answers depending on the science in question. Ask this question of someone working at string theory or some other highly theoretical parts of contemporary physics, and you would probably get the reply that this aim of their colleagues doesn't preclude their being real scientists. Ask it, however, of someone trying to discover how the population of caymans in the Amazon basin has responded to the encroachment of civilization over the last fifty years, or whether the population of 'touconderos' has been constant over the last twenty years, and you might get a very different response. ('Haven't you got anything better to do than ask silly questions?—why don't you go bother someone else?') This suggests that there may be several different aspects or parts of science, some with one aim and some with another. Better, it suggests, that there are several different activities that go under the name 'science'; these activities are related to each other by similarity and analogy. Perhaps the concept of science is one of those cluster concepts called to our attention by Thomas Aquinas and Ludwig Wittgenstein.

Indeed, doesn't this seem pretty obvious? Suppose van Fraassen is right: what distinguishes a given human intentional activity from others is its criterion of success. But then clearly there are many different activities, projects, enterprises, lurking in this neighborhood. From one perspective, this is trivially true: scientists studying the impact of deforestation on caymans will be engaged in a project the criterion of success of which involves reference to caymans; not so for those asking the same question about 'touconderos'. Of course, there are other activities in which both groups are engaged: studying the impact of deforestation on one or another form of wildlife, for example. So there are groups of activities that are hierarchically arranged. Of course, it doesn't follow that for just any pair of such activities a and b there is another activity engaged in by anyone who engages in either a or b, just as it is not the case that for just any games a and b there is a (different) game engaged in by anyone who plays either a or b.

There is clearly a project the criterion of success for which involves producing true theories; there is clearly another where the criterion of success involves producing theories that are empirically adequate, whether or not they are also true. So there are at least two activities here. The question separating the constructive empiricist from the realist is the question, 'which of these two activities is science?' The realist asserts the former and the constructive empiricist the latter. Of course, a presupposition of the dispute is that science is just *one* project, or enterprise, or activity. This seems to be what van Fraassen thinks:

> Those scientists with their very different motives and convictions participate in a common enterprise, defined by its own internal criteria of success, and this success is their common aim 'inside' this cluster of diverging personal aim. How else could they be said to be collaborating in a common enterprise? The question is only what that defining criterion of success is.

So the assumption is that all these scientists are engaging in a common activity; this activity is such that its aim is either the provision of true theories or the provision of empirically adequate theories (i.e., its criterion of success is either the one or the other); and the question before the house is just what the criterion of success actually is.

But is this assumption obvious, or even true? Perhaps there are at least two different enterprises, two intimately related but different enterprises. Perhaps some people engage in the one and some in the other. Perhaps there is a difference across individuals within a given science; perhaps there is also a difference across different sciences. Further, perhaps both of these activities are properly called 'science'. We have several different possibilities here. First, it may be that there is just one activity in the relevant neighborhood: science, whose aim is either what the Constructive Empiricist says or what the Realist says (but not both): one activity with disagreement about what its aim really is. Second, it may be that science encompasses both: there is a single game or activity, science, which can be played by playing either of these others, as with poker: stud poker and draw poker. Third, there may be no single game here: there are two separate games, the realist game and the constructive empiricist game; these games are analogically related (as with chess and checkers, perhaps) but distinct; there is no game which is the union of these two; but both fall under the extension of the term 'science' and the concept of science. Still a fourth possibility is that the term 'science' is multiply ambiguous. And I suppose there is still a fifth possible suggestion here—namely, that there isn't any answer to this question and no fact of the matter as to which of the proposed suggestions is in fact true.

Which of these suggestions is correct? And how would we tell? Is the question which is correct itself a scientific question? If not, is it a *factual* question? Well, let us assume that the question here really is a factual question: it *looks* as if there ought to be a fact of the matter about this, even if it also looks hard to see what the fact of the matter is. And let us also assume without argument that the term is not multiply ambiguous. Which of the three remaining possibilities seems most plausible? It is not easy to mount strong or convincing arguments here. Van Fraassen's assumption, however—that there is just one aim for science—seems to me relatively unlikely, and for two reasons. Among both realists and constructive empiricists there are people of enviable accomplishment and profound acquaintance with science, people of great ability who have spent their entire lives studying and thinking about science. Is it likely that some of these people could be just wrong about the aim of the activity in which they are engaged, or about which they have been thinking for these many years? I should think not. The second reason is this: it is extremely hard to mount negative arguments here. For example, it is extremely hard to mount an argument for the conclusion that an enterprise where you aim at empirical adequacy, rather than truth, is not really science; but it is equally hard to mount an argument for the conclusion that an enterprise where you seek truth, rather than just empirical adequacy, is not science. It seems that one is initially inclined to call 'science' any activity that is (1) a systematic and disciplined enterprise aimed at finding out truth about our world[10] and that (2) has significant empirical involvement. Any activity that meets these vague conditions will initially count as science.

But then what about all those proposed constraints? I suggest that the following is the best way to think about the matter. There are a large number of analogically related enterprises, all satisfying (1) and (2). For each of the proposed constraints, there is an activity falling under the concept of science the aim of which is in fact characterized by that constraint; and for each or at any rate many of the proposed constraints there is another activity falling under the concept of science the aim of which does not fall under that constraint. Further, when people propose that a given constraint pertains to science just as such, to all of science, so to speak, they are ordinarily really endorsing or recommending one or more of the activities the aim of which is characterized by that constraint. So when someone declares that the aim of science is to produce true theories (not just empirically adequate theories) he is most charitably understood as endorsing scientific activities whose aim is in fact the production of

---

10. But what about the constructive empiricist and the instrumentalist? Well, at any rate they are aiming at true predictions, or theories that make true predictions, even if not at true theories.

true theories. He is recommending those activities, suggesting that in some way they are superior to the alternatives. And one who claims instead that the aim of science is the provision of empirically adequate theories is best understood as endorsing scientific activities whose aim is in fact the provision of such theories. Neither, I suggest, is charitably thought of as insisting that every scientific activity is constrained in the manner in question.

Now, how does this work out with Methodological Naturalism? Well, there are *some* scientific activities that are indeed constrained by MN, so that a person whose activity is not constrained by MN would not be engaged in those activities at all. This would be the element of truth in the claims of Ruse and Murphy to the effect that it is true by definition that science is constrained by MN. What is true by something like definition is that certain scientific enterprises currently carried out are in fact characterized by MN, and characterized by it in such a fashion that you cannot engage in them without conforming to MN. But of course there are other scientific activities that are not so constrained. So, for example, a theory according to which God periodically adjusts the orbits of the planets, or has created life specially, or has intelligently designed certain features of the natural world would or could fall under that general concept of science, but not under any of the cluster of scientific activities or enterprises characterized by MN. And those who insist that MN really does characterize science *tout court* are best understood as recommending or endorsing enterprises characterized by MN as superior, in some way, to those activities not so characterized.

Defeaters for Christian Belief?

We must now return to our target question: given that 'Simonian' science is indeed successful science, and given that it is incompatible with Christian belief, and given the esteem in which the Christian holds science, how should Christians think about such science? Should it induce intellectual disquiet, for Christians—a sort of cognitive dissonance? To put things less metaphorically, does the fact that Simonian science comes to conclusions incompatible with certain Christian beliefs—does that fact give Christians a defeater for those beliefs? I am substantially out of time, but the answer, in a word, is 'No'. To see why, we need the notion of an evidence base.

My evidence base is the set of beliefs to which I appeal to in conducting an inquiry. Suppose I am a detective investigating a murder. Someone floats the hypothesis that 'the butler did it'; I happen to know that the butler was in Cleveland, 300 miles away at the time of the murder. I will then reject this hypothesis. Alternatively, I may know that the butler is seventy years old and was a mile from the scene of the crime six minutes before the time of the crime, with no automobile, bicycle, horse, or other means of transportation in addition to his own two feet. I also know that only a very small proportion of seventy-year-old men can run a mile in six minutes. Then I won't simply rule out the hypothesis that the butler did it, but I will assign it (initially, at any rate) a low probability.

Of course, there is much more to say about evidence bases, but no time now to say it. And the next thing to see is that MN is really a constraint on the evidence bases involved in those scientific enterprises it characterizes. Now, Simonian science is characterized by MN—of either the strong or the weak sort. Suppose it is the strong sort. Then the relevant point is that the evidence base of the inquiry in question includes the denial of central Christian (and indeed) theistic beliefs. But then of course the fact that this inquiry comes to conclusions incompatible with Christian belief would be neither surprising nor an occasion for consternation or dismay. It would certainly not constitute a defeater for Christian belief.

So, suppose, on the other hand, that what is involved in Simonian science is weak MN. Then the important thing to see is that the evidence base of Simonian science is only a part, a subset, of the Christian believer's evidence base. That latter includes the beliefs to be found in the evidence base of Simonian science, but it also includes more. It includes belief in God and belief in Jonathan Edwards' 'great things of the Gospel'. And that means that Simonian science need not provide the Christian theist with a defeater for those of her beliefs incompatible with Simonian science. For what the success of Simonian science really shows is something like this: that with respect to its evidential base its conclusions are probable, or sensible, or approvable as science or as good science. What it shows with respect to the Christian's evidential base, therefore, is that from the perspective of *part* of that evidential base the Simonian conclusions are probable, or sensible, or approvable. That is, with respect to part of her evidential base some of her beliefs are improbable. But that need not give her a defeater for those beliefs. For it can easily happen that I come to see that one of my beliefs is unlikely with respect to part of my evidence base, without thereby incurring a defeater for that belief. You tell me you saw me at the mall yesterday; I remember that I wasn't there at all, but spent the entire afternoon in my office, thinking about evolutionary psychology. Then, with respect to part of my epistemic base—a part that includes your telling me that you saw me at the mall—it is unlikely that I was in my office all afternoon; but that fact doesn't give me a defeater for my belief that that is where I was. My knowledge of your telling me that you saw me at the mall doesn't constitute a defeater for my belief that I wasn't there.

Another example: imagine a group of whimsical physicists who try to see how much of physics would be left if we refused to employ, in the development of physics, anything we know by way of memory. Perhaps something could be done along these lines, but it would be a poor, paltry, truncated, trifling thing. Suppose, further, that General Relativity turned out to be dubious and unlikely from this point of view. And now consider physicists who do physics from the usual scientific epistemic base, and furthermore believe the results: would they get a defeater for General Relativity upon learning that it was unlikely from the perspective of truncated physics? Surely not; they would note, as a reasonably interesting fact, that there was indeed a conflict: the best way to think about the subject-matter of physics from the standpoint of the *truncated* epistemic base is incompatible with the best way to think about that subject-matter from the perspective of the *whole* scientific epistemic base. But, of course, they take the perspective of the scientific epistemic base to be normative here; it is the right perspective from which to look at the matter. As a result, their knowledge of the way things look from that truncated base doesn't give them a defeater for the beliefs appropriate with respect to the whole scientific base.

I submit that something similar goes for Simonian science and the Christian epistemic base. For the Christian, Simonian science is like truncated physics. Concede that from the point of view of the evidence base of Simonian science, constrained as it is by methodological naturalism, Simonian science is indeed the way to go (and, of course, perhaps it isn't). This need not give the Christian a defeater for those of her beliefs incompatible with Simonian science; for the evidence base of the latter is only part of the Christian's evidence base.

But isn't this just a recipe for intellectual irresponsibility, for hanging on to beliefs in the teeth of the evidence? Cannot a Christian always say something like this, no matter what proposed defeater presents itself? 'Perhaps B (the proposed defeatee) is improbable or unlikely with respect to part of what I believe', she says, 'but it is certainly not improbable with respect to the totality of what I believe, that totality including, of course, B itself.' No, of course not; if that were proper procedure every putative defeater could be turned aside in this way and defeat would be impossible. But defeat is not impossible; it sometimes happens that I *do* acquire a defeater for a belief B I hold, by learning that B is improbable on some proper subset of my evidence base. According to Isaiah 41: 9 God says 'I took you from the ends of the earth, from its farthest corners I called you. I said, "You are my servant"; I have chosen you and have not rejected you.' One who believes R, the proposition that the earth is a rectangular solid with ends and corners, on the basis of this text, will have a defeater for these beliefs when confronted with the scientific evidence— photographs of the earth from space, for example—against them. At any rate, she will have a defeater for R if the rest of her noetic structure is at all like ours. The same goes for someone who holds pre-Copernican beliefs on the basis of such a text as 'the earth stands fast; it shall not be moved' (Ps. 104: 5); the same also goes for someone who believes on the basis of the Genesis account that the earth or the universe is only 10,000 years old or so. But then what is the difference? Why is there a defeater in these cases, but not in the case of Simonian science? How is it that you get a defeater in some cases of this sort but not in others? What makes the difference?

To sharpen the question a bit, we must ask what sort of defeat is relevant here. Defeaters can be variously divided and classified; one important distinction is that between rationality defeaters and warrant defeaters. Very roughly speaking, a rationality defeater for a belief B is a belief D such that, given my noetic structure, my total set of beliefs, desires, and the like, when I come to hold D, I can no longer rationally continue to hold B. To advert to a classical Chisholmian example, I look into a field, see what looks like a sheep, and form the belief 'there is a sheep in this field'. You, whom I know to be the shepherd and a trustworthy man, come along and tell me that there aren't any sheep in that field, although you own a dog that from this distance looks like a sheep. I then have a defeater for my belief that there is a sheep there. Of course, defeat is relative to noetic structure; if I happen, oddly enough, to believe that I and I alone know that dogs are really sheep in disguise, then I won't have a defeater here. But those of us who don't believe this or anything relevantly similar will acquire a defeater for the belief that there is a sheep there; and, if I continued to hold that belief, it will be by way of some kind of cognitive defect, some failure of proper function.

Rationality defeaters must be distinguished from warrant defeaters, circumstances that result in my belief's failing to have warrant in a state of affairs in which it would otherwise have it. Another classic example, this one to illustrate warrant defeat: I am driving through southern Wisconsin, see what looks like and in fact is a barn, and form the belief 'Now that is a fine barn!' In an effort to mask their poverty, however, the natives have erected a large number—four times the number of real barns—of barn facades: fake barns that look just like the real thing from the highway. As it happens, I am looking at a real barn. Nevertheless, my belief that it *is* a barn lacks warrant; it is only by virtue of the sheerest good luck that I form this belief with respect to a real barn. There is no failure of proper function here; nothing in the situation suggests that I am not carrying on in a perfectly rational fashion in forming that belief. But clearly enough the belief, though true, has little warrant for me; at any rate it doesn't have enough to constitute knowledge.

All rationality defeaters are warrant defeaters; the converse, of course, doesn't hold. A rationality defeater, furthermore, will be a belief; a warrant defeater need not be, but will ordinarily be just some feature of the environment, as in the barn case above. One need not be aware of warrant defeaters, and in the typical case of warrant defeaters that are not also rationality defeaters, one is not aware of them; a rationality defeater, however, is ordinarily a belief of which one is in fact aware. Finally, if you come to know about a situation that constitutes a warrant defeater for a belief you hold, then you typically have a rationality defeater for that belief.

Our question has been this: given my respect for science, does my knowledge of the success of Simonian science constitute a defeater for those of my Christian beliefs with which some conclusion of Simonian science is in conflict? Here, pretty clearly, it is rationality defeaters that are relevant.[11] I have claimed that I do not get a defeater here, although I would get a defeater if I believed R, that the earth is a rectangular solid, on the basis of that text from Isaiah and were presented with photographs of the earth from space. What makes the difference? Here is an unhelpful answer: the one case conforms to the definition of rationality defeat, and

11. That is because we are stipulating that I am aware of the success of Simonian science and its conflict with some Christian belief B. If I weren't aware of both, however, it could be that my belief B would be subject to a warrant defeater that wasn't also a rationality defeater.

the other one doesn't. In the case of Simonian science, I learn that such science comes to conclusions inconsistent with Christian belief, and I also believe that Simonian science is good science; nevertheless I can rationally continue to hold Christian beliefs (although of course I can't also accept those conclusions of Simonian science inconsistent with them). But I can't rationally continue to believe R, once I see those photographs and realize that in fact they are photographs.[12] That is the difference.

But that may leave you a bit dissatisfied. Is there anything further that can be said? *Why* is there a defeater in the one case and not in the other? Well, perhaps we could proceed along the following lines. Consider some Christian belief B incompatible with Simonian science—for example, the belief that Mother Teresa was perfectly rational in behaving in that altruistic manner. The question is whether the addition of A, the belief that Simonian science is successful science (and that it contains the denial of B), is a defeater for B. We have added A to my evidential base EB_{me}; and now the right question, perhaps, is this: is B epistemically improbable or unlikely with respect to that new evidential base? If it is, perhaps we have a defeater; if not, not. Of course, B might initially be a member of EB_{me}, in which case it will certainly not be improbable with respect to it. But if that were sufficient for A not being a defeater of P, no member of the evidential base could ever be defeated by a new discovery; and that cannot be right. So, let us delete B from EB_{me}. Call the result of deleting B from my evidential base 'EB_{me} reduced with respect to B'— 'EB_{me}-B', for short. The idea—call it 'the reduction test for defeat'—is that A is a defeater for B just if B is relatively improbable—epistemically improbable—with respect to EB_{me}-B.

Of course, it won't work to delete only B from EB_{me}—we must also delete conjunctions that include B—for example, the conjunction of B with two plus one equals three. We must also delete all the beliefs in EB_{me} that entail B—for example, beliefs of the sort *(If R then B) and R*. Still further, we shall also have to deal with pairs of beliefs that entail B, since it might be that I hold a pair of beliefs that together entail B but do not happen to believe their conjunction. (Maybe I have never thought of them

12. Of course, there is still the relativity of defeat to noetic structure; there are some noetic structures with respect to which those beliefs would not be a defeater for the belief that R. (For example, I might believe, for some reason, that space is pervaded by an aether-like substance that causes photographs of cubical objects to appear spherical, or I might believe that the camera in question had the unusual property of photographing cubes in such a way that they look like spheres.)

together.) Should we delete one member of each such pair? But here we run into a problem: in general, there will be no unique way of following this procedure, and different ways of following it can yield significantly different results. So let us resort to the vague way out (vagueness is all the rage these days): let us say that EB_{me}-B is any subset of EB_{me} that does not entail B and is otherwise maximally similar to EB_{me}. Now, could we say the following: could we say that I have a defeater for B if and only if B is epistemically unlikely with respect to EB_{me}-B, i.e., if and only if A and B satisfy the reduction test for defeat?

Well, this test gives the right result in the present cases. First, consider our question about Simonian science and Christian belief. Recall that B is the proposition that Mother Teresa was perfectly rational in behaving in that altruistic fashion. B, we are assuming, is incompatible with Simonian science. To apply the proposed criterion, we must ask whether B is improbable (henceforth I will suppress the 'epistemically') with respect to EB_{me}-B—where, of course, EB_{me}-B includes A, the proposition that Simonian science is successful science. The answer, I should think, is that B is not improbable with respect to EB_{me}-B. For that body of beliefs includes the empirical evidence, whatever exactly it is, appealed to by the Simonian, but also the proposition that we human beings have been created by God and created in his image, along with the rest of the main lines of the Christian story. But, with respect to *that* body of propositions, it is not likely that if Mother Teresa had been more rational, smarter, she would have acted so as to increase her reproductive fitness rather than live altruistically. But then the proposed defeatee—namely, that Mother Teresa was perfectly rational living as she did—is not improbable on that evidential basis. Hence, on the proposed reduction test, the fact that Simonian science is more likely than not with respect to the scientific evidential base does not give the Christian theist a defeater for what she thinks about Mother Teresa.

Now, compare the case of the person who first believes the earth is a rectangular solid on the basis of the biblical verse I mentioned above, and then acquires the evidence, including photographs, that the earth is spherical. Consider her new evidential base reduced with respect to the proposed defeatee—i.e., the proposition that the earth has corners. With respect to this reduced evidential base, the proposition that the earth has no corners is very likely. For that reduced evidential base contains or includes all of our reasons for supposing that in fact the earth doesn't have corners. And what does it include on the other side, i.e., what does it include by way of support for the belief that the earth has corners? Only what would be, presumably, the rather tentative thought that in the passage in question God was intending to teach us that the earth has corners. But, clearly there are other perfectly plausible ways of construing that passage. On balance, therefore, she will conclude that in fact that is not what the passage in question is intended to teach. Hence, in this case, unlike the case of Simonian science, the reduced evidential base provides evidence, indeed powerful evidence, against the proposed defeatee, and the proposed defeatee is improbable with respect to the reduced evidential base.

So, the reduction test gives the right result in the present case. But it cannot be right in general. Perhaps, indeed, it states a necessary condition of rationality defeat: perhaps, wherever I get a defeater for a belief B by way of acquiring a new belief A, B will be relatively improbable with respect to EB_{me}-B. But this condition is nowhere nearly sufficient for defeat. And the reason is of the first importance. For it might be, clearly enough, that B has a lot of warrant on its own, warrant it doesn't get from the other members of EB_{me} or indeed any other propositions; B may be *basic* with respect to warrant. But then the fact that it is unlikely with respect to EB_{me}-B doesn't show for a moment that the belief is not perfectly rational.

Consider an example: the police haul me in, accusing me of slashing the tires of your car again. At the police station I learn that the department chairman, a man of impeccable probity, claims to have seen me in the parking lot, lurking around your car at the time (yesterday mid-afternoon) the crime occurred; I am also known to resent you (in part because of your article in the department newsletter claiming that in church I slyly withdraw money from the collection plate under the guise of contributing). I had means, motive, and opportunity; furthermore there have been other such sordid episodes in my past; the evidence against me convinces everyone in the department (except the post-moderns). However, *I* recall very clearly spending the entire afternoon skiing in Love Creek County Park. My belief that I was skiing there then is not based on argument or inference from other propositions. (I do not note, for example, that I feel a little tired, that my ski boots are damp, and that there is a map of Love Creek in my parka pocket, concluding that the best explanation of these phenomena is that I was skiing there.)

So, consider EB_{me}-P, my evidential base diminished with respect to P, the proposition that I did not slash your tires. With respect to EB_{me}-P, P is epistemically improbable; after all, I have the same evidence as everyone else for not-P, and everyone else is quite properly (if mistakenly) convinced that I did slash your tires. Still, I certainly do not have a defeater, here, for my belief that I did not do it. And the reason, of course, is that P has for me a source of warrant independent of the rest of my beliefs: I *remember* it. In a case like this, whether I have a defeater for the belief P in question will depend, on the one hand, upon the strength of the intrinsic warrant enjoyed by P, and, on the other, the strength of the evidence against P from EB_{me}-P. Very often the intrinsic warrant will be the stronger (husband, in flagrante delicto, to wife: 'who are you going to believe—me or your lying eyes?'). But it is not automatically the case, of course, that the intrinsic warrant of P overcomes the evidence from EB_{me}-P; if the latter is strong enough I may have to conclude that the source of the apparent warrant of P is deceiving me. In the case of the slashed tires, for example, perhaps the department chairman, assorted grad students, and the chaired professor most distinguished for probity and judiciousness unite in declaring that they *saw* me slash those tires. In that case I will have to conclude that my memory has let me down; perhaps I have repressed memory of the whole unpleasant episode.

By way of conclusion: a serious Christian is committed to a high view of science: science is important, and is a manifestation of the image of God in us human beings. A fair number of theories and proposals from evolutionary psychology (David Sloan Wilson, E. O. Wilson, Herbert Simon, and others) are incompatible with Christian belief. Call such science 'Simonian' and suppose that it is or will become *good* science: does it follow that Christians have a defeater for those beliefs of theirs incompatible with such science? I answer that it does not. That is because Simonian science is constrained by Methodological Naturalism; but then the relevant scientific evidence base is only a proper subset of the Christian's evidence base. This means that Simonian science constitutes a defeater for Christian belief only if (but not if) they satisfy the Reduction Test for Defeat; but they do not.

8

Scientific Explanations of Religion and the Justification of Religious Belief

Michael J. Murray

Over the last decade psychologists, anthropologists, and evolutionary theorists have put forward a variety of models aimed at giving an empirically grounded if not testable scientific explanation of religion (see Dennett 2006; Barrett 2004; David Sloan Wilson 2002; Boyer 2001b). These explanations, drawing on resources from a variety of disciplines, aim to explain how human minds, with particular cognitive structures and arising through particular evolutionary trajectories, are drawn to religious beliefs and practices across times and cultures. Psychological explanations of belief formation (even religious belief formation) are not new. What is also not new is the claim that scientific explanations of religious belief serve in some way to undermine the justification for those beliefs. Sometimes, defenders of these scientific explanations are quite clear about these purported implications—and here Freud comes to mind as perhaps the most famous example, illustrated by the title (and the contents) of his discussion of religion in *Future of an Illusion*. However, most contemporary defenders of cognitive and evolutionary models of religious belief have been more cautious—or, at least, subtle—than Freud. Although Daniel Dennett, Pascal Boyer, Scott Atran, David Sloan Wilson, and others are not willing to come right out and say that these explanations pull the justificatory rug out from under the religious believer, they surely imply it. By giving sections of his book subtitles like 'Explaining Airy Nothing' Boyer, for example, is sending a message that is clear and not exactly subtle.

Less subtle still are folks like Paul Bloom who, in a recent *Atlantic Monthly* article entitled 'Is God an Accident?' (Bloom 2005), argues that religious belief is 'an incidental by-product of cognitive functioning gone awry', and Jesse Bering who (while perhaps merely grandstanding) is quoted as saying that with such research 'We've got God by the throat and I'm not going to stop until one of us is dead.'[1] For Bering, the deliverances of evolutionary psychology are 'not going to remain in the privileged chapels of scientists and other scholars. It is going to dry up even the most verdant suburban landscapes, and leave spiritual leaders with their tongues out, dying for a drop of faith.'[2]

Are Bloom and Bering right? Do these models show that religious beliefs, to turn a phrase of E. O. Wilson and Michael Ruse, are nothing but 'a trick fobbed off on us by our genes?' Our first reaction to such a question should be: well, if they do, it is not clear how. These models, if correct, show *not one thing more* than that we have certain mental tools (perhaps, selected, or, perhaps, 'spandrels') which under certain conditions give rise to beliefs in the existence of entities which tend to rally religious commitments. But, pointing that out does nothing, all by itself, to tell us about whether those beliefs are *justified* or not. After all, we have mental tools which, under certain conditions, give rise to belief in the existence of palm trees and electrons. We do not regard those belief-forming mechanisms as unreliable nor (typically) the beliefs formed as unjustified. Let us be clear then: the mere fact that we have beliefs that spring from mental tools selected for by natural selection is, all by itself, totally irrelevant to the justification of beliefs that spring from them. So, what is it about religious beliefs, formed by the working of various psychological mechanisms and honed by natural selection, that makes us think that religious beliefs are epistemically suspect? This chapter considers the four most interesting arguments that might be offered for this claim.

Argument 1: Religious Beliefs are Unjustified Because they Spring from a Mechanism Known to Produce Many False Positives

Argument 1 can be developed as follows:

1. *Broward–Palm Beach New Times*, 9 Mar. 2006.   2. Ibid.

On the most widely endorsed cognitive psychological account of the origins of religious belief, those beliefs are spawned—or at least nurtured—into existence by a mental tool often described as a 'hypersensitive agency detection device' or HADD. HADD is triggered by various environmental stimuli including apparently purposeful motions (dots moving on a screen), configurations of matter (crop circles), or physical processes (dark clothes flapping in the breeze at twilight) with no apparent natural or agentive cause. When triggered, HADD spawns belief in unseen agents that are taken to be the causes of the motions, configurations, or processes. Evolutionary theorists hypothesize that such a mental tool would be adaptive since it would lead our ancestors to be especially sensitive to cues that might signal a predator. Furthermore, it would be adaptive for HADD to err on the side of excessive false positives since the cost of these would, for obvious reasons, be much greater than the cost of any false negatives. And indeed it does err in this way, thus explaining our tendency immediately to assume that bumps in the night are caused by some*one*.

In light of the fact that HADD is hyperactive in this way, it generates many false positives and is thus unreliable. Of course, beliefs that are outputs of a mechanism known to be unreliable are unjustified, at least unless those beliefs have some sort of independent evidence supporting their truth. Thus, religious beliefs, spawned by HADD and not supported by independent evidence (and that covers the religious beliefs embraced by most folks) should be rejected as unreasonable or unjustified.

While this argument might be modified into a formidable objection, in this form it falls short of the mark. For the argument to succeed, two additional claims would need defending. First, we would need a defense of the claim that HADD indeed plays an important role in the formation of those beliefs. If HADD were rarely or minimally involved in the formation of religious belief its tendency toward unreliability (if such there be) might not have any serious impact on the justification of religious belief on the whole. Unfortunately for the defender of this argument, advocates of evolutionary and cognitive psychological explanations of religion firmly disagree over the importance of HADD in explaining religious belief. Justin Barrett (2004), Stewart Guthrie (1993), and Daniel Dennett (2006) hold that HADD plays an important role while others, such as Pascal Boyer (2001b), argue that its role is minimal. For Boyer, other cognitive tools carry the greatest share of the load in explaining the origin and contours of religious belief while HADD, when involved at all, only tends to raise our confidence that religious agents act in our environment. If

Boyer is right, even if HADD is typically unreliable, that fact would be insufficient for us to conclude that religious beliefs too are unreliable and so unjustified.

More problematically, for the argument to succeed the critic of religious belief would have to show, second, that HADD is unreliable specifically in the contexts in which religious beliefs are formed. HADD might be unreliable when I hear creaking noises in the abandoned house down the block, but might be quite reliable when I hear a whistled tune in the hall. Is HADD more like the former or the latter when it comes to religious belief? Merely asking the question makes it plain that the reliability of HADD can only be assessed with reference to the contexts in which it is activated. This is no surprise since similar assessments are required in the cases of other belief-forming mechanisms as well. My visual system is generally reliable in helping me form beliefs about my physical environment... except in low light conditions, or when it comes to things that are very distant or small, or when I have taken LSD, or... Similarly, HADD is quite reliable as a belief-forming mechanism in some conditions and not in others.

Perhaps in those cases where HADD generates beliefs in agents entirely on its own it is susceptible to a percentage of false positives that renders it unreliable and the beliefs generated by it unjustified. But HADD often functions in conjunction with other cognitive tools; indeed, it is these other cognitive tools that allow us to assess the relevant evidence further, and to determine that HADD sometimes causes error. The important question, then, is: is HADD highly liable to error when, operating in conjunction with other belief-forming mechanisms, it generates or supports beliefs in or about agents? Initially it seems that in such contexts HADD is, in fact, often *reliable*. When you hear footsteps in the hall outside your room, or a knock on the door, or what appears to be the sound of a bouncing ball in the apartment above you, you form beliefs in unseen agents, and you are right. Of course, it is open to the critic to claim that the contexts in which beliefs in supernatural or religious agents are formed are significantly different from the contexts in which beliefs in these more mundane agents are formed. But this is a claim that would have to be argued for. And it is hard to see how such an argument would go without simply begging the question against the religious believer.

Argument 2: Religious Beliefs are Unjustified Because they are Produced by Mechanisms that Generate Mutually Exclusive Beliefs

This second argument goes as follows:

> Whatever cognitive tools are involved in spawning religious belief, one thing is clear: the beliefs spawned are obviously mutually incompatible. Any cognitive tools which give rise to mutually incompatible beliefs in this way are obviously unreliable, and any beliefs arising from them would then have to be taken to be unjustified (at least absent some sort of independent evidence of their truth). As a result, religious beliefs arising from these tools cannot be reasonably accepted absent independent justification.

One aspect of this argument is obviously correct: religious beliefs across times and cultures are in large measure mutually inconsistent. But, for this argument to succeed it would have to presume something that is just as obviously false—namely, that the mental tools identified by cognitive scientists give rise to these inconsistent beliefs *all on their own*. When environmental conditions stimulate the various mental tools that are taken to be involved in religious cognition—HADD, Theory of Mind, memorability and transmissibility via minimal counter-intuitiveness, etc.—the outputs of these tools are still highly non-specific. HADD tells me there is 'an agent'; my beliefs about what sorts of fauna inhabit these parts lead me to conclude that the agent is a bear or a tiger or the bogeyman. If you conclude that it is a bear and I conclude that it is the bogeyman this does not show *HADD* to be unreliable, it shows that my mom was wrong about the bogeyman. Likewise, no one doubts that divergent cultural traditions play an enormous role in giving religious concepts their specific contours. If the mutually exclusive aspects of these beliefs creep in from cultural sources this does nothing to undermine the reliability of these cognitive tools, it just shows that the cultural traditions are false.

Here an analogy would be helpful. Contagion avoidance is a well-defined and adaptive cognitive tool that leads us to have aversive beliefs about and feelings toward waste products, corpses, rotting food, and so on. In so far as the contagion avoidance tool is involved in generating beliefs, it does so only by inducing us to believe that the object in question has *some feature or other* which should compel us to avoid it. On its own, it does nothing to specify what that feature *is*. So, when those who form these aversive beliefs/desires about corpses are asked to explain or justify them, the justifications will be widely divergent. Some might say that the corpses are potential sources of pathogenic infection; others fear possession by the soul of the deceased, and so on. Many of these explanations will be incompatible with one another, but none of that speaks to the reliability of the contagion avoidance tool. That tool is simply a mechanism that shapes a part of the belief—the part that indicates that there is a threat worthy of avoiding here. Thus, as far as the contagion avoidance tool goes, it functions reliably.

What this shows is that for this second argument to succeed one would need to show that the mutually incompatible aspects of these beliefs arise from the workings of the cognitive tools, and not the accretions or specifications that are introduced through cultural influences. It seems unlikely that this is the case.

Argument 3: Religious Beliefs are Unjustified Because, if these Accounts are Right, the Beliefs do not have the Proper Relationship to the Object of the Belief

When I have heard scientists trying to articulate an argument for the unjustifiability of religious belief from the cognitive psychology of religion the argument most commonly offered goes something like this:

> Cognitive psychological accounts of religion can account for the origin of religious belief in a way that makes no reference to and requires no causal connection with supernatural reality. However, properly justified belief requires that the target of the belief be causally connected to the belief itself in certain ways. Since these accounts show us that none of those ways is in fact in play in the origins of religious belief, beliefs so generated are unjustified.

Scientists offering this argument are making some philosophical assumptions which need to be made explicit before we can go on to assess the argument. Philosophers who are concerned about questions of the justification of belief fall into two basic categories: internalists and externalists. Internalists argue that whether or not a belief is justified depends entirely on facts 'inside the head' (for example, facts about the extent to which the belief is properly supported by sensory states or other beliefs one has). Externalists argue that justification depends on whether or not the belief has the right relation to facts in the external world. For some, the right relation consists only in reliability (does the belief-forming mechanism typically succeed in 'getting things right'?) while for others the right relation will require that there be certain causal connections between the external world and the belief formed. I point this out only to make it clear that even if these psychological accounts do show that there is no direct causal connection between religious beliefs and their target only some epistemological theories would take that to be relevant to the justification of those beliefs. Exernalists will think that the unreliability of beliefs formed in this way— unreliability revealed by the mutually incompatible outputs—shows us that religious beliefs must be unjustified. Internalists, on the other hand, will be content to hold that beliefs formed in this way might still be justified since nothing about the beliefs 'in the head' of the religious believer conflict or fail to cohere in ways that would undermine those beliefs.[3] As a result, these accounts of the origins of religious belief will raise concerns about justification primarily for externalists.

So should externalists conclude, if evolutionary accounts of religious belief are right, that those beliefs are unjustified? To answer this question we need to understand exactly what is supposed to be problematic, by the externalist's lights, about beliefs formed in this way. It is this: in cases like this our having the belief is *entirely independent of whether or not the belief is true*. When this is the case, the justification of the belief is undermined. We can illustrate the problem as follows. Imagine that I am sitting in the psychology lab, staring at my hand, and I have a belief that my hand is in front of my face. Little do I know that on the other side of the wall behind me a researcher is pointing a device in my direction that emits radiation of a sort that causes subjects both to go blind and to have a belief that there is a hand in front of their face. *The device* is in fact the cause of my belief. In this case, then, though my belief might be *true*, it would be unjustified since *even if there were no hand there* I would still believe that there was. That is a problem, since, when beliefs are caused by such processes, we have no reason to think that the process is getting things right (or not).

One might think that if this is sufficient to undermine the justification of the hand-belief, then religious belief is in trouble—at least if the evolutionary or cognitive psychological accounts of it are correct. After all, those accounts seem to show that purely natural forces, acting in purely natural fashion, generated minds which, through purely natural stimuli, generate (purely natural) religious belief. And if that is right, then religious belief

---

3. Of course, were the religious believer to come to believe or know that the religious beliefs of others spring from a similar mechanism and none the less generate conflicting outputs, that additional belief might render one's religious beliefs unjustified.

would, it seems, exist *whether or not there is any supernatural reality*. It seems that the cases are perfectly analogous.

That line of reasoning just elucidated is right if and only if the following claim is true:

> (1) Whether or not there is a God (or other supernatural reality), human minds, honed by such-and-such evolutionary mechanisms, would exist and would hold religious beliefs.

If (1) is true, religious beliefs are as unjustified as the radiation-induced hand-belief (again, on the assumption that I am not in possession of independent evidence for the truth of the belief). So, the key question now becomes: is (1) true?

I don't think so. I, for example, don't think there would be a universe if there were no God. I don't think the universe would be fine-tuned for life if there were no God. And I don't think there would be any actual life, believers, human beings, or religion either if there were no God. I might be wrong of course. But let us remember that it is the person arguing against religious belief that bears the burden of defending (1). Good luck to them. I have no idea how one would argue for its truth aside from arguing that I am wrong on the claims noted in this paragraph.

However, some scientist critics of religious belief would likely not be satisfied with this response. For them, the argument can be extended in a way that goes something like this:

> The above response is the sort of response one would expect to get from a theist who thinks that God orchestrated the creation of the universe, the origin of life, the emergence of humanity, human minds, and religion, all through various evolutionary mechanisms. The alternative would be to hold that the explanations of all of these things could be given in entirely natural- istic terms. The theist seems to think that there are no grounds for picking between the positions and thus no way of coming to favor the naturalists' stance. As a result, we have no better reason for thinking that religious beliefs arise in entirely natural ways (as affirmed by (1)), than we do for thinking that religious belief is a put-up job orchestrated by God. But that's not right. We *do* have reason to favor the naturalist explanation, and the reason is: it is more parsimonious! Thus, while it is possible that the supernaturalist/theist is right, it is more reasonable to assume that the naturalist is right.

The argument aims to press the superiority of the naturalist explanation on grounds of simplicity. But while simplicity is a scientific virtue, it is (only) a *ceteris paribus* virtue. And all other things are rarely equal. When we choose between competing hypotheses, we also need to take into account the other virtues of the competitors as well as (or perhaps we should say, including) the extent to which the hypotheses cohere with our overarching view of the world. To borrow a famous philosophical example, it is, all other things being equal, simpler to assume that there are no other minds but my own (and that the appearance that other things have minds is just an illusion) than it is to accept that there are many minds. But we don't accept the 'one mind' over the 'many mind' hypothesis because such a hypothesis doesn't cohere with many other things to which we are committed. Both the Christian and the naturalist are reasonably committed to the reality of 'other minds'. The Christian might be committed to the idea that all humans have minds because all humans are created in the image of God. The naturalist/physicalist might be committed to the idea that all humans have minds for other reasons, perhaps a belief that things that are physically alike are alike in other respects (including mental ones) and thus that all humans (like me) have minds. In either case, other considerations override considerations of parsimony when it comes to choosing between the one mind and the many mind hypotheses.

How does this affect the argument above? The answer is this: the theist might say that the belief that God is the remote cause of supernatural beliefs fits in quite well with other reasons they have for thinking that religious belief is true (for example, that without a God many things just don't make sense: the existence of objective morality, the fact that there is something rather than nothing, the fact that the universe is fine-tuned for life, and so on). For them, the theistic explanation of these facts would be more reasonable even if not simpler. Of course, for the naturalist, things might be different. However, all of this shows simply that psychological explanations of belief of the sort we have been considering cannot—just on their own— undermine the justification of religious belief.

Argument 4: Religious Beliefs are Unjustified Because the Mechanism that Produced them was not Properly Subject to the Winnowing Power of Natural Selection

Some might be inclined to argue that we can only regard belief-forming mechanisms as reliable when they are subject to the right sort of winnowing by natural selection. This argument would go as follows:

While some belief-forming mechanisms honed by natural selection can be supposed to be reliable, others cannot. The ones that can are those that produce beliefs 'visible' to natural selection—beliefs about the physical world generated by the operation of the senses, for example. If my visual system produces beliefs that are largely incorrect, natural selection will catch up with me. Because of this, I can have some confidence that my visual systems are reliable. But supernatural beliefs generated by HADD and other cognitive tools are not subject to the winnowing power of natural selection in this way. If these cognitive tools were to mislead us systematically about the nature of supernatural reality, natural selection would do nothing to cure us of these illusions (except under certain highly unusual circumstances—think Jim Jones and the People's Temple). As a result, we have no reason to think that their reliability would have been similarly honed. We ought thus to regard religious belief so spawned to be unreliable.

A number of scientists seem attracted to this line of reasoning.[4] This argument displays three fundamental flaws. The first flaw is simply that many of our non-religious basic beliefs just don't have the sort of connection to fitness that our imaginary critic claims. Consider our belief in the reality of the external world. If our belief in the reality of the external world was, after all, false (because, say, it was caused in us by Descartes's evil deceiver), would there be anything to intrude into our illusion and 'winnow it'? There is no reason to think so. If our belief in other minds turned out to be errant, would there be any fitness costs involved that would 'winnow it'? It doesn't seem so.

Second, it assumes that natural selection can indeed winnow reliable from unreliable belief-forming mechanisms. Unfortunately, there is no reason to think this. The only way that natural selection can winnow these belief-forming mechanisms is by winnowing the behaviors that they produce. Behaviors, in our case, arise from the interplay of beliefs *and desires*. Because of this, false beliefs can be as adaptive as true beliefs *as long as they are paired with affective systems that, together with the false beliefs, give rise to adaptive behaviors like feeding, fleeing, fighting, and reproducing.* Since false beliefs can be as adaptive as true ones there is no reason to think that natural selection will select for reliable belief-forming mechanisms and against unreliable ones.

What is the upshot? It is that if the only force for honing our belief-forming mechanisms is natural selection we have no reason to think that any of our belief-forming mechanisms are reliable when it comes to truth.

4. Atran offers something like this (2002a: 182–3) as does Wilson in his contribution in this volume.

But things are indeed worse than we have been pretending here. If our imaginary critic's account is right there is positive reason to think that these mechanisms spun from natural selection are downright *unreliable*. If natural selection is blind to the alethic (i.e., truth-conducive) reliability of belief-forming mechanisms, it would be an incredible stroke of luck if the adaptive mechanisms we have are *also* reliable alethically. The low probability thus gives us reason to think that we have lost the alethic lottery. As a result, our critic's claim that only belief-forming mechanisms that are honed by natural selection can be taken to be reliable is entirely unsupported.

The third flaw is that even if our imaginary scientist is right about the role evolutionary pressures play in giving us true beliefs about our environment there is no reason to think that evolutionary pressures would lead us to false beliefs concerning religious reality. We can see this by hypothesizing that theism is true, and that God created the world in such a way that biological complexity and diversity evolved in much the way evolutionary scientists believe it did. The theist might then look on these evolutionary accounts as providing us with a description of the way in which God configured evolutionary history to make belief in supernatural reality easy or natural for us. If the theist is right about this—that is, if that is the way things really are—then our coming to believe that there is supernatural reality is something that leads us to true belief (and it does so precisely because those beliefs are true). God, on this view, set up the natural conditions so that, *pace* the objection, natural selection *does* select for reliable religious belief-forming mechanisms.

9

Evolutionary Accounts of Religion: Explaining and Explaining Away

Michael J. Murray and Andrew Goldberg

Explaining Religion: What Sort of Explaining?

In his first-century BCE work *De Natura Deorum* the Roman philosopher Cicero recounts the explanation offered by Epicurus for the fact that 'nature has imprinted an idea of [the gods] in the minds of all mankind'. His explanation was one that was at one level 'naturalistic' and at another level 'theological'. He described it this way:

> As infinite kinds of almost identical images arise continually from the innumerable atoms and flow out to us from the gods, so we should take the keenest pleasure in turning and bending our mind and reason to grasp these images, in order to understand the nature of these blessed and eternal beings.
>
> (Cicero 1986: 87, 90)

The explanation is naturalistic in virtue of appealing to a natural sequence of causes that, it is claimed, generate the belief. Yet Cicero sees no conflict in yoking theological explanations to natural ones, arguing that the natural process of atomic bombardment occurs for the sake of allowing human beings to take pleasure in their understanding of the gods.

While a number of naturalistic explanations of religious belief have been offered in the intervening centuries (Freud and Marx providing perhaps the two best-known examples), the most recent, and controversial, explanations have come from the domains of evolutionary and cognitive psychology.

Unlike Cicero's account, these contemporary psychological accounts have a great deal of empirical evidence in their favor. Furthermore, and again unlike Cicero, psychologists offering these explanations commonly claim (but rarely argue) that these accounts of religion render any possible parallel theological explanation false or at least unwarranted. The task of this chapter is to summarize some of these accounts, point out some of their weaknesses as scientific accounts of religion, and consider just how much of religion such explanations can explain away.

Boiled down to a single slogan, the Darwinian theory of evolution contends that characteristics evolve because they help the organisms that have them survive, reproduce, and increase the frequency of their genes in subsequent generations. Once one grasps the theory it can easily become a parlor game to hypothesize about how many of the characteristics we see in organisms might be accounted for in Darwinian terms. Zebras run quickly because doing so allows them to avoid predators; great white sharks detect aquatic electrical discharges because it helps them find prey; and so on. Yet, even Darwin recognized that some characteristics of organisms seem to defy such explanations. The peacock's tail seems to render it gratuitously vulnerable to predators. How could such a characteristic persist? In addition to puzzling morphological traits like peacock coloration, a number of (heritable) organismic behaviors can be identified which likewise seem to detract from an organism's fitness. Honey bees sacrifice their lives by stinging intruders that strike the hive, for example. Darwin himself puzzled over the anomalous nature of such traits and behaviors, and he proposed a variety of supplementary explanations for them—explanations aimed at showing their consistency with his overarching theory.

Over the last decade or so a number of evolutionary psychologists have turned their attention to another form of behavior (and accompanying belief) that is common among human beings and that initially seems at least as intractable from an evolutionary perspective as peacock coloration and kamikaze honey bees once did: religious belief and behavior. Religion is, it seems, a Darwinian anomaly. On the one hand, religion is so pervasive across times and cultures that it appears to be a fixed feature of human culture. And yet, on the other hand, religion also apparently involves human beings believing 'nearly incoherent falsehoods' that in turn spawn behaviors, i.e., religious practices, with extraordinarily high fitness costs. In this way, religious behavior appears eminently maladaptive. Evolutionary psychologist Scott Atran describes what we might call the evolutionary 'problem of religion' as follows: 'Religion is materially expensive and unrelentingly counterfactual and even counterintuitive. Religious practice is costly in terms of material sacrifice (at least one's prayer time), emotional expenditure (inciting fears and hopes), and cognitive effort (maintaining both factual and counterintuitive networks of beliefs)' (2002a: 6). A number of theorists have thus turned their attention toward explaining the evolutionary problem of religion.

Before we look at just how evolutionary explanations are invoked to explain religion it is worth asking what such explanations aim to explain exactly, and what the general form of the explanation will be. What is to be explained, we are told, is 'religion'. Unfortunately, evolutionary psychologists are often not very forthcoming about their own definitions of religion. Perhaps that is not especially problematic. As Paul Griffiths once quipped, 'Defining religions is a little like writing diet books or forecasting the performance of the stock market: there's a good deal of it about and none of it seems to do much good' (2002: 31). None the less we should be clear about what they take themselves to be explaining. What phenomenon is it that they take to be pervasive across times and cultures on the one hand and yet apparently maladaptive on the other? Many seem happy with a characterization of religion like the one supplied by Atran: 'Religion is (1) a community's hard-to-fake commitment (2) to a counterfactual and counterintuitive world of supernatural agents (3) who master people's existential anxieties, such as death and deception' (2002a: 4).[1]

And what form will such explanations take? One might be initially skeptical of the prospects of scientific or evolutionary account of *belief*. Can the mechanisms of variation and selection go any distance toward explaining why we hold religious beliefs or any particular beliefs at all? After all, there would seem to be something downright weird about giving an evolutionary explanation for specific beliefs such as 'that there is a computer in front of me'. Can evolutionary mechanisms somehow explain or account for that? Certainly not in any specific sense. But while appeal to our evolutionary history might not be able to explain why we have specific token beliefs it might be able to explain belief formation at a more

---

1. Some attempts at offering scientific explanations of religion take on the more modest goal of explaining the origins or persistence of one or another practice belief that seems characteristic of religion. So, for example, some will focus on the pervasiveness of religious ritual performance (see Whitehouse 2004a and McCauley and Lawson 2002, for example) while others will focus on cross-cultural acceptance of human immortality (Bering 2002b).

general level. For example, appeal to variation and selection seems likely to be useful when we try to explain why we have *cognitive equipment that allows us to form sensory beliefs when our sense organs are appropriately stimulated*. Such equipment allows us to have an awareness of our environment, and beliefs formed on the basis of such awareness would prove enormously adaptive. If there were some corresponding evolutionary explanation for the fact that we have the cognitive equipment that *suffices for us to form religious beliefs (and practices) when appropriately stimulated* then we will likewise have an evolutionary explanation for our having these capacities.

One might initially expect that explanations of this sort would seek to find the adaptive advantages enjoyed by organisms with religious beliefs and claim that religious beliefs exist because of the adaptive advantages conferred. But 'evolutionary explanations' of traits don't always work by citing specific *adaptive advantages* of the trait in question. While some traits might be explained in terms of their direct fitness benefits others will be explained by benefits that are much more indirect. For those not familiar with how evolutionary explanations of this sort work, an informal example or two will prove useful. Some male baboons, for example, display a willingness to be enlisted to fight an aggressor against the troop even when the aggressor poses no risk to the individual. What explains this willingness to court danger needlessly? The answer is that those same baboons are later successful in recruiting help from others when they are the direct target of aggression (Packer 1977: 441–3). Such 'I will-scratch-your-back-if-you-scratch-mine' behavior is not uncommon in the animal world and it provides us with one example of how traits can develop by offering indirect benefits.

In addition, traits can be explained as wholly non-adaptive *by-products* of other mechanisms that are adaptive. Traits of this sort are often called 'spandrels'. Traits are treated as 'spandrels' when at least one of the following two conditions is met: either (a) natural selection is blind to the trait in question or (b) the trait can be explained in terms of some feature of its history that does not depend on selection pressures.[2] Traits satisfying the

---

2. A commonly (though recently controversial) example of a 'spandrel' is female orgasm among primates. While female orgasm is possible in a number of female primates, it is typically manifested only after lengthy stimulation. Such a trait is a 'spandrel' since it satisfies both conditions. Since primate copulation never lasts twenty minutes, female orgasm is never manifested and thus can't be selected for or against. But it is further true that given the homology between the male penis and the female clitoris, there is a clear explanation of the origin of the trait, though that explanation does not depend on 'selection pressures'. This example springs from widely discussed research performed by Frances Burton on macaques (1970: 180–91).

first condition carry neither a fitness benefit nor a fitness cost. As a result, their persistence in the population is due to other traits of which they may or may not be inevitable by-products. For example, even organisms that might be extraordinarily fit by virtue of having certain adaptive traits will at the same time have other traits with no fitness consequences (either by chance—attached earlobes, for example—or as inevitable by-products, such as an ability to dance ballet as a result of a well-toned musculature). The fitness neutral traits will tend to become more widespread in the population as well in virtue of their connection with other traits on which it can now piggyback. Traits satisfying the second condition may carry fitness costs (or benefits) though these costs and benefits play no role in the origin or persistence of the trait. Instead, such traits arise as by-products of other traits where these other traits have fitness advantages that dwarf the benefits or costs of the by-product.

Since biological traits admit of more than one type of evolutionary explanation it should come as no surprise that evolutionary explanations of religion also come in more than one variety: those which take religion to be adaptive, those which take religion to have indirect adaptive benefits, and those that regard religion as a 'spandrel'. It is interesting to note, however, that the leading evolutionary theorists of religion are, for the most part, 'spandrelists'.[3] These non-adaptationists argue that religion is to be explained as a mere by-product brought about by a chance interaction of otherwise adaptive cognitive tools. Atran, for example, claims: 'Religions are not adaptations and they have no evolutionary functions as such. Religion did not originate exclusively or primarily to: cope with death, keep social order, recover security of father, displace sexual gratification, provide causal explanation, provoke intellectual surprise.' None of these, he claims, is necessary or sufficient (Atran 2002a: 12).

The Standard Model

Though evolutionary accounts of religion differ on the importance of adaptationism in explaining religion, all agree on this: the human mind has a suite of cognitive mechanisms that collaborate in specifiable and

3. Both Atran and Boyer insist on this point strenuously. See Atran 2002a: 12 and Boyer 2001a: chap. 1. However, Atran wavers on this point, sometimes arguing that adaptive advantages play no role in the origin of religion, though they may play a role in its persistence (see, most notably: Atran 2005: 54).

predictable ways to generate religion pan-culturally.[4] The beliefs carry with them both a commitment to the ontological *reality* of what they represent and a commitment to their *importance* that is manifest both cognitively and affectively. Two questions thus become crucial: what characteristics allow religious concepts to play this special role? and what cognitive mechanisms allow us to generate such religious ideas? On what is now called the 'standard model', religious ideas are able to play their special role because they have the following characteristics:

a. They are *counter-intuitive* in ways that make them optimally suited for recall and transmission.

b. They spring from cognitive mechanisms that generate beliefs about *agents and agency*.

c. They are *inference rich* and thus allow us to generate narratives about them that enhance their memorability, make them attractive as objects of ritual, and increase our affective reaction toward them.

d. They typically represent the religious entities as *minded agents who*, because of their counter-intuitive character, *stand to benefit us* in our attempt to maintain stable relationships in large interacting groups.[5]

Religions are, by nature, communal, and thus religious ideas are ideas shared by a community. In order for religious ideas to become communal they must have characteristics which make them memorable and readily transmissible. As it happens, human minds are structured in such a way that ideas of certain sorts are more naturally memorable and transmissible than others. In particular, human minds find it very easy to remember and talk about ideas that are strange. But, not any old sort of strangeness will do. Rather, only strangeness that involves specifiable sorts of deviations from our innate ontological categories seems to do the trick.

Human beings are naturally inclined to sort objects they encounter into ready-made or native ontological categories such as: animal, plant, inanimate natural object, artifact, etc. This 'folk-ontology' allows us rapidly to classify objects in our environment, and such computational simplicity

4. The outlier here is David Sloan Wilson. On Wilson's view, practices that confer group fitness advantages lead their practitioners to retrodict religious beliefs which are capable of sustaining the practice. So the specific shape of the religious belief depends on the specific nature of the adaptive practice that requires support. This thesis is defended in his *Darwin's Cathedral* (Wilson 2002).

5. This list is adapted from Boyer 2001a.

confers fitness advantages. However, empirical data demonstrate quite conclusively that when we encounter ideas of particulars which violate our
native general ontological categories in minimal ways, the ideas are highly
memorable and liable to transmission (Boyer 2001a: chap. 2; Barrett 2004:
chaps. 2–4). If religious ideas are going to be remembered and successfully
transmitted they will need to take advantage of cognitive dispositions of
just this sort. We can thus predict that (in many cases) successfully shared
religious ideas will be strange in carefully specified and in what evolutionary
theorists describe as 'minimally counter-intuitive' (MCI) ways. Such a
prediction should lead us to expect that central religious concepts will
violate our native cognitive categories, though not massively so. Harvey
Whitehouse explains the role of such concepts as follows, 'MCI concepts
will, all else being equal, be easy to recall in all human societies . . . on this
view we should expect concepts of ghosts and witches [MCI concepts]
to be globally recurrent, whereas concepts of statues made of cheese or
that can see into the future will be either localized or entirely absent from
human cultures' (Whitehouse 2004: 31; see also Boyer 2001a: chap. 2;
Pyysiäinen 2002: 113; Barrett 2004: chap. 2). The latter concepts will not
be fit objects of religious attention and devotion because they fail to satisfy
the MCI test; such concepts in fact violate our native ontological categories
in massive ways, thereby making them harder to remember and transmit.
As a result, we can expect the entities which are central to religious belief
to be strange, but strange 'within specifiable boundaries'. As Barrett puts it,

> A tree that hears prayers is a religious concept and Minimally Counterin-
> tuitive. But a tree that hears prayers you'll make next week is not a reli-
> gious concept and is more than minimally counterintuitive—not only has
> expectations on trees been violated but also our intuitive assumptions about
> communication. A person who can foretell the future is a religious concept
> (and minimally counterintuitive), but a person who vanishes whenever you
> look at him, knows how many insects are in the Amazon basin at any given
> moment, and sustains itself on crude oil, is not a religious concept. It is
> massively counterintuitive.[6]

The minimally counter-intuitive nature of religious ideas might explain
why those ideas routinely display certain general features, but it still leaves us
to wonder about their *origins*. According to (b), religious ideas are spawned
from an online cognitive tool aimed at agency detection. Humans are,

6. Presentation at the Nature and Belief conference, Calvin College, Grand Rapids, Mich., Nov.
   2005.

thankfully, equipped with specialized cognitive mechanisms that hypoth-esize the existence of *agents* when we detect special sorts of stimuli in our environments. When, for example, we see 'unnatural' configurations in nature (crop circles or runs through the underbrush), or unnatural types of motion (rustling bushes), or unnatural sounds (things going bump in the night) we naturally hypothesize the existence of unseen agents as their source. This 'hypersensitive agency detection device' (HADD), enhances fitness since it leads us to be especially wary in circumstances where, for example, predators might be on the prowl. Of course, such cognitive mechanisms are less adaptive when they are less sensitive, more adaptive when more sensitive. As a result, such a mechanism will tend toward greater sensitivity and thus tend to produce a fairly high number of false positives (those beliefs about ghosts in the attic are, inevitably, always wrong). Concepts of supernatural beings thus arise at least in part as a way of explaining natural phenomena that trigger our HADD. Justin Barrett explains the role of HADD in religious cognition as follows:

> Our minds have numerous pattern detectors that organize visual information into meaningful units. HADD remains on the lookout for patterns known to be caused by agents. If this patterned information matches patterns . . . known to be caused by agents, HADD detects agency and alerts other mental tools . . . More interesting is when a pattern is detected that appears to be purposeful or goal directed and, secondarily, does not appear to be caused by ordinary mechanical or biological causes. Such patterns may prompt HADD to attribute the traces to agency yet to be identified: unknown persons, animals, or space aliens, ghosts, or gods.
>
> (Barrett 2004: 37)

Once we generate counter-intuitive ideas via HADD, other cognitive tools can enhance their significance in the ways described in (c) and (d). Let us begin with (d). As our primate ancestors began to live in larger interacting groups it became highly valuable to be able to predict the behaviors of others in the group. Since these behaviors are motivated by beliefs and desires of the agents, having the ability to represent those beliefs and desires not only allowed for prediction of behavior but also for the cultivation of strategies for outsmarting others to gain resources—strategies such as deception. If I understand how your actions are motivated I can seek to hijack those motivations in ways that get you to act for my advantage. Such selective pressures are cited as the explanation for the human ability to attribute mindedness to other human (or human-like) entities and to explain behaviors by appeal to hypothesized beliefs and desires. The cognitive capability has been labeled the Theory of Mind tool.

When we conjoin this tendency to anthropomorphize with (a) and (b) we can predict that human beings will be liable to take HADD-triggering events as occasions to form beliefs about *minded agents* which are the causes of these events. Since many of these natural events (floods, thunder, etc.) could only be caused by very powerful and unseen agents it is natural for us to form beliefs in the existence of *powerful, invisible, and minded agents*, i.e., something very like the objects of religious experience and devotion. And since, returning to (a), *invisible agents* are counter-intuitive, they are memorable and easily transmissible.

In addition to the above characteristics, these powerful, invisible, and minded agents take on greater cognitive and affective salience in light of their 'inference richness' (as noted in characteristic (c) above). Ideas are 'inference rich' when they allow us to construct narratives that can be used to explain otherwise unexplained natural and social phenomena. Since it is easy for us to generate narratives concerning these powerful, invisible agents, such 'proto-religious' ideas have the latent potential to become highly emotionally gripping (see Atran 2002a: 81; Boyer 2001a: 50, 59; Barrett 2004: 15). For example, the standard cognitive model claims that we are highly liable to take these beliefs in minded invisible agents and infer that, since they are not confined by ordinary spatial boundaries they must have *wide-ranging knowledge* of what is happening, even at distant places (and perhaps distant times). Indeed, the inference richness of such proto-religious concepts is enhanced when it comes to supernatural agents because we have a native developmental bias to regard supernatural agents as having (at least) super-knowing and super-perceiving powers.[7] Cross-cultural empirical studies demonstrate quite clearly that the initial human tendency to regard all minded agents as infallible shifts radically at age four in such a way that children no longer regard humans as infallible, though the overwhelming majority still regard gods as such (Richert and Barrett 2005). Such supernatural agents are thus likely to possess information about what I am doing and what others are doing. Hypothesizing supernatural agents with super-knowing powers thereby undermines our beliefs that we can get away with violating social, cultural, or moral norms wholly undetected. Supernatural agents are thus naturally connected with

---

7. See Barrett, Chap. 3 of this volume.

morality because they deter me from trying to 'get away' with norm-violating behavior, and because I can have some confidence that the behavior of others is similarly monitored. Recognition of these formidable powers of supernatural agents thus helps those in large interacting groups to follow the dictates of the social contract and refrain from trying to cheat others (see especially Johnson and Krüger 2004). Atran explains as follows:

> Because human representations of agency and intention include represen-tations of false belief and deception, human society is forever under the threat of moral defection. Simple consent among individuals seldom, if ever, sustains cooperation among large numbers of people over long periods of time . . . Supernatural agents thus *also* function as moral brothers who keep constant vigil to dissuade would be cheaters and freeriders.[8]

Because supernatural agents possess socially potent 'strategic information' these invisible agents take on personal importance making them worth exploiting, pleasing, and/or placating. This in turn further invites us to construct *religious rituals* in which such exploiting, pleasing, or placating can be carried out.[9]

The confluence of the workings of these cognitive mechanisms, it is argued, make us highly liable both to form religious ideas and to sustain them in and through religious rituals and practices.

Notice that there is nothing in the account of the *origins* of religious ideas that involves appeal to the adaptiveness of the ideas themselves. Perhaps these religious beliefs are mere 'spandrels'. Yet one might argue that once such beliefs and practices emerge they can be co-opted for adaptive work. And, indeed, some argue that the primary reason that religion *persists* is that it confers such additional advantages.[10] For example, as we have seen, belief in such agents might tend to generate or supplement our motivation for altruistic or moral behavior. This in turn leads to greater reciprocal cooperation between members of my social group, potentially enhancing both individual and group fitness. If adaptive cognitive mechanisms work

---

8. This line of thought is developed by a number of figures including Day 2005: 92–3; Atran 2002a: 112; Boyer 2001: chap. 4; Pyysiäinen 2004: 50–2; and Boyer 2002: 78–84.

9. We give little attention to the topic of ritual here though the literature presents important arguments concerning the role of ritual in the evolutionary advancement of religious practice. Most important here are the works by McCauley and Lawson 2002; Lawson and McCauley 1990; and Whitehouse 2004a.

10. See, e.g., Hinde 2005: 52 ff.; Pyysiäinen 2004: 45–52; Bering 2004; Johnson and Bering, Chap. 1 of this volume; Sosis 2003; Sosis 2004.

in concert to make religious beliefs likely, and especially if these religious beliefs can be co-opted to do additional fitness-enhancing work, there are strong selective pressures favoring the formation and maintenance of religious beliefs and practices amongst human beings.

However, as noted earlier, the most prominent advocates of the standard model are quite adamant that religion confers no fitness benefits at all.[11] These non-adaptationists argue that religion is to be explained as a mere by-product brought about by a chance confluence of cognitive circumstances. We happen to find counter-intuitive ideas memorable, we happen to attribute mindedness to agents, we happen to engage in HADD, and we happen to have a moral code, the force of which can be bolstered by hypothesized strategic agents. The result, *voilà*, is religious belief and practice.

Assessing the Views

Are these cognitive/evolutionary explanations plausible? If so, they at most show us why we are liable to develop religious ideas, though as noted it won't be much help explaining why religious beliefs take the *very specific* shapes that they do. In this way they are like attempts to give cognitive/evolutionary explanations of our beliefs concerning biological taxonomy. The selective pressures to develop innate taxonomic categories might make it inevitable that we *form* taxonomies—but whether that taxonomy will include separate categories for fishes and aquatic mammals will be decided by factors that have nothing to do with evolutionary pressures on the development of human minds. So, selection pressures won't explain, for example, why Roman Catholics believe in transubstantiation. And those defending the standard model rarely claim explanations that are any more greedy than this.[12]

11. See above, n. 2.
12. For specific disavowals of complete or detailed explanations of religious belief, one can consult Boyer 2002: 76–7, where he writes: 'People take their information about the features of ghosts and spirits and gods, to an overwhelming extent, from socially transmitted information, not from direct experience. Conversely, intrinsically vague experiences are seen through the conceptual lenses provided by what others said about the gods and spirits. To sum up, people know vastly more about gods and spirits from listening to other people than from encountering these mysterious agents.' See also Barrett 2004: 77. The two most notable exceptions are Whitehouse and David Sloan Wilson. Whitehouse's 'Modes Theory' does aim to offer more specific explanations of those conditions under which 'doctrinal' and

Advocates for the standard model do however make bold claims about the origins of religious belief and about the implications of these theories for the truth and justification of religious belief. I will consider both of these issues. First, I will offer some very brief reflections on the adequacy of these accounts of the origin of religious belief on their own terms. Do they offer us a plausible explanation for religion so understood? Second, I will look at the implications of these accounts for the religious believer if true.

On these accounts, religious commitment coalesces around concepts of minimally counter-intuitive-minded agents that are inference rich and which spawn both affective reactions and religious ritual. But, there are a host of such ideas that do not, and seemingly cannot, become the object of religious devotion despite having these same characteristics: the tooth fairy, Mickey Mouse, Batman, SpongeBob, etc. So the problem is: why are there Muslims but not Batman-ians? The question is posed by Pyysiäinen as follows:

> symbolism, as explained by Atran, Sperber and Boyer, cannot be distinguished from mere fiction, such as Mickey Mouse cartoons, without some additional criteria . . . Boyer's earlier work does not contain anything that would allow us to differentiate between religious and nonreligious counter-intuitiveness or between religion and superstition or fiction, although he clearly thinks that these are different categories.
>
> (Pyysiäinen 2004: 45)[13]

The problem is that the list of 'religious' properties is insufficient to distinguish religious ideas from merely strange and MCI ideas that are taken to be fanciful. So what is it that accounts for our commitment to the *reality* of one set of ideas and not the other?

While current theorists have offered no response to this challenge, there are at least two (potentially complementary) responses worth considering. The first goes as follows: defenders of the standard cognitive model argue that counter-intuitive religious beliefs often *arise* in part from the operation of a 'hypersensitive agency detection device' (HADD) which is in general adaptive despite generating a large number of false positives (a relatively harmless fault). In this way, religious ideas have a different origin from that of mere creatures of fiction. This might help solve the Mickey Mouse

'imagistic' religion arises. David Sloan Wilson argues that the specific shape of religious ideas is determined by the practices they are meant to support.

13. The objection is also raised by Hinde (2005: 39–40).

objection since beliefs formed by way of inferences from our agency detection device have two important features. First, they commit the believer to the *reality* of the hypothesized purposeful agent and second, the commitment is accompanied by heightened emotional arousal. A commitment to the *reality* of agents hypothesized by HADD is expected since such a commitment is necessary to explain the adaptive value of HADD in the first place. When I hear a certain sort of rustling in the brush or see 'traces in the grass' or hear things going bump in the night it is adaptive for me to respond in a way that allows me to avoid a potential threat (from a predator, for example). But I will hardly be motivated to engage in the right sorts of avoidance behavior unless I am genuinely committed to the *existence* of the hypothesized agent. Thus, one would expect that beliefs in counter-intuitive entities triggered by the HADD will carry existential commitment, while beliefs concerning counter-intuitive entities encountered first in dreams or works of fiction will not. Such commitment is adaptive in the former case, but not in the latter. Of course, it is part and parcel of the existential commitment to a perceived threat that the belief arouses powerful emotions, such as fear, as well. Believing that the rustling in the bushes signals a real predator leads to a fear that at least in part motivates me to flee. But it is also true that the emotional arousal itself strengthens my commitment to the reality of the hypothesized agent.[14]

Second, for reasons that are still not quite clear human beings exhibit a demonstrable natural tendency to hypothesize the existence of supernatural beings with a cluster of superpowers. Above I referred to empirical work which indicates a developmental tendency to favor belief in the existence of supernatural beings with super-knowing and super-perceiving faculties. But it is equally true that human beings cross-culturally are developmentally biased towards accepting belief in the existence of supernatural beings that are superpowerful, immortal (Gimenez, Guerrero, and Harris, manuscript), and creators (Kelemen 1999). If HADD leads us to hypothesize the existence of supernatural-minded agents and this is coupled with a developmental bias toward belief in beings with superpowers, these two factors taken together make it likely that beings of this sort will become likely objects of religious devotion while Mickey Mouse and SpongeBob will not.

---

14. In the interests of full disclosure it appears that Boyer rejects an account of this sort (2001a: 144–8) while Barrett (2004: chap. 3) defends it.

Yet, even this response will not satisfy all of the relevant worries. Since we are committed, cognitively and emotionally, to the reality of religious entities, and since we are liable to remember and transmit ideas of emotionally arousing MCI agents generated by HADD, and since we are biased toward belief in superpowered, supernatural beings, we undoubtedly possess powerful starting ingredients for religious cognition. But it is also true that any agents hypothesized by the activation of HADD are none the less highly liable to empirical defeat. If I hear a noise in the closet but find nothing there when I look I surrender the belief in the hypothesized agent. If I think I hear something moving in the bushes and then the noise stops I soon give up the belief that there is something there. False positives are common with HADD, and once we detect their falsity (or fail to detect corroborating evidence of their truth) the hypothesized agents are quickly abandoned. So, an important question remains: shouldn't we expect that religious belief would be equally liable to defeat when the religious hypothesis is not confirmed by independent evidence or when we come to discover natural explanations for the events that originally led us to hypothesize supernatural agency? Many 'primitive cultures' invoke agentive explanations for natural phenomena until natural explanations are shown to suffice. Why do those religious beliefs persist even when natural explanations for the 'traces in the grass' are subsequently discovered?

Let us assume that defenders of this model can answer the question of how such false positives are able to survive. There is still the further question of why concepts spawned in this way would amount to anything other than mere objects of predatory fear. These unseen agents would be regarded as nothing more than superpowerful, bizarre, and scary. Why then would these things become the focus of religious devotion? We can imagine one arguing as follows:

> Supernatural concepts don't emerge from HADD ready made for religious devotion. Rather, these unseen agents, hypothesized to be minded, are on occasion taken to be not merely unseen but invisible. In virtue of that, they are counter-intuitive. And such invisible, MCI agents then are understood to have strategic information. This makes the concepts inference rich, allowing them to rally emotional commitment, and makes them fit objects of ritual. This in turn spawns routine activities in which we take ourselves to engage in commerce with these special agents. Combine this with our tendency to believe in supernatural super-beings and we have a recipe for religious belief

and practice. It is only when the confluence of *all* of these factors occurs that religion emerges.

The main problem with this version of the story is that it seems to render the view incapable of explaining what it set out to explain: the *pervasiveness* of religion across times and cultures. If the emergence of religion requires this apparently highly contingent confluence of cognitive circumstances we may have an explanation of why religion sometimes emerges—here and there. But, given the highly contingent nature of the processes described here, it does not seem likely that religion is something we would expect to find everywhere and always. Why would concepts spawned by HADD become layered with all of the additional properties that attend religious concepts?[15] If that were to happen in some cases we could chalk it up to chance. But could we expect this to be common? One could, of course, hypothesize that human cognitive capacities and the environment in which they are placed are calibrated in a way that makes this special outcome likely. But this sort of special pleading raises an important question: why are human cognitive capacities and the human cognitive environment structured in a way that makes religious belief so widespread? Is this special fact about humans and their environment evidence of a form of cosmic cognitive design?

Philosophical Implications of Evolutionary Accounts

Finally, let's turn to a more incendiary question: do such evolutionary explanations undermine the truth of or justification for religious beliefs? The question is important, first, because religious believers tend to feel threatened by scientific 'explanations' of religion. For many of them,

---

15. One might hold that the pervasiveness is explained by common origin. Perhaps this confluence occurred once early in our hominid ancestry and all subsequent manifestations of religion are cultural descendants of this manifestation. This claim would depend on a history of religions that none would accept as far as we know. And it is further disowned by prominent defenders of the view such as, for example, Atran, who says: 'If we reject the unlikely possibility that these thematic occurrences stem from historical contact and diffusion or are spontaneous instantiations of a Platonistic set of innate religious forms . . . then how else could such apparent recurrences independently take place across cultures without specific and strong universal cognitive constraints?' (2002a: 88).

attempts to explain religion are attempts to explain it away.[16] Second, as noted earlier, many evolutionary scientists present their views as if indeed they *do* explain religion away by showing it either to be false outright, or at least superfluous. For example, evolutionary theorist Todd Tremlin remarks that when it comes to theological as opposed to psychological explanations of belief 'the truer "tragedy of the Theologian" is that he or she is shopping second rate wares'. And in his landmark work *Religion Explained* Pascal Boyer exclaims that 'In a cultural context where this hugely successful [scientific] way of understanding the world has debunked one supernatural claim after another, there is a strong impulse [among the religious] to find at least *one* domain where it would be possible to trump the scientist . . . But evolution and microbiology crushed all this . . . ' (Boyer 2001a: 76; see also Pyysiäinen 2001b: 78–9).[17] There are two things to say about the incendiary question.

Thing One

The first thing a philosopher will be inclined to say is: of course, such explanations don't explain religion away. After all, these accounts merely aim to explain the origins of religious beliefs and, as we all learned in our introduction to philosophy courses, an account of a belief's origin tells us nothing about its truth. To think otherwise is to commit the notorious 'genetic fallacy' (a fallacy which, in spite of our context, has nothing to do with genetics). Each philosopher has his favorite way of illustrating this fallacy. Mine comes from the story of Fredrich Kekulé, the somewhat eccentric nineteenth-century German chemist. Kekule is famous for being the first to present chemicals in terms of structural formulas, and more famous for his discovery of the ring structure of the benzene molecule. His great discovery occurred not as a result of hard labor in the lab but from an episode he described as follows:

> I turned my chair to the fire [after having worked on the problem for some time] and dozed. Again the atoms were gamboling before my eyes. This time the smaller groups kept modestly to the background. My mental eye, rendered more acute by repeated vision of this kind, could not distinguish larger

16. For one who reads these accounts this way, see Griffiths 2002: 53–7.
17. Boyer also conveys this message repeatedly with section titles in the book such as 'Giving Airy Nothing a Local Habitation' (2001a: 2).

structures, of manifold conformation; long rows, sometimes more closely fitted together; all twining and twisting in snakelike motion. But look! What was that? One of the snakes had seized hold of its own tail, and the form whirled mockingly before my eyes. As if by a flash of lighting I awoke ... Let us learn to dream, gentlemen.

(Weisberg 1993)

Now this is admittedly a silly reason to believe that benzene has a ring structure. It was, none the less, *his* reason. But his coming to it on silly grounds doesn't undermine the *truth* of the belief. For the same reason, nothing we say or discover about the origins of our religious beliefs is going to make any difference to our assessment of the truth of those beliefs.

One can imagine a critic of religious belief being not entirely satisfied with this response to the incendiary question. Such a critic might respond as follows:

> I concede that evolutionary accounts of religious belief have nothing to tell us about the truth or falsity of the beliefs. But that doesn't mean that these accounts have no bearing on other epistemically interesting issues in the neighborhood. To see how, return to your Kekulé story. We can't infer that Kekulé is wrong about his beliefs about the structure of benzene simply on the basis of the way he came to the belief. But we *can* infer that Kekulé is a crazy nut, and that his beliefs were completely unwarranted—at least until he was able to marshal empirical evidence to support them. The same thing holds true for the religious believer. The evolutionary account of religious belief doesn't undermine the truth of religious belief, but they do undermine the justification for or the *reasonability of* religious belief.

Do 'genetic accounts' such as this one undermine *justification*? Sometimes they do. For example, if we have reason to think that the mechanism at work in generating the belief is, or is likely to be, unreliable, then any beliefs resulting from it would be unwarranted and should be rejected. But what about when we have no grounds for forming a belief one way or the other concerning reliability? Are such beliefs epistemically innocent until proven otherwise?

This is a question too difficult to answer in detail here, so here is a quick answer. Philosophers commonly make a distinction between basic and non-basic beliefs. Basic beliefs are foundational: that is they are those beliefs on which others are based, but which are not themselves based on other beliefs. What would such beliefs be? Our belief in induction, in the reality of the external world, or in other minds—all of these are basic beliefs—beliefs we come to, not on the basis of inference from evidence, but through the basic operation of the human mind. And we feel confident that we are justified in holding these beliefs, even if they themselves are not held on the basis of other beliefs that justify them.

What is interesting here is the striking similarity between standard philosophical examples of basic belief and the psychologists' characterization of religion. Both are pervasive, spontaneously and non-inferentially held beliefs which arise through the basic or native operations of the human mind. Do we have any independent reason to think that the processes that lead to other basic beliefs—belief in induction, other minds, the reality of the external world, etc. are reliable? Of course not. But we intuitively form such beliefs and we find ourselves ineluctably committed to them. That's about all we can say on their behalf. But none of that leads us to call into question the warrant we have for such beliefs. From this we can infer that what holds for these beliefs holds for basic belief and, specifically, in this context, religious belief.

A critic might find this response unsatisfying not because she finds the account of the justification of basic beliefs unconvincing, but rather because she finds the religious belief and other basic beliefs to be disanalogous in one important respect. Earlier I noted that on the standard model religious belief originates, at least in part, through the operation of the agency detection mental tool. However, we also saw that it is good for this tool to be sensitive to an extent that makes it likely to yield a significant number of false positives. If that is right, then it seems fair to conclude that while HADD might be adaptive, it will also be *unreliable*. If religious (basic) beliefs are spawned by such an unreliable mechanism the claim to justification is correspondingly undermined.

Unfortunately for the critic, things are not so simple. If HADD were a mental tool which generated beliefs in specific agents on the occasion of sensing agency signaling states of affairs, then perhaps we should regard such beliefs with suspicion. But HADD simply doesn't function in this way. When human beings hypothesize agents as the cause of some agency signaling state of affairs the content of the belief typically consists in little more than that some agent is or was at work in generating the state of affairs. We hear a funny noise in the basement or we see crop circles and we start to investigate. As time goes by we sometimes discover probable non-agentive explanations for the event or state of affairs that prompted our investigation. In other cases we do not. And when we don't, further investigation and further events often lead us to form more detailed hypotheses about the type of agent involved. I hear a noise in the basement so I investigate. Then I hear a similar noise outside the basement window and infer that whatever caused the original noise has the capacity to move in and out of the house. And so on. After a time, the pattern of noises may converge in a way that leads me to hypothesize the existence of an agent of a specific sort (it is something small enough to crawl in and out of the pet entry in the basement door, for example). Are HADD-spawned beliefs in specific sorts of agents routinely unreliable? I am not sure how we might find out. But there is no reason to think that they are.[18]

Thing Two

The second thing to say in response to the incendiary question is that an account of religion in evolutionary terms does nothing to preclude *other* accounts of those beliefs that might be equally or indeed *more* salient.

For those who are skeptical about this, it will be instructive to consider a fictional parallel. One might imagine a scientific ironist who notices that truly first-rate scientists, while adding to the totality of human knowledge in ways that allow us to harness nature's forces and turn them to our advantage, are routinely unfit in an evolutionary sense. Nerdy, unkempt, and inclined to retreat to sterile and olid laboratories, these scientists are often poor at finding mates and, even when they do find them, poor at offspring production. In light of this, our ironic scientist might ask: what explains the origin and persistence of these evidently maladaptive beliefs and practices of 'empirical science'? He might then frame an 'evolutionary explanation of empirical science' as follows:

> Imagine (he says) a group (Modern Man) which has among its members a subset (the empirical scientists) which aims to cultivate and propagate rules of behavior (scientific research and teaching) which allows the entire group to believe principles and engage in adaptive behaviors which confer a differential

18. Of course sometimes HADD triggering evidence takes us through cycles of affirmation and denial as well. When deer hunting I might hear a sound in the distant brush and form the belief that a deer is present. But then I see and hear nothing further and so surrender that belief. Later, when I visit the spot from which the earlier sounds seemed to emanate, I see deer tracks and see droppings and renew my belief that the earlier sound was indeed caused by a deer. Cases such as these make it uncertain how we are to assess the general reliability of beliefs spawned by HADD. Thanks to Justin Barrett for this example.

advantage on the group as a whole. Members of this smaller community model in their behavior a commitment to these principles and practices in their lives (through laboratory and field research) and in their community. This commitment leads the members of this community often to retreat from the group (to the labs and to scholarly conferences), largely for the purpose of devoting themselves to these principles and practices, even though this is done at the expense of their own in-group fitness. In this retreat they continue to refine these principles and practices by constructing overarching theories—theories which often postulate the existence of entities which are unobservable and not directly falsifiable. These entities and theories serve to make the principles easy to remember, for themselves and for members of their larger group, and give everyone a sense that there is a greater reality to which the group must be responsive if they are to thrive. Because of the resulting differential advantage that this community confers on the group, the practices of this community, and the group of which it is a part, continues to persist as the overall group thrives.[19]

Is this explanation 'true'? Perhaps it is, as far as it goes. But no one is going to be inclined to think that this is the whole truth about the origins and persistence of empirical science. In fact, no one is going to be inclined to think it is even a very important part of the truth. We are instead going to be inclined to say that empirical science—its beliefs and practices— exists and persists because it helps to get us at the truth about the physical world. The evolutionary explanation may be true, but the explanation in terms of truth conduciveness is much more fundamental. The evolutionary explanation might be correct as far as it goes, but it is simply not all that *salient*.

The same is true when it comes to evolutionary explanations of religion. They may be true, as far as they go. But nothing about such explanations undermines, or trumps, explanations in theistic or alethic terms. This was the lesson well learned from Cicero. It may be quite right to say that God created human beings or set in motion natural events which made it inevitable that evolutionary processes would converge upon human beings, with belief-forming mechanisms that make religious belief likely or inevitable. It may then be equally true to say that we are inclined to form religious beliefs *because* they are true. And, as with our evolutionary

---

19. For those who do not recognize the allusion, this account is intended to parallel the account of religion offered by David Sloan Wilson in Wilson 2002.

explanations of empirical science, these latter explanations may be far more *salient*.

In the case of the fictional explanation of empirical science, nothing about our evolutionary explanation sufficed to 'explain empirical science away'. And the same is true *mutatis mutandis* with our evolutionary explanations of religion. Explaining it is not tantamount to explaining it away.

10

Explaining Religious Experience

Charles Taliaferro[1]

The fact that we can die, that we *can* be ill at all, is what perplexes us; the fact that we now for a moment live and are well is irrelevant to that perplexity. We need a life not correlated with death, a health not liable to illness, a kind of good that will not perish, a good in fact that lies beyond the goods of nature.

William James, Varieties of Religious Experience (New York: Collier Books), 123.

There are abundant accounts of why so many of us appear to have an experiential awareness of a sacred, transcendent reality. In *Breaking the Spell; Religion as a Natural Phenomenon*, Daniel Dennett frames his own approach to such religious experiences by asking who benefits (*cui bono*) from them or reports of them. Assuming the 'benefits' include intellectual coherence and cogency and are not narrowed to self-serving, criminal-like goals (who inherits from the victim?), this strategy seems welcome. I see the origins and nature of religious experience as rooted in complex factors, including the drive (recognized by William James, among many others) to seek and find the fulfilling benefits of a relationship to a broader, good, and sacred reality that is (in its most general formulation) theistic. So, part of my own response to the general question of why some of us experience the divine is the somewhat simple response: because there is

1. I thank Michael Murray, Jeff Schloss, Alvin Plantinga, and members of the Department of Philosophy at Bethel College and the Department of Religion at Boston University for comments on earlier drafts of this chapter.

a divine beneficent reality to be experienced or, putting the point more formally, the best account of why some of us experience God includes the reality and activity of an omnipresent God. My reasons for thinking this involves the background belief that when we come to assess religious experience there are some good independent reasons for thinking that theism is both coherent and at least as plausible as its closest competitor (naturalism), and thus, in William James's phrase, a live hypothesis. Given an open-ended philosophical inquiry in which both theism and naturalism are live hypotheses, I believe theism is more cogent in accounting for religious experience (Taliaferro 1994; Taliaferro 1998; Goetz and Taliaferro 2008). In a single chapter, I cannot fully exhibit all the reasons for this background assumption, but what I set out to do is to argue that there are some philosophically interesting problems that afflict an alternative contemporary, popular naturalist project of dismissing the evidential force of religious experience. My focus is on Daniel Dennett's recent project in which naturalism is privileged at the outset and theism is not offered a level playing field.

In this chapter, I argue that Daniel Dennett employs a methodology for explaining religious experience with a structure and a problem similar to that faced by the methodology he employs in his philosophy of mind: in the first he virtually rules out theism in principle, and in the second he definitively and explicitly rules out explanations that involve consciousness, experience, sensations, and other mental phenomena. My contention is that just as his work in philosophy of mind involves begging the question against the first-person perspective, his work in explaining away religious experience involves begging the question against theism. I further argue that there is an inconsistency in Dennett's position, as his critique of theistic accounts of religious experience involves a thesis he rejects in his philosophy of mind—namely, the reality and privileged awareness of our own states of awareness and subjectivity. The fact that in his attack on theistic accounts of religion he resorts to confident first-person perspectives, and so on, is reason to think that his philosophy of mind is problematic. While this chapter may be read as an *ad hominem* argument I hope to use my assessment of Dennett's work to urge that just as our philosophy of mind should be open (in principle) to accepting irreducible conscious explanations, the reality of first-person awareness, and so on, our philosophy of religious experience should be open to accepting theistic explanations. The project of this chapter is in the tradition of Alvin Plantinga's 1967 classic *God and Other Minds*, which seeks to bring insights from the philosophy of mind to bear on our reflection on the philosophy of religion. I begin with some observations about Dennett's characterization of religion and his methodology.

A Starting Point and a Method

In *Breaking the Spell* Dennett offers the following definition of religion: religions are 'social systems whose participants avow belief in a supernatural agent or agents whose approval is to be sought' (Dennett 2006: 9). Dennett then outlines his fundamental thesis about the nature of religion that he claims begs no questions concerning theism or, to use his term, supernaturalism:

> What do I mean when I speak of religion as a natural phenomenon?...I might mean that religion is natural as opposed to *supernatural*, that it is a human phenomenon composed of events, organisms, objects, structures, patterns, and the like that all obey the laws of physics or biology and hence do not involve miracles. And that *is* what I mean. Notice that it could be true that God exists, that God is indeed the intelligent, conscious, loving creator of us all, and yet *still* religion itself, as a complex set of phenomena, is a perfectly natural phenomenon. Nobody would think it was presupposing atheism to write a book subtitled *Sports as a Natural Phenomenon* or *Cancer as a Natural Phenomenon*. Both sports and cancer are widely recognized as natural phenomena, not supernatural...
>
> (Dennett 2006: 24, 25)

The main body of Dennett's *Breaking the Spell* consists in drawing on anthropological-sociological accounts of religion that do not involve any appeal to theism or, in Dennett's preferred terminology, supernaturalism and miracles. Dennett draws on work by naturalists who propose that appealing to invisible, benign forces may well seem to 'believers' to be an important protective strategy in a dangerous world. Dennett employs work by Craig Palmer, Lyle Steadman, David Sloan Wilson, Pascal Boyer, Justin Barrett, with his 'hypersensitive agency detection device' (HADD), Edward Pritchard-Evans, James McLenon, Rodney Needham, and others, including the bizarre work of Julian Jaynes.

Although Dennett does not himself break new ground in accounting for the ways in which religious ideas and ostensible experiences of the divine can be generated, he does bring together an impressive body of extant literature and offers a unified philosophical frame of reference to evaluate its findings. He also offers a specific case of his own employment of hypnotic suggestion to support his view of the natural production of religious experiences. It will be instructive to take note briefly of his overall framework and his anecdotal case.

In terms of framework, Dennett contends that researchers into the nature of religion are faced with being unable to reconstruct the interior beliefs of religious practitioners reliably. On this front, Dennett builds on a lament expressed by Rodney Needham in the course of his study of the Penan in the interior of Borneo:

> I realized that I could not confidently describe their attitude to God, whether this was belief or anything else . . . In fact, as I had glumly to conclude, I just did not know what was their psychic attitude toward the personage in whom I had assumed they believed . . . Clearly, it was one thing to report the received ideas to which a people subscribed, but it was quite another matter to say what was their inner state (belief for instance) when they expressed or entertained such ideas. If, however, an ethnographer said that people believed something when he did not actually know what was going on inside them, then surely his account of them must, it occurred to me, be very defective in quite fundamental ways.
>
> (Needham, cited Dennett 2006: 239)

This inability to access the depths of another's religious state of mind afflicts not just European–North American research into the life of the Penan in the Rainforest, but it afflicts our access to 'the inner minds' of all others, whether in the same community or not. Dennett claims:

> When it comes to interpreting religious avowals of others, *everybody is an outsider*. Why? Because religious avowals concern matters that are beyond observation, beyond meaningful test, so the only thing *anybody* can go on is religious behavior, and, more specifically, the behavior of *professing*. A child growing up in a culture is like an anthropologist, after all, surrounded by informants whose professings stand in need of interpretation. The fact that your informants are your father, and mother, and speak in your mother tongue, does not give you anything more than a slight circumstantial advantage over the adult anthropologist who has to rely on a string of bilingual interpreters to query the informants.
>
> (Dennett 2006: 240, 241)

Dennett commends shifting the research focus away from subjective reports of the sort William James capitalized on in his landmark *Varieties of Religious Experience* or the phenomenological approach to religion of Rudolf Otto to a behavioral analysis of professions and behavior.

Dennett's sources are not just scholarly. In the course of bolstering the thesis that persons may be prone to suggestions by authority figures to believe in the supernatural, he conveys the following story involving his daughter. As this case has a bearing on my claim that there is a conflict between Dennett's philosophy of mind and his critique of theistic accounts of religious experience, I cite the anecdote at length:

> One's parents—or whoever are hard to distinguish from one's parents—have something approaching a dedicated hotline to acceptance, not as potent as hypnotic suggestion, but sometimes close to it. Many years ago, my five-year-old daughter, attempting to imitate the gymnast Nadia Comaneci's performance on the horizontal bar, tipped over the piano stool and painfully crushed two of her fingertips. How was I going to calm down this terrified child so I could safely drive her to the emergency room? Inspiration struck: I held my own hand near her throbbing little hand and sternly ordered: 'Look, Andrea! I'm going to teach you a secret! You can push the pain into *my* hand with your mind. Go ahead, *push! Push!*' She tried—and it worked! She'd 'pushed the pain' into Daddy's hand. Her relief (and fascination) was instantaneous. The effect lasted only for minutes, but a few further administrations of impromptu hypnotic analgesia along the way, I got her to the emergency room, where they could give her the further treatment she needed. (Try it with your own child, if the occasion arises. You may be similarly lucky.) I was exploiting her instincts—though the rationale didn't occur to me until years later when I was reflecting on it.
>
> (Dennett 2006: 130)

I return to this case below.

To his credit, Dennett includes in *Breaking the Spell* an assessment of some positive theistic arguments. He discusses the ontological, cosmological, and design argument. I think this is no mere bypass in his naturalistic critique of religion, for if there are positive independent reasons for thinking there is an all-good Creator-God, his case against there being bona fide experiences of God would be weaker. I comment on Dennett's criticism of theistic arguments in the final section of this chapter.

Preliminary Difficulties

I begin a critical evaluation of Dennett's work by noting a minor problem with his definition of religion as a social system that gives center stage to seeking the approval of a supernatural agent. This definition is too narrow. There are societies and traditions that are widely recognized as religious that do not include an element of seeking supernatural approval. Buddhism— which Dennett identifies as a religion—does not, at least in its earliest Theravada strand, nor is supernatural approval a component in Daoism nor a central concern in some important traditions in Confucianism.

Because very little in Dennett's critique of theistic religious experiences depends on his insistence that religion must involve the supernatural, I will not press the matter further other than taking note that when it comes to arguing that his own position is not religious Dennett seems committed to the idea that religion, *by definition*, must involve a failure of clarity and rationality. Consider the following passage where it appears that the chief reason for Dennett's claim not to embrace a religion is that he does not allow for mystery or the abdication of reason:

> I, too, want the world to be a better place. This is my reason for wanting people to understand and accept evolutionary theory: I believe that their salvation may depend on it! How so? By opening their eyes to the dangers of pandemics, degradation of the environment, and loss of biodiversity, and by informing them about some of the foibles of human nature. So isn't my belief that belief in evolution is the path to salvation a religion? No; there is a major difference. We who love evolution do not honor those whose love of evolution prevents them from thinking clearly and rationally about it! On the contrary, we are particularly critical of those whose misunderstandings and romantic misstatements of these great ideas mislead themselves and others. In our view, there is no safe haven for mystery or incomprehensibility. Yes, there is humility, and awe, and sheer delight, at the glory of the evolutionary landscape, but it is not accompanied by, or in the service of, a willing (let alone thrilling) abandonment of reason. So I feel a moral imperative to spread the word of evolution, but evolution is not my religion. I don't have a religion.
>
> (Dennett 2006: 268)

See also Dennett's profession of 'sacred values' (2006: 23). Because Dennett appeals to so much that comprises standard examples of religion (much of contemporary Christianity involves an appeal to stewardship over the environment, salvation, moral imperatives, the love, glory, awe, and delight in God and nature, and so on) he must assume that *a necessary condition for being a religion is that it involves the abandonment of reason and the establishment of a haven for incomprehensibility, mystery, misunderstandings, and misstatements.* Dennett's key defense of his claim to not be religious seems to be that religion (by definition) includes such a list of 'vices'. Surely this is not a fair definition, acceptable to non-naturalists or to significant numbers of religious practitioners.

I shall argue in the next section, that Dennett's problematic, even question-begging treatment of religion in the above, implied definition is similar to his treatment of intentional explanations and consciousness. To prepare for the next section, however, let us consider further the structure of Dennett's methodology.

Dennett stipulates at the outset that if religion is to be explained the explanation cannot involve a supernatural reality or a miracle. Two modest points need to be made about terminology before directly challenging Dennett. First, 'supernatural' has never been the standard term to describe the God of classical Judaism, Christianity, and Islam. This is partly because the term is often linked with the term 'superstitious' but also because many theists historically have held that God has a nature. In English, the standard term to describe the belief in an omnipotent, omniscient, necessarily existing, omnipresent, everlasting Creator-God who is revealed in human history since the seventeenth century is 'theistic'. While not a great deal hangs on the choice of terms, to avoid both eccentricity and, more importantly, to avoid even hinting that an appeal to God is *ipso facto* superstitious, I commend the use of 'theism' and its cognates rather than 'supernatural'.

Second, the concept of a miracle is somewhat vexing. There are obvious problems with David Hume's concept of a miracle as a violation of the laws of nature (why assume it is a law of nature that the Creator cannot directly cause events like a resurrection to occur?) and if by 'miracle' one means simply an act of God, then for most theists the cosmos itself is a continuous miracle, for the cosmos could not exist for an instant were it not for the creative, conserving act of God. Perhaps Dennett's insistence that accounts of religious experience not involve miracles may be read as requiring that the account of religious experience we seek *not include special acts of God as opposed to God's general, creative conservation of the cosmos.* On this view, the belief that a resurrection took place by God's creative power would be a belief that a miracle occurred, as this is not part of God's general will in all cases of persons who die, whereas the belief that water boils at 212 degrees at sea level would not be a belief in a miracle because this is consonant with God's general, continuous will that there be water, seas, heat, the relevant laws of nature, and so on. But while Dennett *may* be read as counseling that theists simply suspend their belief in only special acts of God, he is more plausibly read as insisting that theists adopt the presumption that an appeal to God (or theism) will play *no essential role whatever in accounting for religion and religious experiences*. Dennett seems to hold that to resort to the belief that God's omnipresent reality partly accounts for the widespread apparent experience of God would be to believe that God has defied the laws of nature. This assumption comes to the fore in the following passage:

> Sports and cancer are the subjects of intense scientific scrutiny by researchers working in many disciplines and holding many different religious views. They all assume, tentatively and for the sake of science, that the phenomena they are studying are natural phenomena. This doesn't prejudice the verdict that they are. Perhaps there *are* sports miracles that actually defy the laws of nature; perhaps some cancer cures *are* miracles. If so, the only hope of ever demonstrating this to a doubting world would be by adopting the scientific method, with its assumption of no miracles, and showing that science was utterly unable to account for the phenomena. Miracle-hunters must be scrupulous scientists or else they are wasting their time—a point long recognized by the Roman Catholic Church, which at least goes through the motions of subjecting the claims of miracles made on behalf of candidates for sainthood to objective scientific investigation. So no deeply religious person should object to the scientific study of religion with the presumption that *it is an entirely natural phenomenon* [emphasis mine]. If it isn't entirely natural, if there really are miracles involved, the best way—indeed, the only way—to show that to doubters would be to demonstrate it scientifically. Refusing to play by these rules only creates the suspicion that one doesn't really believe that religion is supernatural after all.

> (Dennett 2006: 26)

How tentative is Dennett's recommendation that we should assume a natural and thus, for Dennett, a naturalistic account of religion?

I read Dennett as holding that we can only appeal to theism as an explanation of religious experience if there is an utter failure of a naturalistic account of religion, a failure that is so profound that it would 'demonstrate' that religion cannot be natural. Dennett claims that he is not commending a 'prejudice'. But what is the difference between a prejudice against X and commending a stringent, 'scrupulous' presumption against X, without which we are 'wasting our time'? Perhaps a theist should presume (as Dennett suggests Roman Catholic miracle-hunters presume) that explanations of events do not involve miracles as special acts of God (as delimited above, e.g. resurrections) in the absence of strong evidence to the contrary; but why should one scrupulously assume at the outset that there can be no appeal to God whatever unless naturalism is shown to be demonstrably false? Why not assume, instead, that religious experience may be explained *either* naturalistically or theistically and then consider which explanation offers a better account of the phenomena? (As an aside, I do not think that theistic accounts of religious experience require special acts of God or miracles like resurrections or defiling the laws of nature. Many of the cases of religious experience in James's work or in Evelyn Underhill's classic study *Mysticism* involve persons ostensibly experiencing God's goodness, glory, love, greatness; if these cases are authentic they involve more than is encompassed by a description and explanation within the natural sciences, but then so do descriptions and explanations of a Shakespearean scholar or a logician.)

As should be clear, the debate over religious experience that Dennett does not take on is one in which both the theist and naturalist are able to develop their arguments with a comprehensive examination of background beliefs. I briefly take note of this alternative, comprehensive strategy, and then turn to Dennett's philosophy of mind. While naturalism may be thought to be privileged on grounds of simplicity (after all, naturalists posit the cosmos, whereas theists posit the cosmos plus God), philosophers such as Richard Swinburne, Stewart Goetz, and myself have argued that theism has an ideal, greater explanatory unity in accounting for both the very existence of a contingent cosmos and its goodness (see Swinburne 2004; Taliaferro 1994; Taliaferro 2005; Goetz and Taliaferro 2008). By our lights, matter and energy, the very existence of the cosmos and values, the emergence of consciousness, moral and aesthetic properties, and the development of religious experience are all explained, ultimately, by the causal, creative power of God who intentionally sustains a good world. Given a developed, extensive defense of this position, the hegemony of naturalism is problematic. But rather than undertake this larger enterprise here about the comparative power of theism versus naturalism in terms of simplicity and comprehensive explanatory power, I focus on the problem of reconciling Dennett's naturalistic critique of religion with his philosophy of mind, and on what I suggest is a narrow method of accounting for human nature that seems to run parallel to his methodology when it comes to religious experience. I propose that an examination of Dennett's philosophy of mind gives us reason to re-examine his philosophy of religious experience.

The Overall Picture of Consciousness and God

In various works, Dennett contends that truly to explain intentionality and consciousness in humans and other animals we need to account for them in non-intentional, non-conscious terms. In *Brainstorms* Dennett writes: 'the account of intelligence required of psychology must not of course be question-begging. It must not explain intelligence in terms of intelligence, for instance by assigning responsibility for the existence of intelligence in creatures to the munificence of an intelligent Creator' (1978: 83). A similar position is advanced by Dennett in *Consciousness Explained*: 'Only a theory that explained conscious events in terms of unconscious events could explain consciousness at all' (2001: 454). It needs to be appreciated that Dennett's form of naturalism here is not unique to him. Consider Georges Rey's stance:

> Any ultimate explanation of mental phenomena will have to be in *non*-mental terms, or else it won't be an *explanation* of it. There might be an explanation of some mental phenomena in terms of others—perhaps *hope* in terms of *belief* and *desire*—but if we are to provide an explanation of all mental phenomena, we would in turn have to explain such mentalistic explainers until finally we reached entirely non-mental terms.
>
> (Rey 1997: 21)

For Dennett and Rey, explanations of human action and experience in terms of basic, teleological, or purposive powers would not be bona fide explanations. Dennett adopts the same strategy for selves and conscious experience: accounts that either leave the self intact or conceive of subjective experiences as irreducible elements in the world are unacceptable.

Dennett sometimes writes as though persons exist as substantial selves, but he does not allow substantial selves, nor subjective conscious feelings and beliefs, to be part of his ultimate account of the nature and course of reality.

> You've got to leave the first person [substantial self] out of your final theory. You won't have a theory of consciousness if you still have the first person in there, because that was what it was your job to explain. All the paraphernalia

that doesn't make sense unless you've got a first person there, has to be turned into something else. You've got to figure out some way to break it up and distribute its powers and opportunities in the system in some other way.

(Dennett, in Blackmore 2006: 87)

Dennett's methodology is explicitly designed to cut against taking the first-person point of view seriously. By his account, the Cartesian certitude that the self exists over time and has subjective experiences rests on a nearly anti-scientific or at least unscientific approach to human nature. Rather than begin with the certitude of experience and the self, Dennett thinks it comparatively more reasonable to believe in the existence of mass, charge, and space–time. In the following passage, Dennett ridicules David Chalmers' belief that subjective experience exists, likening this to the belief that there is a peculiar entity in the world, cuteness.

> [Compare] Chalmers' proposal [that we are immediately aware of the reality of conscious experience] with [an] imaginary non-starter: *cutism*, the proposal that since some things are just plain cute, and other things aren't cute at all—you can just see it, however hard it is to describe or explain—we had better postulate *cuteness* as a fundamental property of physics alongside mass, charge and space–time. (Cuteness is *not* a functional property, of course; I can imagine somebody who wasn't actually cute at all but who nevertheless functioned exactly as if cute—trust me.) Cutism is in even worse shape than vitalism. Nobody would have taken vitalism seriously for a minute if the vitals hadn't a set of independently describable phenomena—of reproduction, metabolism, self-repair and the like—that their postulated fundamental life-element was hoped to account for. Once these phenomena were otherwise accounted for, vitalism fell flat, but at least it had a project. Until Chalmers gives an independent ground for contemplating the drastic move of adding 'experience' to mass, charge, and space–time, his proposal is one that can be put on the back burner.

(Dennett 2001: 35)

Putting to one side Dennett's sneering language, note the way in which he privileges mass, charge, and space–time over against first-person experience. Dennett offers the following advice to those of us who persist in thinking that there is such a thing as experiential awareness of properties:

> The way I recommend is to ask yourself, 'what am I pointing to? What am I ostending when I say *this*?' What I think you'll find is that you can start elaborating a sort of catalogue of the cases that matter to you at this moment. Maybe it's the particular deliciousness of this taste in my mouth; so what is that deliciousness? Well, I'd like some more, and I can recall it at a later

date, and so on. We're going to take care of all that. We're going to include your disposition to want some more, your capacity to recollect, and even the likelihood that you will find yourself pleasurably recollecting this experience of it. There's a huge manifold of reactive dispositions that you're pointing to when you're saying, 'this very yumminess right now', and what you have to do is recognize that however indissolvable, however unassailable, however intrinsically present that all seems to you, what has to be explained is that it seems to you, not that it is so.

(Blackmore 2006: 88; Dennett's emphasis)

Consider Dennett's method behind these convictions. Dennett insists that evidence for consciousness or the self must be behavioral or third-person. That is why he thinks it is more reasonable to accept the belief in mass and electric charge than experience. But look to where it seems this leads: to the utterly unacceptable conclusion that we are not substantial selves existing over time and that we do not have conscious experiences, but only appear to do so. From the standpoint of what many of us think is an immediate and unproblematic deliverance of common sense, it seems that you and I are persons enduring over time; we have experiences, make choices, and so on. Dennett sometimes asserts (with indignation) that he by no means denies selves and experiences, but I know of no other way to interpret his position than as a form of eliminativism. Dennett eliminates the explanatory role and the reality of conscious experience and the self in his final theory of what exists. In my view, such an eliminativism radically undermines the very practice of science (Taliaferro 1994). I suggest that science simply would not be possible without assuming the reality of first-person perspectives, the substantial existence of scientists themselves, and the reality of conscious, subjective experience. In *The Primacy of the Subjective* Nicholas Georgalis forcefully argues that the third-person, 'scientific' point of view is not possible without presupposing a first-person position:

Advocates of a strictly third-person methodology must be implicitly employing data or information gained from their first-person perspective in order that they may have some clue as to what to investigate from a third-person perspective, to even know what is being 'talked about' when subjective states are at issue.

(Georgalis 2006: 84)

A similar point has been made against behaviorists or neo-behaviorists by H. H. Price, Galen Strawson, Thomas Nagel, Colin McGinn, and others.

If this were an essay in philosophy of mind, multiple arguments would now need to come into play that would adjudicate between those of us who privilege the first-person versus the third-person. I have argued elsewhere against Dennett—for example, in Taliaferro 1994 and Goetz and Taliaferro 2008; but here I want to connect philosophy of mind with Dennett's approach to religious experience. Consider three points in response to Dennett's combined philosophy of mind and philosophy of religious experience. First, in his philosophy of mind, Dennett is reluctant to allow for the primacy of subjective conscious experience, but quite the opposite seems to going on in *Breaking the Spell*. In Dennett's extension of Rodney Needham's uncertainty about the mindset of others, Dennett seems to hold that a subject herself has a much greater grasp of her own thoughts than those of others. When Dennett describes a child growing up in a culture he seems to allow that the child is required to study and interpret the acts of others. He depicts the child as an anthropologist who, presumably, knows her own mind, but only gradually comes to know those of others. This seems to be quite different from Dennett's neo-behaviorism, which supposes that we may be far more certain of mass and charge (posits of physics) than we can be of conscious experience or of our awareness of ourselves as substantial individuals. Dennett might claim that in the case of the child he is using 'folk talk' as opposed to strict, scientific discourse, but in *Breaking the Spell* he appears to give folk talk far more authority and primacy than the language and framework of physics.

Second, once one allows for first-person subjective consciousness, why assume as a methodological position that religious experience cannot count as a form of observation? Recall Dennett's claim that 'religious avowals concern matters that are beyond observation, beyond meaningful test' (Dennett 2006: 240–1). *Breaking the Spell* contains no discussion or reference of any kind to the leading philosophers who have defended an observational approach to religious experience, construing such experiences as themselves forms of observation, perception, or awareness of the divine. Once one sees that Dennett's neo-behaviorism should not be considered axiomatic, there should be some engagement with work by William Alston, Caroline Franks, Keith Yandell, Richard Swinburne, Jerome Gellman, William Wainwright, and others (see Yandell 1993 as representative). If Dennett's philosophy of mind, which eliminates intentional explanations, subjective experience, and the substantial self, is sound, then one may presumably sidestep this literature with a clean conscience. If Dennett's naturalism succeeds with the natural world, why shouldn't his naturalism be the default, privileged position when it comes to explaining religion? But, once one allows that his naturalism is profoundly problematic about human beliefs, experience, and action, it no longer has a claim to be our exclusive method in the account of religion. This observation may be further articulated in terms of broadening the concept of 'explanation'; if the appeal to intentional, purposive explanations should be granted as one possible, viable option in accounting for human behavior, why rule out theistic intentional, purposive explanations in terms of religious experience or in accounts of the cosmos as a whole? Such explanations of the cosmos will best be thought of as philosophical, rather than scientific explanations (Goetz and Taliaferro 2008; Swinburne 2004).

Third, Dennett's account of relieving his daughter's pain challenges his professed skepticism about the beliefs and desires of others. When Dennett writes that 'everybody is an outsider' it seems incredible to think that Dennett himself is much of an outsider when it comes to his daughter. The case actually not only undermines Dennett's professed skepticism about the beliefs and ostensible observations of others but it is also evidence of the open-ended character of experience. I suspect that what the daughter experienced was the loving empathy of a caring father. Put to one side the mechanics by which Dennett expressed this empathy (his profession that he can absorb and remove the pain of another person anatomically) and it seems that we have a plausible case in which the perception of another person's loving care can seem to penetrate into our very being. Religious experiences come in many varieties, but one that is closest to the case Dennett describes is called the co-inherence, an event in which one person can affectively bear the pain of another person. These experiences might well be described in purely secular terms but they feature most prominently in religious contexts of mediation, modeled partly on the belief in Christ as a mediator who is able to bear the suffering and sin of others (I have defended this position in Taliaferro 1989).

To summarize: I suggest that the plausibility of Dennett's neo-behaviorism in philosophy of mind is as plausible (or implausible) as his neo-behaviorism in his philosophical analysis of religious experience, and that some of the views he seems to be committed to in his naturalistic account of religious experience appear to be in conflict with his philosophy of mind.

Proposal

What would be a fair, non question-begging inquiry? As noted earlier, I believe one needs to allow for both naturalism and theism as possible candidates for accounting for religious experiences. Neither should be presumed to be privileged at the outset. In fact, a comprehensive, more wide-ranging method would also not limit the terrain to theism and naturalism but allow for alternative secular non-naturalist accounts of the world (for example, absolute or subjective idealism), Buddhist metaphysics and epistemology, monistic forms of Hinduism, and so on. A fuller, more comprehensive investigation would allow each school of thought its own description and explanation of the wide range of what may be considered religious experience, which can then be subjected to a range of tests. These tests may include internal consistency, a philosophical analysis of the intelligibility of the concepts involved (for example, is a Buddhist concept of the self coherent? is the concept of an incorporeal God intelligible?), coherence with what we reasonably believe in science, history, and other domains, including the philosophical areas of metaphysics, epistemology, and value theory. Given such a broader outlook a naturalistic project like Dennett's should rightly give space to assessing independent theistic arguments, while a theistic project, like Keith Yandell's, which argues for a position more similar to my own (religious experience provides some evidential justification for theism), should include a treatment of the most powerful arguments for naturalism. Regrettably, Dennett only spends about five pages in *Breaking the Spell* in assessing independent theistic arguments. When his objection to the cosmological argument is 'What caused God?' it is tempting to read this material as merely (to use Dennett's phrase about Roman Catholics' inquiry into whether an ostensible miracle can be explained scientifically) going through the motions. Still, Dennett's aim of taking on theistic arguments is precisely the kind of task that needs to be undertaken by naturalists who truly wish to break the intellectual and experiential allurement of a religious world view and practice. It is only on such a wider terrain that we can reasonably form judgments as to whose spell should be broken: the theists' or the naturalists', or some other, alternative religious or secular world view.

I I

Humanness in their Hearts: Where Science and Religion Fuse

Del Ratzsch[1]

This is...not the kind of area in which decisive arguments are available; rather it's the kind of area in which one has had a good day if one manages not to drown.

Jerry Fodor, *In Critical Condition* (Cambridge, Mass.: MIT Press, 1998), 63–4[2]

Introduction

Attempts to relate science and faith have been of perennial interest to the Christian intellectual community. Given recent Western academic history, it is perhaps unsurprising that virtually all such attempts have been fundamentally propositionalistic. The problem has been seen as one of finding, stating, and elucidating the right *principles* of integration; of discovering what *propositions* (and theories) of science should penetrate theology and religious beliefs; of discovering what *propositions* of religious belief and what *doctrines* of theology should carry weight in the scientific context; of figuring out how *contradictions* or apparent *conflicts* between scientific and religious statements should be resolved; of working out how the *claims* of the two could be made *logically consistent*; of constructing *arguments* showing,

1. I am grateful to Alvin Plantinga, Jeff Schloss, Jitse Vandermeer, Joe LaPorte, Stephen Matheson, and Luke Maring for discussion and comments.
2. Fodor is on a different topic here, but the sentiment is spot on.

for example, how science could provide *rational support* for religious beliefs. What I wish to suggest in the following is that that may not be the most productive way to conceive of the problem.

That viable integration should not necessarily be a matter of proposition dynamics is perhaps not really surprising. Our deepest springs are not all propositional—much less propositionally articulable. That religion is not ultimately propositional is a widely attractive view. And one influential conception of scientific theories is the semantic conception according to which theories are structures in n-dimensional state spaces (or sets of models) rather than axiomatically structured collections of propositions. If the two relata of science–religion integration are not wholly propositional, then perhaps the conceptual resources for integration will not be confined to those of relationships among propositions or propositional entities. They might, rather, partially reflect other aspects of the dynamics of human rational cognition. In what follows, I wish to do some initial exploration in that direction.

The Extra-empirical

The picture of a science grounded on a bedrock of pure empirical data, rigidly structured according to as logically rigorous a system of induction as constructable and shorn of all metaphysics, religion, and other perceived conceptual contaminants, reigned as an ideal beginning with its influential early expositor, Bacon. But recent history has not been kind to that view, and despite its still wielding significant inertial underground conceptual clout the erosion of substantive parts of the view is very nearly complete. It is no longer controversial that things other than pure data and reason function within science or that data themselves are not always so pure as once thought. Indeed, other factors—extra-empirical factors—*have* to function in science for science itself to function.

Underdetermination

Empirical data underdetermine scientific theories in that for any body of empirical data, no matter how large or complete, there are always in principle unlimitedly many theoretical interpretations consistent with those data. It follows that no body of empirical data ever logically entails or conclusively confirms *the* relevant correct theory. Empirical data by themselves cannot generate, identify, nor rigorously drive us to some single theory from among all possible competitors. Underdetermination, then, presents us with a forced choice between empirical purity (at a cost of the theoretical) and theoretical legitimacy (at the cost of absolute empirical rigor). Thus, when we *do* single out a particular theory our selection process will of necessity involve extra-empirical factors—factors beyond the purely empirical. A realist science thus cannot survive on just empirical observation and logic but requires richer conceptual resources and is of necessity integrally embedded in a deeper conceptual matrix from which it cannot be cleanly detached intact.

Among the operative presuppositions upon which science unavoidably depends, many are unproblematic, and various of them are so familiar as ordinarily to escape attention. It must be presupposed that there is a real world; that it is largely 'out there'; that it exists largely independent of us; that it persists; that change is real; that events in that world have effects; that there are stabilities and uniformities extending through time and space. The cosmos must be assumed to be to some degree understandable by the minds doing the science. Our grasping of nature's intelligibility (in any realist sense) requires a significant isomorphism between patterns defining the phenomena understood, and patterns in and of our cognitive structures. And for our senses to be a means by which we acquire scientifically essential contingent data those faculties must be in some general sense reliable with respect to aspects of the real world.

None of the above is perceived as seriously problematic. As it turns out, however, the above collection is still profoundly inadequate. Science can be *pursued* only if it has some aim, some goal(s). All such are, of course, value-steeped (and historically variable). Such goals and values are not forced upon us by reality but involve human decision. And, since what *methods* are appropriate is linked to what goals are being pursued, 'scientific method' itself may be partially shaped by such choices. Assumptions concerning what specific approaches to a nature available to investigators of our sort are likely to be successful will be inescapable as well. Defining the very category of 'scientific'—let alone selecting specific theories within that category—requires norms restricting the explanatory and descriptive concepts legit-imately deployable, the types of inferences permissible, and the obligatory structure of a 'good' explanation. For instance, in the early modern period, theories whose dynamics were not mechanical, whose ontology was not corpuscular, whose forces were not contact were dismissed as beyond the proper scientific pale.

Although historically unstable, the catalog of such norms and indicators typically includes empirical adequacy, accuracy, breadth, elegance, coherence, fruitfulness, predictiveness, simplicity, beauty, unifying or systematizing power, inherent plausibility, explanatory power, interestingness, and the like.

Such characteristics are not easily formally definable, come in a wide range of degrees, often come into conflict, can be given a variety of relative weights and rank orderings, admit of varying procedures for conflict resolution, and so forth. Assessments of such characteristics are highly disputable, and are not straightforwardly, rigorously, empirically driven, algorithmic, rule-governed, nor neatly axiomatizable.

And the science that we do, the theories we employ, the picture of the world we piece together: human concepts are structural elements of all of them. In doing science we are inarguably limited to concepts for which our human cognitive faculties are competent. Beyond that, at any given moment we are in practice limited to a perhaps fairly small subset of those humanly graspable conceptual resources. We have not yet thought of everything humans can think of, and what we have thought of arises out of human-mediated resources. Some even of those materials will have very human histories—some as human creative inventions, some having histories with roots well beyond the domain of the laboratory. After all, nature cannot simply dictate theoretical concepts or theories. And other human choices—religious, philosophical, and even political—have affected the scope and content of such resources.

Humanness and deeper matters

But structures of our humanness factor in at even deeper levels—levels of which we are typically not even aware.

Perception

Interests, mindsets, enthusiasms, expectations, and so forth obviously might affect what is perceptually noticed, attended to, or singled out as significant.

But at present many believe that some human factors are partially *constitutive* of the very experiences of perception themselves.

As presently conceived, perception involves more of the observer than merely mechanically operating sensory faculties, and some of that additional involvement is active. Such activity can grow out of anything, from very specific theory-based expectations through broader conceptual commitments, or background mindsets, to full-blown world views. And it is not that such factors merely direct or filter perception but that they partially shape the very content of some perceptual experiences. Thus, when veteran telescopic observers draw detailed diagrams of canals on Mars, when reputable professional physicists write technical papers reporting properties of the lines generated by their N-ray diffractors, when early professional followers of Darwin discuss observations of *Bathybius haeckelii*, or when early microscopists produce sketches of homunculi, we need not necessarily dismiss it as invention, self-delusion, or deceit. And when the two sides of nineteenth-century disputes over heredity systematically report different observed behavior of chromosomes during meiosis we need not necessarily attribute it either to incompetence or to desperate efforts to save face by the losing side. If perception is indeed an active process, it may well be that in all these sorts of cases the scientists in question were perfectly *accurately* reporting the actual *contents* of their conscious observational experiences.[3] And if, as some argue (à la Kant; Kuhn), the constitutive activity of the subjective is preconscious, so that even our most basic perceptual experiences are simply presented to us already actively shaped and completed, then there is diminished prospect of self-correction (see, e.g., Feyerabend 1975: 73, 78). Our awarenesses and experiences come to us in *some* degree shaped, screened, assessed—with a pre-interpretational cast to them. That is emphatically *not* to endorse the counsel of critical and epistemic unconditional surrender according to which cognition (or worse, reality or truth) is 'interpretation all the way down', whatever that ultimately comes to. But it *is* to say that within our cognition some tinge of (pre)interpretation is never completely absent.

Where might such preconscious content come from? On modular theories, essential information structures are built into the operation of the brain itself. For instance, Steven Pinker regarding vision:

---

3. According to Jeff Hawkins and Sandra Blakeslee, there are about ten times as many paths from the brain to the senses as in the reverse direction (Hawkins and Blakeslee 2004: 25). Concerning 'filling in', see, e.g., ibid.: 117 and *passim*.

[O]ptics is easy, but inverse optics is impossible. Yet your brain does it every time you open the refrigerator and pull out a jar. How can this be? The answer is that *the brain supplies the missing information*, information about the world we evolved in and how it reflects light.

(Pinker 1997: 28; see also de Sousa 1987: 191, 194)

Such built-in preconscious specialized information is essential for solving otherwise unsolvable inverse problems in other areas as well (e.g., kinematics), and constitutes part of Pinker's case for modularity. This, of course, amounts to a neurophysiological solution to underdetermination.

Intelligibility

A key task of the scientific enterprise is that of making parts of the world *understandable*, or *intelligible*, to us. The concept *understanding* is extremely difficult to explicate. But the basic idea is straightforward: understanding something involves removal of at least some of its mystery. The process of coming to understand something involves a transition from mystery to sense-making. What seems to make *sense* is, of course, tightly connected to such important epistemic factors as background beliefs, conceptual matrix, theory commitments, paradigms, and even world views. But what seems to make sense is also notoriously dependent upon psychological circumstances, mental condition, levels of various substances in the brain and so forth.

But there is something even more fundamentally human at work here as well. Identification of sense-making, or intelligibility, presents itself to us experientially as a particular *feel*, a particular *seeming*, that defines our conviction that something makes sense, that we have gripped the correlation of reality to cognition. The presence of this experiential dimension may explain why our talk in this area is so often metaphorical—we 'see' it, the 'light dawns', we 'grasp' the matter, and so on. And we cannot get behind or underneath this experience to examine its credentials. Any evaluation of its credentials would have to employ resources and procedures whose justification would ultimately track back at least in part to that experiential dimension itself—the support for those credentials would have to strike us as themselves making sense. As with our other faculties of cognition, at some point and in some circumstances it must simply become a human brute given of the process. This general point was behind the remark of the physicist Sir Denys Haigh Wilkinson that even on purely scientific questions, after having done all the science we can do, finally we 'cannot do more than say "this makes me feel good; this is how it has to be" ' (Wilkinson 1977: 22). Others have made similar observations (Bonner 1988; Kosso 1998: 27–8; Polanyi 1946: 9; Putnam 1987: 22). In fact, Paul Thagard even includes a 'happiness node' in his computational scheme for justification of theories (Thagard 2002: 246–7).

It appears relatively clear that this experiential dimension can be triggered by any number of (suspect or completely unsuspected) human factors. Things that make *intense* sense in dreams, or to the intoxicated, or to the mad, are often utterly indescribable in ordinary discourse. Not only is this 'sense' faculty thus not infallible but there is apparently no non-circular procedure for justifying reliance upon it. There is thus apparently some internal experiential faculty of human cognition upon which we cannot escape placing a crucial dependence, but into whose inner workings (and propriety) we cannot look.[4]

So the whole idea of understanding (scientific or otherwise) rests upon an involuntary endorsement of the objective legitimacy of specific *human inner phenomenal experiences* associated with particular things having a genuinely sense-making appearance. That we are not dealing here with some 'objective' human-free process seems amply clear. Thus, one of the foundational aims of science and its key operative faculties may not even be *definable* in human-free terms. That is not to say that it does not work, is unreliable, should be ignored, is irrational to trust, or anything of the sort. I believe none of those to be true. But its workings seem to be largely involuntary, we have little clue as to how it works or why the things that trigger it do so, and it seems to be both profoundly human and inevitably (maybe even essentially) affected by a wide variety of human factors and foibles.

Explanations

Explanations are what supply the materials which allow that 'seeing'. And a good explanation must supply the sort of materials which, in the complicated human cognitive context in question, will trigger that shift from mystery to sense. Such shifts are mediated by a complicated, enmeshing system of outlooks, stances, theoretical commitments, expectations,

---

4. 'Nearly all important thinking takes place outside of consciousness and is not available to introspection' (Fauconnier and Turner 2002: 33). See also ibid.: 18, 72, and *passim*.

sensitivities, psychologies, and the like. Many of the relevant factors we can easily identify. But not all may be explicitly identifiable. And various of the crucial components do not seem to be propositional.[5]

Reason

It is tempting to think that, whatever other domains of human cognition may be human-colored, at least *reason*—especially such rigorously rational pursuits as mathematics, logic, and 'scientific reasoning'—will not be tainted. But that seems unlikely.

Human intuition

As paradoxical as it may sound, even our most rigorous reasoning rests at bottom upon human intuitions. Formal reasoning (mathematics, formal logic, etc.) cannot proceed without at least some basic axioms, derivation procedures, formation and transformation rules, and other inferential resources. Those in their turn can be justified only as basic givens which have the property of just seeming right (or necessarily true, self-evident, incorrigible, etc.), or which when employed in ways sanctioned by the system itself generate results which exhibit some required virtue (consistency, etc.). But, either way, there will be an ultimate dependence upon some human capacity for registering or recognizing the special character involved. That capacity might be some judgment concerning consistency or coherence, or concerning the rational unacceptability of contradictions. Or it might be an unshakable sense that the foundational logic operations that *seem* absolutely right to us really *are* absolutely right—that our inability to imagine how denials of such intuitions could even be thinkable testify to their absolute legitimacy. Or it might be something else entirely. Mathematician Keith Devlin notes (more or less apologetically) that 'If you push me to say how I know [that Hilbert's proofs are correct], I will end up mumbling that his arguments convince me and have convinced all the other mathematicians I know.'[6]

Here we find shared *human convictions* at the very heart of mathematics. And speaking of our 'precision intelligence' Pinker says:

5. According to Steven Weinberg, even *beauty* is part of what it is to *be* an explanation (1992: 149, also 90, 131, 165).
6. *Discover*, Jan. 2004, p. 36: '2003: Mathematicians Face Uncertainty'.

No rational creature can consult rules all the way down; that way infinite regress lies. At some point, a thinker must *execute* a rule because he just can't help it; it's the human way, a matter of course, the only appropriate and natural thing to do—in short an instinct.

(Pinker 1997: 185)

So we deal here with not merely convictions, but *instinct*. Indeed, the credentials in question may not always even rise to the level of instinct. Von Neumann is often quoted as claiming that 'in mathematics you don't understand things, you just get used to them'.

But whatever starting-point we pick will have a similar status—complete and unavoidable dependence ultimately upon some faculty or set of faculties, some intuition(s) that we human beings have. There simply is no other way to get any such project off the ground—or even onto the runway to begin with. That will hold true of any rational project—logic, mathematics, and scientific reason included.

Emotion

Clearly, emotion could be involved in science in conceptually superficial (although practically consequential) ways—choice of research problems and so forth. Emotion may be involved in more surprising ways in the prosecution of science. Although interpretation of some of the data is controversial, Fiedler and Bless suggest that,

Positive emotional states facilitate active generation, whereas negative emotional states support the conservation of input data. In other words, positive moods should encourage the application of prior knowledge structures (schemas, stereotypes, scripts) to infer new information beyond the available data. In contrast, negative mood states should induce a conservative set to adhere to the input data as carefully as possible.

(Fiedler and Bless 2000: 147)

(That might explain why one never hears of a jovial positivist.) It seems thus clear that Joseph Forgas is correct in his contention that '[A]ffective states have a widespread, automatic and largely unnoticed influence on both the content, and the process of cognition' (Forgas 2000: 109).[7] Emotion may operate even more substantively in certain types of rational

---

7. Forgas has also done some research suggesting that eyewitness observations are more accurate if one is in a bad mood.

decision-making.[8] A number of neurophysiologists (e.g., Antonio Damasio; Oliver Sacks; V. S. Ramachandran), on the basis of both laboratory and clinical studies, have argued that people lacking appropriate emotional functioning can be incapable of full normal cognizing in some cases and in particular seem to be unable to make rational decisions in cases involving their own welfare. On the view advanced, what we typically take to be rational behavior, especially in practical decision-making, is an outcome of complex interactions among a number of systems of neural systems. Among the components involved are systems associated with emotion (e.g., the amygdala and other parts of the limbic system). What has recently apparently emerged is that certain sorts of rationality are compromised or absent in the absence of emotion—that when the 'emotion' systems are damaged, or otherwise without effective function, the sort of rational decisions essential to normal social functioning and even to some types of personal welfare are not made. Without functioning emotion, the 'decision-making landscape' is flat, leaving the person involved with less than sufficient reason to pick any one goal or strategy over any other. Indeed, Damasio argues (in connection with his 'somatic marker hypothesis'[9]) that, were emotion not involved in such decisions, practical decisions in real time would generally be impossible. It was thus, he argues, a near evolutionary necessity that nature 'built the apparatus of rationality not just on top of the apparatus of biological regulation, but also *from* it and *with* it' (Damasio 1999: 128).[10]

And various structures in the brain (e.g., tonically active neuron sites in the caudate) directly integrate reason inputs (from the prefrontal cortex) with emotion inputs (from the amygdala).[11] Although Damasio does not argue explicitly for it, he suspects that other types of rationality beyond the practical (and he specifically includes scientific reasoning and mathematics) function essentially like the rationality of practical decision-making.

8. There is a significant literature arguing that emotions contain judgments or other cognitive components and can thus be in some sense rational—e.g., Robert Solomon, Bennett W. Helm, and others.

9. This theory is developed in Damasio 1994 and discussed also in Damasio 1999: 41 and 2003: 148. Damasio concludes that 'Well-targeted and well-deployed emotion seems to be a support system without which the edifice of reason cannot operate properly.'

10. Damasio also speaks of the 'mind . . . so closely shaped by the body' at Damasio 1999: 143.

11. See, e.g., Schwartz and Begley 2002: 67 and Pinker 1997: 371 ff. for discussion.

Emotion may be involved even more deeply in some ways. Ramachandran and Blakeslee discuss a variety of fascinating cases (Blakeslee and Ramachandran 1998: chap. 8). In fact, on some views, emotion structures are involved in consciousness itself (Hamer 2004: 100 ff.). There is even some evidence that evaluation of the logical validity of simple syllogisms involves different combinations of neural systems depending upon the emotional salience of the *topic* of the syllogism (Goel and Dolan 2003). In any case, on a number of levels, reason and emotion seem to function as a not wholly dissolvable unit.

Emotion can even—properly, on some views—run deep in what are de facto more specifically science-relevant directions.[12] For instance, Thagard has recently argued that one important and legitimate factor in theory justification in science is whether or not acceptance of the theory maximizes coherence—including *emotional* coherence (see Thagard 2002: 235–50; also Clore and Gasper 2000: 24 ff.). And Christopher Hookway has recently argued that emotion in some cases runs close to the cognitive heart of science. According to Hookway, felt emotional responses can be one way that intuitively applied but unarticulated *epistemic* evaluative criteria present themselves to us cognitively. If that is the case, then given that some individual criteria—not to mention the complete catalog of criteria—may be not only unarticulated but propositionally unarticulable, i.e., it may be that 'effective *epistemic* evaluation could turn out to be *impossible* without ... appropriate emotional responses' (Hookway 2002: 257, my emphasis; a related position is taken in Clore and Gasper 2000). Further, in scientific investigations *some* sort of stopping procedures are essential both because theories are in principle subject to massive underdetermination and because investigative, experimental, and explanatory regresses threaten in the absence of applicable stopping points. Emotion constitutes a mechanism for stepping out of the regress: '[T]he end of inquiry must be regulated by an emotional change' (Hookway 2002: 258). And given that relevant emotion may be how unarticulated *epistemic* criteria present, that need not undermine the rationality of such procedures. Emotion can not only stop the regress, but 'Emotional judgments ensure that our reflections stop at the right place' (Hookway 2002: 257).

---

12. According to van Fraassen (2002), emotion provides an essential impetus in Kuhnian revolutions. Van Fraassen summarizes the view succinctly at 2005: 93.

Various people (e.g., Ronald de Sousa) argue that '[E]motions apprehend an axiological level of reality' (de Sousa 1987: 301). If that is true, and if we indeed live in a coherently integrated cosmos which embodies axiological realities, then not only may human reason functionally depend in part on emotion, but science's capability of zeroing in on actual truth may thus depend upon emotion as well. In any case, to the extent that experiences of emotion tie into reality, or to the extent that they are essential even to scientific rationality, to that extent they cannot be dismissed as *mere* subjectivity, wholly irrelevant to truth.

Somato-kinetics

Damasio believes that even the *body* gets involved in reason in ways so substantive that, he claims, the body 'contributes a *content* that is part and parcel of the workings of the normal mind' (Damasio 2004: 226). That sounds extremely odd, but, remarkably, in responding to a question concerning the 'internal or mental images...mathematicians make use of, whether they are motor, auditory, visual, or mixed', Einstein responded that 'the psychical entities which seem to serve as elements in thought... are, in my case, of visual and some of muscular type' (Hadamard 1945: App. II, pp. 142–3). And, as it turns out, Einstein was not alone here.[13] Of course, to the extent that our concepts are shaped or determined by contingent human neurophysiological—and neuromuscular—structures (rather than contingent human sociohistorical structures) which have (allegedly) resulted from contingent—even accidental—vicissitudes of our history, they may have tilts bearing no substantive relationship to anything whatever. It is not at all obvious that the substantive contents of various concepts generated by a physiology driven by biochemistry in turn driven by physical laws and randomness must be related either to each other or to relevant aspects of nature in any truth-preserving or truth-reflecting ways. And, even if it *did* appear obvious, that appearance might itself be a mere epiphenomenon of neurophysiological quirks. As the biologist and one-time Marxist J. B. S. Haldane remarked:

> [I]f my mental processes are determined wholly by the motions of atoms in my brain, I have no reason to suppose that my beliefs are true. They may be

---

13. In Roe 1952: 145–7, Anne Roe reports that 19% of the social scientists in her study reported 'kinesthetic elements, that is, feelings of muscular tension' involved in their thinking (oddly, none of the physical scientists did). See also Giere 1988: 136.

sound chemically, but that does not make them sound logically. And hence I have no reason for supposing my brain to be composed of atoms.

(Haldane 1928: 220)

(Nor any reason for, for example, supposing any of Dawkins's anti-religious memes to be true.)

Here, then, is another place for characteristically human but non-propositional input into science—one would anticipate that Alpha Centaurians (or even different human genders), with vastly different bodies presumably supplying a different *content*, would reason in different, or perhaps even incommensurable, ways.

Tacit recognition of a role for the body within abstract cognition itself may underlie the conviction of Kuhn and others that hands-on training is an *essential* part of science education, that relevant aspects of scientific pursuits may not even be expressible—much less reducible to propositions—but may be part of a very literal somatic 'feel' that guides a significant part of scientific activity (what Karin Knorr-Cetina calls an 'action/cognition mesh' (1981: 4)). And, of course, many religions take *acts* of worship to be essential to the grasping of the very *content* of religious faith itself.

Gedanken models

Some (even including Freud) have argued that reasoning (of at least some types) is not propositional, but involves direct mental manipulation of mental models. For instance, Nancy Nersession argues that key types of reasoning 'developed as a means of simulating possible ways of manoeuvering within the physical environment' (2002: 152, 146). Such reasoning processes are, she claims, 'modal in format and employ perceptual and possibly motor mechanisms in processing' (2002: 140). On this view, '[t]he reasoning process is through model manipulations and involves processing mechanisms used in perceptual-motor activity'. Such reasoning would again introduce an implicit physical and non-propositional motif into the operation of reason itself (Pinker 1997: 335).

Other

Various people have argued for the involvement of other factors and faculties as well. For instance, it has recently been argued by Fauconnier and Turner that many of our deepest cognitive processes rest ultimately on our faculty of imagination (see Fauconnier and Turner 2002: 6, 8, 89, 95, 115, and *passim*). And, of course, the roles of culture, social structures, and the like are frequently cited in this context. Much of that is familiar, and I will not pursue such suggestions here.

Personhood and individuality

All of the above human factors have potential consequences for human cognition—from perception to common sense to the most delicate tweaks of our theorizing. What might be the consequences of all this humanness here? Looking at nature through night-vision goggles, everything is tinged green. Looking at reality through human-cognitive goggles, everything is tinged—what? We can abstract away the greenness, being able to isolate it by contrast with other experiences as an artifact of the system. In the human-cognitive case, we apparently have no abstraction-permitting contrast—*all* our experiences are human-mediated. And this humanness cannot be purged from science.

Science-relevant factors get even more specific. Physicists both past and present have been struck by an aesthetic dimension in nature. Nature's laws have often been cited for their symmetry, their elegance, their order, their unity, their exquisite meshing, and for the harmonies sung by their mathematical structure. All of those have been taken as constituting part of their *beauty*. This aesthetic dimension is perceived as so fundamentally infused into the structure of law that many physicists take beauty to be a pointer toward truth (e.g., Polkinghorne 1984: 57–8).

But, surely if *anything* is deeply rooted in our individual humanness it is our appreciation of what is and is not beautiful or elegant.[14] If our sense of the beautiful serves among the indispensable evaluative procedures within science then deep human factors figure into selection of descriptive and explanatory content within those areas.

Even such seemingly tractable, no-nonsense values as 'empirical adequacy' have their murkier side. In practice, adequacy often operates among a cluster of such ill-definable principles as that of 'enoughness'—convictions concerning whether the data are precise enough, numerous enough, close enough to predicted values, whether a theory is accurate enough, simple

---

14. Some argue that aesthetic appreciation contains an ineliminable emotional component.

enough, powerful enough, better enough than alternatives, supported by data strongly enough, whether essential concepts are clear enough, non-metaphysical enough, whether the picture generated fits well enough with other conceptual commitments, and so forth. On none of those fronts is there a definitive cut-off point or rigorous—or even statable—algorithm for resolution.[15] Thus, here in what was once supposed to be the heart of scientific empirical rigor one finds individual human inklings, urges, intuitions, and inclinations—and indefinable and contentious ones at that.

Even personal psychologies function here. According to Damasio, the participation of the person is deep, with one's very *sense of self* ... influenc[ing] the processing of whatever gets to be known' (emphasis mine, Damasio 1999: chap. 1, and *passim*; see also Wentzel van Huyssteen 1999: chap. 3, e.g., pp. 174–6; and chap. 4). That accords with some further remarks from Wilkinson:

> How do we then choose between alternative scientific hypotheses when we have used up all our scientific criteria? We are, of course, left face to face with ourselves. The only remaining criterion is what seems right to us ... in the deepest seat of human feeling ... [I]n science, we sift and exhaust the evidence and then choose because we feel. Man's essential humanity must become, at this stage, not integrated with, but a replacement for, science until new data come along to permit the taking up again of the scientific method ...
>
> (Wilkinson 1977)[16]

It thus looks as though some deeply intertwined, unitarily melded features of our humanness and even of individual personhood lie deep in the center of science. As Polanyi once remarked, the personal dimension is 'no mere imperfection but a *vital component* of knowledge' (Polanyi 1946: preface).

Cognitive Terrain

How exactly ought we to think about all this? I don't know how we should think about all this *exactly*, but I want to develop an analogical way of

---

15. Ronald Giere argues that 'the necessity for dealing with values or interests is explicit from the start' (1988: 161).

16. We are *always* in a situation of having less than complete data.

thinking *approximately* about the above factors and their implications for various aspects of cognition. Indeed, it is not clear how other than analogically one *can* approach non-propositional matters in cognitive contexts. In fact, some have held that there are truths which can be expressed in no other way than analogically or narratively.[17]

Think of the underlying structure of one's cognition as a *terrain* with a variety of hills, peaks, valleys, and other contours.[18] Just as water flows preferentially in some directions and resists others on a physical terrain, so inferences, intuitions, and convictions might tend to flow in some directions rather than others on a cognitive terrain. Or, just as strange attractors may make arrival at a specified region nearly inevitable on a mathematical terrain, a cognitive terrain might contain some conceptual depression into which every interpretation of every experience or bit of data eventually slid. (Think of conspiracy theories, paranoia, or deep philosophical commitments.) And, just as some physical landscapes cannot support some buildings, some types of theories might not sit stably upon some types of cognitive terrain.

One consequence is that there will be various inbuilt undertows in our cognition. Sometimes those undertows can even carry our thinking and inferences in directions which we wouldn't consciously and intentionally approve. Numerous studies have shown that the ordinary logical, mathematical, probabilistic, and physical reasoning even of those trained in relevant fields does not always conform to the formal rules they (and we) rationally endorse. Perhaps, as Thomas Huxley once remarked, 'What we call rational grounds for our beliefs are often extremely irrational attempts to justify our instincts' (Blakeslee and Ramachandran 1998: 152).[19]

---

17. I think that Iris Murdoch held something like this (see Murdoch 1971: 34). Some postmodernists can be read in this direction—e.g., Wentzel van Huyssteen cites Jean-François Lyotard as holding that narratives can provide types of knowledge unavailable in any other way. And if I read parts of Haraway 1990 correctly she is suggesting that this is the way scientific theories sometimes carry their content. Andrew Newberg and Eugene D'Aquili note (in connection with their 'cognitive imperative') that 'we cannot help but to organize the world and our experience of the world by creating stories and ultimately myths to help perform this function' (2001: 191, n. 8). That may be connected with the fact (according to, e.g., Dennett) that narratives—stories—carry more effective convincing power than does, e.g., argumentation (Dennett 1995: 12).

18. Others have arrived at similar pictures, and speak of conceptual topologies, conceptual landscapes, etc.

19. William James and others have made similar remarks.

In some sense, reality, via those of our contacts with it to which we causally respond, projects onto our cognitive terrain, and the picture modeled there will depend both upon the character of the projection and upon the antecedent shape of the terrain. Of some of those projections we are aware—those would constitute a subset of our experience, sensory and/or otherwise. There will be many projectings of which we are unaware and no doubt many such of which we cannot even in principle be aware, even though they may affect features of that terrain. Clearly, not merely the character of the resultant picture, but whether or not the resultant picture reflects, is in some sense isomorphic to, or in some sense mirrors, reality, and depends upon the character of the projection, the terrain, and the projection/terrain interaction. (It is, of course, possible that reality is such that no projection upon any possible terrain could mirror that reality, in which case the character of *truth* in any sense available to us becomes problematic if not inscrutable. That may be one way to read Kant.)

Principles governing interactions between our cognitive structures and (contacts with) the reality outside of us, as well as principles governing the internal dynamics of our reactions to and processings of such contacts, and principles dictating the effects of such contacts, reactings, and processings upon our cognitive terrains are, of course, themselves parts of the standing order of the reality independent of us. (It may be possible for our cognitions—or other effects—to affect the given structures and processes of reality, but even if so the principles according to which such changes occur would themselves belong to the reality beyond our reach.)

Depending upon the relevant governing principles and upon how fine-grained the effects they dictate, it may be that no two human beings have *exactly* the same cognitive terrain, or that no one person has *exactly* the same cognitive terrain for any time longer than the minimum stimulus processing time. The picture of reality any individual has will depend upon interactions between the factors which define one's individual personhood and the reality which impinges upon that personhood. The resultant combined package may be individually unique. Certainly, the package of experiences, precise corner of reality, etc. will be unique, and if each such feature/factor has the requisite sort of effect, then unless some details get swamped or unless the causal correlates follow some many–one mapping, the resultant terrains will be individually unique. But, depending upon the relevant degree of fine-grainedness, there may be overlaps in terrain—we may all experience the moon in roughly identical, similar, isomorphic, or equivalent ways, for instance. But, even so, there may be individual differences, gender differences, or cultural differences, and there would almost certainly be species differences.

I take any individual's cognitive terrain to be (ideally) a single, unified entity comprised of the relevant melded ingredients. Not only do cognitive scientists tend to talk that way in related areas, but the unity and comprehensive character of individual terrains is at least suggested by a variety of correlations between apparently disparate parts of the thinking of a wide range of experimental subjects. The integrated character of cognitive terrains would further suggest that wider social and historical matters— including religious belief—would have their effects on not only directions and reception, but on the contents of science as well. I take that to be right, although claims in this area are routinely overinflated and undersupported.

Cognitive Terrains and Science

As mentioned above, some research indicates that a flat emotional terrain leaves one rudderless and incapable of *practical* rational decisions. Similarly, a flat extra-empirical conceptual terrain leaves one theoretically rudderless and incapable of *theoretical* rational decisions.[20] But, more fundamentally, scientific content is compromised on a metaphysically flat conceptual terrain as well. Of course, epistemic values and various other of the presupposed principles glossed early on provide some of the required relief features for a science-permitting conceptual terrain, but they are not sufficient—the non-propositional factors cataloged above have a role as well. Thus:

(1) A 'non-flat' conceptual terrain is essential to science.
(2) The terrain in question is human-shaped.

Those I take to be beyond dispute. The first represents in part the demise of Baconianism and Positivism, the second some of the insights (often overblown) of the post-Kuhn era. It is crucial to recognize also that:

20. And note that some philosophers of science take scientific reasoning to be more closely akin to decision-making than to inference. See, e.g., Giere 1988: p. xvi.

(3) There may be only a very small part of the possible cognitive terrain state-space which can display (or model) truth/nature.

Think of a flat grid with a number of separate irregular closed loops of varying size irregularly placed. It might very well be impossible to assign any rhyme, reason, pattern, or meaning to those loops. But, suppose that the grid was a 3-dimensional terrain, with a projection rising through and filling each loop, contoured in such a way that every segment of every loop was at a uniform height, precisely at the same level as every other loop. Significations now begin virtually to leap out of the grid—for example, a contour map of an erosional field cutting through a specific geological horizon which has left a number of peaks projecting above that horizon—a reading that the most complete two-dimensional description and equations would never have hinted at. That significance would have been masked— indeed non-existent—over the vast majority of possible grid terrains. Only a very particular *sort* of terrain would display the right revealing picture. In the case of a conceptual terrain, the flat scenario would be like a situation of underdetermination, that situation being remedied by the collection of extra-empirical factors from earlier discussion constituting an elevation dimension.

Of course, physical structures cannot just hover detachedly and independently above the underlying terrain—and scientific theories aiming at making nature's projections onto our conceptual terrain intelligible cannot just hover detachedly and independently above the underlying cognitive terrain. Theory stability requires that theories *fit* the relevant terrain.

If genuine scientific understanding involves (or just is) an isomorphism between our cognitive theoretical structures and reality, then not just any old cognitive terrain will permit intelligibility.[21] Think of it this way: nature in some sense projects onto our cognitive terrain, and only if we have cognitive contours upon which nature's loops can be properly signifyingly projected will we get any purchase upon truth.[22] And contours and tilts built into or developed within that terrain will have significant effects for what theories are even thought of (e.g., the traditional context of discovery), thought to be worth exploring (e.g., Laudan's context of pursuit),

---

21. Charles S. Peirce, for instance, spoke of the necessity for a 'sufficient affinity between the reasoner's mind and nature's' (1931: 121).
22. That 'projection' will, of course, itself be mediated by our own sensory–cognitive systems— themselves affected by that terrain.

thought to make prima facie sense (e.g., Berger's plausibility structures), thought to be likely (e.g., Bayesian prior probabilities), thought to be supported (e.g., the traditional context of justification), and a variety of other scientifically consequential matters.

Peirce wondered why and how the mind, looking for scientific hypotheses could so quickly zero in on a truly vanishing fraction of all possible hypotheses which yet—if science indeed moves toward truth—contained theories which were on the right general track. Mind, Peirce said, somehow has a 'natural adaptation to imagining correct theories', a 'power of guessing right' after a mere few trials, while 'leaving the vast majority of possible hypotheses unexamined'.[23] Induction, chance, standard inferences, and other formalisms do not provide any answers here.[24] (This is a bit reminiscent of the ability of human chess grand masters to beat computers such as Deep Blue—which have the capacity to analyze 100 million chess positions per second—i.e., the ability to single out better moves without (it seems to me) processing anywhere remotely near that number of alternatives.)

But the right sort of cognitive terrain would automatically (and preconsciously) exclude the vast bulk of misdirected hypotheses (and chess moves), and might even provide a tilt at least isomorphic to the right sort of hypothesis. Hookway argues specifically that emotion can help with the necessary exclusionary pruning function.[25] De Sousa also argues that emotion constitutes a partial solution. Indeed, he says, emotions are 'indispensable' to that solution, and thus 'their existence grounds the very possibility of rationality at [the] more conventional levels [of, for example, lines of inquiry and preferred inference patterns]' (1987: 192 ff, 203).

As noted, many of the extra-empirical matters are not only noncognitive and non-propositional, but are involuntary as well. We do not control the structure of our intuitions, the basic character of our emotions, our neurophysiology, our biochemistry, the innate principles of terrain modification, and so forth.[26] So, if we have any hope of getting our

---

23. Peirce, Aristotle, Galileo, and others have held versions of this view.
24. This is, in effect, what de Sousa refers to as the 'philosopher's frame problem'.
25. Hookway 2002: 261. (One version of this solution casts emotion as involving state-space search procedures. See Dylan Evans, 'The Search Hypothesis of Emotion' (Evans and Cruse 2004: 179–91).)
26. And if it is ultimately only stories—narratives—that convince, then even scientific explanations will be subject to the sort of non-formal constraints which satisfactoriness of narrative imposes. The shape of such satisfaction requirements are, of course, part of the underlying terrain.

science right, that will rest in part on the hope that the deep, involuntary, non-cognitive matters that shape our cognitive terrain have done so in appropriate ways. Science depends upon cognitive fine-tuning just as our existence depends upon cosmic fine-tuning.

And the fact that that underlying cognitive fine-tuning is partially non-propositional may be one reason why earlier attempts to axiomatize science (or parts of it) were so sterile. It also ties in with Kuhn's contention that some crucial scientific sensitivities cannot be learned except by doing—important parts of the terrain are carved and absorbed only somatically, kinesthetically, tactilely[27] (or even, says Thagard, through 'a kind of contagion of taste and enthusiasm' (2002: 235–50)). The general process is familiar from ordinary experiences such as learning to ride a bicycle, or to fly by the seat of one's pants. (That latter is not an empty metaphor—anaesthetize the buttocks and one literally cannot fly the same way.[28]) We think of those as skills involving the often-ignored 'knowing how' district of epistemology, but science is—inescapably—part skill.

Terrain changes partially involve processes of which we are not in direct conscious control and of which we are probably not fully aware, since the terrain itself is not an object in normal investigation, but is rather a lens through which investigation takes place—a lens which when functioning properly is transparent to us. Alterations over time of a world view, of an ethos, or feedback effects of specific practices—all such things can gradually re-sculpt the terrain to the point that theories and beliefs that used to fit snugly now raise conceptual blisters.[29] That is one reason why when one reads older science one sometimes senses that the whole thing is just ineffably wrong—the old structure simply no longer sits stably on our current terrain. The structure was constructed for a terrain to which we no longer resonate. And we often cannot put a finger on exactly what the problem is, for the simple reason that part of the old terrain is in places we no longer *have* fingers for. We thus experience the epistemological equivalent of phantom itches.

---

27. On the flip side, Robert Solomon (2003: 187) argues that emotion has propositional content— even using the phrase 'kinesthetic judgments'.
28. This delightful bit of information comes via David Van Baak. For a nice informal discussion of the role of the buttocks in flying, see Budd Davisson at <http://www.airbum.com/articles/ArticleUsingButt.html>.
29. Schwartz and Begley cite some evidence that certain sorts of cognition can even alter neurological structures: '[M]ental effort and acts of will [have] the power to regulate the circuitry of [the] brain' (2002: 93).

That sort of experience is not, however, without significance. I take the rationality (not necessarily the truth) of a theory to consist in its having the appropriate fit to the underlying terrain. It is that *fit* to terrain that generates the right 'feel' of a theory—recall Wilkinson—and misfit may generate a 'feeling of unease' (Cairns-Smith 2002: 32–3). This is evocative of Wolfgang Pauli's remark that 'the deepest pleasure in science comes from finding ... a home for some deeply felt, deeply held image' (Kauffman 1993: p. vii) and Polanyi speaks of 'enjoying [the structure of mathematics] as a dwelling place for our understanding' (1959: 38). That phenomenal *experience* becomes the (or at least *our*) bottom-line marker for rationality itself.

But science-permitting terrains may have an even more intriguing feature.

Cognitive Fine-tuning: Origin?

If the terrain in question must be so exquisitely fine-tuned (at least for any plausible realism), exactly how does that fine-tuning arise?

Natural selection as sculptor?

It is widely assumed that evolution sculpted our human cognitive terrain in ways appropriate to the material reality around us, that being why science is reliable, tracks truth, and so forth. Were the relevant evolutionary processes *guided*, that might very well be the case. But that purely unguided processes would be capable (let alone likely) to do the job is less obvious.[30] And, even if one could provide a naturalistic evolutionary justification for the reliability of common-sense perceptions and conceptions, that would not automatically translate into reasons for trusting the *theoretical* deliverances of human epistemological projects—such as science.[31]

---

30. Evolutionary theories of mind are not at the moment what one would call exact science. As David Sloan Wilson remarks: '[The] diversity of ideas ... about the evolution of human mentality ... probably exceeds the diversity of phenomena to be explained and yet show no signs of reducing itself' (1990: 39).

31. Alvin Plantinga, Marjorie Grene, Noam Chomsky, Thomas Nagel, and others have argued this.

In short, a purely naturalistic evolutionary history would provide few grounds for suspecting that a resultant human cognitive terrain would exhibit the cognitive fine-tuning necessary for theoretical accuracy. In the cosmic fine-tuning case, attempts to sidestep conclusions of cosmic guidance typically involve multiplying varying universes—overwhelming the odds. It is far from obvious that such a strategy works even in the cosmic case (see Ratzsch 2005) but that it would work in the present case is even less likely. The evolutionary production of vastly many cognitive variants would not materially raise the probabilities of the right sort of *theoretical* terrain emerging triumphant for the simple reason that there seems to be essentially nothing there for selection to get a grip *on*. An ability to romp through Fourier series did not, so far as anyone knows, have any bearing whatever upon differential reproductive success in the Pleistocene.[32] Indeed, according to Scott Atran, such things might even be maladaptive (Atran 2002b).

Science-essential sculpting is on some views an evolutionary 'spandrel'.[33] But, if science is (or arises out of) an evolutionary 'spandrel', and if religion is, as some others (e.g., David Sloan Wilson) allege, a fitness-enhancing product of group selection, then evidently religion is or has been evolutionarily more important to human flourishing than is science. That will be true *even if*—serendipitously—our *theoretical* science (including evolutionary theory) has some connection to truth.[34]

Michael Ruse and E. O. Wilson have argued that a (false) belief in the objectivity of morality fosters fitness and has been favored by evolution (Ruse and Wilson 1993). David Sloan Wilson has argued that a (false) belief in religion fosters group fitness and has been favored by evolution (David Sloan Wilson 2002). If Scott Atran is right, evolution has apparently favored a (false) belief in what nearly amounts to its own denial.[35] Non-theistic evolution apparently does not merely lack an interest in truth—truth taking

---

32. Plantinga, Polkinghorne, Peirce, Pinker, Wilson, and many others have also made this point.

33. On some views, the capacities underlying science might be not merely an evolutionary 'spandrel', but a 'spandrel' of a 'spandrel' (Gopnik and Gylmour 2002: 117).

34. Some evolutionary 'explanations' of science and of religion start from the bald—and unsupported—assumption that theism is false. See, e.g., Bulbulia 2004b.

35. Atran cites empirical evidence suggesting that a strong, universal tendency to believe in biological essences emerges spontaneously early in childhood. The result of this evolutionarily generated tendency—the essentialist bias to understand variation in terms of deviance—is undoubtedly a hindrance to evolutionary thinking, even for 'students and philosophers of biology' (Atran 2002a: 41–72).

the hindmost, as Patricia Churchland famously put it—but in important instances seems to have a vested interest in falsehood. That should be of some concern to its advocates.

Atheism doesn't hold much promise here either

Actually, the prospects for any sort of philosophical naturalism—and specifically materialism—providing the requisite resources are questionable as well. Although I will not pursue the issue here, Alvin Plantinga has recently argued that there may be inescapable self-generated defeaters for any such naturalism in this context, and there are other significant questions which arise straightforwardly.[36] If Plantinga is right, the prospects here are none to minus slim. Dennett lauds Darwinian evolution as a 'universal acid' (Dennett 1995: *passim*) but the acid may be more universal than Dennett suggests—dissolving even its own case for itself.

In any case, what would a doctrinaire non-theistic science look like—a science that was truly non-theistic and not one which merely appropriated historically theistic-shaped science while gluing on a thin veneer of non-belief? An exercise in hypothetical comparative science may be revealing here. Well-known Stalinist, Maoist, Marxist, and Nazi theoretical disasters provide at least some cautions here. And the upshot for science itself could be grim indeed. The Stalinist theorist Nickolai Bukharin once claimed that pure science was a morbid symptom of class society (Polanyi 1967: 3). And we all—including the later-executed Bukharin—know the standard Stalinist response to things and people perceived as 'morbid symptoms of class society'.

Atheism, materialism, naturalism, and the like simply do not automatically carve scientifically fertile cognitive terrains.

Enter Religion

Given that, I suggest a fourth principle concerning cognitive terrains:

(4) The 'fine-tuned' cognitive terrain required by science is theism-shaped.

---

36. See Plantinga 2002. Being committed to a view which generates its own undefeatable defeaters puts one in a position for which Plantinga proposed the technical term of being 'epistemically screwed'.

Paul Dirac once remarked that 'Nature's fundamental laws...control a substratum of which we *cannot* form a mental picture without introducing irrelevancies' (emphasis mine, Polanyi 1967: 88). Where do these 'irrelevancies' originate, and what are they? Nature cannot, of course, simply dictate our scientific concepts. Scientific concepts frequently if not typically originate elsewhere in human experience and cognition and then are deployed in theoretical contexts. Given that on most tellings our cognition is not keyed to theoretical events and processes (e.g., think quantum mechanics), those concepts are nearly always deployed *metaphorically*.

The core metaphors are often teleological. The pervasiveness of teleological concepts in science has been often noted, and has deep historical and conceptual roots. Historian of biology Timothy Lenoir suggests that biologists cannot manage without them (Lenoir 1982: p. ix). Midgley argues that it is unlikely that even our (scientifically crucial) imagination can work without notions of teleology. So, when grappling with alien theoretical matters there simply is no viable alternative to 'metaphorical redescription'—some of those metaphors being teleological.

But, things go deeper. Historically there were close connections between science and theology (and religious belief). The story of one such connection involving the early rise and history of science is well known. Very briefly, central aspects of the traditional doctrines of creation and divine voluntarism were explicitly taken by major (indeed most) early scientists to imply that the cosmos (being structured around God's wisdom) was rational and intelligible, that we (being created in God's image) could in principle comprehend that creation, that our senses and cognitive faculties (being designed for knowing) were basically reliable, but that we (being finite) could not just deduce a priori what and how God would have created. Since God had created not only rationally but *freely*—in a (contingent) way not evident to us a priori that we had actually to *look* if we wanted to know what God had done—our investigation of nature had to be fundamentally empirical. Those perceived implications provided key conceptual and methodological resources involved in the birth, early growth, and internal economy of modern science.

Of course, it might be that even if religion was instrumental in getting science up and running, that science has long since left any such connection behind. But, despite widespread assertions that science and its theistic heritage are separable, it is not at all clear that that is true. A cosmos which is (as science must assume) coherent, uniform, intelligible—and even beautiful—and containing scientists whose cognitive and sensory faculties are suitably shaped to that reality, looks *structurally* remarkably like a creation scenario—a cosmos as artifact, deliberately created with wisdom and containing creatures who can (partially) understand the cosmos because the minds with which they are attempting to understand it in some ways parallel—resonate to—the mind whose wisdom is built into that cosmos.

But shapings and shadings from the wider conceptual context of science penetrate deeper into science than just gross structure. Not only do some weight-bearing components of science have historical theological pedigrees, but some metaphors—for instance, biological 'design', cosmic fine-tuning, or even *law*—exhibit ultimately theological tints. Strenuous efforts are made to excise the conceptual 'irrelevancies'— both teleological and theological—of the relevant metaphors, but that, according to Mary Midgley, is often impossible: 'These words are indeed metaphors. But they are not optional, disposable metaphors. They cannot be replaced at will by literal and "objective" language. Like many metaphors, these *form part of the thought*' (emphasis mine, Midgley 1992: 10).

Teleological and theological undertones apparently cannot be wholly removed from scientific concepts, and even end up constituting part of the very *substance* of some concepts (see Ratzsch 2004).

Religion, Terrains, and Science

Physicist Paul Davies notes that 'science began as an outgrowth of theology' but then claims—surprisingly—that, 'all scientists, whether atheists or theists...accept an essentially theological worldview' (Davies 1995: 138). Is any such disposition actually evidenced in the cognitive landscape of scientists? Some anecdotal evidence is intriguing. Astronomer Fred Hoyle made this startling observation: 'I have always thought it curious that, while most scientists claim to eschew religion, it actually dominates their thoughts more than it does the clergy' (quoted in Davies 1993: 223).

There is a potentially significant result from more formal studies of scientists. Liam Hudson summarized results of one study as follows:

> Scientists and non-scientists differ significantly in their reactions to descriptions of nature. Compared with non-scientists, scientists show a marked preference for metaphors of nature which are anthropomorphic—with certain significant exceptions. They *reject* anthropomorphic metaphors if these suggest nature as threatening or anarchic.
>
> (Hudson 1966: 148)

Note that this 'marked preference' is for conceptual structures reflecting a *benign* (not threatening), *faithful* (not anarchic), *person*. And note that it is a preference generated in the cognitive structures of those in deepest informed contact with nature—scientists—whose cognitive terrain is presumably most subject to sculpting by (or being driven by?) nature itself.

That looks awfully like an integration of science and theism. Why should that sort of integration be evident in the birth and rise of science itself, and why should it *still* be visible in the tacit world view (Davies), and in the conceptual preferences and/or propensities of (Hudson) contemporary scientists—even the unbelieving ones? There are, I think, two significant and related factors.

First, if the cosmos *is* a creation, and unless that creation differs from all other known (or conceivable?) artifacts in lacking an inbuilt intelligibility keyed to the mind and purposes of the artificer, then in our attempts to understand the structure of the cosmos either we are and our science is unteachable (i.e., science is not self-corrective), or else, to adapt a phrase from John Polkinghorne, our science itself will eventually become laced with subtle 'rumors of divinity'.

But, if science fits firmly (only?) on a theism-shaped terrain, and if science's foundational structure is forced by its search for coherence to conform to the underlying terrain, then any fully satisfactory science may de facto have a theistic foundation and shape. This is *not* to say that only believers will get science ultimately right—only that any ultimately successful science will involve an *implicit* practicing conceptual theism. Science depends upon a fund of absolutely indispensable presuppositions which not only grew out of a theistic context but still look awfully like the weight-bearing members of a creation—intelligibility, coherence, reliability, beauty, and the rest of the familiar list. And, as just seen, there is some reason for suspecting that science cannot be hermetically insulated from the harmonics which that structure might generate while still reaping the pay-offs of exactly that structure.

Nature itself may, via any science which is truly empirical, drive the cognitive terrain (even of those who resist) in theism-shaped directions. That may be why the militant atheist and Nobel laureate Francis Crick felt compelled to warn fellow biologists not to trust their own biology-driven intuitions: 'Biologists must constantly keep in mind that what they see was not designed, but rather evolved' (Crick 1988: 138).

Second, cognitive terrain is *integrated*, and theism-shaped conceptions cannot be quarantined in some conceptual backwater. In general, cognitive terrains are nearly seamless. In discussing their theory of conceptual blending, Fauconnier and Turner say: 'A mental space consists of elements and relations activated simultaneously as a single, integrated unit' (2002: 104). Indeed, it is a constitutive integration:

> Our mental world is not an amorphous collection of relations and formal structures. Rather, it is inherently shaped by the rich topology of conceptual integration networks and mental spaces, including vital relations and their compressions. This landscape of conceptual integration networks is not something that gets superimposed onto [our] apprehension of basic meaning and form. It is the very way in which meaning and form, and hence the mental world itself, are constructed.
>
> (Fauconnier and Turner 2002: 394)

Grounding for a science/religion interaction may be already present in a creation-sculpted terrain—a terrain highly tilted toward an integral science/theism unity. It should again be noted that beyond the metaphoric preferences just discussed some of the more basic human cognitive structures which are irremovably and properly infused into science are among those stereotypically associated with religious belief—emotion, feels, intuitions, faith, deep cognitively formative stances and ethoi, values, goals, commitments to principles and praxes beyond the empirically determinable.

Furthermore, if *feels* (or *intuitions* or *emotions* or the like) really do constitute bedrock of science itself, one cannot demonstrate any substandard rationality of religious belief merely by citing emotion, subjective experience, interpretation, etc. as constituting components of religious belief—unless one is willing to see scientific rationality sink alongside it (see also Wentzel van Huyssteen 1998: 154, 155). As Larry Laudan has argued, '[T]he presence of [philosophical, religious, and moral issues in science] may be entirely rational; [indeed] the suppression of such elements may itself be irrational and prejudicial' (Lauden 1977: 132). Attempts both clearly to separate science and religion and to assign science and religion vastly different levels of rational warrant will at the least be complicated.[37] The constitutive integration of such religious-shaped entities into science not only opens some fundamental possibilities for religion/science interactions, but may make such interactions inevitable. Indeed 'interaction' may be too separationist a term. Just as some tendencies of thought, inference, and reason are simply presented to consciousness as faits accomplis, pre-shaped by deeper, unrecognized cognitive terrain structures, so, I am claiming, a deep mutually constitutive interweaving of human science and underlying conceptual structures—including religious structures—is also a cognitive fait accompli by the time the tip of the content and direction of science surfaces to formal scrutiny.

An inescapably unified science/religion picture will arise out of the unity of the traditionally disparate aspects of human personhood itself, the unity of the multi-hued ingredients of rationality itself, and the unity of scientific and religious truth within the cosmos itself. Given that a single, unitary cognitive terrain underlies all our cognitive procedures—including both science and religion—the same fundamental structures and processes of rationality are of necessity imposed on, or better, partially constitutive of, both science and religion.

And the embodied structures of rationality are not axiomatizable, formalizable, rule-reducible, nor necessarily even fully propositional. Conceptual decisions and inferences—including theory evaluation and choice—are reason-conducive decisions and inferences channeled by non-stable terrain-determinates of rationality—determinates which do indeed frequently exhibit 'rumors of divinity'.

---

37. Fauconnier and Turner argue that the capacity for what they call 'double scope conceptual integration', acquired roughly 30,000 years ago, was the common trigger for the human capacities for science, art, language, and religion (2002: 186).

Conclusion

Definitive and constitutive features of our humanness not only lie at but comprise part of the very core of both science and religion (or at least the core of our cognitive faculties underpinning both). In fact, some of the exact same human factors are constitutive in both cases. And some of those factors are not religiously peripheral, but are *precisely* among those traditionally taken to be definitive of specifically religious belief and commitment. Scientific thought rests on an agent-shaped foundational terrain which constitutes part of the structure of scientific thought, and that structure (and whatever content it drives) partially configures scientific theories. And the reality mapped (or 'mirrored') can only be cognized via subtly agent-based, teleological, even theological, metaphors—despite ongoing insistent attempts to strip them from science. And, if Midgley is right concerning metaphor and content, then that implicit theism will constitute part of the very content of scientific thought—content which cannot simply be quarantined within some confined region, such as a context of discovery. All of this suggests that cases for

(a) science systematically undercutting religion;

(b) science and religion being hermetically quarantined from each other;

(c) science automatically taking rational precedence over religion; and

(d) science being conceptually and intellectually autonomous;

are misguided.

Once one commits to (at least a Reformed view of) the doctrine of creation—that an integrated cosmos, to be seen aright for any distance along any of its dimensions must ultimately be seen whole—it becomes plausible that complementarity, dialog, autonomy, and other such traditional models of science/religion relationships can be seen as far too impoverished and timid. If the cosmos is a deliberate creation—and surely that is a *factual* question and not one to be simply a priori decreed by late-arriving humans in a small corner of the cosmos, or to be decided by stipulated methods unequal to the task—then science may inescapably bear the implicit but none the less consequential imprint of that fact, regardless of whether it is overtly recognized and acknowledged as such or not. Indeed, it may be that although we can think in superficially atheistic ways, really *thinking* about the *cosmos* may be an irreducibly theistic undertaking.

That idea fits nicely with an intriguing remark made by the twentieth-century biologist Edwin Chargaff:

> If [a scientist] has not experienced, at least a few times in his life, this cold shudder down his spine, this confrontation with an immense, invisible face whose breath moves him to tears, he is not a scientist.
>
> (Newberg and D'Aquili 2001: 154)

Not only can one glimpse that orthogonal reality from within science, but, says Chargaff, one is not yet even a scientist if one does not.

12

Theology and Evolution: How Much Can Biology Explain?[1]

John Haught

...with me the horrid doubt always arises whether the convictions of
man's mind, which has been developed from the mind of the lower animals, are of any value or at all trustworthy. Would any one trust in the convictions of a monkey's mind, if there are any convictions in such a mind?

Charles Darwin, Letter to W. Graham, 3 July 1881, *The Life and Letters of Charles Darwin*,
ed. Francis Darwin (New York: Basic Books, 1959), 285.

In 1715 Isaac Watts wrote a Christian hymn beginning with this stanza:

> That made the mountains rise
> That spread the flowing seas abroad
> And built the lofty skies.
> I sing the wisdom that ordained
> The sun to rule the day;
> The moon shines full at his command
> And all the stars obey.

In 1975 Kenneth Boulding offered a new version:

> What though the mountains are pushed up
> By plate-tectonic lift,
> And oceans lie within the cup
> Made by the landmass drift.
> The skies are but earth's airy skin
> Rotation makes the day;
> Sun, moon, and planets are akin
> And Kepler's Laws obey.   (Boulding 1981: 112–13)

---

1. This essay is a condensation and adaptation of several chapters of my Haught 2006.

Boulding does not say whether the sentiments expressed in his update are really his own, but his tongue-in-cheek rendition expresses succinctly the world view known as 'scientific naturalism'. This label is apparently the invention of Charles Darwin's famous advocate Thomas H. Huxley (1825–95) (Numbers 2003: 266). It is the belief that nature is all there is and that science alone can make sense of it. Some scientific naturalists are willing to keep singing the old hymns. Even though the lyrics no longer ring true they still warm the heart. Others, however, insist that it is time to stop singing them altogether. There can be no harmonizing of Watts's stanza with Boulding's. Nature is enough.

Naturalism comes in many flavors but in philosophical discourse today the term generally signifies a Godless view of the universe. For example, when the philosopher Owen Flanagan states that the mission of contemporary philosophy is to make the world safe for 'naturalism' he clearly means safe for atheism (Flanagan 2002: 167–8). And in the popular religious writings of C. S. Lewis 'naturalism' is taken as the repudiation of each and every theological interpretation of the world (Lewis 2001). Its core teachings are these (Hardwick 1996):

(1) Outside of nature, which includes humans and their cultural creations, there is nothing.

(2) It follows from (1) that nature is self-originating.

(3) Since there is nothing beyond nature, there can be no overarching purpose or goal that would give any lasting meaning to the universe.

(4) There is no such thing as the 'soul', and no reasonable prospect of conscious human survival beyond death.

(5) The emergence of life and mind in evolution was accidental and unintended.

What I am calling 'scientific naturalism' accepts these five tenets, but adds two more:

(6) Every natural event is itself a product of other natural events. Since there is no divine cause, all causes are purely natural causes, in principle accessible to scientific comprehension.

(7) All the various features of living beings, including humans, can be explained ultimately in evolutionary, specifically Darwinian, terms. This belief may be called 'evolutionary naturalism'.

Is scientific naturalism a reasonable world view? Let me assume, for the sake of discussion, that you are a scientific naturalist, and allow me to speak to you directly. As you have been reading this chapter your mind has been following an invariant sequence of cognitional acts. (1) You have *attended* to and experienced the words and sentences I have penned. (2) Then you have tried to *understand* what I am saying, looking for something intelligible. (3) Finally, if you have understood anything I have written so far, you have probably also asked whether my understanding is correct, or at least whether your own understanding of my ideas is accurate. In either case you have spontaneously subjected your understanding and mine to critical questioning. And your spirit of criticism may have led you to the *judgment* that I am either right or wrong (Lonergan 1967: 221–39).

So your mind has spontaneously unfolded in three distinct acts of cognition: experience, understanding, and judgment. Since you are capable not only of insight and critical reflection but also of acting in the world, you are called upon at times to decide what course of action to follow. So, *decision* is a fourth cognitional act. Elsewhere I say much about decision and whether naturalism can provide an adequate account of our moral life (Haught 2006: 141–66) but my focus here will be on understanding the first three levels of cognition.

You may never have noticed it before, but your mind *cannot help* executing the three distinct but complementary acts: experience, understanding, and judgment. This is because there are persistent and ineradicable imperatives at the foundation of your consciousness. These imperatives, along with the associated cognitional acts, are these:

(1) Be attentive! → experience
(2) Be intelligent! → understanding
(3) Be critical! → judgment

The fourth set (not examined here) is:

(4) Be responsible! → decision

These cognitional acts, along with the imperatives that give rise to them, make up what I shall be calling *critical intelligence* (following Bernard Lonergan). It is not enough to call your mental functioning simply 'intelligence', since you can be intelligent, insightful, and even ingenious without being right. It is your *critical* intelligence, concerned as it is with *true* understanding that I wish to highlight. An even fuller designation of your mental life would be 'open, critical, and responsible intelligence', but here I shall be satisfied with the simpler label.

The imperatives to be attentive, intelligent, and critical flow from a single deep longing that lies at the heart of each person's intellectual life. Since ancient times this longing has been known as *the desire to know.* It is the root of science and all other rational pursuits. Science, for example, begins with *experience*, propelled by the imperative to be open and attentive. We may call this the empirical imperative. It turns the scientist's mind toward data that science needs to understand. And if scientists reach insight into, or *understanding* of, the data, they express it in propositions known as hypotheses and theories. But science does not stop there, since not every bright idea is a true idea. A third imperative—be critical!—prods the scientist to reflect on whether the hypotheses or theories are correct. Scientific understanding must be subjected continually to verification (or falsification). Only after undertaking a rigorous criticism of one's ideas, often requiring evaluation by others or publication in peer-reviewed journals, will it be appropriate to render at least a tentative *judgment* that one's scientific ideas are true or false.

Science, of course, is much more nuanced than this. I wish only to make the point that scientific procedure illustrates how closely the human mind adheres to the threefold cognitional structure and its persistent imperatives. But this invariant pattern is also operative in common sense, philosophy, and other forms of cognition. It has been operating in you all the while you have been reading this chapter. You have experienced the words and sentences I am expressing—following the imperative to be attentive. You have then tried to understand the words and sentences—following the imperative to be intelligent. And now—in obedience to the imperative to be critical—you are asking whether what I'm saying is true. So you can immediately identify the threefold cognitional pattern in the actual performance of your own critical intelligence this instant. For the moment it does not matter how your mind evolved, or what the cultural factors in its genesis may have been. These are important issues also, but for our immediate purposes it will be helpful to notice only how your critical intelligence is functioning presently.

Perhaps you have never attended to your mental operations in this immediate way before. You may never have turned your attention to the fact that your mind is continually prodded by hidden imperatives. Yet, even if you have never adverted to them in the past, you will now discover that you cannot escape them. You may at times have failed to obey the imperatives to be attentive, intelligent, and critical, but their presence has been operative even when their voice has been muffled. If you are now doubting what I have just said it is because you are being attentive, intelligent, and critical—in response to your own mind's imperatives. No matter how many doubts and uncertainties you have about everything else you cannot deny the threefold cognitional structure of your own critical intelligence without employing it even in the act of doubting it.

The next point I want to make, then, is that you cannot help *trusting* in the imperatives of your mind. Without having made a tacit act of faith in your own critical intelligence you would not have bothered to follow me up to this point. You would not have asked whether I am making any sense, or whether I may be pulling the wool over your eyes. Your whole cognitional performance depends on a deeply personal confidence in your own intelligence and critical capacities. Unless you had already placed some degree of trust in your cognitional ability you would hardly even have bothered to ask any questions at all. But how do you justify this trust? I can imagine that seasoned philosophers or scientific thinkers, after reading what I am writing in this chapter, will try to refute the claims I am making. But such refutation will arise only because my critics also trust their own minds' imperatives to be attentive, intelligent, and critical. And if my critics espouse scientific naturalism can this world view adequately ground the cognitional confidence that underlies their own judgment that I am wrong?

Is Naturalism True?

If you embrace the belief system known as scientific naturalism, have you ever asked whether it coheres logically with the invariant structure of your cognitional life? Let me put my question another way: is the essentially mindless, purposeless, self-originating, self-enclosed universe of scientific naturalism large enough to house your own critical intelligence? If not, truthfulness compels you to conclude that naturalism is an unreasonable creed. Your formal understanding of the world—your world view, if you will—must not be such as to contradict the way the mind functions when it seeks knowledge of the world. Nor must your world view have the effect of subverting the confidence that underlies the thought processes that give rise to that world view. That Charles Darwin himself considered this to be a serious consideration is evident in the citation given at the head of this chapter.

So, does scientific naturalism support or subvert your desire to know? I don't know what your own response will be, but after struggling with this question for many years I have concluded that the universe as conceived by scientific naturalism is quite clearly incompatible with the critical intelligence with which I attempt to understand that universe. More strongly stated—a consistent acceptance of scientific naturalism logically impairs the trust that underlies my attempts to understand and know the world. Only those views of reality that are logically consistent with, and lend support to, the desire to know and the mind's imperatives can be called truthful.

Truth can be defined as the objective or goal of the pure desire to know; and the fundamental criterion of truth is fidelity to the desire to know and obedience to the imperatives of the mind. So, at the very least, in order to pass the test of reasonableness any belief system that you cling to must be congruent with your desire to know and the imperatives of your mind. If a specific set of beliefs fails to support the interests of your desire to know, or if it undermines the confidence and trust in the cognitional imperatives that lead you toward open-minded and critical exploration of reality, then it is inconsistent with the fundamental criterion of truth—namely, fidelity to the desire to know.[2]

Can you, then, consistently and coherently claim to be both a naturalist and, at the same time, completely faithful to your own desire to know? Not only naturalists but religious believers also need to ask whether their explicit beliefs correspond to the interests of the mind's imperatives. If not, then these beliefs must be declared unreasonable also, and lovers of truth must disown them. What one believes to be ultimate reality must not function in such a way as to contravene the restless longing for truth that we have just identified as the desire to know. Hence, one might also examine religious beliefs, and not just naturalism, from the point of view of whether and how these may be serving the interests of the desire to know, or perhaps following other desires. Not a few studies have argued, after all, that religion can indeed satisfy the desire for pleasure (Freud 1989), consolation (Marx 1964), revenge (Nietzsche 1990), or meaning (Frankl 1959; Berger 1990;

---

2. As I have mentioned already, my inquiry is guided by Bernard Lonergan's ideas even though my terminology and applications of his theory of knowledge are not always his.

Shermer 2003). And the severest critics of religion have argued in effect that if belief in God is inconsistent with the desire to know, then it must be abandoned. I would agree. Seldom, however, has scientific naturalism been subjected to the same rigorous standard of authentication.

In real life, as each of us knows, the desire to know must continually compete with opposing tendencies. While it is essentially pure and detached, in our actual existence the desire to know is always entangled with other longings. We have to struggle throughout our lives to decouple the innate intentionality of the desire to know from other urges that promise easy but evanescent satisfaction. As the Danish philosopher Søren Kierkegaard puts it, 'it is far from being the case that men in general regard relationship to the truth as the highest good, and it is far from being the case that they, Socratically, regard being under a delusion as the greatest misfortune' (Kierkegaard 1954: 154–5). None the less, it is possible, as you can tell from the exercise with which I opened this chapter, to identify the imperatives of your own mind and their intention to put you in touch with reality. Once again, *reality* means that which is intended by your desire to know. If you are still questioning whether this is true, it can only be because your own desire to know is at this moment seeking to know what is *really* the case. So the evidence is right there in front of you at this very instant.

Moreover, as further reflection will show, the desire to know intends nothing less than the *fullness* of being. This is why any arbitrary imposition of boundaries on the desire to know is an act of violence, inconsistent with truth-seeking. The desire to know is *anticipatory* rather than possessive. It is most at home where there is an openness to a limitless horizon of being, and it begins to feel cramped whenever it hears phrases such as 'enough', 'nothing but', or 'all there is'.

Linking Intelligence to the Emergent Universe

It is not necessary at this point to specify the evolutionary, cultural, historical, and social processes that went into the making of your critical intelligence, important and fascinating as all this may be. For now it is sufficient simply to be fully aware, first, of the presence of a desire to know at the core of your own being and, second, that this desire is as much a part of the natural world as are trees and toads. Your critical intelligence is not hovering somewhere outside of nature. It *is* nature, in the same way that stars and rivers are nature. It should not be hard for the naturalist to accept this premise, since nature is supposedly all there is. However, since critical intelligence is so intimately entangled with the rest of nature—a point that both biology and cosmology have confirmed in great detail—what we can find out by looking closely at critical intelligence will also be relevant to understanding *the whole natural world* with which it is so intimately interlaced.

In fact, the most illuminating access each of us has to the natural world is the portal of our own critical intelligence; so why leave this emerald of evolution out of our picture of nature as though it were not part of it? Science generally does just that, and for its limited purposes such a methodological exclusion seems appropriate. But how could we profess to be *fully* open to the data of experience—in obedience to the mind's first imperative—if we deliberately refused to focus on what, to each critically intelligent subject, is the most stunning of nature's inventions? My point is that if we do attend fully to our critical intelligence, and if we try seriously to integrate it into our understanding of nature, the naturalistic approach to the world will be exposed as insufficiently attentive, intelligent, and critical.

In terms of natural history, of course, it is clear that our critical intelligence emerged from a universe that was formerly lifeless and mindless. But in order to account for the trust each of us places in our critical intelligence it is not enough to assert that the ultimate ground of our desire to know is a lifeless and mindless causal past. If the ultimate cause of mind is mindlessness we would still need to look for reasons sufficient to explain why we should trust our minds here and now, as Darwin himself insinuates. Fully justifying the obvious acts of faith that we place in our critical intelligence requires that we situate human cognitional life, and along with it the whole universe, in a more spacious environment than the one laid out by scientific naturalism. I believe it will be essential to call upon theology to accomplish this expansion.

A Richer Empiricism

If we truly intend to understand the *universe*, we can no longer pretend that it has no essential connection to critical intelligence. And once we re-establish the connection between the latter and nature as a whole it will be possible to see more clearly that the same horizon of truth and being that arouses the imperatives of the mind has also been hiddenly involved in *cosmic* history throughout. The work of fashioning the cerebral apparatus that underpins human consciousness has been going on, as it now appears, for some fourteen billion years. And so the emergence of critical intelligence must be located within the context of the larger cosmic epic. Likewise, the cosmic story cannot be told well if we leave out any mention of the recent eruption of a restless desire to know.

Modern naturalism, however, fails to explore in sufficient depth the intimate connection between critical intelligence and its cosmic matrix. In a crudely physicalist sense, of course, naturalists agree that mind is part of nature. But they seldom look closely at what is implied about the cosmos in the *actual performance* of critical intelligence. Indeed, naturalism's typical portrait of the universe is one in which critical intelligence is virtually absent from the seamless web of natural phenomena. The philosophical difficulty arising from this virtual exiling of mind from nature is that it leaves naturalism with no illuminating explanatory categories to account robustly for what is most obvious in the experience of each of us—our actual intelligent functioning. After imaginatively sweeping the cosmos clean of subjects the explanatory program of naturalists, including many neuroscientists and cognitive scientists today, is to show how subjective consciousness—which we all know performatively to be quite real—can come into existence out of a natural process divested from the start of any traces or anticipations of mind. To set the problem of mind's existence up in the manner of this essentially materialist outlook is to prepare the stage for magic rather than explanation.

The habit of looking away from the subjectivity near at hand, as though it does not really exist in nature, is being shored up today by a Darwinian naturalism that regards only the historical or algorithmic past as adequate for understanding the present.[3] However, without denying the importance of historical or evolutionary accounts, a rich empiricism surveys the history of life and the natural world without ever turning away its eyes, even for a moment, from the present actuality of our own critical intelligence. Any adequate explanation of nature must explain *all* of its outcomes, and in doing so it does not help matters to place in brackets the novel emergent

3. Daniel Dennett's work is the most explicit example in Dennett 1995.

reality of mental existence and then try to account for it solely in terms of what is purely mindless.

A richer empiricism, on the other hand, is so sensitive to the mind's imperative to be open to the full range of experience that it always keeps the fact of our critical intelligence in the foreground as it looks backward into nature's past. Scientific naturalism sidesteps this stereoscopic approach. This is why, in the end, it finally has to resort to magic in its own accounts of intelligence. Expelling subjectivity completely from its visual field at the outset, naturalism can only meet defeat when it approaches the irreducible fact of critical intelligence.[4] Scientific naturalism does not possess the conceptual tools to bridge the gap between the third-person language about physical or evolutionary causes on the one hand, and the first-person discourse of intelligent subjects about their inner experience on the other. As the naturalist philosopher John R. Searle admits, these disparate perspectives point to two different modes of existence: 'Conscious states have a subjective mode of existence in the sense that they exist only when they are experienced by a human or animal subject. In this respect they differ from nearly all the rest of the universe.' It is not helpful, however, when Searle goes on to suggest that a scientific study of mind can in some sense bridge the gulf between the subjective and objective. After all, the sciences, including neuroscience, are inevitably third-person approaches. Scientific objectivity can help explain why minds fail, and it can uncover the physical conditions required for mental functioning. But an objectifying study of mind can never lead incrementally to the experience of being a critically intelligent subject (Searle 2004: 135–6).

Instead of stretching and straining a fundamentally materialist naturalism to fit the amazing feats of mind, as Searle does, I suggest that it is time for philosophers of mind to look for a world view that can encompass both critical intelligence and the entire cosmic process in a way that avoids the de facto dualism to which many of them, including hard materialists, have become resigned. The perspective I am laying out here is one that starts by looking closely at the structure of critical intelligence. Only after undertaking a general empirical survey inclusive of subjective existence can one expect to understand the cosmos in its fullest dimensions. Simply reciting the usual evolutionary factors is scarcely enough to help us understand how mindless objects can be transformed into sentient, intelligent, and

4. Colin McGinn, a self-avowed naturalist, resignedly admits as much in McGinn 1999.

critical subjects. A richer explanatory framework is needed to avoid the appeal to miraculous leaps. Explanatory adequacy must somehow make the categories of intelligence and subjectivity fundamental to the makeup of true being, rather than derivative aspects of an originally senseless reality.

Naturalists, of course, will not agree with my proposal. They will not give up their belief that the fundamental causes of intelligence are themselves completely unintelligent. This means, however, that naturalists are compelled to explain intelligent subjectivity ultimately in terms of processes and events that lack both intelligence and subjectivity. How then can the appearance of sorcery be avoided? A series of blind and unintelligent causes of mind, no matter how temporally prolonged and gradual in cumulative effect, would never add up to a sufficient reason for putting the kind of confidence in their own intellectual functioning that naturalists in fact do when they offer such an account. Given the story they tell about the unconscious physical foundations and mindless evolutionary fashioning of their own minds, naturalists must look elsewhere to justify the colossal confidence they place in their own minds. Calling mind a fluke, as some evolutionists do, will hardly suffice. As long as they ground their own critical intelligence *ultimately* either in blind natural selection or a series of accidents, or both, I can see no reason why anyone, least of all they themselves, could ever trust so unflinchingly the operations of their own critical intelligence. Naturalists will tell me that their position is true and mine is false. They are completely confident that the mind can be naturalized, that is, fully explained in terms of what is physically or cosmologically earlier-and-simpler than mind. But what is there in this fundamentally unconscious cosmic background, or in the cultures that this unconscious foundation brought into being through the mediation of minds, that could have instilled in them their cognitional confidence?

After many years of looking at naturalistic writings I have yet to find a reasonable answer. Instead I find magic everywhere. In almost every case, to put it bluntly, the naturalist's account of the origin of mind is one in which I am asked to believe that the lustrous gold of critical intelligence 'emerges' from the dross of pure mindlessness without also being shown how such alchemy actually works. Invoking the ideas of deep time and emergence to 'explain' how matter can become minds does nothing to dispel the aura of miracle that hovers over the whole show. The naturalist's actual, here-and-now intellectual performance is so utterly discontinuous with the set of materials out of which it is said to have been processed that it places in serious doubt any claim that naturalism is a reasonable philosophy of nature.

Notice, however, that I am not at all denying the power and importance of evolutionary explanations. I am only questioning the coherence of evolutionary naturalism. I have said nothing to discredit or discourage the ongoing scientific search for the details of the story that led up to the birth of intelligence. Evolutionary accounts are essential to adequate understanding of all living phenomena. But, unless a stereoscopic empiricism and a richly layered method of explanation are allowed to supplement the conventional scientific way of seeing and understanding, evolutionary accounts will still sound like sheer divination. A more radically empirical method of inquiry and a proportionately expansive metaphysics are needed.

The Need for Theology

A fuller explanation of nature, one that can account for the element of anticipation in life, emergence, evolution, and intelligence, requires, in addition to scientific study, the illumination of a theological world view. The place of theological explanation is to make ultimate sense of the anticipatory aspect of both nature and mind. It can give a good reason for the existence of a realm of *potentiality* that allows the world to be anticipatory. This potentiality, though not actual, is not the same as sheer nothingness, and so it must have a ground in reality. Theology gives the name God to the source and reservoir of all possibilities. It is the abiding presence of new possibilities on the horizon of the cosmic and evolutionary future that arouses our own sense of anticipation, and at least in some analogous way the leaning of all things toward the future. Rather than reducing the fact of our own subjective anticipation to a ghostly shadow hovering over a mindless universe, theology can make anticipation fundamental to *everything* going on in nature. Anticipation is what bears the universe along as it reaches out toward fuller being. No doubt, the actualizing in cosmic history of explicitly conscious instances of anticipation is all very uncertain and frothed with contingency. Historically speaking, there can be no doubt that the cosmos was devoid of actual intelligent subjects until recently. From the point of view of natural history the road from primal radiation to the emergence of thought has not been smooth or devoid of setbacks. But the domain of possibilities that eventually drew forth conscious anticipation has been present and quietly influential always.

Of all natural phenomena our minds are perhaps the most fragile, at least from a physicalist point of view. But their fragility is in direct proportion to their splendor, and their splendor is inseparable from the fullness toward which they aspire but cannot own. Like a flower blossoming momentarily in bright sunshine, critical intelligence feels the call of being, meaning, goodness, beauty, and truth only for a season. But in its response to this transcendental environment the restlessness of the whole universe rushes toward the future. In the mind's anticipation of truth, goodness, and beauty the entire cosmic process is drawn toward the goal it has silently sought perpetually.

To the naturalist, obviously, the appeal to such a theological understanding will seem to be an unwarranted leap. But here my leap, if you want to call it that, consists only of ensuring that all necessary and relevant categories for robust explanation are loaded in at the beginning rather than invented in midstream during the explanatory process. We are obliged after all to understand *the totality* of nature, and this includes critically intelligent subjectivity. The merit of theological explanation is that it has no need to invent ad hoc concepts to explain critical intelligence. Something causally proportionate to this inestimably precious phenomenon has always been silently, persuasively, and non-coercively proposing new possibilities to the cosmic process. When critical intelligence did eventually arise in cosmic history it was ultimately because the universe had been charged with the ingredients for its arrival from the moment of creation—'in the beginning was the Word'. Moreover, the advantage of a theological understanding is that it can explain, in a way that naturalism cannot, why the intelligent subject spontaneously puts so much trust in the desire to know. Trust, after all, can flourish only where there is something to value, and value has to be rooted in what is imperishable. I can conceive of no fuller justification of the trust underlying cognitional performance than a theological vision of reality that attributes to truth, meaning, goodness (and beauty) something of the eternal. 'It fortifies my soul to know / That, though I perish, Truth is so.'[5]

---

5. From Arthur Hugh Clough's poem 'With Whom Is No Variableness, Neither Shadow of Turning' (1862).

Scientific naturalists will persist in claiming that they have already included human intelligence in their very non-theological picture of nature. Darwin, they will contend, has done so in his sweeping vision of life, explaining intelligence as a product of natural selection. But Darwin never claimed to have explained critical intelligence as such; and even in the *Descent of Man* he has to limit his study to external behavioral traits. No objectifying science has ever yet penetrated the world of the subject, nor can it by definition. Naturalists still pretend that the 'insideness' of intelligence is irrelevant as far as enlightened thought is concerned, but in doing so they have exiled the most stunning of all emergent cosmic phenomena from the range of those data that are essential to a full understanding of nature. There is nothing to complain about in such a procedure so long as one remains aware of how much it leaves out, and there need be no objection to the fact that science itself cannot talk about subjectivity. It is only when scientific method, which justifiably abstracts from notions like subjectivity and intelligence, is taken as the sufficient foundation for an entire world view that objections must be raised.

It is hard to understand how naturalists, whose vision of the cosmos intends to be comprehensive, can appropriately suppress attentiveness to anything so empirically accessible as the mind's anticipation of truth. And so it is all the more worthy of attention that recent developments in the fields of astrophysics, scientific cosmology, and biochemistry now render such exclusion much more dubious than it may have seemed only half a century ago. Those naturalists who are aware of recent studies of the early universe can no longer sever critical intelligence from the cosmos as casually as they did earlier in the modern period. It now turns out that the precise physical conditions that would allow intelligent, truth-seeking beings to emerge came into play at the first moment of the Big Bang universe itself. The universe was never *essentially* mindless.

In an expectant way the cosmos, it now appears, was always enveloped by the potential to become subjective. Even at a time when there were no actual intelligent human subjects around to understand and know it, the universe was already infused with a mind-arousing intelligibility that would become the congenial evolutionary habitat for critical intelligence. This pervasive cosmic intelligibility must have had something to do with the fact that critical intelligence eventually arose in cosmic history. Just as the existence of photons had something to do with the evolutionary emergence of eyesight many times independently during terrestrial evolution, so also

an environing cosmic intelligibility had to have been a causal factor in
the emergence of intelligent subjects able to adapt to that environment.
Hence a *full* account of the emergence of critical intelligence has to look
for an ultimate explanation of why the universe is intelligible at all. A
candid openness to that question cannot exclude theology as the source
of a reasonable response.

The salient question is whether the improbable paving of the cosmic
path toward the creation of minds could ever be explained adequately in a
purely naturalistic way. Naturalism's answer, of course, is a clear affirmative.
'Nature is enough' will be the refrain here in cosmology as it has been
in biology. The mindless interplay of accident and impersonal physical
necessity across immensities of time in a multiverse can allegedly account
for the improbable set of cosmic conditions and constants that give the
appearance of having been set up for mind. The Darwinian exposé of
living design as only *seemingly* intelligent has now begun to shape even
the naturalist's cosmology. These days Down House is casting its shadow
over naturalists' thoughts about the universe as well as life (Smolin 2001;
Rees 2001).

Yet, if one takes critical intelligence as a fact of nature, the appeal to cosmic Darwinism as an *ultimate* explanation only drags the naturalist project
down deeper into the alchemical vortex. The upshot is that everything in
nature still emerges out of an original, though now vaster, mindlessness.
Such a setting only exacerbates the incongruity between the ultimate
unintelligibility of the enlarged cosmic kitchen and the emergent mind
that is cooked up in it. And wherever enormous explanatory gaps show
up, the temptation to magic lags not far behind. The naturalist hope is
that by multiplying universes and extending the amount of time available
for accidents to become adaptive it is possible to build a universe whose
environmental conditions are suitable for intelligent subjects. Yet, at bottom
such a universe still remains ultimately unintelligible, and that means it can
never be an adaptive habitat for an *unrestricted* desire to know.

What is needed is an understanding of the universe, or perhaps the
multiverse, in which the desire to know can be taken as a smoothly
natural extrusion of nature rather than the gnostic intrusion for which
the naturalist's austere picture of the cosmos inevitably prepares the way.
Falling back time and again only on the combined notions of chance,
temporal amplitude, and physical necessity, naturalism has not made the
actual existence of mind any more intelligible—rather, much less so—than

before. For naturalism to succeed as ultimate explanation it must be able to link critical intelligence, with its anticipation of a fullness of truth and being, to the cosmic process in a way that is more credible, less loaded with leaps, and more intuitively rational than those of its theological adversaries. So far it has not done so.

Conclusion

Pierre Teilhard de Chardin writes: 'Our world contains within itself a mysterious promise of the future, implicit in its natural evolution . . . that is the final assertion of the scientist as he closes his eyes, heavy and weary from having seen so much that he could not express' (Teilhard de Chardin 1968: 55–6). As I reflect on my own desire to know and try to follow its instinctive orientation toward a *fullness* of being, truth, goodness, and beauty, I can expect to find a satisfactory setting for this desire only in some version of a theological—and specifically eschatological—understanding of reality. Such a world view could be declared illusory by definition only if it frustrated or failed to support the unfolding of my desire to know. But, religious hope, including belief that my critical intelligence is in some sense imperishable, can only serve to shore up my natural inclination to *value* the mind in such a way as to encourage me to surrender humbly to its imperatives. Hope can serve the cause of truthfulness if it encourages me to remain faithful to my desire to know in the face of all apparent frustrations.

I conclude then that a *sufficient* ground for trusting my desire to know cannot be found exclusively by looking back to the causal past but only by taking into account the mind's innate anticipation of a fullness of being, meaning, truth, goodness, and beauty looming on the horizon up ahead. Minds are naturally and irremediably anticipatory, oriented toward a fulfillment that only an endlessly open future can bring. Moreover, critical intelligence is embedded in a long unfolding of life, emergence, evolution, and cosmic becoming whose own orientation has always been deeply anticipatory. The world, Teilhard writes, 'rests on the future . . . as its sole support' (Teilhard de Chardin 2002: 239). The forward thrust of nature as observed in its various phases of emergence is not a fiction that humans wishfully invent. Rather, it is a general hallmark of cosmic process. It comes to light most explicitly in the emergence of the desire to know, but a leaning toward the future is a fundamental feature of all of nature, one that finds a full flowering in religious hope for a final fulfillment of nature, persons, and history.

Natural occurrences, not to mention human creativity, become intelligible only if one does more than just take note of the causal history that leads up to them, or of the atomic constituents ingredient in them. To appreciate the full reality of emergent phenomena it is necessary to attend also to their present openness to future transformation. Everything in nature, as a recently chastened physics now has to admit, is open to future outcomes that defy scientific prediction on the basis of what has already occurred in the realm of the earlier-and-simpler (Laughlin 2005). This freedom from absolute determination by the past is part of their identity just as it is part of our own. Why, ultimately, nature has this general openness to possibility the natural sciences do not say. Scientific method has characteristically understood things primarily in terms of what has led up to them or, reductively, in terms of the allegedly 'fundamental' physical units that make them up. It has been able to make only very general—though technologically useful—predictions based on the past habits of nature. But it has not laid out in fine-grained specificity what actual future and especially long-range cosmic outcomes will be like.

What science deliberately leaves out is the question of why the universe is open in the first place to the dawning of new possibilities. This may not be a properly scientific question in any case, but theology at least has an appropriately explanatory role to play here, not only in accounting for why the universe exists at all, but also in speculating about why nature remains open to future transformation. In saying this I am not making room for a god-of-the-gaps that would ever compete with scientific understanding. My approach challenges naturalism, but in no sense does it compete with science. The hard work of science still remains to be done, and theology can never be a substitute for this effort.

My point is simply that the later-and-more of nature, as the above reflection on critical intelligence has shown, cannot be fully understood by telling the scientific story of how it arose out of the earlier-and-simpler. Learning how mind appeared in the history of nature is fascinating in its narrative content. But if nothing else were involved in explaining the reality and power of mind than conceptually and imaginatively cobbling together a series of mindless antecedents and components, then the essential feature of critical intelligence will still have been overlooked—namely, its *present* anticipatory openness to a fullness of being, meaning, and truth up ahead. And by leaving this dimension of anticipation out of our understanding of mind we would also have diminished our understanding of the wider universe.

Of course, one can always deny verbally that there is anything 'more' involved in critical intelligence than its material constituents. Perhaps minds, like everything else in life, are *really* just simplicity masquerading in the guise of complexity, as Peter Atkins claims (Atkins 1994: 200). However, this declaration is self-refuting since it implies logically that the complex mind that makes such a claim is itself *really* nothing more than the earlier-and-simpler mindless stuff from which it arose. And if the roots of Atkins's own mind have such a physically lowly status, where then did he acquire the colossal *trust* in his mental powers that allows him to assume now that we should listen to him? Tracing the causes of present phenomena all the way back into the remotest past and all the way down to the elemental levels of cosmic stuff leads the mind only toward the incoherence of sheer multiplicity. Only by looking toward future syntheses of the world's elemental units does intelligibility start to show up. For, nothing in our evolving world can make complete sense until it has reached its terminus (Teilhard de Chardin 1969: 66). Full intelligibility, therefore can only coincide with an Absolute Future, a goal that we can approach here and now by cultivating the virtue of hope (Rahner 1969: 59–68).

Temporal passage, physical determinism, and Darwinian selection, though essential to the ongoing creation of life and mind, are not alone enough to account for the anticipatory bearing of critical intelligence, nor for that of the entire natural world in which our minds are embedded. Each natural entity, in addition to comprising physically simpler and historically antecedent factors, is also open, though not without constraints, to being transformed by a realm of new possibilities looming on the horizon of the future. I have called nature's openness to possibility *anticipation*, a concept that each of us can understand immediately since it is the dynamic core of our own critical intelligence. And although scientific discourse under-standably shies away from such terminology a stereoscopic empiricism is obliged to employ analogies like anticipation in order to arrive at a realistic and expansive understanding of nature. Some degree of anticipation—that is, openness to possibility—is a *fundamental* feature of nature, and not something that drops in out of the void only after the emergence of the human mind.

Of course, the quality of anticipation in nature needs an explanation also, and it is here that I would locate the relevance of theology to my inquiry. Such an explanation would focus on the notion of *possibility*. Possibility, in Latin, is *potentia*, a term that can be translated as potency or power. Power, though, is not limited to efficient or mechanical causation. There is also the *power of the possible* that allows room in nature for anticipation, cosmic emergence, and eventually the desire to know. Without an inherent openness to future possibility everything would be frozen in its present state and nothing new could ever happen. Unlike scientific naturalism, which views the future as a void to be filled in by the forward rush of aimless events out of the past, a theology of nature features the openness of the world to surprising new modes of being. The world's openness to novelty is due not to an absolute emptiness stretching up ahead but to an array of possibilities that come to greet the present, as it were, from out of the future, carrying it away from entrapment in what has been. There is a 'power of the future' whose appropriate name is God, and whose central action is the 'arrival of the future' (Pannenberg 1977: 58–9; Peters 1992).

Religious hope, I dare say, arises from the same anticipatory desire to *know* that underlies all conscious intentionality, including scientific inquiry. Even in all its ambiguity, religious anticipation of a final end to all confusion can hardly be completely alien to a critical intelligence whose very definition is a search for ever deeper intelligibility and truth. The widespread religious longing for ultimate fulfillment does not contradict but arises simultaneously with the unrestricted desire to know. Indeed, the cognitional ancestry of our irrepressible trust in the desire to know is intertwined with the religious tendency to look for ultimate fulfillment. To disentangle the two desires, I believe, runs the risk of killing them both.

13

Cognitive Science and the Evolution of Religion

A Philosophical and Theological Appraisal

Nancey Murphy[1]

Introduction

I intend to reflect theologically on the arguments of Pascal Boyer and others who provide cognitive-science accounts of the origin and persistence of religion. The book that launched the cognitive science of religion (CSR) into prominence, and that introduced me to the field, is Pascal Boyer's *Religion Explained: The Evolutionary Origins of Religious Thought*. It is a fascinating account and for a Christian who dabbles in theology very thought-provoking. Frankly, as he is applying his theories to what Westerners often call primitive religions, I am saying: 'Yes, yes—this explains those strange beliefs and practices;' but then, 'Wait a minute. This doesn't apply to us Christians!'

---

1. This chapter fits into a much larger work in progress for me. I recently presented a paper at a conference in honor of John Hedley Brooke which I entitled 'Naturalism and Theism as Competing Large-scale Traditions'. That paper was a schematic treatment of what I hope to do at book length. I begin with Alasdair MacIntyre's claim that the only way to understand the intellectual world is to see it as a competition of major traditions, embodying different world views, different forms of life, and even slightly different accounts of the nature of rationality. In this light I argue that in today's intellectual world there is no reason to think that the question of God can be settled by means of short philosophical arguments, for or against. The audiences such arguments are intended to convince live in different worlds, and will only be convinced by being persuaded to abandon their entire intellectual traditions in favor of another.

So, the apologetic task in our day is in part to address other world religions. However, my particular interest is to address what I call the modern scientific naturalist tradition. One aspect

So, one way a Christian can appropriate Boyer is to say that in so far as his theories are correct they explain other religions. But, as Karl Barth claimed, *religion is* a human phenomenon, while Christianity is something different altogether. I plan to take a different tack, though. I am going to try out the hypothesis that Boyer is giving an account of the *human* contributions to Christianity as well. Yet, from a theological standpoint, his naturalistic account is necessarily incomplete; it leaves God out of the picture.

Here is how I shall proceed. In the first section I will give an overview of some of Boyer's work. Next, I will use Arthur Peacocke's conception of theology, as the top science in the hierarchy of the sciences, to think in abstract terms about how theology should relate to CSR. In the second section I will present Catholic modernist George Tyrrell's theological account of the development of religion and then show how neatly Boyer's work can be adopted into it. In the final section I will suggest some of the ways Christianity can benefit from this adoption, both theologically and practically.

Pascal Boyer and the Cognitive Science of Religion

An important feature of Boyer's work is what he calls 'turning the question of the origin of religion upside down'. We tend to seek for one origin of the many religions. Instead, he says, we need to recognize the *vast* number of *potential* religious concepts, beliefs, and practices, and then explain why the ones that exist have survived. Is there something that religious concepts have in common that explains why they have been preserved and passed down to new generations?

The aspect of Boyer's work that seems most often to catch people's attention is his theory of religious concepts as 'minimally counter-intuitive'.

. of a competition between rival traditions is to see whether one can explain the rival's point of view better than the rival can itself. Since its beginnings in the eighteenth century with David Hume and Baron d'Holbach the naturalist tradition has claimed to be better able to explain the existence of Christianity and the other religions than Christians can explain themselves. It has attempted to do so by means of a number of accounts of the natural causes of religious belief, and by classifying Christianity as but one instance.

My interest in writing this chapter is due to the fact that CSR has replaced Freud, Marx, and others as the current best explanation of religion. So, to defend the Christian tradition it is necessary either to show that CSR's explanations fail or that we can happily accept a lot of them as partial explanations and incorporate them in a helpful way into our own theological world view. So this is a brief account of what I see as the philosophical import of CSR.

From cognitive science, Boyer introduces the idea of a template that allows for quick development of more particular concepts. We have only a small number of templates: PERSON, ANIMAL, ARTIFACT, POLLUTING SUBSTANCE, NATURAL OBJECT. The template ANIMAL, for example, specifies variables that need to be filled in to create a new concept, such as a *giraffe*: its general body shape, what it eats, where it lives, how it reproduces. But the template itself carries a great deal of tacit knowledge. For example, if one female giraffe bears live young, then all will be expected to do so.

Boyer's thesis regarding religious concepts is that they are anomalous, in that they add a special tag that violates one or a few characteristics contributed by the template. Some examples: a spirit violates the PERSON template by adding to it that it has no body. A statue to which one prays uses the ARTIFACT template but adds anomalous cognitive powers. An omniscient God is created from the PERSON template with added special cognitive powers.

Boyer and others have done research in several cultures to show that concepts that are anomalous in these minimal ways are more likely to be recalled by the subjects than either normal concepts or concepts that do not fit a template at all. So he claims that from among an effectively infinite number of possible religious concepts the ones we find in the world have survived and spread because they have this feature of minimal anomalousness. They are concepts that are easily formed by slight alteration of a template and they happen to be more memorable simply as a result of how the human mind or brain works.

In addition, we have inference systems that are turned on by different kinds of entities. These are sometimes called cognitive modules; some examples are: an agency-detection system, closely related to a system for detecting goal-directed movement; a system for keeping track of who's who; and systems dealing with the physics of solid objects, physical causation, and linking function to structure. To the extent that religious concepts have enough in common with ordinary concepts, they set off these inference systems, and this makes some sets of beliefs about the relevant entities natural, and therefore likely to be understood, remembered, elaborated in specific ways, and passed on to others.

There are two further aspects of Boyer's work that I will present here; these regard morality and religious practices. Boyer says that a typical assumption by and about religious believers is that belief in gods or spirits comes first, and then both religious practices and moral prescriptions follow.

Boyer argues that in fact morality and religious practices take priority, and both of these make religious belief more plausible. For example, corpses are highly anomalous because two different inference systems give conflicting answers to how we should deal with them. The system that detects animate beings recognizes that they are no longer alive, but the person-file system cannot suddenly be shut off. So the corpse is an object that needs to be disposed of, yet this is still uncle Joe. Religions incorporate assorted elaborate rituals to satisfy these conflicting needs and attitudes. When rituals are related to concepts of gods or spirits, participation makes belief in the spirits easier to acquire.

Regarding morality, Boyer cites studies showing that very small children, in different cultures, develop remarkably similar moral intuitions. By the age of three they can distinguish between moral and conventional rules. He claims that our evolution as a social species is sufficient to explain our shared morality. However, without knowing about evolution, humans through the ages have needed some other explanation. Spirits or gods, who know what we are doing to whom, and who are interested parties in the transactions, make a highly credible explanation.

In short, human brains have evolved to work in ways that suited us for survival in our early environments. Religious concepts, beliefs, practices, and rituals are natural by-products of these cognitive processes.

Now, as I pointed out at the beginning, our response to Boyer could be to try to evaluate the extent to which his claims are adequate to some sorts of religion—but maybe not all, and especially not mine. Animism and totemism seem to be explained easily: the NATURAL OBJECT and ARTIFACT templates, respectively, are tagged with anomalous cognitive and agential powers. There is actually quite a lot in Christianity that can be *described* in Boyer's terms: angels and demons, some forms of sacramental beliefs and actions. But, of course, we will not take him in this case to have offered an *adequate explanation.*

How To Relate Theology and Cognitive Science

I have found Arthur Peacocke's model for relating theology to the sciences to be the most useful. He has taken the widely accepted model of the hierarchy of the sciences, and adapted it in two ways. First, the original use of the hierarchy was to argue for reductionism. We are now in the midst of a significant world view shift, as reductionism is being replaced by

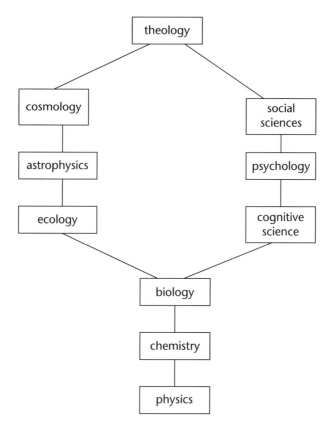

Figure 13.1. The locations of cognitive science and theology

an understanding of the hierarchy that recognizes the emergence of more complex systems. In these systems there often emerge new causal patterns that exercise 'downward' constraints on the parts of the system itself. We can call this whole–part constraint, as Peacocke preferred, or downward causation, in recognition that the system represents a higher level in the hierarchy than its components.

Peacocke's second innovation was to argue that theology, being the science that studies the most complex of all systems—namely, God in relation to the world—should be placed at the top of the hierarchy. George Ellis and I developed this idea, creating a branching hierarchy with the natural sciences above biology in one branch and the human sciences in the other. This allows me to represent the locations of cognitive science and theology. See Figure 13.1.

Our general understanding of the relations among sciences in the hierarchy is that, first, the higher-level science must be consistent with the findings of the ones below. Second, the higher level is underdetermined by the lower. Third, lower-level sciences often raise what Ian Barbour calls 'boundary questions': questions that can be formulated at one level but cannot be answered without insights from a higher-level science.

On this account, theology needs to be consistent with CSR, or at least with those claims of CSR that are well-supported. Clearly, though, from a theological perspective we should expect cognitive-science explanations of religion to be radically incomplete because it does not take divine action into account. But, if we do take divine action into account, can we then reconcile a theological account of the origin and persistence of religion with the phenomena that CSR claims to explain? In order to answer this I need to present a credible account of the role of divine action in the development of religion.

George Tyrrell's Account of the Development of Religion

Tyrrell was born in Dublin in 1861. He was the most prolific theologian of the Catholic modernist movement, lasting from about 1890 to 1910. This was an attempt to reconcile the Catholic heritage with the thought of the modern world, especially to respond to the crisis created by biblical criticism, and to replace a theological epistemology based on authority by one congruent with empiricism.

Tyrrell elaborated a model of religion and its development with places for divine action and religious experience; scripture, narrative, and historical data; morality, ritual, and sentiment; metaphor and mystery; dogma and theology; first- and second-order language; and, finally, church authority and tradition.

As his views developed over time, he first criticized the scholastic theologians of his day, who were treating scripture as a book of theology and attempting to deduce further conclusions from it. He explained the distinction he wished to draw between theology and the 'deposit of faith' by means of an analogy. Just as scientific knowledge about nature is distinct from nature itself, so theology, with its abstract categories, is distinct from the life of the faithful which is its job to explain, and different in kind from the common beliefs of the faithful, expressed in 'vulgar' 'anthropomorphic' language. The Scriptures—the deposit of faith—partake of this common level of expression.

Next, Tyrrell addressed the development of religious knowledge. The world, he asserts, is more than the natural world. The non-physical part of reality constitutes a 'higher plane'; it is the realm of freedom, will, and love—the 'spiritual' world. Human faculties are well suited for accumulating knowledge about nature and history, but we only grasp dimly the realities of the spiritual world. We do so by experiment.

The experiment begins with the construction of moral codes. In his early work he took this to be human invention. Individuals are faced with situations and have to decide both how they ought to feel about them and how they ought to act. After a time of observing the outcomes of these individual experiments, society is able to formulate a code regarding morality and sentiment. The truth of these schemes is their adequacy for the guidance of life and the prediction of the consequences of one's actions. Religious knowledge is then an attempt to formulate hypotheses about the spiritual world that account for the truth of the moral code.

Later he merged his accounts of revelation and of knowledge by experiment. Regarding both, he says that what is given from 'beyond' and serves as the basis for all religious knowledge is a drive or impulse to adjust oneself to the 'whole' that transcends the natural world. This drive resembles an instinct, and allows for recognition of courses of action or thought that move one into closer harmony with the spiritual world. As society develops a code of behavior, sentiment, and piety on the basis of this instinct, its members reflect upon this mode of life and develop 'some picture, idea, and history of the world to which this code strives to adjust our conduct' (Tyrell 1907: 207). Thus, religious belief grows up to account for the religious life; by providing an imagined view of the spiritual world it explains religious practices and sentiments. He says:

> So far, then, revelation (considered objectively) is a knowledge derived from, as well as concerning, the 'other world', the supernatural. But its derivation is decidedly indirect. What alone is directly given from above . . . is the spiritual craving or impulse with its specific determination, with its sympathetic and antipathetic responses to the suggestions, practical or explanatory, that are presented to it . . . To find the object which shall explain this religious need and bring it to full self-consciousness is the end and purpose of the whole religious process.

> (Tyrell 1907: 207)

First-order expressions of these experiences of the spiritual world and of attempts to visualize it—including those in Scripture—are in poetic or 'prophetic' language, which is symbolic, imaginative, imprecise. Christian dogmas are of this order. Theological questions arise in the attempt to systematize and unify the first-order knowledge of religion and reconcile it with other knowledge, including science.

Of these three elements—revelation, dogmatic expression, and theological explication—only the revelatory experience itself is guaranteed truth. Furthermore, this truth is of a practical kind—it is truth about how to live; it is approximative and preferential—it is not guaranteed to be absolute or ultimate, but only to be the alternative that moves closer to ultimate truth.

Figure 13.2 is my picture, in diagrammatic form, of Tyrrell's model. The yes/no experiences are the impulses that form the basis of revelation. Over time and within a community they lead to the formation of patterns of worship, morality, and sentiment. They are also expressed in the first-order imagistic, metaphorical language of dogmas. The patterns of worship, sentiment, and morality need explanation: Why are *these* the correct way to feel, to worship, to act? Hypotheses are formed, again metaphorically, about the spiritual world and they are confirmed in so far as they meet the test of conforming the community experientially to that reality. Scripture

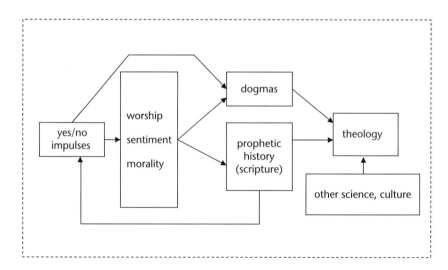

Figure 13.2. The impulses that form the basis of revelation in Tyrrell's model

includes the first-order language of those who knew Christ personally. Prophetic history is a kind of narrative that tells spiritual truths and may or may not also be objectively historical. Theology comes after the first-order language and is the attempt to formulate belief and practice into a consistent system. It needs to be informed by science and the rest of culture.

Parallels with Current Cognitive Science

Despite the one hundred year time gap, Tyrrell shared with contemporary cognitive science of religion the understanding of religion as a natural phenomenon, developing in history according to 'natural laws of religious psychology'. He recognized the tendency of religious representations to be distorted by these psychological laws, and noted that Catholicism is not a 'rational, purified religion' but rather an eclectic mixture, a jumble of levels, not all logically consistent.

So, the integration of CSR into Tyrrell's theological account of religion turns out to be surprisingly easy. What CSR provides is the natural laws of religious psychology. Tyrrell's and Boyer's theories (along with many other contributions to CSR that I have not been able to include here) are complementary.

In addition to the complementarity, there is significant overlap between Tyrrell's and Boyer's descriptions of religion and its development. They agree that the only language we have for religion is drawn from the natural world and has to be adapted. Tyrrell says that religious language is metaphorical, and linguistic theorists point out that when a metaphor is used there are always ways in which that which is being described is like the original application, but also in important ways *not* like it. So, this is a more general theory of religious language than Boyer's, but Boyer's provides dramatic instances that fit under Tyrrell's theory.

Both agree that practices and moral codes are prior to religious belief; religious beliefs are invented to explain and justify the codes and practices. A major point of difference, though, is in their accounts of the sources of moral codes. Boyer takes the sociobiologists' line and argues that our evolutionary past accounts for a universal set of moral intuitions. Tyrrell first claimed that we build moral codes slowly by trial and error. When faced with a choice, we take one of the options and then see what its consequences are for getting along in society. But, more importantly, for Tyrrell, this is just the beginning of moral formation. The important developments are those that result from sensitive believers whose lives are shaped by the yes/no impulses that come from the Spirit.

And this brings us to the critical point where theology has to go beyond cognitive science: the issue of divine action. Boyer claims that his account explains how religions come to be and (implicitly) that this is *all* there is to it. The theologian insists that there is another agent involved, although one not entirely in control of the process.

Notice, though, the pressure that this claim puts on Christians to be able to give an account of God's special divine action. Divine action has been a problem for Christians throughout the modern period—ever since it came to appear that, with a combination of natural laws and initial conditions, all natural events would have sufficient natural explanation.

A number of participants in the theology–science dialog have attempted to find ways to understand special divine action that do not require intervention in the sense of violation of laws of nature. I have followed Robert Russell and others in arguing for quantum divine action. This is the view that God determines what would otherwise have been intrinsically indeterminate events at the quantum level. Quantum divine action has many critics, but as the discussion stands at the moment, none is taken to be definitive.

Now, many theologians evaded the problem of divine action by emphasizing a dualist account of humans, and postulating that God works in the world only by communication to souls or minds. Many of you know that I am famous (or infamous) for rejecting dualism in favor of a non-reductive physicalist account of humans. Thus, however crude or incongruous it may sound, I argue that God communicates with us by orchestrating events in our brains at the quantum level to produce subtle effects on our thoughts, imaginations, and emotions.

It is possible, in fact, to integrate my theory of religious experience with Tyrrell's. Tyrrell says: 'what alone is directly given from above, or from beyond, is the spiritual craving or impulse with its specific determination, with its sympathetic and antipathetic responses to the suggestions, practical or explanatory, that are presented to it . . . ' Here is my physicalist translation of Tyrrell's account of communication with God. Either by deliberate reflection or spontaneously—and perhaps this happens just as the cognitive scientists describe—an idea of God or spiritual things comes to mind, or a plan of action. This means that a complex neural assembly has been activated. God's response is to affect the brain by means of an orchestration of events at the quantum level so as to produce either a positive or negative impulse.

Notice that this whole process is dependent on culture and language. The richer the religious culture the more sophisticated and appropriate the images and symbols may be, and the more discerning the plans for action. With *fewer* resources, God's ability to communicate is proportionately decreased. Tyrrell says that this form of direction is *approximative and preferential* rather than direct.

This theory helps to explain the persisting variety of religions, and the fact that religious experiences are almost always consistent with the expectations and beliefs of the tradition to which the devotee belongs. God does not produce the experience; culture and imagination do— and now we can add that they may well do so in the first instance as a consequence of the way cognitive operators work. God merely ratifies or vetoes, and, even then, only when the human subject is sensitive to the impulses.

So this is an account of the origin of at least some religious representations. If it has merit, this justifies my claim that there is a further level of analysis beyond the individual and the cultural—namely, the theological— that needs to be taken into account in the development and persistence of religion. Yet, this does not preclude any of the analyses put forward by cognitive scientists. The spread, distortion, and maintenance of such representations are indeed matters open to scientific investigation, as Tyrrell recognized in his own day.

Practical and Theological Benefits of CRS

There are a number of other issues in Boyer's writings that would have been worth mentioning here. There are also a number of other authors in the field with useful studies and theories for Christian scholars to consider. For example, Jason Slone has developed a theory of theological incorrectness. He points out that the actual beliefs elicited from subjects on the spur of the moment tend to differ from their communities' orthodoxy, and this happens in rather predictable ways. For example, people tend to imagine God much more anthropomorphically than theologians do. Boyer himself provides good advice to evangelists: 'avoid bombarding people with cogent and coherent arguments for particular metaphysical claims and . . . provide them instead with many occasions where the claims in question can be used to produce relevant interpretations of particular situations' (Boyer 2001b: 317). So we could read this literature for practical advice likely to produce more effective ministries.

I want to mention two theological uses of these ways of thinking. First, it is often said that Jesus can be understood as purifying the Judaism of his day. Cognitive science theories of the sorts of religious beliefs that come naturally to people give us a perspective for evaluating this claim. Here are just two suggestions. First, Boyer has a chapter on how people come to attribute misfortune to God. While Christians do not reject the possibility that some human suffering is punishment for sin, notice that in the story of the man born blind Jesus contradicts the assumption that his blindness must be a consequence of either his or his parents' sins.

Second, much of what scientists call religion, Christians would call magic. Cognitive scientists take it to be a feature of all religion that it is an attempt to control God or other spiritual beings. Jesus follows a long line of prophets in rejecting the view that rituals have direct causal effects on God. The sacrifices God requires are justice and mercy.

A second major use of CSR is to develop a theology of other religions. This is an important issue at my institution, Fuller Seminary. We have decided that no one with a Master's-level education in theology should be ignorant of other religions. But, we struggle with the question of how to include courses on religion that neither take a view, common in the past, that religions other than Christianity are demonic, nor present other religions as somehow on a par with Christianity.

I believe that knowledge of humans' natural tendencies to create religious ideas and practices can be incorporated into such a study. But the study would include what we (claim to) know about how the Spirit works in our own fallible human minds. I think this would put us in a position to look at another religion, much as I have suggested Jesus did with his own Judaism, and to ask whether we see signs of the Spirit of Jesus working similarly to purify that religion.

Conclusion

What I have tried to do in this chapter is not to critique current research in CSR, although surely a lot of it does need to be criticized. Rather, I have tried to show that it is no threat to Christian belief, since it can handily be *complemented* by a theological account of the development of religion. Furthermore, I hope I have convinced you that it is interesting material that Christians ought to know about, and that it is a potentially valuable source of insights for Christian scholars and practitioners.

14

Moral Psychology and the Misunderstanding of Religion[1]

Jonathan Haidt

Morality is one of those basic aspects of humanity, like sexuality and eating, that can't fit into one or two academic fields. Morality is unique, however, in having a kind of spell that disguises it and protects its secrets. We all care about morality so passionately that it is hard to look straight at it. We all look at the world through some kind of moral lens, and because most of the academic community uses the same lens, we validate each other's visions and distortions. I think this problem is particularly acute in some of the new scientific writing about religion.

When I began to study moral psychology, in 1987, it seemed that developmental psychology owned the field. Everyone was either using or critiquing the ideas of Lawrence Kohlberg (1969), as well as his general method of interviewing kids about dilemmas (such as: should Heinz steal a drug to save his wife's life?). Everyone was studying how children's understanding of moral concepts changed with experience. But in the 1990s two books were published that triggered an explosion of cross-disciplinary scientific interest in morality, out of which has come a new synthesis—very much along the lines that E. O. Wilson (2000 [1975]) had predicted in the controversial last chapter of his landmark volume *Sociobiology: The New Synthesis*.

---

1. This chapter is adapted from an essay first published at <http://www.edge.org>.

The New Synthesis in Moral Psychology

The first was Antonio Damasio's *Descartes' Error* (1994) which showed a broad audience that morality could be studied using the then new technology of functional magnetic resonance imaging (fMRI), and also that morality, and rationality itself, were crucially dependent on the proper functioning of emotional circuits in the prefrontal cortex. The second was Frans de Waal's *Good Natured* (1996), published just two years later, which showed an equally broad audience that the building blocks of human morality are found in other apes and are products of natural selection. These two books came out just as John Bargh (1994; Bargh and Chartrand 1999) was showing social psychologists that automatic and unconscious processes can and probably do cause the majority of our behaviors, even morally loaded actions (like rudeness or altruism) that people think they are controlling consciously.

Furthermore, Damasio and Bargh both found, as Michael Gazzaniga (1985) had years before, that people couldn't stop themselves from making up post hoc explanations for whatever it was they had just done for unconscious reasons. Combine these developments and suddenly Kohlbergian moral psychology seemed to be studying the wagging tail, rather than the dog. If the building blocks of morality were shaped by natural selection long before language arose, and if those evolved structures work largely by giving us feelings that shape our behavior automatically, then why should we be focusing on the verbal reasons that people give to explain their judgments in hypothetical moral dilemmas?

In my early research (Haidt and Hersh 2001; Haidt, Koller, and Dias 1993) I told people short stories in which a person does something disgusting or disrespectful that was perfectly harmless (for example, a family cooks and eats its dog, after the dog was killed by a car). I was trying to pit the emotion of disgust against reasoning about harm and individual rights. I found that disgust won in nearly all groups I studied (in Brazil, India, and the United States), except for groups of politically liberal college students, particularly Americans, who overrode their disgust and said that people have a right to do whatever they want, as long as they don't hurt anyone else.

These findings suggested that emotion played a bigger role than that the cognitive developmentalists had given it. These findings also suggested that there were important cultural differences, and that academic researchers may have inappropriately focused on reasoning about harm and rights because we primarily study people like ourselves—college students, and also children in private schools near our universities whose morality is not representative of the United States, let alone the world.

The 1990s was therefore a time of synergy and consilience across disciplines. Inspired by the work of Damasio, de Waal, and Bargh, I wrote a review article titled 'The Emotional Dog and its Rational Tail' (Haidt 2001), which was published one month after Josh Greene's enormously influential *Science* article (Greene, et al. 2001). Greene et al. used fMRI to show that emotional responses in the brain, not abstract principles of philosophy, explain why people think various forms of the 'trolley problem' (in which you have to choose between killing one person or letting five die) are morally different. The year 2001 may therefore have been a tipping point—a year when the zeitgeist shifted away from the study of moral reasoning and decisively toward the multidisciplinary study of moral emotions and intuitions. Most people who study morality today read and write about emotions, the brain, chimpanzees, and evolution, as well as reasoning.

This is exactly what E. O. Wilson had predicted in 1975: that the old approaches to morality, including Kohlberg's, would be swept away or merged into a new approach that focused on the emotive centers of the brain as biological adaptations. Wilson (2000 [1975]: 563) even said that these emotive centers give us moral intuitions, which the moral philosophers then justify while pretending that they are intuiting truths that are independent of the contingencies of our evolved minds. And now, thirty-three years later, Josh Greene (2008) just published a paper in which he uses neuroscientific evidence to reinterpret Kantian deontological philosophy as a sophisticated post hoc justification of our gut feelings about rights and respect for other individuals. I think E. O. Wilson deserves more credit than he gets for seeing into the real nature of morality and for predicting the future of moral psychology so uncannily. He is in my pantheon, along with David Hume and Charles Darwin. All three were visionaries who urged us to focus on the moral emotions and their social utility.

I recently summarized this new synthesis in moral psychology (Haidt 2007) with four principles:

1. Intuitive primacy but not dictatorship

This is the idea, going back to Wilhelm Wundt (1907) and channeled through Robert Zajonc (1980) and John Bargh (1994) that the mind is driven by constant flashes of affect in response to everything we see and hear. Our brains, like other animal brains, are constantly trying to fine-tune and speed up the central decision of all action: approach or avoid. You cannot understand the river of fMRI studies on neuro-economics and decision-making without embracing this principle. We have affectively valenced intuitive reactions to almost everything, particularly to morally relevant stimuli such as gossip or the evening news. Reasoning by its very nature is slow, playing out over the course of many seconds that follow the initial flash of affect. Studies of everyday reasoning (Kuhn 1991) show that we usually use reasoning to search for evidence to support our initial judgment, which was made in milliseconds. But I agree with Greene (2008) that sometimes we can use controlled processes such as reasoning to override our initial intuitions. I just think this happens rarely, maybe in 1 or 2 per cent of the hundreds of judgments we make each week.

2. Moral thinking is for social doing

This is a play on William James' pragmatist dictum that thinking is for doing, updated by newer work on Machiavellian intelligence. The basic idea is that we did not evolve language and reasoning because they helped us to find truth; we evolved these skills because they were useful to their bearers, and among their greatest benefits were reputation management and manipulation. Just look at your stream of consciousness when you are thinking about a politician you dislike, or when you have just had a minor disagreement with your spouse. It is as though you are preparing for a court appearance. Your reasoning abilities are pressed into service generating arguments to defend your side and attack the other. We are certainly able to reason dispassionately when we have no gut feeling about a case, and no stake in its outcome, but with moral disagreements that is rarely the case. As David Hume said long ago, reason is the servant of the passions.

3. Morality binds and builds

This is the idea—stated most forcefully by Emile Durkheim—that morality is a set of constraints that binds people together into an emergent collective entity. Durkheim focused on the benefits that accrue to individuals from being tied in and restrained by a moral order. In his book *Suicide* Durkheim (1951 [1897]) alerted us to the ways that freedom and wealth almost inevitably foster *anomie*, the dangerous state where norms are unclear and people feel that they can do whatever they want. Durkheim didn't talk much about conflict between groups, but Darwin thought that such conflicts may have spurred the evolution of human morality. Virtues that bind people to other members of the tribe and encourage self-sacrifice would lead virtuous tribes to vanquish more selfish ones, which would make these traits more prevalent.

Of course, this simple analysis falls prey to the freerider problem that George Williams (1966) and Richard Dawkins (2006 [1976]) wrote so persuasively about. But I think the terms of this debate over group selection have changed radically in the last ten years, as culture and religion have become central to discussions of the evolution of morality. I will say more about group selection in a moment. For now I just want to make the point that humans do form tight, cooperative groups that pursue collective ends and punish cheaters and slackers, and they do this most strongly when in conflict with other groups. Morality is what makes all of that possible.

4. Morality is about more than harm and fairness

In moral psychology and moral philosophy, morality is almost always about how people treat each other. Here is an influential definition from Elliot Turiel (1983: 3): morality refers to 'prescriptive judgments of justice, rights, and welfare pertaining to how people ought to relate to each other'. Kohlberg thought that all of morality, including concerns about the welfare of others, could be derived from the psychology of justice. Carol Gilligan convinced the field that an ethic of 'care' had a separate developmental trajectory, and was not derived from concerns about justice. Turiel's definition encompasses Kohlberg and Gilligan; moral psychologists since the 1980s have been in general agreement that there are two psychological systems at work, one about fairness/justice, and one about care and protection of the vulnerable. And if you look at the many books on the evolution of morality, most of them focus exclusively on those two systems, with long discussions of Robert Trivers' (1971) reciprocal altruism (to explain fairness) and of kin altruism (Hamilton 1964) and/or attachment theory (Bowlby 1969) to explain why we don't like to see suffering and often care for people who are not our children.

But if you try to apply this two-foundation morality to the rest of the world you either fail or you become Procrustes. Most traditional societies care about a lot more than harm/care and fairness/reciprocity. Why do so many societies care deeply and morally about menstruation, food taboos, sexuality, and respect for elders and the Gods? You can't just dismiss such concerns as social conventions. If you want to describe human morality, rather than the morality of educated Western academics, you have to include the Durkheimian view that morality is in large part about binding people together.

The Five Foundations of Morality

From a review of the anthropological and evolutionary literatures, my collaborators and I (Haidt and Graham 2007; Haidt and Joseph 2004) concluded that there were three best candidates for being additional psychological foundations of morality, beyond harm/care and fairness/reciprocity. These three we label as in-group/loyalty (which may have evolved from the long history of cross-group or subgroup competition, related to what Kurzban, Tooby, and Cosmides (2001) call 'coalitional psychology'); authority/respect (which may have evolved from the long history of primate hierarchy, modified by cultural limitations on power and bullying, as documented by Boehm (1999)), and purity/sanctity, which may be a much more recent system, growing out of the uniquely human emotion of disgust, which seems to give people feelings that some ways of living and acting are higher, more noble, and less carnal than others.

My collaborators and I think of these foundational systems as expressions of what Sperber (2005) calls 'learning modules'—they are evolved modular systems that generate, during enculturation, large numbers of more specific modules which help children recognize, quickly and automatically, examples of culturally emphasized virtues and vices. For example, academics have extremely fine-tuned receptors for sexism (related to fairness) but not sacrilege (related to purity). Virtues are socially constructed and socially learned, but these processes are highly prepared and constrained by the evolved mind. We call these three additional foundations the 'binding' foundations, because the virtues, practices, and institutions they generate function to bind people together into hierarchically organized interdependent social groups that try to regulate the daily lives and personal habits of their members. We contrast these to the two 'individualizing' foundations (harm/care and fairness/reciprocity) which generate virtues and practices that protect individuals from each other and allow them to live in harmony as autonomous agents who can focus on their own goals.

My colleagues Jesse Graham, Brian Nosek, and I have collected data from about 30,000 people so far on a survey designed to measure people's endorsement of these five foundations. In every sample we have looked at, in the United States, in other Western countries, and even among our Latin American and East Asian respondents, we find that people who self-identify as liberals endorse moral values and statements related to the two individualizing foundations primarily, whereas self-described conservatives endorse values and statements related to all five foundations. It seems that the moral domain encompasses more for conservatives—it is not just about Gilligan's care and Kohlberg's justice; it is also about Durkheim's issues of loyalty to the group, respect for authority, and sacredness.

I hope you—the reader—will accept that as a purely descriptive statement. You can still reject the three binding foundations normatively—that is, you can still insist that in-group, authority, and purity refer to ancient and dangerous psychological systems that underlie fascism, racism, and homophobia, and you can still claim that liberals are right to reject those foundations and build their moral systems using primarily the harm/care and fairness/reciprocity foundations. But please accept for the moment that there is this difference, descriptively, between the moral worlds of secular liberals on the one hand and of religious conservatives on the other. There are, of course, many other groups, such as the religious left and the libertarian right, but I think it is fair to say that the major players in the new religion wars are secular liberals criticizing religious conservatives. Because the conflict is a moral conflict, we should be able to apply the four principles of the new synthesis in moral psychology.

Applying the New Synthesis and the Five Foundations to the New Atheism

In what follows I will take it for granted that religion is a part of the natural world that is appropriately studied by the methods of science. Whether or not God exists (and as an atheist I personally doubt it), religiosity is an enormously important fact about our species. There must be some combination of evolutionary, developmental, neuropsychological, and anthropological theories that can explain why human religious practices take the various forms that they do, many of which are so similar across cultures and eras (see, e.g., Atran 2002a; Boyer 2001b). I will also take it for granted that religious fundamentalists, and most of those who argue for the existence of God, illustrate the first three principles of moral psychology (intuitive primacy, post hoc reasoning guided by social utility, and a strong sense of belonging to a group bound together by shared moral commitments).

But because the New Atheists talk so much about the virtues of science and our shared commitment to reason and evidence, I think it is appropriate to hold them to a higher standard than their opponents. Do these New Atheist books model the scientific mind at its best? Or do they reveal normal human beings acting on the basis of their normal moral psychology?

1. Intuitive primacy but not dictatorship

It is clear that Richard Dawkins (2006 [1976]) and Sam Harris (2006) have strong feelings about religion in general and religious fundamentalists in particular. The passions of Dawkins and Harris do not mean that they are wrong, or that they cannot be trusted. One can certainly do good scholarship on slavery while hating slavery. But the presence of passions should alert us that the authors, being human, are likely to have great difficulty searching for and then fairly evaluating evidence that opposes their intuitive feelings about religion. We can turn to Dawkins and Harris to make the case for the prosecution, which they do brilliantly, but if we readers are to judge religion we will have to find a defense attorney. Or at least we'll have to let the accused speak.

2. Moral thinking is for social doing

This is where the scientific mind is supposed to depart from the lay mind. The normal person (once animated by emotion) engages in moral reasoning to find ammunition, not truth; the normal person attacks the motives and character of her opponents when it will be advantageous to do so. The scientist, in contrast, respects empirical evidence as the ultimate authority and avoids ad hominem arguments. The metaphor for science is a voyage of discovery, not a war. Yet, when I read the New Atheist books, I see few new shores. Instead I see battlefields strewn with the corpses of straw men. To name three:

(i) The New Atheists treat religions as sets of beliefs about the world, many of which are demonstrably false. Yet, anthropologists and sociologists who study religion stress the roles of ritual and community much more than of factual beliefs about the creation of the world or life after death. The New Atheists take religion too literally, which makes it easy for them to identify logical inconsistencies but hard for them to see the personal and societal benefits of religion.

(ii) The New Atheists assume that believers, particularly fundamentalists, take their sacred texts literally. Yet ethnographies of fundamentalist communities (such as Ault (2005)) show that even when people claim to be biblical literalists, they are in fact quite flexible, drawing on the Bible selectively—or ignoring it—to justify humane and often quite modern responses to complex social situations.

(iii) The New Atheists all review recent research on religion and conclude that it is an evolutionary by-product, not an adaptation. They compare religious sentiments to moths flying into candle flames, ants whose brains have been hijacked for a parasite's benefit, and cold viruses that are universal in human societies. This denial of adaptation is helpful for their argument that religion is bad for people, even when people think otherwise. I quite agree with these authors' praise of the work of Pascal Boyer (2001b) and Scott Atran (2002a), who have shown how belief in supernatural entities may indeed be an accidental output of cognitive systems that otherwise do a good job of identifying objects and agents. Yet, even if belief in gods was initially a by-product, as long as such beliefs were heritable and had consequences for behavior then it seems likely that natural selection operated upon phenotypic variation and favored the success of individuals and groups that found ways (genetic or cultural or both) to use these gods to their advantage—for example as commitment devices that enhanced cooperation, trust, and mutual aid.

3. Morality binds and builds

Dawkins (2006 [1976]) is explicit that his goal is to start a movement, to raise consciousness, and to arm atheists with the arguments they will need to do battle with believers. The view that 'we' are virtuous and our opponents are evil is a crucial step in uniting people behind a cause, and there is plenty of that in the New Atheist books. A second crucial step is to identify traitors in our midst and punish or humiliate them. There is some of that too in these books—atheists who defend the utility of religion or who argue for disengagement or détente between science and religion are compared to Chamberlain and his appeasement of Hitler.

To my mind an irony of Dawkins's position is that he reveals a kind of religious orthodoxy in his absolute rejection of group selection. David Sloan Wilson (2002) has supplemented Durkheim's view of religion (as being primarily about group cohesion) with evolutionary analyses to propose that religion was the conduit that pulled humans through a 'major transition' in evolutionary history. Dawkins (2006 [1976]), along with Williams (1966) and most critics of group selection, acknowledges that natural selection works on groups as well as on individuals, and that group selection is possible in principle. But Dawkins relies on Williams's argument that selection pressures at the individual level are, in practice, always stronger than those at the group level: freeriders will always undercut Darwin's suggestion that morality evolved because virtuous groups outcompeted selfish groups.

Wilson (2002), however, makes the case that culture in general and religion in particular change the variables in Williams's analysis. Religions and their associated practices greatly increase the costs of defection (through punishment and ostracism), increase the contributions of individuals to group efforts (through cultural and emotional mechanisms that increase trust), and sharpen the boundaries—biological and cultural— between groups. Throw in recent discoveries that genetic evolution can work much faster than previously supposed, and the widely respected work of Richerson and Boyd (2005) on cultural group selection, and suddenly the old consensus against group selection is outdated. Religiosity is a heritable trait, one that makes little sense as an individual-level adaptation for outcompeting one's less-religious neighbors. Religiosity makes a lot of sense, however, as a group-level adaptation for binding individuals together, solving the freerider problem, and outcompeting less cohesive groups.

It is time to examine the question anew. Yet Dawkins has referred to group selection in interviews as a 'heresy', and in *The God Delusion* he dismisses it without giving a reason. In chapter 5 he states the standard Williams freerider objection, notes the argument that religion is a way around the Williams objection, concedes that Darwin believed in group selection, and then moves on. Dismissing a credible position without reasons, and calling it a heresy (even if tongue in cheek), are hallmarks of standard moral thinking, not scientific thinking.

4. Morality is about more than harm and fairness

In *Letter to a Christian Nation* Harris (2006: 8) gives us a standard liberal definition of morality: 'Questions of morality are questions about happiness and suffering . . . To the degree that our actions can affect the experience of other creatures positively or negatively, questions of morality apply.' He then goes on to show that the Bible and the Qur'an, taken literally, are immoral books because they are not primarily about happiness and suffering, and in many places they advocate harming people.

Reading Harris is like watching professional wrestling or the Harlem Globetrotters. It is great fun, with lots of acrobatics, but it must not be mistaken for an actual contest. If we want to stage a fair fight between religious and secular moralities, we cannot eliminate one by definition before the match begins. So here is my definition of morality, which gives each side a chance to make its case: *moral systems are interlocking sets of values, practices, institutions, and evolved psychological mechanisms that work together to suppress or regulate selfishness and make social life possible* (Haidt 2008).

In my research I have found that there are two common ways that cultures suppress and regulate selfishness, two visions of what society is and how it ought to work. I will call them the contractual approach and the beehive approach. The contractual approach takes the individual as the fundamental unit of value. The fundamental problem of social life is that individuals often hurt each other, and so we create implicit social contracts and explicit laws to foster a fair, free, and safe society in which individuals can pursue their interests and develop themselves and their relationships as they choose. Morality is about happiness and suffering (as Harris says, and as John Stuart Mill said before him), and so contractualists are endlessly trying to fine-tune laws, reinvent institutions, and extend new rights as circumstances change in order to maximize happiness and minimize suffering. To build a contractual morality, all you need are the two individualizing foundations: harm/care, and fairness/reciprocity. The other three foundations, and any religion that builds on them, run afoul of the prime directive: let people make their own choices, as long as they harm nobody else.

The beehive approach, in contrast, takes the group and its territory as fundamental sources of value. Individual bees are born and die by the thousands, but the hive lives for a long time, and each individual has a role to play in fostering its success. The two fundamental problems of social life are attacks from outside and subversion from within. Either one can lead to the death of the hive, so all must pull together, do their duty, and be willing to make sacrifices for the group. Bees do not have to learn how to behave in this way but human children do, and this is why cultural conservatives are so heavily focused on what happens in schools, families, and the media.

Conservatives generally have a more pessimistic view of human nature than do liberals. They are more likely to believe that if you stand back and give kids space to grow as they please, they will grow into shallow, self-centered, undisciplined pleasure seekers. Cultural conservatives work hard to cultivate moral virtues based on the three binding foundations: in-group/loyalty, authority/respect, and purity/sanctity, as well as on the universally employed foundations of harm/care and fairness/reciprocity. The beehive ideal is not a world of maximum freedom, it is a world of order and tradition in which people are united by a shared moral code that is effectively enforced, which enables people to trust each other to play their interdependent roles. It is a world of very high social capital and low anomie.

It might seem obvious to you that contractual societies are good, modern, creative, and free, whereas beehive societies reek of feudalism, fascism, and patriarchy. And, as a secular liberal I agree that contractual societies such as those of Western Europe offer the best hope for living peacefully together in our increasingly diverse modern nations (although it remains to be seen if Europe can solve its current diversity problems). I just want to make one point, however, that should give contractualists pause: surveys have long shown that religious believers in the United States are happier, healthier, longer-lived, and more generous to charity and to each other than are secular people (Brooks 2006; Myers 2000). Most of these effects have been documented in Europe too. If you believe that morality is about happiness and suffering, then I think you are obligated to take a close look at the way religious people actually live and ask what they are doing right. Don't dismiss religion on the basis of a superficial reading of the Bible and the newspaper. Might religious communities offer us insights into human flourishing? Can they teach us lessons that would improve well-being even in a primarily contractualist society?

You cannot use the New Atheists as your guide to these lessons. The New Atheists conduct biased reviews of the literature and conclude that there is no good evidence of any benefits except the health benefits of religion. Here is Daniel Dennett (2006: 55) in *Breaking the Spell* on whether religion brings out the best in people:

> Perhaps a survey would show that as a group atheists and agnostics are more respectful of the law, more sensitive to the needs of others, or more ethical than religious people. *Certainly no reliable survey has yet been done* that shows otherwise. It might be that the best that can be said for religion is that it helps some people achieve the level of citizenship and morality typically found in brights. *If you find that conjecture offensive, you need to adjust your perspective.*

I have italicized the two sections that show ordinary moral thinking rather than scientific thinking. The first is Dennett's claim not just that there is no evidence, but that there is *certainly* no evidence, when in fact many widely available surveys have shown for decades that religious practice is a strong predictor of charitable giving. Arthur Brooks (2006) recently analyzed these data and concluded that the enormous generosity of religious believers is not just recycled to religious charities. Religious believers give more money than secular folk to secular charities, and to their neighbors. They give more of their time, too, and of their blood. Even if you excuse secular liberals from charity because they vote for government welfare programs, it is hard to explain why secular liberals give so little blood. The bottom line, Brooks concludes, is that all forms of giving go together, and all are greatly increased by religious participation and slightly increased by conservative ideology (after controlling for religiosity).

These data are complex and perhaps they can be spun the other way, but at the moment it appears that Dennett is wrong in his reading of the literature. Atheists may have many virtues, but on one of the least controversial and most objective measures of moral behavior—giving time, money,[2] and blood to help strangers in need—religious people appear to be morally superior to secular folk.

My conclusion is not that secular liberal societies should be made more religious and conservative in a utilitarian bid to increase happiness, charity, longevity, and social capital. Too many valuable rights would be at risk, too many people would be excluded, and societies are so complex that it is impossible to do such social engineering and get only what you bargained for. My point is just that every longstanding ideology and way of life contains some wisdom, some insights into ways of suppressing selfishness, enhancing cooperation, and ultimately enhancing human flourishing.

But, because of the four principles of moral psychology it is extremely difficult for people, even scientists, to find that wisdom once hostilities erupt. A militant form of atheism that claims the backing of science and encourages 'brights' to take up arms may perhaps advance atheism. But it may also backfire, polluting the scientific study of religion with moralistic dogma and damaging the prestige of science in the process.

2. I note that Brooks excludes giving to political causes, where it could be the case that atheists give more.

15

Does Naturalism Warrant a Moral Belief in Universal Benevolence and Human Rights?

Christian Smith

I want in this chapter to consider the kind of morality we would have reason to believe if it were the case that we inhabit a naturalistic universe. In particular, I want to consider whether in a naturalistic cosmos we would have reason to believe—as very many modern people in fact do—in universal benevolence and human rights as moral facts and imperatives.

By naturalistic I refer to the metaphysical belief of naturalism—namely, a belief in the universe as consisting of energy and matter only, in which no transcendent, supernatural, divine being exists as creator, sustainer, guide, or judge. A naturalistic universe is one that has come to exist by chance—not by design or providence—exclusively by purposeless natural forces and processes. There is no ultimate, inherent meaning or purpose. Any meaning or purpose that exists for humans in a naturalistic universe is constructed by and for humans themselves. When the natural forces of entropy eventually extinguish the human race—if some natural or human-made disaster does not do so sooner—there will be no memory or meaning, just as there existed none before human consciousness evolved. This naturalistic universe is the reality that mainstream natural science tells us we actually do in fact inhabit. Naturalism is not only a methodological assumption of contemporary science. It is also the standard metaphysical world view assumed, promoted, and protected by contemporary science.

What about benevolence and rights? Modern people tend to believe strongly that all human persons everywhere possess inalienable human rights to life, certain freedoms, respect of conscience, and protection against unwarranted or arbitrary violations of personal property and choices by the government or other persons. The enjoyment of these rights, it is widely believed, is not contingent upon being smart, attractive, wealthy, strong, or any other conditional quality or situation. Simply being a human person endows one with such rights and entitles one to their respect by others. Such basic human rights are such that they place a moral duty on people to honor, protect, and defend not only their own rights but also the rights of other people if they are able to do so. Further, many modern people believe in universal benevolence, that is, belief in the inherent moral goodness of sustaining the lives, reducing the suffering, promoting the health, and increasing the well-being of other people, including strangers, and perhaps particularly of the weak and vulnerable. Again, in principle, benevolence is commonly believed valid for every person of both sexes in all nations, races, religions, social classes, and ethnicities—whether other people are similar to us or not, it is widely believed that it is morally good to protect their lives and relieve their sufferings.

Such beliefs may seem idealistic. But they are also woven into the institutional and cultural fabric of many contemporary societies and the international system. It is because of the belief in universal benevolence and human rights that nations often come to the aid of distant disaster victims, that hospitals try to save and improve the lives of the sick and diseased, and that people give money to alleviate victims of famine, flood, and epidemics. It is ultimately because of these moral beliefs that the United Nations and many NGOs and individual advocates work to curtail the spread of AIDS in Africa and elsewhere, to provide clean drinking water to remote third world villages, and to organize for the release of prisoners of conscience and the end of torture. Such beliefs also often form the background against which many people try to treat others—including strangers and those who are different in various ways—with respect, courtesy, tolerance, and sometimes kindness. In fact, the ideas of universal benevolence and human rights has given rise to myriad important features of contemporary life, from the globally significant United Nations Universal Declaration of Human Rights to established legal protections afforded criminal suspects, to the heartsickness that many ordinary people feel on hearing news of disaster, injustice, and tragedy, even among strangers who live far away. In short, universal benevolence and rights are central features of modern moral sensibilities.

The question that I address in this chapter is: if we in fact live in the naturalistic cosmos that much of science tells us we occupy, do we have good reasons for believing in universal benevolence and human rights as moral facts and imperatives? In addressing the issues such a query raises, it is helpful to distinguish three different questions. The first is, can and do people who do believe that we live in a naturalistic universe also believe in universal benevolence and human rights and act upon such beliefs? The answer, obviously, is yes: many believers in naturalism are also passionate and devoted believers in human dignity, universal benevolence, and human rights. That answer is so clear, in fact, that simply asking the question risks insulting such people, though it is a point worth clarifying up front.

The second question is this: do people who believe that we live in a naturalistic universe *have good reason* to believe in universal benevolence and human rights—that is, are they rationally warranted in asserting and championing such moral claims and imperatives? Asked differently, does the moral belief in universal benevolence and human rights fit well with and flow naturally from the facts of a naturalistic universe? This is the question that I wish to address in this chapter. The answer that I will consider is: No, if we are intellectually honest we will see that a belief in universal benevolence and human rights as moral fact and obligation does not make particular sense, fit well with, or naturally flow from the realities of a naturalistic universe. One who believes in a naturalistic cosmos is, it seems to me, perfectly entitled to believe in and act to promote universal benevolence and human rights, but only as an arbitrary, subjective, personal preference—*not* as a rational, compelling, universally binding fact and obligation. The person who lives in a naturalistic universe may certainly *choose* to affirm universal benevolence and human rights. But they might equally reasonably choose some other, quite or even radically different moral position. At bottom, they do not occupy moral grounds for making compelling and binding claims on others on behalf of universal benevolence and human rights. This may be an unpopular argument and I may in fact be wrong, though I currently cannot see how or why. But, for the record, I am quite open to see so.

The third question is: *if* my answer to the second question is correct— that intellectual honesty does not grant residents of a naturalistic universe warranted moral belief in universal benevolence and human rights—will human societies and cultures who want to believe in them anyway, for whatever reasons, be able, notwithstanding the lack of warrant, to sustain such beliefs over the long run? If my answer to the second question is in fact wrong, then this is not a concern. In that case, people who want human societies to affirm and institutionalize the belief in universal benevolence and human rights should in this case be able to appeal to the reasonable warrant, the good fit, the natural inference that such beliefs represent in a naturalistic universe. But if my answer to the second question is convincing, then social practices grounded on belief in universal benevolence and human rights are potentially endangered. In theory, they would be in grave danger. However, the third question is not about theory. It is about whether *in real practice, as human cultures and societies actually tend to function*, universal benevolence and human rights would in fact be in danger. The answer to this question, it seems to me, is: maybe, maybe not. I think one can reasonably argue both ways. We simply may not be in a position to know until the answer is an accomplished fact one way or another. Sociological considerations tend to make me think that over time such beliefs will erode. But, more on this later. First, I engage the second of the questions posed above.

Historical Transcendent Accounts

I have said that I am inclined to believe that if we are intellectually honest we must concede that a belief in universal benevolence and human rights as moral fact and obligation does not make particular sense, does not fit well with, does not naturally flow from the realities of a naturalistic universe. Perhaps it is worth mentioning that I actually do not wish this to be the case. Given the institutional authority of naturalism in modernity, especially in science, the future of human societies would be more securely like what I believe they should be—namely, institutionally committed to universal benevolence and human rights—if these did make reasonable sense in a naturalistic universe. But, I do not see how they do. If anything, it appears to me that a naturalistic universe naturally gives rise to quite different moral commitments, ones quite objectionable to those who believe in benevolence and rights.

But, if so, why or how is it that so many modern people do appear to believe in universal benevolence and human rights? Answering this (fourth) question is not the focus of this chapter, but does provide a key background assumption for my argument. The best answer—one which many if not most believers in naturalism can and do readily recognize—points us in a historical direction, toward the metaphysics and moral teachings of religious teachings, perhaps particularly Judaism and Christianity. Many ancient civilizations and cultures readily accepted and practiced different forms of slavery, infanticide, and sometimes human sacrifice. Many took for granted innate inequalities between different groups of people. In general, few possessed the cultural resources to develop a strongly humanistic morality of the kind we widely affirm today. By contrast, the transcendent monotheism of ancient Judaism introduced a set of uncommon ethical sensibilities that were crucial in the eventual development of the culture of benevolence and rights. These included sacred beliefs in all human persons being made 'in the image of God'; in God liberating the Hebrews from oppressive Egyptian slavery; in Yahweh as a God of justice, righteousness, equity, and loving-kindness; in Yahweh as the only true God over all the people and nations of the earth; and in the Promised Land as a place of abundance but also social justice, economic equity, and judicial integrity. Yahweh abhorred infanticide and human sacrifice, demanded justice for the poor, and set legal limits on ill treatment of servants and criminals. Over centuries, Judaism developed a keen self-critical consciousness through recurrent prophetic condemnations of injustice, exploitation, and neglect of the poor, the needy, widows, strangers, aliens, and the unjustly accused. Judaism also evolved a universal vision of God's chosen people on a mission not to conquer the nations but to serve as the people through whom all of the nations might come to know God's love and righteousness and so stream to God's throne for worship.

Christianity, whether viewed as an offshoot of or the fulfillment of Judaism, inherited this ethical legacy and added to it the demanding teachings of Jesus on love for enemies, universalizing the 'neighbor', self-sacrificial giving, the disciples' worldwide mission, the sacred value of caring for the physical needs of others, and the dignity and importance of women, children, and 'sinners'. The Christian Apostles further taught the duty to share material wealth, respect for the consciences of others, the priority of persuasion over force, and the power of God's kingdom to dissolve divisive social distinctions—'in Christ there is neither Jew nor

Greek, male nor female, slave nor free', St Paul declared, 'all are one in Christ Jesus' (Gal. 3: 28).

Of course, both Jews and Christians have over millennia recurrently failed to live up to their own moral teachings—sometimes miserably so and with dreadful consequences. But Jewish and Christian teachings—on sin, repentance, forgiveness, and restitution—have also provided the grounds for bad conscience, prophetic condemnation, penitence, and self-correction. And the moral teachings of these religious traditions—canonized in sacred scriptures and elaborated in the practices of religious communities—have through centuries of Jewish diaspora and Christendom been diffused and embedded as deep structures in the moral cultures of entire societies and civilizations. The Enlightenment and modernity shattered Christendom and largely disestablished Christianity. But the Enlightenment and modernity have also carried on and developed in mostly secular forms the long humanistic moral tradition launched and fostered by millennia of Jewish and Christian tradition. That is, they have attempted to establish Christian and Jewish moral values on a non-theistic footing. In short, the widespread beliefs of modern people—whether religious or not—in universal benevolence and human rights can be traced to deep cultural roots in specific religious traditions which for millennia have nurtured a particular vision of universal human dignity, responsibility, and accountability. As a counterfactual matter—politically incorrect perhaps but I think nevertheless historically demonstrable—few if any other ancient human cultures appear to have possessed the embryonic metaphysical and moral cultural material from which could have evolved the robust commitment to universal benevolence and human rights that many moderns today embrace. In any case, regardless of what might have otherwise developed with regard to benevolence and rights, in fact what actually *did* develop was in large measure the cultural and institutional fruit of deep historical Jewish and Christian roots. And at the heart of those traditions was the belief in a transcendent personal God who is the source, governor, and judge of moral order and action.

Implicit in this account and relevant for the argument below is my assumption that sustaining belief commitments to ideas and practices that are difficult and costly requires an account or narrative that satisfactorily explains to neophytes and doubters the reality and reasons behind the belief commitments themselves. Beliefs with demanding and challenging implications and consequences need at least implicit rationales for people to embrace and act on them over the long run. Such beliefs will not perpetuate themselves over time without explanation. When skeptics ask why anyone should care about someone suffering on the other side of the world or in some hospital or foreign war zone, those who believe that we all should care must have an answer, an account to offer explaining why. 'Because each human person is made in the image of God' has, for example, been one historically compelling account. Whether explanations such as 'Because "society" says so' and 'You would wish others to care for you if you were suffering' might continue to serve as an effective account may be questionable.

Another premise of my argument worth surfacing here is that many people are not naturally and predominantly altruistic, self-giving, considerate of the needs of others, and more committed to truth and justice than their own welfare. This is not a grand position on philosophical anthropology but a general empirical observation that I think is quite defensible and relevant to this chapter's discussion. Most people have not only bright sides with capacities for genuine good, but also dark sides with capacities for deep selfishness, self-deception, and indifference toward the needs of others. It is precisely this fact that helps generate in the first place the problem of benevolence and rights addressed in this chapter.

I will proceed in this chapter to address the second question posed above by taking the role of the skeptic who does not see why, if the universe is the naturalistic one science tells us it is, we should have a moral commitment to universal benevolence and human rights. Why should we not simply realize that such a commitment is grounded in an illusory religious metaphysics, reject that commitment as ill-informed, and formulate alternative moral commitments that are more consistent with the real universe in which we actually live? I will emphasize what seems to me to be an intellectually coherent and honest case based on naturalism, even at the expense of perhaps violating deeply held moral convictions and sensibilities.

Naturalism and Morality

Recall the features of a naturalistic universe. There is no divinity, no transcendent natural law, no ultimate spiritual meaning or destiny that transcends human invention during the blip of cosmic time humans have occupied. Reality consists of various conglomerations of infinitesimally small particles pulled together by physical forces but which are in a constant state of flux. There exists only matter and energy—atoms, molecules, cells, organisms, light, heat, radiation. Everything existent is working itself out by natural forces that are not designed, intended, nor morally weighted. Everything simply is. Some forces and processes generate certain outcomes, others generate others. Complex substances have slowly evolved. Life has very improbably evolved. Conscious and self-conscious human beings have even more improbably evolved. Evolution through natural selection relies on functional mutation and selective survival. But it also relies on massive death and extinction. Most of the living species that ever inhabited planet earth, including some proto-human groups, are now vanished. In the future many other living entities will go extinct. Eventually, sooner or later, one way or another, all life on earth will be extinguished. And energy, matter, and natural forces will simply continue to play themselves out indefinitely.

In the meantime, lo and behold, one species, human beings, has by odd chance developed cognitive, emotional, and volitional capacities that result in their making valuations and judgments of a moral character. By 'moral' here, following Charles Taylor, I mean understandings about what is right and wrong, good and bad, worthy and unworthy, just and unjust, which are believed to be established not by people's own actual desires, decisions, or preferences, but by sources believed to exist apart from them, providing standards by which people's own desires, decisions, and preferences can themselves be judged. Viruses, ticks, and foxes do not create and live in moral worlds. But human beings, it so happens, do.

Furthermore, the potential range of human moral perceptions, categories, valuations, and judgments is immense. That humans are morally oriented animals per se does not itself specify the content of human morality. In fact, within very broad functional boundaries, humans can believe, have believed, and sometimes do believe in an immense variety of different kinds of moral world views and commitments. There is no one single moral system that is hardwired into humanity. Humans are not naturally or automatically humanistic liberal Democrats, for example, or slave-trading racists. They have to become such things through socialization by other people and social institutions that believe in and maintain such moral systems. The recurrent existential human question, therefore, is what *ought* we to rightly believe morally? What *is* true with respect to morality?

If we are able to slough off the superstitions and errors of pre-modern mythologies about spirits and gods and heaven and hell, what honest, cogent answer might we give to this perennial moral question? What might we be warranted in believing is right and wrong, good and bad, worthy and unworthy for *homo sapiens* scratching out an existence on the skin of this tiny planet spiraling around in what appears to be an empty and inherently purposeless cosmos? Would such facts call for a moral commitment to universal benevolence and human rights? I am afraid, as far as I can see, that they would not.

To begin with, let us first observe that a naturalistic universe does not offer any moral guidance per se at all. The heavens, contrary to what the ancient Psalmist wrote, do not declare the glory of holy God. Things just are what they are. More specifically, evolution provides no moral orientation whatsoever. For many years evolutionists believed that they could squeeze the doctrine of Progress out of evolution. But it did not take long to realize that evolution is simply an account of change, not progress or 'advance'. Organisms do tend to 'want' to survive. But on evolutionary grounds per se we cannot say that it was morally good or bad that the dinosaurs lived or died, for instance. It simply happened. And if humanity were to be extinguished by a global plague, survived only by bacteria, that too would, on evolutionary terms, be morally neither right nor wrong. It simply would be what happened. The last dying humans might regret and grieve it, but in a naturalistic universe that would not make the fact immoral. The fact would simply be that some bacteria could survive and humans could not. So, assuming naturalism, if morality is to be acquired at all, it must be acquired from the human mind, not from a naturalistic universe. Moral facts and values are simply not natural givens existing 'out there' for humans to recognize and embrace. They are, rather, human constructions that people must invent, believe, more or less live by, and enforce among each other.

Survival Morality?

This brings us back to the question: which moral beliefs ought contemporary and future humans create, believe in, and live by, and why? Might the nearly universal drive of organisms to *survive* provide a clue? Perhaps, but it is not clear what that clue might actually suggest. It might help if we could posit a normative 'species solidarity rule' stating that each organism ought to be committed to the survival of its own species. That at least might give us a fixed starting-point from which to build out an evolution-based morality. Unfortunately, using such a rule would rely on a preexistent moral obligation in order to explain the existence of moral obligations. We would then have to explain: where did that rule come from and why ought any member of a species believe and act on it? In fact there are human persons who believe that humans are the doom of the world and should relinquish their planetary dominance for the sake of the survival of other animal and plant species. If they are morally wrong in this, is it because they have violated the species solidarity rule? Alternatively, one might say that such a 'rule' is not actually normative but merely descriptive, that members of species in fact just do happen to be 'committed' to the survival of their species—and this may perhaps provide the basis of moral reasoning. But that is wrong too. Members of some animal species fight and destroy each other. Members of other species endanger themselves to protect the lives of members of other species. Are dolphins tending toward evolutionary immorality when they save swimming humans from sharks? Are trained St Bernards, when they save humans buried in avalanches? Are humans evolutionarily immoral in diverting resources that could help save the lives of vulnerable humans in order to instead save animals on the endangered species list? I do not think so. This hardly seems to me a promising approach to explaining universal benevolence and human rights.

But let us try harder to derive morality from survival. Let us posit that for humans 'the moral' is that which facilitates human survival. It is moral to care for the sick because doing so fosters human survival. It is moral to share one's food with the hungry because that increases likelihood of human survival. Etc. The question then is: whose survival? The survival of an individual? A nuclear family? A kinship group? A tribe? An ethnic group? A 'nation'? A 'race'? The entire human species? Which and why exactly? If the subject of survival is the individual organism and its family or kin, then it is not at all clear why universal benevolence should be a moral fact and obligation. Individuals, clans, and tribes can simply take care of themselves and rightly be indifferent about the suffering or survival of others of their species who are just as likely to be competitors as cooperators. If, on the other hand, the subject of survival is the human species, then it is not at all clear why universal human rights should be a moral fact and obligation.

In many cases, humanity as an animal species would be much better off and could potentially evolve higher levels of reproductive fitness if its most deformed, diseased, stupid, retarded, criminal, incorrigibly unproductive, and otherwise functionally useless and defective members were simply cut off from society and left to die. What within the parameters of naturalistic evolution exactly would be wrong with eugenics, for instance, is not all that rationally clear. Such ideas may and I hope do cause revulsion in us. But my argument is simply that naturalism cannot well explain that revulsion.

Back to the question of deriving morality from survival and the problem of specifying whose survival: natural selection as a process operates through the survival and deaths of individual organisms. Neither saber-tooth tigers nor manta rays ever joined in solidarity together to enhance their species' reproductive fitness. They simply survived and died as individual organisms subject to the purposeless forces of nature. If anything, they often competed with one another for individual survival. If individuals managed to survive, then the species survived. If individuals did not, then the species did not. So, which human moral system might be derived from the drive to survive? It depends again on *whose* survival. Some advocates of 'evolutionary ethics' derive human ethics from the drive toward species survival. But that again is viciously circular, in *presupposing* a moral rule making right the survival of the species over the tribe or family or individual, rather than explaining the existence of that rule in the first place. Nothing whatsoever in a naturalistic cosmos generally, or in evolutionary natural selection specifically, it seems to me, produces or could produce a preferred moral imperative for humans to devote themselves to species survival. If anything, in trying to get from survival to morality, naturalistic evolution would suggest that what is 'right' for humans to do is that which enhances individual and immediate family survival. And that does not lead to universal benevolence and rights.

About here in this discussion, advocates of 'evolutionary ethics' point out that human beings are dramatically unlike other species on the earth in that we possess not only bodies capable of physical survival but also brains capable of complex forms of reasoning, anticipation, creativity, forethought, imagination, and planning. This, they say, is precisely where morality comes into play. Humans are not merely struggling to survive on the earth. They are also able to perceive and reflect on the earth's general history and condition, explain to themselves the causes and consequences of events, forecast alternative futures dependent upon different conditions, and make real choices that have consequences. Such superior cognitive capacities conjoin with sophisticated emotional and volitional abilities to generate moral categories, valuations, judgments, and action. Fine. All of this is true. But how does it necessarily lead to the humanistic morality of universal benevolence and human rights? Such complex human capacities could just as easily lead to a warrior ethic of tribal or national conquest and dominance. To derive the kind of universal humanistic morality that many embrace today from the sheer facts of complex human cognitive capacities requires demonstrating a consistent functional benefit such a morality provides to reproductive fitness. But universal benevolence and human rights simply do not demonstrably provide such a benefit. With natural selection, even aided by the complex capacities of human cognitive ability, reproductive fitness is most evidently enhanced when individuals seek their own material advantage and that of their family, kin, and tribe—that is, their local 'in-group'—those on whom safety, security, health, and future depend. Interactions with others beyond one's in-group might be peaceful and friendly, but only for strategic instrumental reasons, not because of any universal morality. Nothing about the human capacity for complex reasoning, forethought, or planning per se naturally leads to universal benevolence and belief in human rights. The quest for survival, no matter how well aided by the powers of the human brain, simply cannot rationally get us to a genuine belief in the moral obligation of universal benevolence and the existence of inalienable human rights. Something else is required to produce those—if not a transcendent God, then some other account or explanation.

One possibility that might work if its premise were actually true is to posit that humans possess a natural, innate sympathy for most or all other humans simply by virtue of their humanity. Rousseau made a move like this. Unfortunately, the preponderance of evidence falsifies the premise, at least the version of it that would be required to build on it a robust belief in universal benevolence and rights. History and experience show that, while people may often feel sympathy for other people, those feelings are also very often overwhelmed by the all too familiar forces of self-interest, insecurity, rivalry, greed, enmity, and revenge. It seems just as easy and likely if not easier and more likely to become estranged from and even hostile toward others who are different than to care for them and seek their good. The power of innate sympathy is often feeble compared to other, less-kindly human capacities. But *even if* natural sympathy were a common, overpowering human impulse, that itself would not create the ontological existence of inalienable human rights and moral obligations of universal benevolence. Again, widespread subjective feelings simply do not and cannot give rise to moral facts and obligations. To get from one to the other requires the recognition of an ontological fact of rights and obligations the independent existence of which our feelings might only suggest. For our widespread moral belief in universal benevolence and human rights does not oblige us to act in response if and when we feel sympathy toward others. The belief requires that we act regardless of how we may feel. In fact, the belief itself actually claims the authority to change how we actually *do* feel to more closely align with how we ought to feel. The moral fact of universal rights itself calls us to learn emotional responses in respect of those existent rights of others.

A Social Contract Account?

An alternative way to account for the moral obligations of benevolence and rights is to posit some sort of social contract that simply creates and implements them. Again Rousseau is relevant here. The idea is that the moral facts and duties involved in universal benevolence and human rights are not ontologically independent realities derived from God, natural law, or any other transcendent source, to which humans respond or conform. Rather, benevolence and rights are ultimately human historical and cultural inventions that social collectives so happen for their own reasons to have decided to agree to define, embrace, and enforce. And by the power of a Durkheimian 'conscience collective' they have come to appear to subsequent generations to have an ontologically independent, transcendent, even sacred character calling for obedience.

This social contract account may very well be correct. It certainly comports with a naturalistic universe. But such an account also gives up most of the ground needed to sustain a belief in benevolence and rights, by shifting these from moral facts and imperatives to stable but ultimately contingent human agreements. The vulnerability is that if a commitment to rights and benevolence is understood as merely the outcome of a social agreement then two consequences follow. First, little prevents individuals who come to believe this from selectively violating the agreement if it served their advantage and they can get away with it. Second, nothing prevents the members of any given society from deciding that they want to rewrite the social contract in ways jettisoning rights and benevolence. Nothing larger could or arguably even should constrain the individual 'moral freerider' or the collective social contract rewriters. If benevolence and rights are ultimately only institutionalized historical constructions, then they can be individually circumvented when possible or collectively deconstructed if social circumstances seem to merit such a revision. Why should the sensibilities and agreements of generations long dead necessarily govern our lives and those who live in the future unless it is clear how and why universal benevolence and rights serve our and their real interests? In this way, the social contract account opens the door for universal rights and benevolence to join in the dustbin of history the belief in a flat earth and the divine right of kings, if social conditions and events were to so lead people to make that move.

Furthermore, if social contract is indeed the real source of our belief in rights and benevolence, then the enlightened few who understand this fact are also inevitably led to a position that contradicts every known principle, instinct, and experience about moral education that humans have ever had—namely that greater and better moral education fosters more moral living. If the morality of rights and benevolence that people normally act upon because they believe they are real moral facts and obligations are really only historically agreed-upon human constructions, then it would be better for moral educators to hide this fact from the masses and perpetuate the contract by allowing people to think morality is more than contract. It would be better intentionally to mislead and keep people in the dark in order to get them to act morally. And that is a very strange if not perverse position in which to be.

But, again, all of this simply avoids answering the basic moral question: what *ought* human persons rightly to believe is morally true? For the social contract account is not a normative defense of the validity of benevolence and rights, but rather only a descriptive explanation for their existence and social power. The social contract account works in a naturalistic universe precisely by shifting the question away from what is normatively real and true to how empirically we came to believe what we believe. Whether or not the contract story adequately answers its own descriptive question about empirical sources, it does not and cannot compel people to believe in benevolence and rights as *moral truths* which they are obliged to act upon even sometimes to their own detriment. Morality has to do with what is right and wrong, good and bad, etc., which are believed to be established not by humans' own actual desires, decisions, or preferences, but by sources believed to exist apart from them. The social contract account simply redefines benevolence and rights to be not matters of morality but rather of social convention. If and when people come to see these 'morals' as mere social conventions, the main thing that will then compel their conformity in action is the threat of greater harm for not conforming. And that is not a prescription for sustaining a robust culture of universal benevolence and human rights.

Naturalism's Morality

Before proceeding further to interrogate what I think are failed attempts to derive and defend a serious moral commitment to universal benevolence and human rights from a universe defined by naturalism, I wish to turn now to spell out an alternative moral vision that seems entirely justifiable given the parameters of naturalism. Suppose we could completely eliminate from our minds and practices the enduring cultural and institutional influences of the Jewish and Christian metaphysics and moral orders that naturalism tells us are false. Suppose we could also eliminate the other culturally humanistic traditions, such as Enlightenment humanism, that have been at least indirectly dependent on transcendent or theistic metaphysics and moralities as sources of their viewpoints helping to form our contemporary moral conceptions about benevolence and rights. If we could thus 'start from scratch' in a naturalistic universe, not confused by superstitions and errors, and if we could exercise complete intellectual honesty in considering the moral beliefs and commitments that would be fitting for and reasonably defensible in a naturalistic universe, what kind of morality might we come up with? What moral order would make sense, given naturalism's picture of reality? Remember, 'moral' means understandings about what is right and wrong, good and bad, worthy and unworthy, just and unjust, which are believed to be established not by people's own actual desires, decisions, or preferences, but by sources believed to exist apart from them, providing standards by which people's own desires, decisions, and preferences can themselves be judged.

Well, one is hard pressed to come up with an answer, because it is not clear that in a naturalistic universe there *are* normative sources that exist apart from people. Matter and energy are not a moral source. They just exist and do what they do. The natural processes that govern the operation of the cosmos are not moral sources. They are simply the givens of physics, elemental facts of natural reality lacking inherent meaning or purpose or normativity. Positive and negative electrical charges, for instance, do not attract one another because that is right or just, they do so simply because that is just how they work. The evolutionary development of substances and life forms is not a moral source. These also just happen as they happen. What then in naturalism's cosmos could serve for humans as a genuine moral guide or standard having a source apart from human desires, decisions, and preferences and thus capable of judging and transforming the latter? I cannot think of any.

Some may claim that human morality should at the very minimum conform to the basic direction and mechanisms of physics and evolution. That, at least, would bring some consistency to the entire matter. What such a claim leaves unexplained, however, is where the 'should' in that sentence came from. Why should humans conform in this way? Why shouldn't humans who are endowed with complex cognitive, emotional, and volitional powers do whatever they want to do? Why should not the 'should' of such a naturalistic morality just as well be that every existent entity is free to be and do whatever it is able and wants to be and do? Molecules are and should be molecules to their full extent without unnatural normative constraints, even when they conglomerate massively and smash into and destroy other material entities. Jellyfish should be jellyfish to their full capacities without unnatural moral constraints, even when they sting, kill, and consume other living sea creatures. And humans should simply be humans to their full capabilities without unnatural moral constraints, even if this means acting out in any way whatever of which one's ideas, feelings, and desires make one capable. The ought would simply be seeking consistency with the is and its capacities. What would be wrong with that?

Still, others will insist that what we know about evolution does provide us with some moral parameters, even if we cannot think of evolutionary change as advance or progress. This is arguable. But let us consider it and see where it takes us. What moral direction might our knowledge about evolution provide us? The central moral maxim that such an approach would seem to offer would be something like this: *Each organism should do whatever it can and needs to do to survive and thrive.* (Again, it is not clear where the 'should' in that sentence comes from, but let us set that issue aside for a moment.) If reproductive fitness is enhanced by engaging in cooperative social life, then that is good; if reproductive fitness is enhanced by antisocial selfishness, than that is good too. If survival is facilitated by care for the sick and weak, then that is right; but if survival is aided by leaving the sick to die, then that is right. Whatever organisms can do to survive and thrive is good, right, true, and just. This may be the closest to what we might devise as a consistent evolutionary ethic. Obviously, it accomplishes nothing by way of securing the moral commitment to universal benevolence and human rights.

Another approach to examining what an intellectually honest naturalistic morality might look like is to ask what exactly would be morally wrong with actions and practices that would violate most ordinary contemporary people's sense of benevolence and rights. Can naturalism provide coherent reasons for rejecting them? Consider, for instance, the following proposals, all of which would arguably enhance in various ways the reproductive fitness of humanity as a species:

- All elderly persons who have finished their productive and reproductive decades and are now living out their last years as dependent invalids in expensive hospitals and 'assisted living' facilities should be removed from social and medical support and allowed to die. This policy would particularly apply to the suffering, terminally ill, and those whose life savings or family members cannot cover the cost of their care. Half of all medical costs today are said to be spent on people's last six months of life. Why? Let the dying die. Use those resources for more productive purposes.

- Cities and municipalities should be authorized to round up all inveterate drug addicts, incorrigible drunks, and long-term homeless people and either deploy them in socially beneficial projects of forced labor or simply euthanize them. Such people are socially unproductive, destructive, and hopeless and have forfeited their 'right' to life.

- Babies who are born with incapacitating physical or mental defects should be let to die—their parents can try again to have healthy babies to replace them. Parents, especially in societies with high-population pressures, who give birth to healthy but unwanted babies, should also be allowed to let them die. Better to have societies populated by wanted and well-cared-for children.

- All persons convicted of serious criminal offenses, especially multiple offenses and multiple convictions, should, if they are allowed to live, be involuntarily sterilized so that they do not pass on their potentially criminal genetic material to future generations.

- Long-term patients in mental hospitals and insane asylums who show no promise of recovery from their serious illnesses should be euthanized.

- Penal systems should return to more punitive arrangements and practices not only to serve as expensive protective holding tanks for criminals but proactively punish criminals for their offenses, as a means to raise the costs of crime and so deter other prospective criminals from wrongdoing.

Of course, such suggestions will deeply violate the moral sensibilities and commitments of many contemporary readers. But that is primarily because most modern readers are the heirs of millennia of cultural moral traditions rooted in transcendent monotheism that gave compelling accounts of universal human dignity and destiny that unfolded historically in complex and dialectical ways that now demand universal benevolence and respect for human rights. But what if the naturalist world view is true? What if those cultural traditions were built on error? What if transcendent monotheism turns out to be a myth? What if our actual human situation is one of accidental species existence lived out in solitude on this minor planet rotating away toward eventual oblivion in an inherently purposeless, meaningless, and standardless cosmos that operates according to impersonal and uncaring physical forces? Does it matter then that demented old people are left to die? Is it 'wrong' forcibly to bar criminals from having children? Would it be an injustice to allow a severely retarded baby to die, to be replaced it is hoped by another, healthy, baby? If so, on what grounds? By what standard? Why does it matter? Who in the long run would know or care or enforce any consequence?

In a naturalistic universe, not everyone would have to become savages or cunning egoists. In such a universe, any given person might be free simply to choose to want to be a caring, self-sacrificing humanist. A naturalistic morality could afford people such a choice. But, again, such a commitment must also have the status of an arbitrary, subjective, personal preference. No account could be given within the bounds of naturalism as to why such a commitment ought to be binding on others. If others wished instead to embrace full-scale eugenics and a ruthless survival-of-the-fittest culture, that would be legitimate and defensible as well. Lacking a moral standard truly external to human ideas, feelings, and desires by which those ideas, feelings, and desires could be judged, it is not clear why we would not have to accept most every innate expression of human thought, affect, and will as morally licit. What else would humans have upon which to construct being and action? Moreover, in a naturalistic universe, those smarter, stronger, more attractive and charismatic people with the capacity by force or deception to foist their ideas, feelings, and desires on others would be entitled to do so. Perhaps they might even compel others to embrace and internalize their own preferred moral views and practices, such that others came to believe that they were ontologically and universally good, right, true, and just. Why not? Those who can, will. In the end, however, a widespread belief that those moral views were true and universal would itself not make them so. At bottom, they would simply be some dominant people's imposing of their arbitrary views on other more compliant people.

In short, naturalism, when taken with all seriousness and honesty, would most likely simply liquidate our standard concept of morality. 'Morality' itself—as involving standards external to our own thoughts, emotions, and desires—would have to dissolve or transmute into some other different thing. Even if we provisionally allow ourselves to smuggle into our considerations a normative 'should' that is actually alien to naturalism, the moral orientation we then derive is oriented to practical functionality and unequal merit in human survival and reproductive fitness. Universal benevolence and human rights are nowhere near explained or secured. And if we resort to free human choice for belief in benevolence and rights we also so redefine them as arbitrary subjective preferences holding no more inherent authority or attraction than an alternative commitment to warrior conquest and glory, pitiless strategic egoism, sadism, or utter relativistic nihilism. They are all equally legitimate potential personal inclinations.

Other Deficient Accounts

All of this is nuts, some readers may be saying by now. Moral philosophy has produced numerous rational ethical systems that do not appeal to transcendent metaphysics yet point to the truth and goodness of benevolence and rights. Were that this were so. It is true that moral philosophy has generated such moral systems, but philosophy has also just as effectively pinpointed their intellectual faults and failures. All versions of such rational, non-transcendent moral philosophies, it turns out, fail to account successfully for universal benevolence and rights in one or both of two ways. Either they surreptitiously smuggle in assumptions and commitments from the Judeo-Christian or some other moral heritage or they simply fail on their own terms as rational systems justifying universal benevolence and rights. I have already discussed such problems with the social contract attempt to ground benevolence and rights above. Here I briefly examine four other possibilities.

Utilitarian moral reasoning appears entirely compatible with a naturalistic universe, as it appeals only in its moral calculations to human pains and pleasures, defining the moral good as that which produces the greatest happiness for the greatest number. Doesn't utilitarianism as a philosophy focused on human happiness offer us a moral system capable of underwriting universal benevolence and human rights? Well, no, actually. For one thing, utilitarianism is incapable on its own terms of explaining why anyone *should* actually be committed to the happiness of the greatest number. Why not—given utilitarianism's assumption of hedonic individualism—simply be concerned with one's own pleasure and happiness? If what we humans are is simply bundles of phenomenally experienced pain and pleasure that constitute happiness and unhappiness, why be obliged to maximize general happiness? Motivating utilitarian calculations to that end, note, requires a prior moral commitment to maximal collective human happiness—a commitment which utilitarianism itself cannot produce or justify. Furthermore, even if we grant the maximum collective happiness premise, utilitarianism is blind to inalienable human rights. In fact, if feeding members of a minority religious group to lions for the stadium entertainment of the masses would increase the overall bottom-line happiness of the collective, then doing so would be moral in utilitarian terms—the increased happiness of the masses would simply outweigh the lost happiness of those fed to the lions. In the end, since pleasure and happiness are simply on a qualitatively different plane than innate human rights, utilitarianism is unable to get us from the former to the latter. If anything, utilitarianism endangers the latter, as we see in the writings of Princeton utilitarian ethicist Peter Singer.

What about Kantian ethics? Immanuel Kant's categorical imperative teaches that we should '*Act so as to treat humanity, whether in your own person or in others, always as an end, and never merely as a means*', in order that we may fulfill the general formula of the moral law—namely, '*Act so that the maxim may be capable of becoming a universal law for all rational beings*'. Surely this rationally explains why all persons ought to respect and respond to the obligations of universal benevolence and human rights? Well, unfortunately, not really, at least not again without first smuggling in a prior moral commitment not itself derived or justified by Kantian ethics. The main problem with Kant's ethic for our purposes here, as Alasdair MacIntyre has shown in *After Virtue*, is its failure finally to explain why anyone ought to be committed to following it in the first place. Kant's system may work well as a moral guide for the person *who is already committed for other reasons to* universal benevolence, fairness, justice, kindness, and so on, and is looking for a handy rule by which to make specific moral decisions. Such was the case for Kant himself, who came to his philosophical work having already absorbed and taken for granted the moral commitments and sensibilities of his own Lutheran cultural upbringing. Kant never doubted what the content of a good moral life looked like. What Kant's moral philosophy provided were concise rules for making rational choices in the pursuit of living out such established moral commitments—rules which did not have to appeal directly to God or the Bible. But what Kant's moral system did not provide was an account of why anyone ought to be committed to following those moral commitments in the first place. Suppose then that you are inclined toward serious rational egoism and not benevolence. In that case, the right thing for you to want is actually not to treat all other people as ends and not means. Rather, the right thing for you to want is for everyone else to treat you as an end, but for you to be free selectively to treat other people as means if and when that serves your self-interest— which often it clearly can and does. Kant therefore may be helpful to those who are already committed to living a moral life characterized by respect, duty, reasonableness, and munificence. But for people living in a world without transcendence and a universe without larger meaning or purpose and who are looking for a good and compelling reason to believe in universal benevolence and human rights, Kant comes up short. Against many disagreeable alternative moral viewpoints, what Kant can say in riposte is that they violate respect for reason and good will—hardly a vigorous argument against such rivals, who simply counter, 'Who gives a damn? Go to hell with your good will!' In short, Kant *presumes* respect for reason and good will rather than rationally necessitating and justifying them. The naturalist challenge requires a better account than Kant can give.

Next, consider the argument of John Rawls in his 1971 book, *A Theory of Justice*, which argues the case for political liberalism and equality on immanent grounds making no reference to transcendence metaphysics. Rawls defines justice as fairness, asking us to consider what kind of social arrangements we would wish to see established if in starting from the very beginning all of us were operating behind a 'veil of ignorance', not knowing who would occupy which social position or enjoy what outcomes in society. Rawls argues that, under these conditions, people's rational desire would be to want a society of equality and fairness in which no people were systematically, dramatically disadvantaged or privileged relative to others. In effect, it is better in a pure 'lottery' system to play it safe and end up with a middling position in an equal social system than to gamble and risk ending up in a disadvantaged position in an unequal social system. Echoing Kant, Rawls's case implies that if I would not want a particular social situation for myself then I should also not want that same situation for someone else. As an abstract mental exercise, Rawls's argument may seem to work. But the flaw in his argument is that it has very little to do with our actual social reality. We are *not* in fact starting from the very beginning, we do *not* actually live behind a veil of ignorance, and most people in reality *do* know their likely positions and outcomes in society. Rawls asks people, on the basis of artificial 'as if' assumptions, voluntarily to agree to a fair and equal social order that would require the privileged to give up wealth and power on behalf of others. Here we have another version of an elegant moral philosophy's success crucially depending on *presupposing* moral goodness in people, rather than actually necessitating and justifying the moral goodness that the philosophy needs to succeed. Rawls is (to borrow an image from Peter Berger) trying to move a stalled bus by pushing it forward while standing inside of it. It doesn't work. Achieving liberal fairness and equality among the people who actually populate planet earth requires a moral and intellectual traction that Rawls's mental experiments presume but do not provide. Again, the uncooperative can simply say, 'screw your liberal Harvard fairness, I'm looking out for number one'.

Some may protest here by observing that my objections to these standard moral philosophies presuppose some pretty antisocial people not willing simply to go along with benevolence and respect for others' rights. Yes, quite right, that is precisely the point. It turns out that in the world we live in there are plenty of such people around. Moreover, there are antisocial capacities if not propensities in nearly all people, myself included. Neither optimism nor 'Up with People' rallies will be enough to address the moral challenge. If universal benevolence and human rights as moral facts and imperatives are to be sustained in this world that will require credible explanations and accounts that legitimize practices and institutions compelling enough to override the parochialism, selfishness, and enmity that real existing humans are so very capable of generating among themselves and against each other. 'All you need is love' and 'Everybody get together' turn out to be *very* big orders. The question then is: what metaphysically or otherwise grounded morality can generate such love and solidarity in a world so lacking in love and solidarity? I am afraid that none of Bentham, Mill, Kant, or Rawls has the answer.

Finally, let us briefly consider the position that we might call 'self-evidential moral platonism', of which the work of University of Wisconsin moral philosopher Russ Shafer-Landau is a good example. Shafer-Landau rejects moral relativism and defends objective moral realism, not by appeal to a divine person or transcendent command, but by arguing that moral principles simply exist. They just are. Moral truths simply describe the nature of the distinctly moral world as it is, just as the laws of physics and chemistry describe what is true about aspects of the material world that they address. People don't invent these moral principles, nor do they necessarily derive from the command of God. They simply are what they are. For any reasonable person of good will, moral truths will be self-evident. Any normal person, for instance, will simply know that it is immoral to torture a child for entertainment.

What might we say about such an argument? Shafer-Landau has done a great service in deconstructing many prevalent yet problematic arguments for moral relativists. Doing justice to his sophisticated, impressive, but arguably problematic argument is well beyond the scope of this chapter. For present purposes, suffice it to say that if Shafer-Landau's self-evident moral Platonism works, then naturalism as I have described it here is in trouble. Shafer-Landau asserts the real self-existence of moral principles and facts possessing real normative authority. And these do not consist of evolving matter and energy. Once that move is granted, it seems to me, naturalism begins to unravel, as Charles Lamore has also shown in his anti-naturalist book *The Morals of Modernity*. Having opened the door to the existence of immaterial Platonic moral principles and facts, there is no obvious reason, for instance, why further considerations of immaterial natural laws or divine beings should be automatically ruled out of bounds. In fact, if I read him correctly, Shafer-Landau is open to these possibilities, even if he may not be dependent upon them for his essential argument. Thus, if evolutionary naturalism as a coherent program is to work, then Shafer-Landau must be wrong. They cannot both be admitted.

But Can We Sustain it Anyway?

Here I would like to return to address the third question posed at the outset: *if* my answer to the second question as argued in this chapter is correct—that intellectual honesty does not grant residents of a naturalistic universe warranted moral belief in universal benevolence and human rights—will human societies and cultures who want to believe in them anyway, for whatever reasons, be able, notwithstanding the lack of warrant, to sustain such beliefs over the long run? I think the answer to this is arguable. On the one hand, human cultures demonstrate amazing capacities to carry on institutional practices long after their animating sources have withered. Max Weber's *The Protestant Ethic and the Spirit of Capitalism*, for instance, illustrates how the sixteenth- and seventeenth-century Protestant Reformation's 'worldly asceticism' gave rise to theological and spiritual categories and practices that arguably helped foster the emergence of modern capitalism, which has since continued as the world's most powerful social institution despite the receding of doctrines about predestination, salvation, and hell. Weber may be mistaken on some of his historical details, but the larger theoretical point still holds—cultural ideals and practices often survive the environments that produced them, can transpose into novel parallel forms, and frequently have long shelf lives. Perhaps belief in universal benevolence and human rights has taken on a cultural life of its own, apart from the transcendent metaphysics that helped give it birth, and will be able to carry on through appeal and inertia into the human future indefinitely.

At the same time, sociological understanding also suggests that beliefs and ideas require institutional resources to sustain. Values, categories, norms, and viewpoints do not operate like perpetual-motion machines. Entropy is always at work. Alternative values, categories, norms, and viewpoints

are always competing for adherents. In order for belief commitments—
especially challenging and costly commitments—to endure over time and
space they must benefit from institutionalized resources and customs to
reinforce and validate them. Resources are scarce and tend to gravitate
to compelling ideas and opportunities to generate more resources. Time
and again, in the historical record of cultural change, beliefs and values
once prized have come to seem outmoded, irrelevant, passé, not worthy
of allegiance. We cannot predict whether this would happen to the now
widely accepted belief in universal benevolence and human rights if and
when more and more people come to grasp and internalize the full meaning
of life in naturalism's universe. But if my argument above is valid and if our
common belief in benevolence and rights were gradually or suddenly to slip
away, that would—in my view—be a tragedy of unspeakable proportions.
I shudder to think of my grandchildren and their children and beyond
having to live in such a world. For this reason, I suggest it is worth our
reconsidering the necessary metaphysical and cultural bases of the moral
facts and obligation to which we are committed, now, while they are still
understood and practiced, even if for flimsy reasons.

Conclusion

Let me be clear about the claims of this chapter. My argument has not
demonstrated that we do not live in a naturalistic universe. We very well
may. My argument only concerns the reasonable consequences for our ideas
about morality if that is the case. Neither has my argument established the
truth of transcendent monotheism. That was not the point. My more limited claim is simply that transcended monotheism was a crucial condition
in giving rise historically and culturally to our current commitments to
benevolence and rights. Furthermore, I am obviously not suggesting that
only Judaism and Christianity foster people's acting morally. Certain significant standards of substantive morality—against unjust killing, lying, stealing,
and so on—are (contra absolute cultural relativists) found in and supported
by every human culture. Rather, this chapter speaks more precisely to
the much higher standard of morality demanded by universal benevolence
and human rights. Belief in these is not in fact universal—although many
moderns, myself included, would like them to become so—and therefore
needs explaining and defending.

Let us suppose then that we are interested in sustaining and strengthening the modern moral commitments to universal benevolence and human rights. Let us say that we want on moral grounds to eliminate slavery, child abuse, political imprisonment and torture, the sex trade, and the like. Let us agree that we ought to live in a world in which people and nations do what they can to stop disease epidemics, aid the victims of catastrophe, and oppose the gross exploitation of the poor, no matter where and to whom these happen. And let us suppose that it is not only perhaps beneficial but also truly good for people to be interpersonally kind, thoughtful, and fair to other people. The question is: what kind of moral culture do we need to vindicate those commitments and practices? The necessary condition for these having evolved into existence as we know them in the first place was the historical emergence of transcendent monotheism, first in Judaism and later continued by Christianity. The key question we now face, I suggest, is whether the metaphysical world view of naturalism that has in many quarters displaced transcendent monotheism as the predominantly authorized truth about reality can provide the intellectual and emotional foundation to sustain this belief in benevolence and rights. I know there are smart people who think it can. But I simply cannot see, for reasons explained above, how that is so. I fear that in a naturalistic universe universal benevolence and human rights will in due time go the way of the dinosaur. We may hope that I am wrong. But hope itself is not enough. What we also need is an articulation of some truly rational and compelling account for high moral standards of benevolence and rights—if indeed such an account exists. Nothing short of this is needed for the sake of our children, grandchildren, and all future generations who we want to live in humanistic, not inhumane societies.

16

Evolutionary Social Constructivism

Narrowing (but Not Yet Bridging) the Gap

David Sloan Wilson[1]

Evolution and social constructivism are two subjects that for most people are separated by an enormous gap. Evolution is about genes and behaviors adapted to the distant past that limit what we are and can become in the future. Social constructivism is about culture and our almost unlimited capacity to define what we are and can become in the future. The gap between these two positions often appears so great that the people on each side have little constructive to say to each other. Most social constructivists are not like 'Creationists' who deny the fact of evolution, but they do marginalize its relevance to the point where it might as well be false. Most evolutionists interested in human behavior do not deny the fact of culture but they don't have a consistent story to tell about it and in many cases its relevance is also marginalized to the point where it might as well not exist.

Evolutionary social constructivism is a fitting term for the attempt to bridge this gap (David Sloan Wilson 2004). It recognizes that people live in a world largely of their own making but regards evolution as an essential subject for understanding how we became so different from other animals and how the process of social construction operates in the present day. Recent books by evolutionists who are reaching across the divide include *The Symbolic Species* (Deacon 1998), *The Imagined World Made Real: Towards*

---

1. I thank Charles Harper for bringing Smith's book to my attention, along with Robert Bellah and Elliott Sober for useful discussion.

a Natural Science of Culture (Plotkin 2003), *Niche Construction: The Neglected Process in Evolution* (Odling-Smee, Laland, et al. 2003), *Animal Traditions: Behavioural Inheritance in Evolution* (Avital and Jablonka 2001), *Hierarchy in the Forest: Egalitarianism and the Evolution of Human Altruism* (Boehm 1999), and my own *Darwin's Cathedral: Evolution, Religion, and the Nature of Society* (David Sloan Wilson 2002). A recent book by a sociologist reaching across the divide is *Moral, Believing Animals: Human Personhood and Culture* (Smith 2003).

This chapter briefly summarizes the evolutionary side of the bridging effort and then examines Christian Smith's effort in more detail. As the title of his book implies, Smith has distanced himself from extreme relativism and recognizes the need for a theory of human nature that transcends cultural differences: 'Despite the vast differences in humanity between cultures and across history, no matter how differently people narrate their lives and histories, there remains an underlying structure of human personhood that helps to order human culture, history, and narration' (Smith 2003: 3–4). Unfortunately, Smith's effort to develop this thesis is not informed by the most relevant evolutionary literature and does not independently converge upon it. I will attempt to identify and correct the discrepancies, so that the two bridge-building efforts can meet in the middle.

The Evolutionary Side of the Bridging Effort

In *Darwin's Cathedral* I described the study of culture from an evolutionary perspective this way:

> Although culture has for many decades been envisioned as an evolutionary process, there is little agreement about its precise nature, importance, or relationship to genetic evolution. The most severe critics of sociobiology rely upon culture as an alternative, which they think can be studied without reference to evolution (e.g., Sahlins 1976). Some biologists regard culture as a handmaiden of genetic evolution that evolves the same phenotypic adaptations, only faster (e.g., Alexander 1979; 1987). Other biologists try to decompose culture into gene-like units that do not necessarily benefit their human hosts (e.g., Dawkins 1976; Blackmore 1999). Instead, they act more like disease organisms as they spread from head to head.
>
> (David Sloan Wilson 2002: 28)

Given such a lack of consensus, it must be acknowledged that the study of culture from an evolutionary perspective is still in the rank speculation stage. Isolated facts might be scientifically well established, but these have not been put together into any kind of big picture that can be said to be scientifically established, in the sense that Darwin's theory has for the study of non-human species. Nevertheless, when it comes to both evolution and intellectual inquiry the past is a poor guide to the future. A number of developments in evolutionary biology during the last few decades are leading to a conception of cultural evolution that might prove robust and moreover converges with central themes of social constructivism. A short list of these intertwining developments includes the following.

Human uniqueness and symbolic thought

The idea that we are different from all other creatures is a central tenet of Western thought. The list of supposedly unique attributes is almost endless, including language, tool use, intelligence, morals, and aesthetics. Clearly, many of the ideas that pre-date Darwin by centuries must be revised in light of the fact that we are recently derived from primate ancestors and the enormous amount of information now known about non-human species. The general trend in evolutionary research has been to show that claims of human uniqueness were greatly exaggerated. Nevertheless, we clearly are unique in some respects so the challenge is to identify the real differences, not to deny any differences at all. In *The Symbolic Species* Deacon (1998) presents a sophisticated argument that our species is unique in its capacity for symbolic thought. According to Deacon, thinking symbolically doesn't require an especially large brain or even a different brain from that possessed by our primate ancestors. In fact, it is actually possible to teach a chimpanzee or bonobo to think symbolically, more like us than their own kind. The problem is that it requires an arduous training process that has no counterpart in nature. Moreover, symbolic thought interferes with more basic forms of associative learning that are adaptive in most natural environments. If I pair the sound of the word 'cat' with an actual cat in a conditioning experiment, mice will learn to associate the two, but if I then say the word 'cat' many times without a cat actually being present, the object and its symbol will become dissociated again. In contrast, I can say the word 'cat' to you a million times and you will still associate it with a cat. More generally, symbolic thought requires symbols and what they stand for to remain associated in the mind even when they are not associated in the real world. Symbolic thought is like a lofty peak in an adaptive landscape that can be climbed only by first crossing a valley of low fitness. What made humans unique was a natural environmental context that made symbolic thought adaptive in its initial stages, allowing us, and us alone, to cross over to the new adaptive peak. Of course, social constructivism requires the capacity for symbolic thought. As Durkheim put it, 'in all its aspects and at every moment of history, [human] social life is only possible thanks to a vast symbolism' (Durkheim (1995) [1912]: 223). Deacon's thesis therefore represents an important part of the new bridge connecting evolutionary biology with social constructivism.

Darwin machines: evolutionary processes built by evolution

All organisms—even bacteria and protozoa—are designed to be flexible, adaptively changing their properties within their own lifetimes in response to environmental change. In his panoramic review of brain evolution across the animal kingdom, Allman actually begins with a discussion of bacteria:

> Some of the most basic features of brains can be found in bacteria because even the simplest motile organisms must solve the problems of locating resources and avoiding toxins in a variable environment. Strictly speaking, these unicellular organisms do not have nervous systems, but nevertheless they exhibit remarkably complex behavior: They sense their environment through a large number of receptors and store this elaborate sensory input in the form of brief memory traces. Moreover, they integrate the inputs from these multiple memory sensory channels to produce adaptive movements. The revolution in our understanding of genetic mechanisms has made it possible to determine how these brainlike processes work at molecular level in bacteria.
>
> (Allman 1999: 3)

One way to accomplish this kind of adaptive flexibility is with a system of rigid if-then rules, similar to tax preparation software. It cues you for just the right information, which it puts together in just the right way correctly to calculate your taxes. Similarly, organisms can be designed to receive just the right environmental cues, which are processed in just the right way to produce the adaptive phenotypic response. There is nothing open-ended or creative about this process.

Another way to accomplish adaptive flexibility is illustrated by the mammalian immune system. Disease organisms are too numerous and evolve too fast with their short generation times to be combated with a set of rigid if-then rules. Instead, the immune system is a fast-changing evolutionary process in its own right, in which antibodies are produced at random and selected according to their ability to bind to antigens. The immune system is an evolutionary process, built by evolution.

This kind of adaptive flexibility extends beyond the immune system. Gerald Edelman, who received the Nobel prize for his work on the immune system, went on to develop a similar conception for the human brain (Edelman 1988; Edelman and Tonomi 2001). Deacon (1998) provides a lucid account of how brain development is fundamentally a Darwinian process, with growing axons competing for receptor sites. At a functional level, symbolic thought can be envisioned as a Darwinian process in a virtual world of mental representations.

Plotkin's (1994a) term 'Darwin machine' aptly describes two essential features of an evolutionary process built by evolution. The word 'machine' indicates that the evolutionary process must be highly managed to lead to biologically adaptive outcomes. Anyone who has studied the immune system knows that it is mind-bogglingly complex in its genetic innateness. Antibodies that match antigens reproduce more, not by a lucky coincidence, but because the immune system is constructed that way. Nevertheless, the word 'Darwin' indicates that the process remains evolutionary despite being highly managed, with all the implications of evolution played out on a new stage. Open-ended and creative solutions to recent environmental challenges is perhaps the most important implication, but we should also expect the same kinds of historical contingencies and other constraining factors that cause adaptations to fall short of perfection in genetic evolution.

Social constructivists often associate evolution with an incapacity for change, in contrast to their own belief in the human potential for change. These associations only make sense if by 'evolution' we mean genetic evolution. When we include Darwin machines, the social constructivist position itself becomes evolutionary. Furthermore, genetic innateness can be seen positively as the complex machinery that makes rapid evolution possible. The idea that we can understand the human potential for change without paying attention to genetically innate mechanisms becomes as absurd as trying to study the immune system as if it were not genetically innate. With Darwin machines, the bridge from evolutionary biology to social constructivism has been considerably extended.

Groups as units of selection and adaptation

An important part of the sociological tradition is to view societies and cultures as organic wholes, whose properties cannot be reduced to their individual parts. This kind of holism fell upon hard times in both biology and the social sciences during the middle of the twentieth century. In the social sciences, the principle of methodological individualism claimed that all properties of societies can be reduced to the properties of their members and are not properly understood until this reduction has taken place (Watkins 1957). Rational choice theory offered a specific agenda in which individuals are assumed to behave as utility maximizers. In evolutionary biology, a consensus emerged that groups can evolve into adaptive units in principle but almost never do in reality. The reason is that group-level adaptations require a process of among-group selection, which is almost invariably weak compared to within-group selection (Williams 1966). As a separate argument, all adaptations were claimed to evolve at the level of genes, even when they benefited individuals or groups as vehicles of the genes (Williams 1966; Dawkins 2006 [1976]).

Despite the dominance of these ideas during recent intellectual history, much has happened in evolutionary biology to undermine their authority. One of the most important developments has been labeled 'major transitions of life'. It used to be thought that evolution takes place entirely by small mutational change, but now a second pathway has been identified in which social groups become so integrated that they become a new higher-level organism. One of the first to propose this radical new theory was Lynn Margulis (1970), who claimed that eukaryotic cells—the nucleated cells of all organisms other than bacteria—are actually symbiotic communities of bacteria whose members led a more autonomous existence in the past. Now it appears likely that similar transitions, from groups *of* organisms to groups *as* organisms, have occurred throughout the history of life, right down to the origin of life itself as social groups of cooperating molecular reactions (Maynard Smith and Szathmary 1995; Michod 1999).

Each transition requires a solution to the same kinds of social dilemmas that abound in human life. For example, consider a primordial cell in which the genes exist as independently replicating units. Some genes participate in the economy of the cell, producing resources that all can use. Other genes selfishly use these resources to replicate without contributing to the economy of the cell. The selfish genes are favored by within-group selection (they are more fit than solid-citizen genes within the same cell) while the solid citizen genes are favored by among-group selection (groups with an above-average frequency of solid-citizen genes contribute more to the total gene pool than groups with a below-average frequency). As long as within-group selection remains strong the cell will not function adaptively. The evolution of chromosomes neatly solved this problem by binding the genes together into a single structure that replicates as a unit. Chromosomes greatly reduce differential replication within the cell, making among-cell selection the primary evolutionary force. Notice that this represents a feedback process between traits that alter the parameters of social evolution (chromosomes) and traits that evolve on the basis of the alteration (solid citizen genes). This is what is meant by the term 'niche construction', which can be regarded as a close cousin of social constructivism.

The major transitions of life forever dispel the notion that higher-level selection is invariably weak compared to lower-level selection. Eukaryotic multicellular organisms such as you and me are shining contradictions of that claim. More generally, if the organisms of today are the social groups of past ages, then the concept of the social groups of today as *like organisms*, at least to a degree, no longer appears so outrageous. Indeed, when natural selection is carefully partitioned into within- and among-group components, group selection can be shown to be an important force in many species, even when it does not result in full-fledged 'superorganisms'. In other words, many traits in the organic world evolve by increasing the fitness of collectives, relative to other collectives, rather than by increasing the fitness of individuals, relative to other individuals within collectives (Sober and Wilson 1998).

These developments in evolutionary biology provide a new background for the study of human evolution. People have always existed in many kinds of groups that merge and split for various activities. In any given context, traits can evolve by benefiting individuals relative to others in the same group, or by benefiting the whole group relative to other groups. Furthermore, traits comparable to chromosomes can evolve that reduce the possibilities for within-group advantage, concentrating natural selection at the between-group level. Cultural anthropologist and primatologist Chris Boehm (1999) has developed this thesis in his book *Hierarchy in the Forest*.

According to Boehm, moral systems are the human analog of chromosomes, reducing the potential for individuals to profit at the expense of other members of the same group and converting the whole group into a potent unit of selection and adaptation. Consider the effects of moral systems on the three ingredients of natural selection: phenotypic variation, fitness consequences, and heritability. Behaviors that are strongly prescribed or proscribed by a moral system simply will not vary within the group as much as they would otherwise (unless variation per se is part of the norm). On the other hand, groups that adopt different norms can vary tremendously from each other. In technical terms, moral systems dramatically alter the partitioning of phenotypic variation within and among groups. These phenotypic differences also make a difference: murder, theft, adultery, rape, self-sacrifice on behalf of others, slacking, and most other behaviors that arouse moral passions are clearly relevant to basic survival and reproduction. Finally, moral systems are often elaborately constructed to replicate themselves from person to person and group to group through narratives and other practices deemed sacred. In short, moral systems have a transformative effect on the fundamental ingredients of natural selection, largely (although by no means entirely) converting social groups into functionally adaptive units, even when they are composed of genetically unrelated individuals.

These developments concerning levels of selection are intertwined with the other developments concerning symbolic thought and Darwin machines, giving them a collective dimension that would be missing otherwise. So many aspects of human life are collective, including the other- and group-oriented nature of morality, language, and any symbol that is not the personal invention of a single individual. Group-level functionality was taken for granted until the middle of the twentieth century, when it was denied altogether or viewed through the distorted lens of individualism. Now we are on the verge of achieving a complex but comprehensible middle ground, in which group-level functionality does exist, but only when special conditions are met. The collective dimension extends the bridge from evolutionary biology to social constructivism.

Adaptation and rational thought

Rational thought has a special status in the social sciences, in part because it provides the core of logical and scientific reasoning and in part because its barebone assumption of utility maximization provides the basis for endless theorizing. Rational thought is often treated as the gold standard against which other forms of thought are judged. Religious thought in particular is found so wanting by this standard that it becomes well-nigh incomprehensible.

In contrast, evolutionary theory judges all forms of thought in terms of what they cause organisms to do. Rational thought leads to adaptive outcomes in some contexts, which is why it has become part of our mental toolkit. It does not lead to adaptive outcomes in all contexts, which is why it is not the only tool in our mental toolkit. There is also a historical argument for why rational thought is only one tool in our toolkit—because it is a recent tool and most of the other tools are more ancient. Once these evolutionary factors become the basis for evaluating modes of thought, a host of alternatives to rational thought become explicable in terms of what they cause people to do. Emotions are evolved mechanisms for motivating adaptive behavior that are far more ancient than the cognitive processes associated with rational thought. We might therefore expect moral systems to be designed to trigger powerful emotional impulses, linking joy with right, fear with wrong, anger with transgressions. We might expect stories, music, and rituals to be at least as important as logical arguments in orchestrating the behavior of individuals and groups. Imaginary beings and events that never happened can provide blueprints for action that far surpass factual accounts of the natural world in clarity and motivating power. These other-worldly forms of thought, which include but are not restricted to religion, cannot completely eclipse rational thought, which is superior in some contexts, but the reverse statement is equally true.

Social constructivists are themselves uncomfortable with the gold standard of rational thought, but they don't have a standard to replace it, other than the absence of standards associated with relativism. Adaptation, or rather adaptationism appropriately conceived (which acknowledges that not everything is adaptive) therefore provides a new way of thinking about alternative modes of thought, extending the bridge from evolutionary biology to social constructivism still further.

It should be obvious that these developments in evolutionary biology reach toward themes that have always been central to social constructivism. Let us now see how one sociologist reaches in the direction of evolutionary biology.

Christian Smith's Bridging Effort in *Moral, Believing Animals*

Earlier I stressed the current lack of consensus among evolutionary biologists on the subject of culture. Christian Smith reveals a similar lack of consensus among sociologists, who remain just as much in the rank speculation stage as far as the big picture is concerned, however well they have documented pieces of the puzzle. The conception of human nature and society that Smith is trying to establish within his own discipline includes the following elements. There is a universal human nature that transcends cultural differences. There is a core of truth in earlier sociological traditions (such as the work of Talcot Parsons) that needs to be preserved and built upon. Human culture is fundamentally a moral order and people are inescapably moral agents. There is more to morality than altruism. Norms do not exist as isolated packets but as part of a complicated normative system. People have a propensity for self-centeredness in addition to their inescapably moral natures. People are, fundamentally, believing animals who convey their beliefs largely through narratives. Stories shape people in addition to people shaping stories.

This conception of people, society, and culture is highly compatible with the developments in evolutionary biology that I have reviewed—so close that it seemed as I read Smith's book that the bridge might be nearing completion. Alas, as soon as Smith started writing about biology and evolution (2003: 33–43) it became clear that the gap was still large in his own mind and his own effort to bridge the gap was proceeding in a different direction. According to Smith, the positions that he associates with sociobiology and evolutionary psychology are fatally flawed for a number of reasons. They attempt to explain moral systems as genetically adaptive. They tend to reduce morality to altruism. They cannot explain altruism toward non-kin. They have difficulty making the jump from genes to conscious and self-conscious people acting with moral intentions, and once this jump is made the basic assumptions of sociobiology and evolutionary psychology become unnecessary. They cannot provide a substantive account of morality and will lead to dire moral consequences if they become widely accepted.

Despite this negative account, which can be regarded as a bridge-demolishing effort, Smith acknowledges that we are biological creatures whose moral, believing properties must have come from somewhere. His positive account portrays morality as a by-product of human intelligence. Our abilities to anticipate the consequences of our actions, to make value judgments, and to choose among alternative courses of action combine to make us moral. Special emphasis is placed on self-consciousness as a capacity to step outside ourselves, preventing us from using our other mental capacities for more narrow utilitarian purposes.

Before I criticize these ideas, I want to express solidarity with Smith in two respects. First, there is much within evolutionary biology worth criticizing. Authors such as Buss (1999) and Cosmides and Tooby (2003) scarcely mention morality in their account of human nature and others such as Alexander (1987) attempt to reduce it to a form of self-interest, which is a non sequitur. The concept of selfish genes is entirely metaphorical and amounts to little more than newspeak for 'anything that evolves by genetic evolution'. Morality is often simplistically equated with altruism. Inclusive fitness theory, with its emphasis on genealogical relatedness, does make altruism toward non-kin appear problematical. I agree with Smith that these are problems that need to be solved before we can understand morality from an evolutionary perspective. Far from denying these problems, I and many of my colleagues have been stressing them ourselves.

Second, I largely share Smith's basic conception of human nature, society, and culture, as I have already recounted briefly here and in more detail elsewhere. My criticisms center not on the basic vision but on how it can be squared with evolutionary theory. Continuing the bridge building metaphor, I imagine myself as a person on one side of the gap calling over to Smith on the other side: 'Hey! We're over *here!*'

In this spirit, I will now attempt to show why Smith is heading in the wrong direction and how his bridge-building efforts can be redirected.

Adaptation vs by-product explanations of morality and religion

Any trait studied by evolutionary biologists can be an adaptation that enhances survival and reproduction or a non-adaptive by-product of the evolutionary process (or a combination of both). Smith is committed to a by-product interpretation of morality, which causes him to reject evolutionary accounts based on adaptation. His commitment extends beyond evolutionary considerations because he rejects all utilitarian and functional accounts of morality.

To see why Smith's rejection of functionalism is premature, we need first to distinguish between individual-level and group-level functionalism. Consider three of Smith's own examples. A woman returns a wallet to its owner even though she could have kept it without being detected. A citizen goes to the trouble of casting a vote whose impact on the election will be negligible. A soldier sacrifices his life in battle for comrades and country. These are intended as examples of people acting against their interests but in each case it is obvious that societies of people who act in these ways will function better than societies whose members behave otherwise.

As for these examples, so also for the more basic principles of morality. 'Do unto others' is the quintessential summary of morality that can be said while standing on one foot and is an excellent guide for a well-functioning society. All of the Ten Commandments that are not about serving one's God are obviously functional at the societal level. The many hundreds of more detailed commandments that comprise Jewish law and have counterparts in other religious traditions are similarly functional at the society level. In most cases it makes little difference whether we interpret 'function' biologically or in the everyday sense of the word. At the most basic level, human welfare consists of such things as food, water, shelter, and freedom from persecution that are biologically adaptive. Moreover, the laws of the Hebrew Bible in particular are a sociobiological dream come true in their injunctions to be fruitful and multiply and more detailed commandments pertaining to reproduction. I am making these claims casually here but treat them more seriously in *Darwin's Cathedral* and will return to the question of how they can be established scientifically to a skeptic's satisfaction below. At the very least, Smith's statement that religion 'does not produce any obvious material benefit' (2003: 95) cannot be taken as self-evident.

Another element of morality and religion that Smith regards as non-utilitarian is their categorical nature:

> In these and all like cases, actions are performed at least in part because they affirm and express commitments to what are understood to be right, good, worthy, just and so on. And these are understood to entail imperatives independent of the actor's own personal wishes and inclinations, and not because they might achieve some other valued outcome or benefit.
>
> (Smith 2003: 10)

Once again, what appears non-utilitarian at the individual level and over the short term can emerge as highly utilitarian at the societal level and over the long term. In his book *Passions within Reason*, evolutionarily informed economist Robert Frank explains how seemingly irrational commitments can be adaptive. Suppose that you are the sort of person who is unable to tell a lie, either by your nature (e.g., you cannot prevent yourself from blushing) or because you have locked yourself into a social convention. If others know that you cannot tell a lie you will be sought out as a valuable social partner. Similarly, suppose that you steal a 100-dollar briefcase from me knowing that it will cost me 300 dollars to get it back. If I am narrowly utilitarian you can steal from me with impunity, but if I am the kind of person who will avenge your transgression no matter what my cost you will not steal from me in the first place. These utilitarian explanations of commitment devices have become popular among evolutionary biologists (Nesse 2001) and sociologists of religion (Iannoccone 1992; Iannoccone 1994) alike and go a long way toward affirming Smith's more general conception of morality as a complex system that goes beyond simple altruism. A system is required to bind individuals into functional groups, especially given their propensity toward self-centeredness, and categorical imperatives are an important part of the system.

I do not mean to imply that moral systems are functional in each and every detail. The process of evolution involves many failures for each success and the results of this winnowing process are seldom completely functional. A sophisticated evolutionary perspective looks for adaptations without expecting them to be everywhere. A glimpse of what Smith is missing by prematurely rejecting adaptationism is provided by his own metaphor of human moral systems as like rafts upon the sea:

> We see, then, that what any people, including ourselves, know about life and the world, about how life ought to be lived, is not founded on an indubitable, universal foundation of knowledge. These are not built on solid piles that have been driven down into a very bedrock of known reality that lies accessible beneath every human person. Rather, all of our knowledge and life practices—however obvious and well-founded they may seem to us—are built like large rafts on beams of particular trusted assumptions and beliefs that themselves float freely in the shifting seas of culture and history. And all of us, in our particular, historical communities of believers float together on those rafts, typically unable to see beyond our rafts to the open sea on which we float and thus accustomed to assuming our raft to be all that exists and is true.
>
> (Smith 2003: 52–3)

This is a wonderful metaphor that deserves to be elaborated. Some rafts are more seaworthy than others. Beneath the rafts floating upon the sea are layer upon layer of rafts on the sea floor that have been accumulating for thousands and even millions of years. Rafts sink or float in part based on luck but in part based on their properties. Only rafts that float give rise to other rafts. If rafts vary in their properties and there is any sense in which they inherit the properties of the rafts from which they are derived, then the three fundamental ingredients of natural selection are present—phenotypic variation, heritability, and fitness consequences. A winnowing process is set in motion, causing the rafts floating upon the sea to accumulate the properties that keep them afloat. Part of what gets winnowed are genes, resulting in a species with an innate capacity to build rafts. Genes are not the only mechanism of inheritance, however, so part of what gets winnowed is culture, conveyed in stories, sacred symbols, and more. In both cases, we can say something about the nature of the rafts by knowing the properties that make rafts seaworthy. There is no guarantee that the winnowing process has stumbled upon all of these design features, but at least we can make educated guesses that can be confirmed or disconfirmed empirically. At the very least, we can be sure that the rafts are not constructed out of tissue paper.

The metaphor can be extended further. Suppose that the winnowing process works rather well. The rafts are not rafts at all but tall ships, elaborately constructed to ply the waters. Furthermore, there are many kinds of ships, since they must extract resources from their environment in addition to staying afloat and there are many ways of doing this. The ships have even crawled out on land and turned into terrestrial vehicles, inhabiting every region of the earth. The incredible diversity of vehicles is based in part on the many subsistence niches that can be occupied and in part on historical factors, since the winnowing process never unfolds in exactly the same way twice, even in identical environments.

All of this is missing from Smith's conception of human nature, society, and culture because he has prematurely rejected evolutionary adaptationism in particular and functionalism in general in his account of morality. His rejection of functionalism is especially odd, given his desire to revive the sociological tradition of Talcott Parsons, one of the most flagrant function-alists of all time. Smith might think that he accepts some form of sociolog-ical functionalism while continuing to reject evolutionary adaptationism, but I argue in detail in *Darwin's Cathedral* that any functionalist account in the social sciences must ultimately be based upon evolution, the only function-endowing process that exists apart from theistic explanations. The late social psychologist Donald Campbell made the same point when he stressed that all things functional were ultimately created by a process of blind variation and selective retention (1960).

So far I have defended the evolutionary position that Smith rejects. What about the evolutionary position that he accepts? Can morality be explained as a by-product of human consciousness and especially self-consciousness? In the first place, this argument is woefully underspecified. No explanation is given for how these human capacities evolved. Are they biological adaptations that serve the selfish interests of individuals and their genes? If so, then why is morality any more authentic as a by-product of a biological adaptation than as a biological adaptation in its own right? If they are not adaptations, how can we explain them as by-products that produce morality as a second-order by-product? In the second place, it leads to a conception of morality that is excessively cerebral, as the following passage makes clear.

> Self-consciousness gives rise to reflective distances between the self and its cognitions, emotions, and desires. And those distances provoke the quest for standards above and beyond the self's cognitions, emotions, and desires by which they might be evaluated as worthy of thinking, feeling, and believing or not. [The philosopher Anthony] O'Hear writes: 'the very fact of being self-conscious about our beliefs, of being in the full sense believers . . . initiates a process in which we search for what is true because it is true, rather than because it serves some interest of ours.'
>
> (Smith 2003: 42)

This passage imagines that our hominid ancestors were just like Immanuel Kant. It makes morality as simplistic in the cognitive realm as altruism makes morality simplistic in the behavioral realm. It even conflicts with the concept of morality that Smith develops elsewhere in the same book, which extends beyond self-conscious awareness into the subconscious bones of our species. Finally, even though there is more to morality than altruism, notice that the entire point of this passage is to explain the enigma of why there is more to human nature than the pursuit of self-interest. There are far better ways to explain the groupish nature of our species than this particular 'just-so story'.

One final comment will complete my discussion of adaptation vs by-product explanations of morality and religion. Utilitarian explanations are often regarded as vulgar, as if morality and religion lose their beauty and majesty as soon as they are shown to be practical. I discuss this strange attitude at the end of *Darwin's Cathedral* and will try to forestall it here with a final elaboration of Smith's raft metaphor. Suppose that you are on vacation aboard a magnificent tall ship, gazing at a glorious sunset, marveling at God's creation. Then the weather turns bad, so bad that within hours you are fearing for your life as the waves crash over the deck and the wind shreds the sails. Miraculously you survive, thanks to the resilience of the ship and the bravery of the crew. Suddenly you realize that the ship and crew have become beautiful, not the elements, and anything about the ship that interferes with its function has become hideously ugly. The stories of Joseph Conrad vividly convey the terror of a storm at sea and it is interesting that he described nautical life as appealing because of its moral simplicity. The problem was to survive.

The moral consequences of adaptationism

Smith regards sociobiology and evolutionary psychology as more than just factually inadequate; he also finds them morally corrosive.

> Sociobiology and evolutionary psychology's particular moral problems may be worth developing a bit, just to be clear about them. When human morality is redefined entirely in relation to reproductive fitness—so that morality is no longer driven by natural law or the will of God or self-evident inherent moral values—then we lose any real moral standard by which to judge actions. Genetic survival and extinction in a competitive environment is all that is. Beyond that we can have nothing evaluative to say about which genes successfully reproduce or how they do it. Indeed, we no longer even possess standards for value judgments about what constitutes progress in evolution. It is finally of no more value that humans survive than do bacteria. Why, on sociobiological grounds, should one be any 'better' than another? Furthermore, if some humans have genetic propensities that enable them to survive and thrive while, or even because, other humans die out, it is difficult, given the sociobiological account, to explain why this should not happen; or why, if it did, anyone should necessarily feel any moral concern or sense of tragedy about it. Some die. Some live. Natural processes work their way out. That is all. If any sociobiology or evolutionary psychology worth considering theoretically gives us any reliable normative direction, it is that the fittest genes should survive and the organisms that carry them should do what they need to do to ensure that outcome. Even then, any notion of 'should' makes little sense, really, since what will happen will simply happen by natural

process. For sociobiology and evolutionary psychology to end up with any serious substantive morality requires smuggling in auxiliary assumptions and commitments that are alien to its own intellectual system . . . Sociobiology and evolutionary psychology's case might be merely amusing, were it not for the monumentally misanthropic practical consequences that should follow any widespread embrace of its program. One can only hope that most moral, believing animals have more sense than to let that happen.

(Smith 2003: 37–8)

The error here is to confine these comments to sociobiology and evolutionary psychology, since Smith is describing the general existential dilemma that applies to any non-theistic account of morality. Smith subsequently makes this clear himself with the following quote from Bertrand Russell.

That man is the product of causes which had no prevision of the end they were achieving; that his origin, his growth, his hopes and fears, his loves and his beliefs are but the outcome of accidental collocations of atoms; that no fire, no heroism, no intensity of thought and feeling, can preserve an individual life beyond the grave; that all the labors of the ages, all the devotion, all the inspiration, all the noonday brightness of human genius, are destined to extinction in the vast death of the solar system, and that the whole temple of man's achievements must inevitably be buried beneath the debris of a universe in ruins—all these things, if not quite beyond dispute, are yet so nearly certain that no philosophy which rejects them can hope to stand. Only within the scaffolding of these truths, only on the firm foundation of unyielding despair, can the soul's habitation henceforth be safely built.

(Russell 1917: 93)

Why Smith should lay these problems at the doorstep of sociobiology and evolutionary psychology is beyond me, since they apply with equal force to his own non-theistic alternatives. Furthermore, theistic accounts of morality have their own problems. In his elegant book *Morality*, philosopher Bernard Williams states: 'it is practically a philosopher's platitude that even if God did exist, that would not, to a clear-headed and moral thinker, make any difference to the situation of morality' (1972: 64). God is regarded as good and just because of criteria for goodness and justice that come from elsewhere. Similarly, in her book *Human Nature after Darwin*, philosopher Janet Richards (2001) shows that less is at stake than meets the eye when it comes to these basic moral and ethical issues. Thankfully, we can concentrate on the empirical question of how we became moral, believing animals without worrying about the entire moral order collapsing on the basis of what we decide.

Science, theism, and the difficulty of testing evolutionary hypotheses

Evolutionary hypotheses are often criticized for being difficult to test, either because they involve events that took place in the distant past or because they are speculative adaptationist 'just-so stories'. This is more than a mundane methodological issue: if evolutionary hypotheses can be tested and falsified with reasonable ease, resulting in the same accumulation of knowledge that we associate with the rest of science, then many arguments that marginalize the importance of evolution collapse. These arguments depend less on the importance of evolution than on the claim that we can never determine the importance of evolution.

With respect to Smith, let's begin with his definition of religions as 'sets of beliefs, symbols, and practices about the reality of superempirical orders that make claims to organize and guide human life' (2003: 98). By superempirical, Smith means 'an ordered reality that is not normally observable with the five human senses'. This term has the advantage of being broader than the usual term 'supernatural'. It has the disadvantage that almost no one would have agreed with it 150 years ago. Prior to Darwin, the Christian conception of God was regarded as an eminently testable hypothesis that could be amply confirmed with the five human senses, either by themselves or when extended by the tools of science. Newton thought that he was studying God's handiwork and one of the main motivations to study natural history was to understand the creator through his creations. Religious beliefs are not *intrinsically* superempirical— they *become* superempirical when they are driven from empirical inquiry by the scientific method. For example, it is perfectly possible empirically for the earth to be young, for each species to be separately created and unchanging through time, for organisms to be elegantly designed in every respect, and for life's afflictions to be part of a benign grand plan when understood in greater detail. These claims *could* be true, but they are disconfirmed by the empirical evidence. In contrast, Darwin's theory caused so many facts to fall into place (despite leaving many questions unanswered) that it compelled acceptance despite its disturbing implications. In short, the scientific method worked well enough for the subject of evolution to completely change the character of religion, forcing it to leave the empirical stage. Modern versions of 'Creationism' mimic the scientific method (the analogy with biological mimicry is worth exploring) but are a farce when examined carefully. The only alternative is to define God and other elements of religion in a way that cannot be falsified empirically—for example, by saying that he set the universe in motion but does not otherwise intervene.

Smith is careful to distance himself from 'Creationism', but his yearning to preserve theism in some form is clear. At first I was taken aback by passages such as the following.

> Why are humans apparently unique among all animals in being profoundly moral animals? It may be impossible to answer this question definitively, but it is worth considering. Some people will say that humans are uniquely moral animals because they are made 'in the image' of a personal, moral God, who created them uniquely to reflect, know, and obey God. Other people will say that humans are moral because of the relatively large brains our species acquired through evolutionary development, which are neurologically capable of depths and complexities of evaluation and emotion unavailable to smaller brained animals. Maybe one or the other of these accounts is right, or maybe both are right.
>
> (Smith 2003: 33)

'What is going on here?' I asked myself as I read this passage. Until this point I had largely agreed with his conception of people as moral, believing animals. Was he seriously proposing the theistic account as a scientific hypothesis that can be pitted against the big brain hypothesis on the basis of empirical evidence? Was he merely being diplomatic toward the religious believers among his readers? Smith clarifies his position in his chapter on religion. He calls theories of religion based on evolution conventional, at least compared to this one.

> Here, by contrast, is a theory that would be truly controversial, daring, and radical: human religions have existed and do exist everywhere because a God really does actually exist, and many humans—especially those not blinded by the reigning narratives of modern science and academia—feel a recurrent and deeply compelling 'built-in' desire to know and worship, in their various ways, the God who is there. Try publishing that, and we will find out who is controversial and daring. Of course, that theory, while not empirically verifiable, would certainly explain a lot. It is a most parsimonious theory. But prevailing assumptions of knowledge production rule it inadmissible. So

we stick with other theories no more empirically verifiable or intellectually
coherent but that at least fit our dominant narrative.

(Smith 2003: 117)

According to this passage, the theistic account is immune to acceptance or
rejection by the usual canons of science because it is superempirical. Nevertheless, it is still called a 'theory' that is 'parsimonious' and 'explanatory',
therefore warranting acceptance in some sense. The evolutionary account is
also immune to acceptance or rejection by the usual canons of science ('no
more empirically verifiable or intellectually coherent'), not because it is
superempirical, but because there is evidently no hope of making scientific
progress on the subject of evolution. Bizarrely, theism's proven weakness
as an empirical theory has been turned into a strength, and the claim that
evolution is hopelessly difficult to study scientifically has become a vital
part of the argument against it. Even though Smith disavows 'Creationism'
and extreme relativism earlier in his book, at the end of the day theism and
evolution become two narratives, with evolution dominant for no good
reason and theism an unfairly persecuted minority. Smith concludes by
adopting 'the parsimonious theistic explanation as my proposed theory'
(2003: 17).

Passages such as these made me wonder if Smith was more intent on
justifying his conception of theism than his conception of people as moral,
believing animals. If so, then he is indulging in an intellectualized form
of 'Creationism' and Oxford University Press should reclassify his book
as theology. If not, then he should be happy to reject his conception
of theism in favor of an evolutionary account that succeeds by normal
scientific standards. To see how such an account is forthcoming, consider
the part of Smith's definition of religion that is not superempirical: 'sets of
beliefs, symbols, and practices . . . that make claims to organize and guide
human life' (2003: 98). This part is functional—surprising, given his earlier
denial that morality has a functional basis. Religions (along with many other
social organizations) are built and designed to tell people what to do. A
system designed for this purpose is necessarily different from one designed
factually to describe the natural world, just as a vehicle designed to move
through water must be different from a vehicle designed to move over land.
Furthermore, religions vary in what they tell their believers to do and this
diversity can be explained with the same theoretical concepts and empirical
tools that work very successfully for the study of non-human species. In this

fashion, Smith's theistic account of morality and religion will go the way of theistic accounts of the natural world.

I have used Smith's book as a vehicle for addressing general issues in sociological and evolutionary theory. *Moral, Believing Animals* begins and ends with a conception of culture, society, and human nature that is not inherently theistic. There is a universal human nature that transcends cultural differences. This nature is moral and believing, giving rise to the cultural diversity that is the hallmark of our species. Establishing this conception within the social sciences (which in some respects involves reviving earlier traditions) will be a great achievement. Squaring it with evolutionary theory will be greater still. Empirically validating the conception so that it becomes the generally accepted 'big picture' for our species will be the greatest achievement of all. Evolutionary social constructivism works toward these goals. Smith's theistic account of morality and religion does not and impedes scientific inquiry in general. I hope that the constructive intent of this chapter with respect to moral, believing animals is evident, even if some demolition with respect to theism was required along the way.

Bibliography

Alcorta, Candace, and Richard Sosis (2005), 'Ritual, Emotion and Sacred Symbols: The Evolution of Religion as an Adaptive Complex', *Human Nature*, 16: 323–59.

Alexander, R. D. (1979), *Darwinism and Human Affairs* (Seattle, Wash.: University of Washington Press).

—— (1987), *The Biology of Moral Systems* (New York: Aldine de Gruyter).

Allen, Collin, Marc Bekoff, and George Lauder (eds.) (1998), *Nature's Purposes: Analyses of Function and Design in Biology* (Cambridge, Mass.: MIT Press).

Allmann, J. M. (1999), *Evolving Brains* (New York: Scientific American Library).

Anderson, Benedict R. O'G. (1991), *Imagined Communities: Reflections on the Origin and Spread of Nationalism*, rev. edn. (London: Verso).

Andreoni, J., W. Harbaugh, and L. Vesterlund (2003), 'The Carrot or the Stick: Rewards, Punishments, and Cooperation', *American Economic Review*, 93: 893–902.

Antes, P., A. Geertz, and R. Warne (2004), *New Approaches to the Study of Religion* (Berlin: Walter de Gruyter).

Ariew, Andrew, Robert Cummins, and Mark Perlman (eds.) (2002), *Functions: New Essays in the Philosophy of Psychology and Biology* (New York: Oxford University Press).

Armstrong, K. (1991), *Muhammad: A Western Attempt to Understand Islam* (London: Victor Gollancz).

Ashbrook, James B. (1994), 'The Cry for the Other: The Biocultural Womb of Human Development', *Zygon: Journal of Religion and Science*, 29: 297–314.

Atkins, P. W. (1994), *The 2nd Law: Energy, Chaos, and Form* (New York: Scientific American Books).

Atran, Scott (1995), 'Causal Constraints on Categories and Categorical Constraints on Biological Reasoning across Cultures', in D. Sperber, D. Premack, and A. J. Premack (eds.), *Causal Cognition: A Multidisciplinary Debate* (New York: Oxford University Press), 205–33.

—— (2002a), *In Gods We Trust: The Evolutionary Landscape of Religion* (New York: Oxford University Press).

—— (2002b), 'Modular and Cultural Factors in Biological Understanding', in Peter Carruthers, Stephen Stich, and Michael Siegal (eds.) (2002), *The Cognitive Basis of Science* (Cambridge: Cambridge University Press).

Atran, Scott (2005), 'Adaptationism for Human Cognition: Strong, Spurious or Weak?', *Mind and Language*, 20: 39–67.

—— and Ara Norenzayan (2004), 'Religion's Evolutionary Landscape: Counterintuition, Commitment, Compassion, Communion', *Behavioral and Brain Sciences*, 27: 730–70.

Ault, J. M. J. (2005), *Spirit and Flesh: Life in a Fundamentalist Baptist Church* (New York: Knopf).

Aunger, Robert (2000), *Darwinizing Culture: The Status of Memetics as Science* (Oxford: Oxford University Press).

Avital, E., and E. Jablonka (2001), *Animal Traditions: Behavioural Inheritance in Evolution* (Cambridge: Cambridge University Press).

Axelrod, R. (1984), *The Evolution of Cooperation* (London: Penguin).

Ayala, Francisco (1987), 'The Biological Roots of Morality', *Biology and Philosophy*, 2: 235–52.

—— (1995), 'The Difference of Being Human: Ethical Behavior as an Evolutionary Byproduct', in H. Rolston III (ed.), *Biology, Ethics, and the Origins of Life* (Boston, Mass.: Jones and Bartlett), 113–36.

Bargh, J. A. (1994), 'The Four Horsemen of Automaticity: Awareness, Efficiency, Intention, and Control in Social Cognition', in J. R. S. Wyer and T. K. Srull (eds.), *Handbook of Social Cognition*, 2nd edn. (Hillsdale, NJ: Erlbaum), 1–40.

—— and Chartrand, T. L. (1999), 'The Unbearable Automaticity of Being', *American Psychologist*, 54: 462–79.

Baron-Cohen, S. (1995), *Mindblindness: An Essay on Autism and Theory of Mind* (Cambridge, Mass.: MIT Press).

Barrett, J. L. (1996), *Anthropomorphism, Intentional Agents, and Conceptualizing God* (Ithaca, NY: Cornell University Press).

—— (1998), 'Cognitive Constraints on Hindu Concepts of the Divine', *Journal for the Scientific Study of Religion*, 37: 608–19.

—— (1999), 'Theological Correctness: Cognitive Constraint and the Study of Religion', *Method and Theory in the Study of Religion*, 11: 325–39.

—— (2001), 'How Ordinary Cognition Informs Petitionary Prayer', *Journal of Cognition and Culture*, 1: 259–69.

—— (2004), *Why Would Anyone Believe in God?* (Walnut Creek, Calif.: AltaMira Press).

—— and Johnson, A. H. (2003), 'Research Note: The Role of Control in Attributing Intentional Agency to Inanimate Objects', *Journal of Cognition and Culture*, 3: 208–17.

—— and F. C. Keil (1996), 'Anthropomorphism and God Concepts: Conceptualizing a Non-natural Entity', *Cognitive Psychology*, 31: 219–47.

—— and E. T. Lawson (2001), 'Ritual Intuitions: Cognitive Contributions to Judgments of Ritual Efficacy', *Journal of Cognition and Culture*, 1: 183–201.

—— R. Newman, and R. A. Richert (2003), 'When Seeing Does Not Lead to Believing: Children's Understanding of the Importance of Background

Knowledge for Interpreting Visual Displays', *Journal of Cognition and Culture*, 3: 91–108.

——and M. A. Nyhof (2001), 'Spreading Non-natural Concepts: The Role of Intuitive Conceptual Structures in Memory and Transmission of Cultural Materials', *Journal of Cognition and Culture*, 1: 69–100.

——and R. A. Richert (2003), 'Anthropomorphism or Preparedness? Exploring Children's Concept of God', *Review of Religious Research*, 44: 300–12.

————and A. Driesenga (2001), 'God's Beliefs Versus Mother's: The Development of Non-human Agent Concepts', *Child Development*, 71: 50–65.

——and VanOrman, B. (1996), 'The Effects of Image Use in Worship on God Concepts', *Journal of Psychology and Christianity*, 15: 38–45.

Baumeister, R. F., E. Bratslavsky, C. Finkenauer, and K. D. Vohs (2001), 'Bad is Stronger than Good', review of *General Psychology*, 5: 323–70.

Behe, M. (1996), *Darwin's Black Box* (New York: Fress Press).

——(2005), 'Design for Living', *New York Times*, Op-Ed, 7 Feb.

Berger, Peter (1990), *The Sacred Canopy: Elements of a Sociology of Religion* (Garden City, NY: Anchor Books).

Bering, J. M. (2002a), 'The Existential Theory of Mind', *Review of General Psychology*, 6: 3–24.

——(2002b), 'Intuitive Conceptions of Dead Agents' Minds: The Natural Foundations of Afterlife Beliefs as Phenomenological Boundary', *Journal of Cognition and Culture*, 2: 263–308.

——(2004), 'The Evolutionary History of an Illusion: Religious Causal Beliefs in Children and Adults', in B. Ellis and D. Bjorklund (eds.), *Origins of the Social Mind: Evolutionary Psychology and Child Development* (New York: Guilford Press).

——(2006), 'The Folk Psychology of Souls', *Behavioural and Brain Sciences*, 29: 453–62.

——and D. F. Bjorklund (2004), 'The Natural Emergence of Reasoning about the Afterlife as a Developmental Regularity', *Developmental Psychology*, 40: 217–33.

——and D. D. P. Johnson (2005), 'Oh Lord, You Hear My Thoughts From Afar: Recursiveness in the Cognitive Evolution of Supernatural Agency', *Journal of Cognition and Culture*, 5: 118–42.

——and T. Shackelford (2004), 'The Causal Role of Consciousness: A Conceptual Addendum to Human Evolutionary Psychology', *Review of General Psychology*, 8: 227–48.

——C. Hernández-Blasi, and D. F. Bjorklund (2005), 'The Development of "Afterlife" Beliefs in Secularly and Religiously Schooled Children', *British Journal of Developmental Psychology*, 23: 587–607.

Bernstein, A. E. (1993), *The Formation of Hell: Death and Retribution in the Ancient and Early Christian Worlds* (Ithaca, NY: Cornell University Press).

Blackmore, Susan (1999), *The Meme Machine* (New York: Oxford University Press).

——(2006), *Conversations on Consciousness* (New York: Oxford University Press).

Blakeslee, Sandra, and V. S. Ramachandran (1998), *Phantoms in the Brain* (New York: Quill).

Bloom, Paul (2004), *Descartes' Baby: How the Science of Child Development Explains What Makes Us Human* (New York: Basic Books).

—— (2005), 'Is God an Accident?', *Atlantic Monthly*, 296: 105–12.

—— (2006), 'My Brain Made Me Do It', *Journal of Culture and Cognition*, 6: 209–14.

—— (2007), 'Religion is Natural', *Developmental Science*, 10: 147–51.

—— and C. Veres (1999), 'The Perceived Intentionality of Groups', *Cognition*, 71: B1–B9.

—— and D. S. Weisberg (2007), 'Childhood Origins of Adult Resistance to Science', *Science*, 316: 996–7.

Boehm, C. (1999), *Hierarchy in the Forest: Egalitarianism and the Evolution of Human Altruism* (Cambridge: Harvard University Press).

Bonner, John Tyler (1988), *The Evolution of Complexity by Means of Natural Selection* (Princeton, NJ: Princeton University Press).

Bonsu, S. K., and R. W. Belk (2003), 'Do Not Go Cheaply into that Good Night: Death-ritual Consumption in Asante, Ghana', *Journal of Consumer Research*, 30: 41–55.

Boulding, Kenneth (1981), 'Toward an Evolutionary Theology', in Jerome Perlinski (ed.), *The Spirit of the Earth: A Teilhard Centennial Celebration* (New York: Seabury Press).

Bowlby, J. (1969), *Attachment and Loss*, i. *Attachment* (New York: Basic Books).

Boyd, Robert, and Peter J. Richerson (1985), *Culture and the Evolutionary Process* (Chicago, Ill.: University of Chicago Press).

—— —— (2001), 'Norms and Bounded Rationality', in G. Gigerenzer and R. Selten (eds.), *Bounded Rationality: The Adaptive Toolbox* (Cambridge, Mass.: MIT Press), 281–96.

—— —— (2005), *The Origin and Evolution of Cultures* (Oxford: Oxford University Press).

—— H. Gintis, S. Bowles, and P. J. Richerson (2003), 'The Evolution of Altruistic Punishment', *Proceedings of the National Academy of Sciences*, 100: 3531–5.

Boyer, P. (1994), *The Naturalness of Religious Ideas: A Cognitive Theory of Religion* (Berkeley, Calif.: University of California Press).

—— (2001a), 'Cultural Inheritance Tracks and Cognitive Predispositions: The Example of Religious Concepts', in Harvey Whitehouse (ed.), *The Debated Mind: Evolutionary Psychology versus Ethnography* (Oxford: Berg Publishers).

—— (2001b), *Religion Explained: The Evolutionary Origins of Religious Thought* (New York: Basic Books).

—— (2002), 'Why do Gods and Spirits Matter at all?' in I. Pyysiäinen and V. Anttonen (eds.), *Current Approaches in the Cognitive Science of Religion* (London: Continuum).

——and P. Lienard (2006), 'Why Ritualized Behavior? Precaution Systems and Action Parsing in Developmental, Pathological and Cultural Rituals', *Behavioral and Brain Sciences*, 29: 1–56.

——and C. Ramble (2001), 'Cognitive Templates for Religious Concepts: Cross-cultural Evidence for Recall of Counter-intuitive Representations', *Cognitive Science*, 25: 535–64.

Brandon, Robert (1995), *Adaptation and Environment* (Princeton, NJ: Princeton University Press).

Brock, S. (2002), 'Fictionalism about Fictional Characters', *Noûs*, 36: 1–21.

Brooke, J. L. (1994), *The Refiner's Fire: The Making of Mormon Cosmology, 1644–1844* (Cambridge: Cambridge University Press).

Brooke, John Hedley, and Geoffrey Cantor (1998), *Reconstructing Nature: The Engagement of Science and Religion* (London: T. and T. Clark).

Brooks, A. C. (2006), *Who Really Cares: The Surprising Truth about Compassionate Conservatism* (New York: Basic Books).

Bulbulia, J. (2004a), 'Religious Costs as Adaptations that Signal Altruistic Intention', *Evolution and Cognition*, 10: 19–38.

——(2004b), 'The Cognitive and Evolutionary Psychology of Religion', *Biology and Philosophy*, 18: 655–86.

——(2005), 'Are There Any Religions?', *Method and Theory in the Study of Religion*, 17: 71–100.

——(2006), 'Nature's Medicine: Empirical Constraint and the Evolution of Religious Healing', in P. McNamara (ed.), *Where Man and God Meet: The New Sciences of Religion and Brain* (Westport, Conn.: Praeger).

——(2007), 'Evolution and Religion', in R. I. Dunbar and L. Barrett (eds.), *Oxford Handbook of Evolutionary Psychology* (New York: Oxford University Press).

Buller, David (ed.) (1999), *Function, Selection, and Design* (Albany, NY: State University of New York Press).

——(2006), *Adapting Minds: Evolutionary Psychology and the Persistent Quest for Human Nature* (Cambridge, Mass.: MIT Press).

Burnham, K. P., and D. Anderson (2002), *Model Selection and Multi-model Inference* (Berlin: Springer Verlag).

Burnham, T., and D. D. P. Johnson (2005), 'The Evolutionary and Biological Logic of Human Cooperation', *Analyse and Kritik*, 27: 113–35.

Burton, F. D. (1970), 'Sexual Climax in Female Macaca Mulatta', *Proceedings of the Third International Congress of Primatology (Basel, Kargher)*, 180–91.

Buss, D. M. (1999), *Evolutionary Psychology* (Boston, Mass.: Allyn and Bacon).

Byrne, R., and A. Whiten (eds.) (1988), *Machiavellian Intelligence: Social Expertise and the Evolution of Intellect in Monkeys, Apes and Humans* (Oxford: Oxford University Press).

Cairns-Smith, A. G. (2002), *Seven Clues to the Origin of Life* (Cambridge: Cambridge University Press).

Calvin, J. (1960), *Institutes of the Christian Religion*, trans. Ford Lewis Battles (Philadelphia, Penn.: Westminster Press).

Campbell, D. T. (1960), 'Blind Variation and Selective Retention in Creative Thought and other Knowledge Processes', *Psychological Review*, 67: 380–400.

—— (1965), 'Variation and Selective Retention in Socio-cultural Evolution', in H. R. Barringer, G. I. Blanksten, and R. W. Mack (eds.), *Social Change in Developing Areas: A Reinterpretation of Evolutionary Theory* (Cambridge, Mass.: Schenkman Publishing Company), 19–49.

—— (1975), 'On the Conflicts between Biological and Social Evolution and between Psychology and Moral Tradition', *American Psychologist*, 30: 1103–26.

Carroll, J. (2004), *Literary Darwinism* (New York, Routledge).

Carruthers, Peter, Stephen Stich, and Michael Siegal (eds.) (2002), *The Cognitive Basis of Science* (Cambridge: Cambridge University Press).

Cavalli-Sforza, L. L., and M. W. Feldman (1981), *Cultural Transmission and Evolution: A Quantitative Approach* (Princeton, NJ: Princeton University Press).

Chagnon, N. A. (1997), *Yanomamo* (Fort Worth, Tex.: Harcourt Brace).

Cicero (1986), *On the Nature of the Gods*, trans. Horace C. P. McGregor (New York: Viking Penguin).

Clayton, P., and J. Schloss (eds.) (2004), *Evolution and Ethics: Human Morality in Biological and Religious Perspective* (Grand Rapids, Mich.: Eerdmans).

Clore, Gerald, and Karen Gasper (2000), 'Feeling is Believing: Some Affective Influences on Belief', in Nico Frijda, Antony S. R. Manstead, and Sacha Bem, *Emotions and Belief: How Feeling Influences Thought* (Cambridge: Cambridge University Press), 10–44.

Clutton-Brock, T. H., and G. A. Parker (1995), 'Punishment in Animal Societies', *Nature*, 373: 209–16.

Cosmides, L., J. Tooby, and J. Barkow (1992), 'Evolutionary Psychology and Conceptual Integration', in J. Barkow, L. Cosmides, and J. Tooby (eds.), *The Adapted Mind: Evolutionary Psychology and the Generation of Culture* (New York: Oxford University Press).

—— —— (2000), 'Consider the Source: The Evolution of Adaptations for Decoupling and Metarepresentation', in D. Sperber (ed.), *Metarepresentation* (New York: Oxford), 53–116.

—— —— (2003), *What is Evolutionary Psychology: Explaining the New Science of the Mind* (New Haven, Conn.: Yale University Press).

Coward, H. (2003), *Sin and Salvation in the World Religions: A Short Introduction* (Oxford: Oneworld).

Coyne, Jerry (1999), 'The Self-centered Meme', *Nature*, 398: 767–8.

—— (2003), 'Gould and God', *Nature*, 422: 813–14.

—— (2007), 'Don't Know Much Biology', *Edge: The Third Culture* <http://www.edge.org/3rd_culture/coyne07/coyne07_index.html>.

Crews, F., J. Gottschall, et al. (2005), *The Literary Animal: Evolution and the Nature of Narrative* (Chicago, Ill.: Northwestern University Press).

Crick, Francis (1988), *What Mad Pursuit* (New York: Basic Books).

Cronk, L. (1994), 'Evolutionary Theories of Morality and the Manipulative Use of Signals', *Zygon*, 4: 117–35.

Csibra, G., S. Bíró, O. Koós, and G. Gergely (2003), 'One-Year-Old Infants Use Teleological Representations of Actions Productively', *Cognitive Science*, 27: 111–33.

Damasio, Antonio (1994), *Descartes' Error: Emotion, Reason, and the Human Brain* (New York: Avon).

—— (1999), *The Feeling of What Happens* (New York: Harcourt).

—— (2003), *Looking for Spinoza* (New York: Harcourt).

—— (2004), 'William James and the Modern Neurobiology of Emotion', in Dylan Evans and Pierre Cruse (eds.), *Emotion, Evolution and Rationality* (Oxford: Oxford University Press).

Darwin, Charles (1872) [1965], *The Expression of the Emotions in Man and Animals* (Chicago, Ill.: University of Chicago Press).

—— (1874), *The Descent of Man and Selection in Relation to Sex*, 2nd edn. (New York: American Home Library).

—— (1959), *The Life and Letters of Charles Darwin*, ed. Francis Darwin (New York: Basic Books).

Davies, Paul (1993), *Mind of God* (New York: Simon and Schuster).

—— (1995), *Are We Alone?* (New York: Basic Books).

Dawkins, Richard (1986), *The Blind Watchmaker: Why the Evidence of Evolution Reveals a Universe Without Design* (New York: Norton).

—— (1993), 'Viruses of the Mind', in Bo Dalhbom (ed.), *Dennett and His Critics: Demystifying Mind* (Cambridge, Mass.: Blackwell), 13–27.

—— (1997), 'Is Science a Religion?', *Humanist*, 57: 26–9.

—— (2006) [1976], *The Selfish Gene*, thirtieth anniversary edn. (Oxford: Oxford University Press).

—— (2007), *The God Delusion* (New York: Houghton Mifflin).

Day, M. (2005), 'Rethinking Naturalness: Modes of Religiosity and Religion in the Round', in H. Whitehouse and R. McCauley (eds.), *Mind and Religion: Psychological and Cognitive Foundations of Religiosity* (Walnut Creek, Calif.: AltaMira Press).

de Sousa, Ronald (1987), *The Rationality of Emotion* (Cambridge: Mass.: MIT Press).

de Waal, F. (1996), *Good Natured: The Origins of Right and Wrong in Humans and other Animals* (Cambridge, Mass.: Harvard University Press).

Deacon, T. W. (1998), *The Symbolic Species* (New York: Norton).

Dennett, Daniel C. (1978), *Brainstorms* (Cambridge, Mass.: MIT Press).

—— (1984), *Elbow Room* (Cambridge, Mass.: MIT Press).

—— (1995), *Darwin's Dangerous Idea* (New York: Simon and Schuster).

—— (2001), *Consciousness Explained* (Boston: Little Brown).

Dennett, Daniel C. (2003), *Freedom Evolves* (New York: Viking).

—— (2006), *Breaking the Spell: Religion as a Natural Phenomenon* (New York: Viking Penguin).

—— (2007), 'Edge: The Reality Club', open letter to H. Allen Orr <http://www.edge.org/discourse/dennett_orr.html#orr>.

Dewey, John (1910), 'The Influence of Darwinism on Philosophy', in *The Influence of Darwin on Philosophy and other Essays in Contemporary Thought* (New York: Peter Smith), 1–19.

Diamond, J. (2005), *Collapse: How Societies Choose to Fail or Succeed* (New York: Viking).

Dole, Andrew, and Andrew Chignell (eds.) (2005), *God and the Ethics of Belief: New Essays in Philosophy of Religion* (Cambridge: Cambridge University Press).

Dudley, M. K. (2003), *A Hawaiian Nation*, i. *Man, Gods, and Nature* (Kapolei, Hawaii: N.A. Kane O Ka Malo Press).

Dugatkin, Lee Alan (1997), *Cooperation in Animals* (Oxford: Oxford University Press).

—— (2001), *The Imitation Factor: Evolution Beyond the Gene* (New York: Simon and Shuster).

Dunbar, R. I. (1998), *Grooming, Gossip, and the Evolution of Language* (Cambridge, Mass.: Harvard University Press).

—— (2005), *The Human Story: A New History of Mankind's Evolution* (London, Faber and Faber).

Durham, William (1992), *Coevolution: Genes, Culture, and Human Diversity* (Palo Alto, Calif.: Stanford University Press).

Durkheim, E. (1951) [1897], *Suicide*, trans. J. A. Spalding and G. Simpson (New York: Free Press).

—— (1995) [1912], *The Elementary Forms of Religious Life* (New York: Free Press).

Earhart, H. B. (ed.) (1993), *Religious Traditions of the World* (New York: Harper Collins).

Edelman, G. M. (1988), *Neural Darwinism: The Theory of Neuronal Group Selection* (New York: Basic Books).

—— and G. Tonomi (2001), *A Universe of Consciousness: How Matter Becomes Imagination* (New York: Basic Books).

Ekman, P. (1975), *Unmasking the Face* (Englewood Cliffs, NJ: Prentice-Hall).

—— (1994), 'Strong Evidence for Universal in Facial Expression: A Reply to Russell's Mistaken Critique', *Psychological Bulletin*, 115: 268–87.

Emery, Nathan J., Nicola S. Clayton, and Chris D. Frith (2007), 'Social Intelligence: From Brain to Culture', *Philosophical Transactions of the Royal Society B*, 362: 485–8.

Evans, Dylan, and Pierre Cruse (eds.) (2004), *Emotion, Evolution and Rationality* (Oxford: Oxford University Press).

Evans, E. M. (2000), 'Beyond Scopes: Why Creationism is Here to Stay', in K. Rosengren, C. Johnson, and P. Harris (eds.), *Imagining the Impossible: Magical,*

Scientific and Religious Thinking in Children (Cambridge: Cambridge University Press), 305–31.

——(2001), 'Cognitive and Contextual Factors in the Emergence of Diverse Belief Systems: Creation Versus Evolution', *Cognitive Psychology*, 42: 217–66.

Fauconnier, Gilles, and Mark Turner (2002), *The Way We Think* (New York: Basic Books).

Fehr, E., and S. Gächter (2002), 'Altruistic Punishment in Humans', *Nature*, 415: 137–40.

————(2003), 'Reply to Johnson, et al.', *Nature*, 421: 912.

——and U. Fischbacher (2003), 'The Nature of Human Altruism', *Nature*, 425: 785–91.

————(2004), 'Social Norms and Human Cooperation', *Trends in Cognitive Sciences*, 8: 185–9.

Feldt, Laura (2009), 'Fantastic Re-collection: Cultural vs Autobiographical Memory in the Exodus Narrative', in Armin W. Geertz and Jeppe Sinding Jensen (eds.), *Religious Narrative, Cognition and Culture: Image and Word in the Mind of Narrative* (London: Equinox).

Festinger, L. (1957), *A Theory of Cognitive Dissonance* (Palo Alto, Calif.: Stanford University Press).

Feyerabend, Paul (1975), *Against Method* (London: Verso).

Fielder, Klaus, and Herbert Bless (2000), 'The Formation of Beliefs at the Interface of Affective and Cognitive Processes', in Nico Frijda, Antony S. R. Manstead, and Sacha Bem, *Emotions and Belief: How Feeling Influences Thought* (Cambridge: Cambridge University Press), 144–70.

Finke, R., and R. Stark (1992), *The Churching of America, 1776–1990: Winners and Losers in Our Religious Economy* (New Brunswick, NJ: Rutgers University Press).

Fishman, A., and Y. Goldschmidt (1990), 'The Orthodox Kibbutzim and Economic Success', *Journal for the Scientific Study of Religion*, 29: 505–11.

Flanagan, Owen (2002), *The Problem of the Soul: Two Visions of Mind and How to Reconcile Them* (New York: Basic Books).

Fodor, Jerry (1998), *In Critical Condition* (Cambridge, Mass.: MIT Press).

——(2000), *In Critical Condition: Polemical Essays on Cognitive Science and the Philosophy of Mind* (Cambridge, Mass.: MIT Press).

Forgas, Joseph (2000), 'Feeling is Believing? The Role of Processing Strategies in Mediating Affective Influences on Beliefs', in Nico Frijda, Antony S. R. Manstead, and Sacha Bem, *Emotions and Belief: How Feeling Influences Thought* (Cambridge: Cambridge University Press), 108–43.

Francis, L. J., and W. K. Kay (1995), *Teenage Religion and Values* (Leominster: Gracewing).

Frank, R. H. (1988), *Passions within Reason: The Strategic Role of the Emotions* (New York: Norton).

Frank, R. H. (2001), 'Cooperation through Emotional Commitment', in R. Nesse (ed.), *Evolution and the Capacity for Commitment* (New York: Russell Sage Foundation), 57–77.

Frankenbery, Nancy, and Hans Penner (1999), 'Clifford Geertz's Long-lasting Moods, Motivations, and Metaphysical Conceptions', *Journal of Religion*, 79: 617–40.

Frankl, Viktor (1959), *Man's Search for Meaning* (New York: Pocket Books).

Freud, Sigmund (1989), *The Future of an Illusion,* trans. and ed. James Strachey (New York: Norton).

—— (1955), *Moses and Monotheism* (London: Vintage).

Frijda, Nico, Antony S. R. Manstead, and Sacha Bem (2000), *Emotions and Belief: How Feeling Influences Thought* (Cambridge: Cambridge University Press).

Gadgil, M., and K. C. Malhotra (1983), 'Adaptive Significance of the Indian Caste System: An Ecological Perspective', *Annals of Human Biology*, 10: 465–78.

Gazzaniga, M. S. (1985), *The Social Brain* (New York: Basic Books).

—— (ed.) (1995), *The Cognitive Neurosciences* (Cambridge, Mass.: MIT Press).

Geertz, Armin W. (2009), 'Gossip as Religious Narrative: Cognitive and Psychological Perspectives', in Geertz and Jeppe Sinding Jensen (eds.), *Religious Narrative, Cognition and Culture: Image and Word in the Mind of Narrative* (London: Equinox).

Geertz, Clifford (1973), 'Religion as a Cultural System', in *The Interpretation of Culture: Selected Essays* (New York: Basic Books), 88–125.

Georgalis, Nicholas (2005), *The Primacy of the Subjective: Foundations for a Unifred Theory of Mind and Language* (Cambridge, Mass.: MIT Press).

Gibbon, Edward (1776), *The Decline and Fall of the Roman Empire* <http://www.ccel.org/ccel/gibbon/decline/files/decline.html>.

Giere, Ronald (1988), *Explaining Science* (Chicago, Ill.: University of Chicago Press).

Gilbert, D. T., R. P. Brown, E. C. Pinel, and T. D. Wilson (2000), 'The Illusion of External Agency', *Journal of Personality and Social Psychology*, 79: 690–700.

Gilbert, G. N. (1978), 'Measuring the Growth of Science: A Review of Indicators of Scientific Growth', *Scientometrics*, 1: 9–34.

Gilovich, T. (1991), *How We Know What Isn't So: The Fallibility of Human Reason in Everyday Life* (New York: Free Press).

Gimenez, M., S. Guerrero, and P. L. Harris (manuscript) *Understanding the Impossible: Intimations of Immortality and Omniscience in Early Childhood.*

Gingrich, Owen (2003), 'Review of *Whitfield's Astrology: A History*', *Isis*, 94: 347–8.

Gintis, H. (2000), 'Strong Reciprocity and Human Sociality', *Journal of Theoretical Biology*, 206: 169–79.

—— (2003), 'Solving the Puzzle of Prosociality', *Rationality and Society*, 15: 155–87.

—— E. Smith, and S. Bowles (2001), 'Costly Signaling and Cooperation', *Journal of Theoretical Biology*, 213: 103–19.

—— (2004), 'Towards the Unity of the Behavioral Sciences', *Politics, Philosophy and Economics*, 3: 37–57.

Goel, Vinod, and Dolan, Raymond (2003), 'Reciprocal Neural Response within Lateral and Ventral Medial Prefrontal Cortex during Hot and Cold Reasoning', *NeuroImage*, 20: 2314–21.

Goetz, Stewart, and Charles Taliaferro (2008), *Naturalism* (Grand Rapids, Mich.: Eerdmans).

Gopnik, Alison, and Clark Glymour (2002), 'Causal Maps and Bayes Nets: A Cognitive and Computational Account of Theory-formation', in Peter Carruthers, Stephen Stich, and Michael Siegal (eds.), *The Cognitive Basis of Science* (Cambridge: Cambridge University Press).

Gottfried, G. M., S. A. Gelman, and H. Schultz (1999), 'Children's Early Understanding of the Brain: From Early Essentialism to Naïve Theory', *Cognitive Development*, 14: 147–74.

Gould, Stephen J. (1997a), 'Darwinian Fundamentalism', *New York Review of Books*, 44: 34–7.

—— (1997b), 'Evolution: The Pleasures of Pluralism', *New York Review of Books*, 44: 47–52.

—— (2002), *The Structure of Evolutionary Theory* (Cambridge, Mass.: Belknap Press).

—— and R. C. Lewontin (1979), 'The Spandrels of San Marco and the Panglossian Paradigm: A Critique of the Adaptationist Programme', *Proceedings of the Royal Society of London (Biological Sciences)*, 205: 581–98.

Grafen, A. (2003), 'Fisher the Evolutionary Biologist', *Statistician*, 52: 319–29.

Greene, J. D. (2008), 'The Secret Joke of Kant's Soul', in W. Sinnott-Armstrong (ed.), *Moral Psychology*, ii. *The Cognitive Science of Morality* (Cambridge, Mass.: MIT Press).

—— et al. (2001), 'An fMRI Investigation of Emotional Engagement in Moral Judgment', *Science*, 293: 2105–8.

Griffiths, Paul J. (1997a), 'Religion', in Charles Taliaferro and Phillip Quinn (eds.), *Blackwell Companion to Philosophy of Religion* (Malden, Mass.: Blackwell Publishing).

—— (1997b), *What Emotions Really Are: The Problem of Psychological Categories* (Chicago, Ill.: University of Chicago Press).

—— (2002), 'Faith Seeking Explanation', review of Pascal Boyer, *Religion Explained: The Evolutionary Origins of Religious Thought*, *First Things* <http://www.firstthings.com/article.php3?id_article=1948>.

Guthrie, Stewart E. (1993), *Faces in the Clouds* (New York: Oxford University Press).

Hackathorn, D. D. (1989), 'Collective Action and the Second-order Free-rider Problem', *Rational Society*, 1: 78–100.

Hadamard, Jacques (1945), *An Essay on the Psychology of Invention in the Mathematical Field* (New York: Dover).

Haidt, J. (2001), 'The Emotional Dog and its Rational Tail: A Social Intuitionist Approach to Moral Judgment', *Psychological Review*, 108: 814–34.

—— (2007), 'The New Synthesis in Moral Psychology', *Science*, 316: 998–1002.

Haidt, J. (2008), 'Morality', *Perspectives on Psychological Science*, 3: 65–72.

——and J. Graham (2007), 'When Morality Opposes Justice: Conservatives Have Moral Intuitions that Liberals May Not Recognize', *Social Justice Research*, 20: 98–116.

——and M. A. Hersh (2001), 'Sexual Morality: The Cultures and Reasons of Liberals and Conservatives', *Journal of Applied Social Psychology*, 31: 191–221.

——and C. Joseph (2004), 'Intuitive Ethics: How Innately Prepared Intuitions Generate Culturally Variable Virtues', *Daedalus*, Fall: 55–66.

——S. Koller, and M. Dias (1993), 'Affect, Culture, and Morality, Or Is it Wrong to Eat Your Dog?', *Journal of Personality and Social Psychology*, 65: 613–28.

Haldane, J. B. S (1928), 'When I am Dead', *Possible Worlds* (New York: Harper and Brothers).

Hamer, Dean (2004), *The God Gene* (New York: Doubleday).

Hamilton, W. D. (1964), 'The Genetical Evolution of Social Behaviour, parts 1 and 2', *Journal of Theoretical Biology*, 7: 1–52.

Hamlin, J. K., K. Wynn, and P. Bloom (2007), 'Social Evaluation by Preverbal Infants', *Nature*, 450: 557–8.

Haraway, Donna J. (1990), *Primate Visions: Gender, Race, and Nature in the World of Modern Science* (New York: Routledge).

Hardwick, Charley (1996), *Events of Grace: Naturalism, Existentialism, and Theology* (Cambridge University Press).

Harris, S. (2006), *Letter to a Christian Nation* (New York: Knopf).

Harrison, E., G. Bromiley, and C. Henry (ed.) (1960), *Wycliffe Dictionary of Theology* (Peabody, Mass.: Hendrickson).

Haselton, M. G., and D. Nettle (2006), 'The Paranoid Optimist: An Integrative Evolutionary Model of Cognitive Biases', *Personality and Social Psychology Research*, 10: 47–66.

Haught, John F. (2006), *Is Nature Enough?: Meaning and Truth in the Age of Science* (Cambridge: Cambridge University Press).

Hawkins, Jeff, and Sandra Blakeslee (2004), *On Intelligence* (New York: Times Books).

Heider, F., and M. Simmel (1944), 'An Experimental Study of Apparent Behavior', *American Journal of Psychology*, 57: 243–59.

Henrich, J. (2004), 'Cultural Group Selection, Coevolutionary Processes and Large-scale Cooperation. A Target Article with Commentary', *Journal of Economic Behavior and Organization*, 53: 3–143.

——and R. Boyd (2001), 'Why People Punish Defectors: Weak Conformist Transmission Can Stabilize Costly Enforcement of Norms in Cooperative Dilemmas', *Journal of Theoretical Biology*, 208: 79–89.

————et al. (eds.) (2004), *Foundations of Human Sociality: Economic Experiments and Ethnographic Evidence from Fifteen Small-scale Societies* (Oxford: Oxford University Press).

Hill, P. C., and K. I. Pargament (2003), 'Advances in the Conceptualization and Measurement of Religion and Spirituality: Implications for Physical and Mental Health', *American Psychologist*, 58: 64–74.

Hinde, R. (1999), *Why Gods Persist* (London: Routledge).

——(2005), 'Modes Theory', in H. Whitehouse and R. McCauley (eds.), *Mind and Religion: Psychological and Cognitive Foundations of Religiosity* (Walnut Creek, Calif.: AltaMira Press).

Hirschfeld, L. A. (1996), *Race in the Making: Cognition, Culture, and the Child's Construction of Human Kinds* (Cambridge, Mass.: MIT Press).

Hirstein, W. (2005), *Brain Fiction: Self-deception and the Riddle of Confabulation* (Cambridge, Mass.: MIT Press).

Hood, R. W., and R. J. Morris (1981), 'Knowledge and Experience Criteria in the Report of Mystical Experience', *Review of Religious Research*, 23: 76–84.

Hookway, Christopher (2002), 'Emotions and Epistemic Evaluations', in Peter Carruthers, Stephen Stich, and Michael Siegal (eds.), *The Cognitive Basis of Science* (Cambridge: Cambridge University Press), 251–62.

Hout, M., A. M. Greeley, and M. J. Wilde (2001), 'The Demographic Imperative in Religious Change in the United States', *American Journal of Sociology*, 107: 468–86.

Hudson, Liam (1966), *Contrary Imaginations: A Psychological Study of the English Schoolboy* (London: Methuen).

Hull, David (1978), 'Sociobiology: Scientific Bandwagon or Traveling Medicine Show?', *Society*, 15: 50–9.

Hume, David (1956) [1757], *Natural History of Religion*, ed. H. E. Root (Palo Alto, Calif.: Stanford University Press).

Humphrey, N. K. (1976), *The Social Function of Intellect: Growing Points in Ethology*, ed. P. P. G. Bateson and R. A. Hinde (Cambridge: Cambridge University Press), 303–17.

——(1992), *A History of the Mind: Evolution and the Birth of Consciousness* (New York, Simon and Shuster).

Iannaccone, L. R. (1992), 'Sacrifice and Stigma: Reducing Free-riding in Cults, Communes, and other Collectives', *Journal of Political Economy*, 100: 271–91.

——(1994), 'Why Strict Churches are Strong', *American Journal of Sociology*, 99: 1180–211.

——D. V. A. Olson, and R. Stark (1995), 'Religious Resources and Church Growth', *Social Forces*, 74: 705–31.

Irons, W. (1996), 'Morality, Religion, and Evolution', in W. Mark Richardson (ed.), *Religion and Science: History, Method, Dialogue* (New York: Routledge), 375–99.

——(2001), 'Religion as a Hard-to-Fake Sign of Commitment', in Randy Nesse (ed.), *Evolution and the Capacity for Commitment* (New York: Russell Sage Foundation), 292–309.

James, William (1902), *The Varieties of Religious Experience* (London: Longmans, Green; repr. New York: Collier Books, 1961).

Johnson, Carl Nils (1990), 'If You Had My Brain, Where Would I Be? Children's Understanding of the Brain and Identity', *Child Development*, 61: 962–72.

Johnson, Dominic (2005), 'God's Punishment and Public Goods: A Test of the Supernatural Punishment Hypothesis in 186 World Cultures', *Human Nature*, 16: 410–46.

——and Jesse Bering (2006), 'Hand of God, Mind of Man: Punishment and Cognition in the Evolution of Cooperation', *Evolutionary Psychology*, 4: 219–33.

——and Oliver Kruger (2004), 'The Good of Wrath: Supernatural Punishment and the Evolution of Cooperation', *Political Theology*, 5: 159–76.

——P. Stopka, and S. Knights (2003), 'The Puzzle of Human Cooperation', *Nature*, 421: 911–12.

Jolly, A. (1966), 'Lemur Social Behaviour and Primate Intelligence', *Science*, 153: 501–6.

Kass, Leon (1985), *Toward More Natural Science: Biology and Human Affairs* (New York: Free Press).

Katz, Leonard D. (ed.) (2000), *Evolutionary Origins of Morality: Cross-disciplinary Perspectives* (Exeter: Imprint Academic).

Katz, Richard (1984), *Boiling Energy: Community Healing Among the Kalahari Kung* (Cambridge, Mass.: Harvard University Press).

Kauffman, Stuart (1993), *The Origins of Order* (New York: Oxford University Press).

Keil, F. C. (1995), 'The Growth of Causal Understandings of Natural Kinds: Modes of Construal and the Emergence of Biological Thought', in D. Sperber, D. Premack, and A. J. Premack (eds.), *Causal Cognition: A Multidisciplinary Debate* (New York: Oxford University Press).

Kelemen, D. (1999a), 'Why are Rocks Pointy? Children's Preference for Teleological Explanations of the Natural World', *Developmental Psychology*, 35: 1440–53.

——(1999b), 'Functions, Goals, and Intentions: Children's Teleological Reasoning about Objects', *Trends in Cognitive Sciences*, 12: 461–8.

——(2004), 'Are Children "Intuitive Theists"?: Reasoning about Purpose and Design in Nature', *Psychological Science*, 15: 295–301.

Kierkegaard, Søren (1954), *The Sickness Unto Death*, trans. Walter Lowrie (Garden City, NY: Doubleday Anchor Books).

Kirkpatrick, Lee (2004), *Attachment, Evolution, and the Psychology of Religion* (New York: Guilford Press).

Knight, N., P. Sousa, J. L. Barrett, and S. Atran (2004), 'Children's Attributions of Beliefs to Humans and God: Cross-cultural Evidence', *Cognitive Science*, 28: 117–26.

Knorr-Cetina, Karin (1981), *The Manufacture of Knowledge* (New York: Pergamon).

Koenig, L. B., M. McGue, R. F. Krueger, and T. J. Bouchard (2005), 'Genetic and Environmental Influences on Religiousness: Findings for Retrospective and Current Religiousness Ratings', *Journal of Personality*, 73: 471–88.

Kohlberg, L. (1969), 'Stage and Sequence: The Cognitive-Developmental Approach to Socialization', in D. A. Goslin (ed.), *Handbook of Socialization Theory and Research* (Chicago, Ill.: Rand McNally).

Kosso, Peter (1998), *Appearance and Reality* (Oxford: Oxford University Press).

Kuhlmeier, V., P. Bloom, and K. Wynn (2004), 'Do Five-Month-Old Infants See Humans as Material Objects?', *Cognition*, 94: 95–103.

Kuhn, D. (1991), *The Skills of Argument* (Cambridge: Cambridge University Press).

Kurzban, R., J. Tooby, and L. Cosmides (2001), 'Can Race Be Erased? Coalitional Computation and Social Categorization', *Proceedings of the National Academy of Sciences*, 98: 15387–92.

Laland, K. N., and G. R. Brown (2002), *Sense and Nonsense: Evolutionary Perspectives on Human Behaviour* (Oxford: Oxford University Press).

Lamore, Charles (1996), *The Morals of Modernity* (Cambridge: Cambridge University Press).

Lansing, J. S. (1993), 'Emergent Properties of Balinese Water Temple Networks: Coadaptation on a Rugged Fitness Landscape', *American Anthropologist*, 95: 97–114.

Lauden, Larry (1977), *Progress and its Problems* (Berkeley, Calif.: University of California Press).

Laughlin, Robert B. (2005), *A Different Universe: Reinventing Physics from the Bottom Down* (New York: Perseus Books).

Lawson, E. T., and R. N. McCauley (1990), *Rethinking Religion: Connecting Cognition and Culture* (Cambridge: Cambridge University Press).

Lenoir, Timothy (1982), *Strategy of Life* (Dordrecht: Reidel).

Lewis, C. S. (1969), 'De descriptione temporum', in Walter Hooper (ed.), *Selected Literary Essays* (Cambridge: Cambridge University Press).

—— (2001), *Miracles* (San Francisco, Calif.: HarperSanFrancisco).

Lewontin, Richard (1997), 'Billions and Billions of Demons', *New York Review of Books*, 44 (1): 28–32.

Lillard, A. S. (1996), 'Body or Mind: Children's Understanding of Pretense', *Child Development*, 67: 1717–34.

Lilly, J. C. (1956), 'Mental Effects on Reduction of Ordinary Levels of Physical Stimuli on Intact Healthy Persons', *Psychiatric Research Reports*, 5: 1–19.

—— (1977), *The Deep Self* (New York, Warner Books).

Lonergan, Bernard, SJ (1967), 'Cognitional Structure', in F. E. Crowe (ed.), *Collection* (New York: Herder and Herder).

Lumsden, C. J., and E. O. Wilson (1981), *Genes, Mind, and Culture: The Coevolutionary Process* (Cambridge, Mass.: Harvard University Press).

McCauley, R. N., and E. T. Lawson (2002), *Bringing Ritual to Mind* (New York: Cambridge University Press).

McCloskey, M. (1983), 'Intuitive Physics', *Scientific American*, 248: 122–30.

McCutcheon, Russell T. (2004), 'Critical Trends in the Study of Religion in the United States', in Peter Antes, Armin Geertz, and Randi Warne (eds.), *New Approaches to the Study of Religion: Regional, Critical, and Historical Approaches* (New York: Walter de Gruyter), 317–44.

McGinn, Colin (1999), *The Mysterious Flame: Conscious Minds in a Material World* (New York: Basic Books).

McGrath, Alister E. (2001), *A Scientific Theology*, i. *Nature* (Edinburgh: T. and T. Clark).

Mackie, J. L. (1983), *The Miracle of Theism: Arguments For and Against the Existence of God* (New York: Oxford University Press).

Margulis, L. (1970), *Origin of Eukaryotic Cells* (New Haven, Conn.: Yale University Press).

Marx, Karl (1964), *Early Writings*, trans. and ed. T. B. Bottomore (New York, McGraw-Hill).

Maynard Smith, John (1982), *Evolution and the Theory of Games* (Cambridge: Cambridge University Press).

—— (1995), 'Genes, Memes, and Minds', review of Daniel C. Dennett, *Darwin's Dangerous Idea: Evolution and the Meanings of Life*, *New York Review of Books*, 42 (19).

—— and E. Szathmary (1995), *The Major Transitions of Life* (New York: W. H. Freeman).

—— and N. Warren (1982), 'Models of Cultural and Genetic Change', *Evolution*, 36: 620–7.

Michod, R. E. (1999), *Darwinian Dynamics* (Princeton, NJ: Princeton University Press).

Midgley, Mary (1982), Foreword to G. Breuer, *Sociobiology and the Human Dimension* (New York: Cambridge University Press).

—— (1992), *Science as Salvation* (New York: Routledge).

Monod, Jacques (1971), *Chance and Necessity* (New York: Knopf).

Mithen, S. (1999), 'Symbolism and the Supernatural', in R. I. Dunbar, C. Knight, and C. Power, *The Evolution of Culture* (New Brunswick, NJ: Rutgers University Press), 147–71.

Morris, B. (1987), *Anthropological Studies of Religion: An Introductory Text* (New York: Cambridge University Press).

Murdoch, Iris (1971), *The Sovereignty of Good* (New York: Schocken).

Murdock, G. P. (1980), *Theories of Illness: A World Survey* (Pittsburgh, Penn.: University of Pittsburgh Press).

Murphy, Nancey (2001), 'Phillip Johnson on Trial' in Robert Pennock (ed.), *Intelligent Design Creationism and its Critics* (Cambridge, Mass.: MIT Press).

Myers, D. G. (2000), 'The Funds, Friends, and Faith of Happy People', *American Psychologist*, 55: 56–67.

Nersession, Nancy (2002), 'The Cognitive Basis of Model-based Reasoning in Science', in Peter Carruthers, Stephen Stich, and Michael Siegal (eds.), *The Cognitive Basis of Science* (Cambridge: Cambridge University Press), 133–53.

Nesse, R. (2001), *Evolution and the Capacity for Commitment* (New York: Russell Sage Foundation).

Nettle, D. (2004), 'Adaptive Illusions: Optimism, Control and Human Rationality', in D. Evans and P. Cruse (eds.), *Emotion, Evolution and Rationality* (Oxford: Oxford University Press).

Newberg, Andrew, and Eugene D'Aquili (2001), *Why God Won't Go Away* (New York: Ballantine).

Newman, G. E., F. C. Keil, V. Kuhlmeier, and K. Wynn (manuscript), 'Sensitivity to Design: Early Understandings of the Link between Agents and Order', *Proceedings of the National Academy of Sciences*.

Newson, L., T. Postmes, S. E. G. Lea, and P. Webley (2005), 'Why are Modern Families Small? Toward an Evolutionary and Cultural Explanation for the Demographic Transition', *Personality and Social Psychology Review*, 9: 360–75.

Nielsen, Kai (2001), *Naturalism and Religion* (Amherst, NY: Prometheus Books).

Nietzsche, Friedrich (1990), *The Birth of Tragedy* and *The Genealogy of Morals*, trans. Francis Golffing (New York: Anchor Books).

Nisbett, R. E., and T. D. Wilson (1977), 'Telling More than We Can Know: Verbal Reports on Mental Processes', *Psychological Review*, 84: 231–59.

Nowak, M. A., and K. Sigmund (1998), 'Evolution of Indirect Reciprocity by Image Scoring', *Nature*, 393: 573–7.

Numbers, Ronald (2003), 'Science without God: Natural Laws and Christian Belief', in David C. Lindberg and Ronald Numbers (eds.), *When Science and Christianity Meet* (Chicago, Ill.: University of Chicago Press).

Oates, Edward (2007), 'Complexity in Context: The Metaphysical Implications of Evolutionary Theory', in John Barrow, Simon Conway Morris, Stephen Freeland, and Charles Harper (eds.), *Fitness of the Cosmos for Life: Biochemistry and Fine Tuning* (Cambridge: Cambridge University Press).

Odling-Smee, F. J., K. N. Laland, et al. (2003), *Niche Construction: The Neglected Process in Evolution* (Princeton, NJ: Princeton University Press).

Orr, H. Allen (1997), 'The Softer Side of Sociobiology', *Boston Review* <http://www.bostonreview.net/BR22.5/orr.html>.

—— (2006), 'The God Project: What the Science of Religion Can't Prove', *New Yorker*, 82: 80–3.

Ostrom, E., J. Walker, and R. Gardner (1992), 'Covenants With and Without a Sword: Self Governance is Possible', *American Political Science Review*, 86: 404–17.

Packer, C. (1977), 'Reciprocal Altruism in Olive Baboons', *Nature*, 265.

Palmer, C. T., and L. B. Steadman (2004), 'With or Without Belief: A New Approach to the Definition and Explanation of Religion', *Evolution and Cognition*, 10: 138–47.

Pannenberg, Wolfhart (1977), *Faith and Reality*, trans. John Maxwell (Philadelphia, Penn.: Westminster Press).

Pascal, Blaise (2004), *Pensées*, trans. W. F. Trotter (Whitefish, Mont.: Kessinger Publishing).

Peirce, Charles Sanders (1931), *Collected Papers*, i, ed. Charles Hartshorne and Paul Weiss (Cambridge: Cambridge University Press).

Peters, Ted (1992), *God—The World's Future: Systematic Theology for a New Era*, 2nd edn. (Minneapolis, Minn: Fortress Press).

Piaget, J. (1929), *The Child's Conception of the World* (New York: Harcourt Brace).

Pinker, Stephen (1997), *How the Mind Works* (New York: Norton).

——(2002), *The Blank Slate: The Modern Denial of Human Nature* (New York: Penguin).

Plantinga, Alvin (1991), 'Theism, Atheism, and Rationality', *Truth Journal*, 3: 1–8.

——(1993a), 'The Main Argument Against Naturalism', *Warrant and Proper Function* (Oxford: Oxford University Press).

——(1993b), *Warrant: The Current Debate* (New York: Oxford University Press).

——(1995), 'Methodological Naturalism', in J. van der Meer (ed.), *Facets of Faith and Science* (Lanham, Mass.: University Press of America).

——(2000), *Warranted Christian Belief* (New York: Oxford University Press).

——(2002), 'Evolutionary Argument Against Naturalism', in James Beilby (ed.), *Naturalism Defeated?* (Ithaca, NY: Cornell University Press), 1–12.

Plotkin, Henry (1994a), *Darwin Machines and the Nature of Knowledge* (Cambridge: Harvard University Press).

——(1994b), *The Nature of Knowledge: Concerning Adaptations, Instinct and the Evolution of Intelligence* (New York: Penguin Press).

——(2003), *The Imagined World Made Real: Towards a Natural Science of Culture* (New Brunswick, NJ: Rutgers University Press).

Polanyi, Michael (1946), *Science, Faith and Society* (Chicago, Ill.: University of Chicago Press).

——(1959), *Study of Man* (Chicago, Ill.: University of Chicago Press).

——(1967), *Tacit Dimension* (Garden City: Anchor).

Polkinghorne, John (1984), *The Quantum World* (New York: Longman).

Porter, Jean (2005), *Nature as Reason* (Grand Rapids, Mich.: Eerdmans).

Poundstone, W. (1992), *Prisoner's Dilemma: John von Neumann, Game Theory and the Puzzle of the Bomb* (New York: Doubleday).

Povinelli, D. J., and J. M. Bering (2002), 'The Mentality of Apes Revisited', *Current Directions in Psychological Science*, 11: 115–19.

Putnam, Hilary (1987), *The Many Faces of Realism* (LaSalle, Ill.: Open Court).

Pyysiäinen, I. (2001a), 'Cognition, Emotion, and Religious Experience', in J. Andresen (ed.), *Religion in Mind* (Cambridge: Cambridge University Press).

——(2001b), *How Religion Works: Towards a New Cognitive Science of Religion* (Leiden: Brill).

——(2002), 'Religion and the Counterintuitive', in I. Pyysiäinen and V. Anttonen (eds.), *Current Approaches in the Cognitive Science of Religion* (London: Continuum).

——(2003), 'True Fiction: Philosophy and Psychology of Religious Belief', *Philosophical Psychology*, 16: 109–25.

——(2004), *Magic, Miracles and Religion: A Scientist's Perspective* (Walnut Creek, Calif.: AltaMira Press).

——and Anttonen, V. (eds.) (2002), *Current Approaches in the Cognitive Science of Religion* (London: Continuum).

Quine, W. V. (1995), 'Naturalism; Or, Living Within One's Means', *Dialectica*, 49: 251–62.

Rahner, Karl (1969), *Theological Investigation*, vi. trans. Karl Rahner and Boniface Kruger (Baltimore, Md.: Helicon).

Ramachandran, V. S., and S. Blakeslee (1998), *Phantoms in the Brain: Probing the Mysteries of the Human Mind* (New York: Quill William Morrow).

Rappaport, R. A. (1979), *Ecology, Meaning, and Religion* (Richmond Calif.: North Atlantic Books).

——(1999), *Ritual and Religion in the Making of Humanity*, Cambridge Studies in Social and Cultural Anthropology, 110 (Cambridge: Cambridge University Press).

Ratzsch, Del (2004), 'Natural Theology, Methodological Naturalism, and "Turtles all the way down" ', *Faith and Philosophy*, 21: 436–55.

——(2005), 'Saturation, World Ensembles, and Design', *Faith and Philosophy*, 22: 667–86.

Rawls, John (1971), *A Theory of Justice* (Cambridge, Mass.: Belknap Press).

Rea, Michael (2004), *World Without Design: The Ontological Consequences of Naturalism* (New York: Oxford University Press).

Rees, Martin (2001), *Our Cosmic Habitat* (Princeton, NJ: Princeton University Press). religioustolerance.org <http://www.religioustolerance.org/ chr_poll3.htm>.

Rescher, Nicholas (1978), *Scientific Progress: A Philosophical Essay on the Economics of Research in Natural Science* (Pittsburgh, Penn.: University of Pittsburgh Press).

Rey, Georges (1997), *Contemporary Philosophy of Mind* (Oxford: Blackwell).

Richards, Janet R. (2000), *Human Nature after Darwin* (London: Routledge).

Richerson, P. J., and R. Boyd (1987), 'Simple Models of Complex Phenomena: The Case of Cultural Evolution', in J. Dupré (ed.), *The Latest on the Best: Essays on Evolution and Optimality* (Cambridge, Mass.: MIT Press), 27–52.

————(1989), 'A Darwinian Theory for the Evolution of Symbolic Cultural Traits', in M. Freilich (ed.), *The Relevance of Culture* (Boston, Mass.: Bergin and Garvey), 120–42.

————(1999), 'Complex Societies: The Evolutionary Origins of a Crude Superorganism', *Human Nature—An Interdisciplinary Biosocial Perspective*, 10: 253–89.

————(2005), *Not By Genes Alone: How Culture Transformed Human Evolution* (Chicago, Ill.: University of Chicago Press).

Richert, R. A., and J. L. Barrett (2005), 'Do You See What I See? Young Children's Assumptions about God's Perceptual Abilities', *International Journal for the Psychology of Religion*, 15: 283–95.

Robinson, P. H., and J. M. Darley (2004), 'Does Criminal Law Deter? A Behavioural Science Investigation', *Oxford Journal of Legal Studies*, 24: 173–205.

Rochat, P., R. Morgan, and M. Carpenter (1997), 'Young Infants' Sensitivity to Movement Information Specifying Social Causality', *Cognitive Development*, 12: 537–61.

Roe, Anne (1952), *The Making of a Scientist* (New York: Dodd, Mead).

Roes, F. L., and M. Raymond (2003), 'Belief in Moralizing Gods', *Evolution and Human Behaviour*, 24: 126–35.

Roof, W. C., and W. McKinney, (1987), *American Mainline Religion: Its Changing Shape and Future* (New Brunswick, NJ: Rutgers University Press).

Rose, Stephen, and Hilary Rose (eds.) (2000), *Alas Poor Darwin: Arguments Against Evolutionary Psychology* (New York: Harmony Books).

Ruse, Michael (1982), *Darwinism Defended* (Reading, Mass.: Addison-Wesley).

—— and E. O. Wilson (1993), 'The Evolution of Ethics', in J. E. Huchinson (ed.), *Religion and the Natural Sciences* (Fort Worth, Tex.: Harcourt Brace Jovanovich).

Russell, Bertrand (1917), *Mysticism and Logic* (New York: Barnes and Noble).

Sahlins, Marshall D. (1977), *The Use and Abuse of Biology: An Anthropological Critique of Sociobiology* (Ann Arbor, Mich.: University of Michigan Press).

Salamon, S. (1992), *Prairie Patrimony: Family, Farming, and Community in the Midwest* (Chapel Hill, NC: University of North Carolina Press).

Sartre, Jean-Paul (1967), *No Exit: Four Contemporary French Plays* (New York: Random House).

Schelling, T. C. (1960), *The Strategy of Conflict* (Harvard, Mass.: Harvard University Press).

Schloss, Jeffrey P. (2004), 'Evolutionary Ethics and Christian Morality: Surveying the Issues', in P. Clayton and J. Schloss (eds.), *Evolution and Ethics: Human Morality in Biological and Religious Perspective* (Grand Rapids, Mich.: Eerdmans), 1–24.

—— (2007), 'He Who Laughs Best: Religious Affect as a Solution to Recursive Cooperative Defection', in Joseph Bubulia, et al. (eds.), *The Evolution of Religion: Studies, Theories, Critiques* (Santa Margarita, Calif.: Collins Foundation Press), 205–15.

Scholl, B. J., and P. D. Tremoulet (2000), 'Perceptual Causality and Animacy', *Trends in Cognitive Sciences*, 4: 299–308.

Schwartz, Jeffrey, and Sharon Begley (2002), *The Mind and the Brain* (New York: Regan).

Searle, John (2004), *Mind: A Brief Introduction* (Oxford: Oxford University Press).

Segerstrale, Ullica (2001), *Defenders of the Truth: The Sociobiology Debate* (New York: Oxford University Press).

Shea, William M. (1984), *The Naturalists and the Supernatural* (Macon, Ga.: Mercer University Press).

Shermer, Michael (2003), *How We Believe: The Search for God in an Age of Science* (New York: Freeman).

Sigmund, K., C. Hauert, and M. Nowak (2001), 'Reward and Punishment', *Proceedings of the National Academy of Sciences of the United States of America*, 98: 10757–61.

Slone, D. Jason (2004), *Theological Incorrectness: Why Religious People Believe What They Shouldn't* (New York: Oxford University Press).

—— (2007), 'The Attraction of Religion: A Sexual Selection Account', in Joseph Bubulia, et al. (eds.), *The Evolution of Religion: Studies, Theories, Critiques* (Santa Margarita, Calif.: Collins Foundation Press).

Smith, Christian (2003), *Moral, Believing Animals: Human Personhood and Culture* (Oxford: Oxford University Press).

Smolin, Lee (2001), *The Life of the Cosmos* (New York: Oxford University Press).

Sober, Elliot, and D. S. Wilson (1998), *Unto Others: The Evolution and Psychology of Unselfish Behavior* (Cambridge, Mass.: Harvard University Press).

Solomon, Robert (2003), *Not Passion's Slave* (New York: Oxford).

Sommers, Tamler, and Alex Rosenberg (2003), 'Darwin's Nihilistic Idea: Evolution and the Meaninglessness of Life', *Biology and Philosophy*, 18: 653–68.

Sosis, R. (2000), 'Religion and Intragroup Cooperation: Preliminary Results of a Comparative Analysis of Utopian Communities', *Cross-Cultural Research*, 34: 77–88.

—— (2003), 'Why Aren't We All Hutterites?', *Human Nature*, 14: 91–127.

—— (2004), 'The Adaptive Value of Religious Ritual', *American Scientist*, 92: 166–72.

—— and C. Alcorta (2003), 'Signaling, Solidarity, and the Sacred: The Evolution of Religious Behavior', *Evolutionary Anthropology*, 12: 264–74.

—— and E. R. Bressler (2003), 'Cooperation and Commune Longevity: A Test of the Costly Signaling Theory of Religion', *Cross-Cultural Research*, 37: 211–39.

—— and B. J. Ruffle (2003), 'Religious Ritual and Cooperation: Testing for a Relationship on Israeli Religious and Secular Kibbutzim', *Current Anthropology*, 44: 713–22.

Spelke, E. S., and G. Van de Walle (1993), 'Perceiving and Reasoning about Objects: Insights from Infants', in N. Elian, W. Brewer, and R. McCarthy (eds.), *Spatial Representation* (New York: Blackwell).

—— A. Phillips, and A. L. Woodward (1995), 'Infant's Knowledge of Object Motion and Human Action', in D. Sperber, D. Premack, and A. J. Premack (eds.), *Causal Cognition: A Multidisciplinary Debate* (New York: Oxford University Press), 44–78.

Sperber, Daniel (1997), 'Intuitive and Reflective Beliefs', *Mind and Language*, 12: 67–83.

—— (2000), 'An Objection to the Memetic Approach to Culture', in Robert Aunger (ed.), *Darwinizing Culture: The Status of Memetics as Science* (Oxford: Oxford University Press), 163–74.

—— (2005), 'Modularity and Relevance: How Can a Massively Modular Mind be Flexible and Context-sensitive?', in P. Carruthers, S. Laurence, and S.

Stich (eds.), *The Innate Mind: Structure and Contents* (New York: Oxford), 53–68.

Spinoza, Benedictus de (1910) [1677], *Ethics* (New York: E. P. Dutton and Co.).

Srinivas, M. N. (1962), *Caste in Modern India, and other Essays* (Bombay: Asia Publishing House).

Stark, Rodney (1997), *The Rise of Christianity: How the Obscure, Marginal Jesus Movement Became the Dominant Religious Force in the Western World in a Few Centuries* (San Francisco, Calif.: HarperCollins).

—— and Roger Finke (2000), *Acts of Faith: Explaining the Human Side of Religion* (Berkeley, Calif.: University of California Press).

Stenger, Victor (2007), *God: The Failed Hypothesis. How Science Shows that God Does Not Exist* (Amherst, NY: Prometheus Books).

Sterelny, K. (2003), *Though in a Hostile World: The Evolution of Human Cognition* (Oxford: Blackwell).

—— (2004), 'Externalism, Epistemic Artifacts and the Extended Mind: The Externalist Challenge', in R. Schantz, *Current Issues in Theoretical Philosophy*, ii. (Berlin, Walter de Gruyter).

—— (2006), 'The Evolution and Evolvability of Culture', *Mind and Language*, 21: 137–65.

—— (2007), 'Social Intelligence, Human Intelligence and Niche Construction', Dicussion Meeting Issue: Social Intelligence: From Brain To Culture, eds. Nathan Emery, Nicky Clayton, and Chris Frith, *Philosophical Transactions of The Royal Society B*, 362: 719–30.

—— and P. Griffiths (1999), *Sex and Death: An Introduction to the Philosophy of Biology* (Chicago, Ill.: University of Chicago Press).

Strassmann, B. I. (1992), 'The Function of Menstrual Taboos Among the Dogon: Defense Against Cuckoldry?', *Human Nature*, 3: 89–131.

Suedfeld, P. (1975), 'The Benefits of Boredom: Sensory Deprivation Reconsidered', *American Scientist*, 63: 60–9.

—— and J. Vernon (1964), 'Visual Hallucination in Sensory Deprivation: A Problem of Criteria', *Science*, 145: 412–13.

Swinburne, Richard (2004), *The Existence of God*, 2nd edn. (Oxford: Oxford University Press).

Taliaferro, Charles (1989), 'The Coinherence', *Christian Scholar's Review*, 18: 333–45.

—— (1994), *Consciousness and the Mind of God* (Cambridge: Cambridge University Press).

—— (1998), *Contemporary Philosophy of Religion* (Oxford: Blackwell).

—— (2005), *Evidence and Faith* (Cambridge: Cambridge University Press).

Taves, A. (1999), *Fits, Trances, and Visions* (Princeton, NJ: Princeton University Press).

Teilhard de Chardin, Pierre (1968), *Writings in Time of War*, trans. René Hague (New York: Harper and Row).

—— (1969), *Christianity and Evolution*, trans. René Hague (New York: Harcourt Brace).

—— (2002), *Activation of Energy*, trans. René Hague (New York: Harcourt Brace Jovanovich).

Thagard, Paul (2002), 'The Passionate Scientist: Emotion in Scientific Cognition', in Peter Carruthers, Stephen Stich, and Michael Siegal (eds.), *The Cognitive Basis of Science* (Cambridge: Cambridge University Press), 235–50.

Thomas, W. I., and D. S. Thomas (1928), *The Child in America: Behaviour Problems and Programs* (New York: Knopf).

Tomasello, M. (1999), *The Cultural Origins of Human Cognition* (Cambridge, Mass.: Harvard University Press).

Tooby, J., and L. Cosmides (2001), 'Does Beauty Build Adapted Minds? Toward an Evolutionary Theory of Aesthetics, Fiction and the Arts', *Substance*, 95: 6–27.

Trivers, R. L. (1971), 'The Evolution of Reciprocal Altruism', *Quarterly Review of Biology*, 46: 35–57.

—— (1991), 'Deceit and Self–Deception: The Relationship Between Communication and Consciousness', in M. Robinson and L. Tiger (eds.), *Man and Beast Revisited* (Washington, DC: Smithsonian).

Turiel, E. (1983), *The Development of Social Knowledge: Morality and Convention* (Cambridge: Cambridge University Press).

—— (1998), 'The Development of Morality', in W. Damon (ed.), *Handbook of Child Psychology*, 5th edn. (London: Wiley), iii. 863–932.

Tyrrell, George (1907), *Through Scylla and Charybdis, or The Old Theology and the New* (London: Longmans, Green and Co.).

van Fraassen, Bas (1980), *The Scientific Image* (Oxford: Clarendon Press).

—— (1989), *Laws and Symmetry* (Oxford: Clarendon Press).

—— (1994), 'Gideon Rosen on Constructive Empiricism', *Philosophical Studies*, 74.

—— (2002), *The Empirical Stance* (New Haven, Conn.: Yale University Press).

—— (2005), 'On Taking Stances', *Harvard Review of Philosophy*, 13: 86–102.

Watkins, J. W. N. (1957), 'Historical Explanations in the Social Sciences', *British Journal for the Philosophy of Science*, 8: 104–17.

Weber, Max 1930 [1904], *The Protestant Ethic and the Spirit of Capitalism*, trans. Talcott Parson (New York: Charles Scribner's Sons).

—— (1978), *The Sociology of Religion* (Berkeley, Calif.: University of California Press).

Weinberg, Steven (1992), *Dreams of a Final Theory* (New York: Pantheon).

Weisberg, R. (1993), *Creativity, Beyond the Myth of Genius* (New York: W. H. Freeman and Co).

Wellman, H., D. Cross, and J. Watson (2001), 'Meta-analysis of Theory of Mind Development: The Truth About False Belief', *Child Development*, 72: 655–84.

Wentzel van Huyssteen, J. (1998), *Duet or Duel?* (Harrisburg, Penn.: Trinity).

—— (1999), *The Shaping of Rationality* (Grand Rapids, Mich.: Eerdmans).

Whitehouse, H. (1995), *Inside the Cult: Religious Innovation and Transmission in Papua New Guinea* (Oxford: Clarendon Press).

—— (2000), *Arguments and Icons: Divergent Modes of Religiosity* (Oxford: Oxford University Press).

—— (2004a), *Modes of Religiosity: A Cognitive Theory of Religious Representation* (Lanham, Md.: AltaMira Press).

—— (2004b), *Theorizing Religions Past: Archaeology, History, and Cognition* (Lanham, Md.: AltaMira Press).

—— and R. N. McCauley (eds.) (2005), *Mind and Religion: Psychological and Cognitive Foundations of Religiosity* (Walnut Creek, Calif.: AltaMira Press).

Whitfield, Peter (2001), *Astrology: A History* (London: British Library).

Wilkinson, D. H. (1977), 'The Quarks and Captain Ahab or: The Universe as Artefact', Schiff Memorial Lecture, Stanford University.

Williams, Bernard (1972), *Morality* (Cambridge: Cambridge University Press).

Williams, George C. (1966), *Adaptation and Natural Selection: A Critique of Some Current Evolutionary Thought* (Princeton, NJ: Princeton University Press).

Wilson, David Sloan (1990), 'Species of Thought: A Commentary on Evolutionary Epistemology', *Biology and Philosophy*, 5: 37–62.

—— (2002), *Darwin's Cathedral: Evolution, Religion, and the Nature of Society* (Chicago, Ill.: University of Chicago Press).

—— (2004), 'Evolutionary Social Constructivism', in J. Gottshcall and D. S. Wilson (eds.), *Literature and the Human Animal* (Evanston, Ill.: Northwestern University Press).

—— (2005), 'Testing Major Evolutionary Hypotheses about Religion with a Random Sample', *Human Nature*, 16: 419–46.

—— and E. Sober (1994), 'Reintroducing Group Selection to the Human Behavioural Sciences', *Behavioral and Brain Sciences*, 17: 585–654.

Wilson, E. O. (2000) [1975], *Sociobiology: The New Synthesis* (Cambridge, Mass.: Belknap Press).

Wundt, W. (1907), *Outlines of Psychology* (Leipzig: Wilhelm Englemann).

Yamagishi, T. (1986), 'The Provision of a Sanctioning System as a Public Good', *Journal of Personality and Social Psychology*, 51: 110–16.

Yandell, Keith (1993), *The Epistemology of Religious Experience* (Cambridge: Cambridge University Press).

Zahavi, A. (1995), 'Altruism as Handicap: The Limitations of Kin Selection and Reciprocity', *Journal of Avian Biology*, 26: 1–3.

—— and A. Zahavi (1997), *The Handicap Principle: A Missing Piece of Darwin's Puzzle* (New York: Oxford University Press).

Zajonc, R. B. (1980), 'Feeling and Thinking: Preferences Need No Inferences', *American Psychologist*, 35: 151–75.

Index

Adaptationism 14–16, **20–22**, 75, 119, 182–3, 188
Agency,
  attribution of 121, 186
Altruism **26–29**, 37, 42, 109, 148, 150, 279, 283, 327–330, 332
Anti-realism 19, 153-
Aquinas, Thomas, St. 148
Atran, Scott 12, 14, 17, 80, 115, **180–181**, **183**, **187–188**, 190, **193**, **237**, 286

Bacon, Francis 151
Barrett, Justin 12, 17, 18, 52, 170, **185–187**, 191, 197, 202
Beauty
  as a theoretical virtue 228–9
Bering, Jesse 21, 50, 75, 89, 119, 124, 169
Boyer, Pascal 44, 82, 120, 168, 170–171, 183–185, **189–191**, **194**, **265–268**, **273–276**, 286

Calvin, John 126, 148
Cavinist theory of religious belief 126
Caprgras syndrome 70
Chalmers, David 210
Cicero 179
Commitment signaling 46–57
Consciousness 201, 209-, 225
  irreducibility of 209–11
Contagion avoidance 172–3
Cooperation 21, **27–43**, 46–51, 106–111
Costly signaling 21, 27, 41, 45, 51
Creationism 6, 12, 121–4
Counterintuitiveness 184–5, 187

Darwin, Charles 1, 4, 54, **101**, 103, 180, **246**, 259, 282, 288
Darwinism
  Popular acceptance of 122

Dawkins, Richard 11, 15, **23–24**, 103–105, 115, 122, 152, 285, **287–288**
Defeaters,
  of religious belief 140, 159–167
  rationality 162–4
  warrant 162–4
Defection
  second order 29, 31
Dennett, Daniel **2–6**, **10**, **13**, 15, 23, 63–64, 68, 152, **200–214**, 230, 238, **290–291**
Dualism 123

Edwards, Jonathan 148
Eliminativism 211-2
Emotion
  and religious experience 13
  and signaling 52–57
  in scientific reasong 223–226
Environment of evolutionary adaptedness 28, 36
Epistemology
  externalism 173–4
  internalism 173
Experience, religious 13, 67–73, 200–1, 212–14
Explanation
  beauty and 228–9
  scientific accounts of religion and 3–9, 197–199
  in science 221–2
  varying evolutionary approaches to 14–16
Evans, Margaret 123

Faith and reason 140
Fitness 21–22
  inclusive 36

Folk theories
    ontology 184–5
Freud, Sigmund 1, 128, 136, **145–148**,
    168, 227, 251, 266
Functionalism 28, 143

Georgalis, Nicholas 211
Green beard effect 33
Group selection 28, 30, 33, 40, **105–108**,
    116, 119, **140–143**, 237, 282,
    287–288, 232–324
Guthrie, Stewart 121

Hard-to-fake-signaling 52, 53
HADD 185–7, 190–192
    and the reliability of religious
        belief 170–1, 196–7

Indirect reciprocity 27
Instinct
    in scientific reasoning 223
Intentionality 209–11
Intuitive dualism 123
Intuitive theism 34
Irrationality in religion 3, 11, 205–6

Johnson, Dominic 21, 50, 85,
    119, 188

Keleman, Deborah 122
Kin Selection **27–28**, 37, 283
Korsakoff's syndrome 70
Kuhn, Thomas 235

Language 35–6, 48

Memes **23–25**, 64, 103, **114–115**, 119
Methodological Naturalism 139, 149–53,
    159–60, 167
Mickey Mouse objection 190–1
Minimal counterintuitiveness 184–5, 187
Miracles 208
    religious experience and 205–6
Modularity
    processing and 219
Monod, Jacques 151
Morality
    supernatural punishment and 30, 188
Murphy, Nancey 152

Naturalism 201–2
    explanations of religion and 6–12,
        207–8, 213–4
    methodological 139, 149–53, 159–60
    ontological 149
    philosophical 129
    vs. supernatural 6–9
Newman, George 122
Nielsen, Kai 3, 11
Norms
    and belief in supernatural
        agency 187–8

Parsimony 175–6
Perception
    as partially constituted by theory 219
    as structured by pre-conscious
        content 219
Pinker, Steven 219–20, 223
Plantinga, Alvin **126–127**, 201–202,
    236–238
Punishment
    Cooperation and 29–45
    Supernatural 29–43
Pyysiäinen, Ilka 190

Realism 153
Reciprocal Altruism **27**, 37, 283
Reciprocity 284, 289
    Indirect **27**
    Strong **28–29**
Religion
    Adaptation and 15–17, 182–3, 188
    As a Spandrel 75, 119, 182–3, 188
    Definition of 12, 181
    Functionalist explanations of 28
    Irrationality and 3, 11, 205–6
    Naturalism and explanations of 6–12,
        207–8, 211–2
Religious Experience 67–73, 200–1,
    212–4
    and miracles 205–6
Reward,
    Supernatural 32–3
Rey, George 209
Ritual 41, 188
    and signaling 54
Ruse, Michael 140–142, 150, **152**, 159,
    169, 237

Second order defection 29
Selection
    group 33
    sexual 20, **103–104**, 115
Sensory deprivation 71
Science
    constraints on 151–9
    extra-empirical factors in 217–29
    presuppositions of 217
    realism v. anti-realism 153–9
    underdetermination of theories
        in 216–29
Signaling
    Commitment signalling 46
    Costly signaling 21, 27, 41,
        45, 51
    Hard-to-fake-signaling 52, 53
Simon, Herbert 140
Sosis, Richard 21, 25, **28–29, 41**,
    51, 54, 120
Spandrel
    Religion as **17–18**, 20, 22,
        25, 68, **119**, 140–142,
        182–183
Social complexity hypothesis 47
Somato-kinetcs
    and reasoning in science 226

Stark, Rodney 6, 10–11, 103, 110–111,
    140–143, 150
Supernatural
    Explanations **6–13,** 175–178
    Punishment **29–43**
    Agents or beings 44–45, 50–51, 54–56,
        68–75, **128–138**, 149–152,
        186–192, 202–207
Supernatural agents
    as norm suporting 187–8

Theology
    as a hard-to-fake signal 52
Theory of Mind 34, 48, 186–7

Underdetermination of theory by
    data 25, 216

van Fraassen, Bas 154–9

Whitehouse, Harvey 18, **185**, 188–189
Wilson, David Sloan 14–15, 27, 116, 140,
    143–148, 184, 189–190, 236–237,
    280, 287
Wish fulfillment 145–6

Yanomamo 31